A Commentary on
The Creed of *al-Imām* al-Ṭaḥāwī

Al-Shaykh Ṣāliḥ al-Fawzān

DAR AL-ARQAM

ISBN: 978 1 8384897 1 7

British Library Cataloguing in Publishing Data
A catalogue record for this book is available from the British Library

First edition: 2014, Second Edition: 2023

Prepared and published by Dar al-Arqam Publishing
Birmingham, United Kingdom

www.daralarqam.bigcartel.com
Email: daralarqam@hotmail.co.uk

Translated by Ilm Translations
Edited by Adnan Karim

If you would like to support our work, donations can be made via:

- www.daralarqam.bigcartel.com/product/donate
- www.patreon.com/daralarqam
- www.paypal.me/daralarqam

Printed in Türkiye by Mega | export@mega.com.tr

بسم الله الرحمن الرحيم

"The house of al-Arqam is the house of Islām"

Al-Ḥākim (d.405 h.) in *al-Mustadrak ʿala al-Ṣaḥiḥayn* (6185)

A COMMENTARY ON

THE CREED OF AL-IMĀM AL-ṬAḤĀWI

Al-Shaykh Ṣāliḥ al-Fawzān

DAR AL-ARQAM

الفهرس

Contents

تقديم الناشر

Publisher's Foreword

The original publication of this translation in 2014 was our first major project. In the years following it, Allah blessed us to continue our work, building upon this original project and completing many more. When the stock from the first print run finished in late 2021, we decided to make a new edition instead of a reprint, intending (via our humble efforts) to give service to the religion of Allah and honour to this work of Shaykh al-Fawzān.

We ask Allah to accept it and keep us sincere.

We would like to thank Nagwan Noaman and her team for their excellent work in translating this book. Though the team disbanded, they completed this excellent work which is still in circulation nearly a decade later. We ask Allah to make it a continuous reward for them.

Dar al-Arqam Publishing
Birmingham, UK
11th October 2022

المقدمة المؤلف

Author's Introduction

All praise be to Allah, the Lord of the worlds, and may the *ṣalāt* and *salām* be on the trustworthy prophet – our prophet Muḥammad, and upon his people, his companions and those who followed them in goodness until the day of resurrection.

What follows are my brief annotations on the treatise *al-'Aqīdat al-Ṭaḥāwi-yyah*, based on transcriptions of lessons I delivered in Ṭā'if. After making some corrections and alterations, I gave permission for it to be published and distributed, seeking benefit from it. If the reader finds any mistake in it, it emanates from me and I request to be informed thereof, and in doing so one shall be rewarded by Allah. I ask Allah that he draws forth from this work benefit for the Muslims.

May the peace and blessings of Allah be upon our Prophet Muḥammad, his people and companions.

Ṣāliḥ b. Fawzān b. 'Abdi 'llāh al-Fawẓān

13/6/1421 (2000)

المتن

بِسْمِ اللهِ الرَّحْمَنِ الرَّحِيمِ

In the Name of Allah, the Most Merciful, the Giver of Mercy

قَالَ الْعَلَّامَةُ حُجَّةُ الإِسْلَامِ أَبُو جَعْفَرٍ الْوَرَّاقِ الطَّحَاوِيُّ - بِمِصْرَ - رَحِمَهُ اللهُ:

The great scholar, Ḥujjat al-Islām, Abū Jaʿfar al-Ṭaḥāwī[1] said in Egypt:

[١] هَذَا ذِكْرُ بَيَانِ عَقِيدَةِ أَهْلِ السُّنَّةِ وَالْجَمَاعَةِ عَلَىٰ مَذْهَبِ فُقَهَاءِ الْمِلَّةِ: أَبِي حَنِيفَةَ النُّعْمَانِ بْنِ ثَابِتٍ الْكُوفِيِّ، وَأَبِي يُوسُف يَعْقُوبَ بْنِ إِبْرَاهِيمَ الْأَنْصَارِيِّ، وَأَبِي عَبْدِ اللهِ مُحَمَّدِ بْنِ الْحَسَنِ الشَّيْبَانِيِّ رِضْوَانُ اللهِ عَلَيْهِمْ أَجْمَعِينَ، وَمَا يَعْتَقِدُونَ مِنْ أُصُولِ الدِّينِ، وَيَدِينُونَ بِهِ لِرَبِّ الْعَالَمِينَ.

1. This is a declaration of the *ʿaqīdah* (creed) of Ahl al-Sunnah wa 'l-Jamāʿah according to the view of the jurists of this religion, Abū Ḥanīfah al-Nuʿmān ibn Thābit al-Kūfī, Abū Yūsuf Yaʿqūb ibn Ibrāhīm al-Anṣārī, and Abū Muḥammad ibn al-Ḥasan al-Shaybāni ﷺ and the principles of faith in which they believed and with which they sought the pleasure of Allah.

الشرح

بسم الله الرحمن الرحيم والحمد لله رب العالمين، وصلىٰ الله وسلم علىٰ نبينا

---

1 The *imām*, the great *ḥāfiẓ*, the *muḥaddith* and *mufti* of Egypt. He was prominent in the study of ḥadīth and *fiqh* - both a compiler and author. He was *thiqah thabt* (highly reliable), a jurist and a man of intelligence. Anyone who observes his writings would know the level and breadth of his knowledge. He died in 321 H. May Allah have mercy on him. See al-Dhahabī, *Siyar Aʿlām al-Nubalāʾ*, vol. 15, p. 27-33.

محمد وعلىٰ آله وصحبه أجمعين.

In the name of Allah, the all Merciful, the most Merciful. Praise be to Allah, Lord of the Worlds. May Allah confer blessings upon our Prophet Muḥammad and upon his family and companions.

أما بعد: فإن العقيدة هي أساس الدين، وهي مضمون شهادة أن لا إله إلا الله وأن محمداً رسول الله، والركن الأول من أركان الإسلام، فيجب الاهتمام بها والعناية بها ومعرفتها، ومعرفة ما يخل بها، حتىٰ يكون الإنسان علىٰ بصيرة، وعلىٰ عقيدة صحيحة؛ لأنه إذا قام الدين علىٰ أساس صحيح صار ديناً قيماً مقبولاً عند الله، وإذا قام علىٰ عقيدة مهزوزة ومضطربة، أو عقيدة فاسدة، صار الدين غير صحيح، وعلىٰ غير أساس، ومن ثم كان العلماء -رحمهم الله- يهتمون بأمر العقيدة ولا يفترون في بيانها في الدروس وفي المناسبات، ويرويها المتأخر عن المتقدم.

To proceed: Creed is the basis of religion. It is the substance of the first pillar of Islam, the testimony that there is no God but Allah and Muḥammad ﷺ is the Messenger of Allah.[2] Therefore much focus has to be given to it. It has to be learned, and so does that which infringes it, so that man becomes discerning and upon the correct belief. Because if someone's faith is based on a correct foundation, it is valued and accepted by Allah; but if it is based on shaky and precarious beliefs, or on incorrect beliefs, then it is not correct and has no foundation. This is why the scholars gave such precedence to creed and why they never slackened in teaching it during their lessons and on special occasions. And the later generations related it from the earlier ones.

كان الصحابة -رضي الله عنهم- ليس عندهم أي شك فيما جاء به القرآن وما

2 According to a ḥadīth related by Ibn 'Umar: The Messenger of Allah ﷺ said: "Islam is based on five (principles): 1. To testify that none has the right to be worshipped but Allah and Muḥammad is Allah's Messenger. 2. To offer the *ṣalāt* dutifully and perfectly. 3. To pay *zakāt*. 4. To observe the fast during the month of Ramadan 5. To perform the *Ḥajj* if one is able." Al-Bukhārī, no. 8 and Muslim no. 16.

جاءت به سنة رسول الله، صلىٰ الله عليه وسلم، فكانت عقيدتهم مبنية علىٰ كتاب الله وسنة رسول الله، صلىٰ الله عليه وسلم، ولا يعتريهم في ذلك شك ولا توقف، فما قاله الله وقاله رسوله صلىٰ الله عليه وسلم اعتقدوه ودانوا به، ولم يحتاجوا إلىٰ كتابة تأليف؛ لأن هذا مسلّم به عندهم ومقطوع به وكانت عقيدتهم الكتاب والسنة، ثم درج علىٰ ذلك تلاميذهم من التابعين الذين أخذوا عنهم، فلم يكن هناك أخذ وردّ في العقيدة، كانت قضية مسلمة، وكان مرجعهم الكتاب والسنة.

The Companions did not possess doubts regarding any part of the Qur'ān or any part of the Sunnah of the Messenger of Allah ﷺ. Therefore their creed was based upon these two sources, and doubts and refrainment never afflicted them in this. Whatever Allah states and whatever His Messenger ﷺ said, they believed and took as their religion; and so they found no need to write books, because the matter was accepted and certain for them. Their creed was the Book and the Sunnah. Their disciples, the *Tābi'ūn* (Successors), learned from them and thus followed the same path. There was no give and take with creed. It was an accepted matter, and their reference was the Qur'ān and Sunnah.

فلما ظهرت الفرق والاختلافات، ودخل في الدين من لم ترسخ العقيدة في قلبه، أو دخل في الإسلام وهو يحمل بعض الأفكار المنحرفة، ونشأ في الإسلام من لم يرجع إلىٰ الكتاب ولا إلىٰ السنة في العقيدة، وإنما يرجع إلىٰ قواعد ومناهج أصلها أهل الضلال من عند أنفسهم، عند هذا احتاج أئمة الإسلام إلىٰ بيان العقيدة الصحيحة وتحريرها وكتابتها وروايتها عن علماء الأمة، فدونوا كتب العقائد، واعتنوا بها، وصارت مرجعاً لمن يأتي بعدهم من الأمة إلىٰ أن تقوم الساعة.

As time passed, the sects and disagreements appeared, and Islām was accepted by those in whose hearts the creed was not firmly grounded, or by those who entered into the religion whilst having deviant ideas, and some new Muslims did not refer to the Qur'ān and Sunnah for matters of creed, instead referring to theories and methodologies that the people of error founded on their own accord. The rise of these occurrences created the need for the Muslim *imāms* to teach and revise the correct creed as well as write it and narrate it from the learned ones of the Ummah. Therefore they wrote literature on creed and were very much concerned with it. This literature became a reference point for the Muslims who would come later, right until the coming of the Hour.

وهذا من حفظ الله تعالىٰ لهذا الدين، وعنايته بهذا الدين، أن قيض له حملة أمناء يبلغونه كما جاء عن الله وعن رسوله، ويردون تأويل المبطلين وتشبيه المشبهين، وصاروا يتوارثون هذه العقيدة خلفاً عن السلف.

This is from Allah's preservation and care for this religion, that He sent trusted bearers of it to convey it according to how it came from Allah and His Messenger ﷺ, and to reject the interpretations of the *mubṭalīn* (invalidators), and the likening [to creation] of the *mushabihīn* (anthropomorphists). They then began inheriting this creed, generation after generation.

ومن جملة السلف الصالح الذين كانوا علىٰ الاعتقاد الثابت عن رسول الله صلىٰ الله عليه وسلم وأصحابه والتابعين، من جملتهم الأئمة الأربعة الإمام أبو حنيفة، والإمام مالك، والإمام الشافعي، والإمام أحمد، وغيرهم من الأئمة الذين قاموا بالدفاع عن العقيدة وتحريرها، وبيانها وتعليمها للطلاب.

Among the righteous Salaf (predecessors) who followed the established creed of the Messenger of Allah ﷺ, his Companions, and the Tābiʿūn (the generation that met the companions but didn't meet the Prophet ﷺ) were the 'four *imāms*': al-Imām Abū Ḥanīfah, al-Imām Mālik, al-Imām al-Shāfiʿī, and al-Imām Aḥmad, as well as other *imāms* who defended and revised this creed, explained it and taught it to their students.

وكان أتباع الأئمة الأربعة يعتنون بهذه العقيدة، ويتدارسونها ويحفظونها لتلاميذهم، وكتبوا فيها الكتب الكثيرة علىٰ منهج الكتاب والسنة، وما كان عليه المصطفىٰ، صلىٰ الله عليه وسلم، وأصحابه رضي الله عنهم والتابعون، وردوا العقائد الباطلة والمنحرفة، وبينوا زيفها وباطلها، وكذلك أئمة الحديث: كإسحاق بن راهويه، والبخاري، ومسلم والإمام ابن خزيمة، والإمام ابن قتيبة،

ومن أئمة التفسير: كالإمام الطبري، والإمام ابن كثير، والإمام البغوي، وغيرهم من أئمة التفسير.

The followers of the four *imāms* maintained this creed, they studied it and dictated it to their students. And they wrote a number of books according to the methodology of the Qur'ān and Sunnah and the way of the Muṣṭafā ﷺ and the Companions and the Tābi'ūn, and they responded to the false and deviant doctrines, clarifying the falsity and incorrectness of them. This was also the way of the ḥadīth masters, such as the likes of Isḥāq ibn Rāhawiyah, al-Bukhārī, Muslim, al-Imām Ibn Khuzaymah, al-Imām Ibn Qutaybah; and of the *tafsīr* (Qur'ānic exegesis) masters, such as al-Imām al-Ṭabarī, al-Imām Ibn Kathīr, al-Imām al-Baghawī amongst others.

وألفوا في هذا مؤلفات يسمونها بكتب السنة، مثل كتاب السنة لابن أبي عاصم، وكتاب السنة لعبد الله بن أحمد بن حنبل، والسنة للخلال، والشريعة للآجري، وغير ذلك.

They wrote works termed as 'the books of the Sunnah' (*kutub al-sunnah*), such as *Kitāb al-Sunnah* by Ibn Abī 'Āṣim, *Kitāb al-Sunnah* by 'Abdullāh ibn Aḥmad ibn Ḥanbal, *al-Sunnah* by al-Khallāl, *al-Sharī'ah* by al-Ājurrī, and so on.

ومن جملة هؤلاء الأئمة الذين كتبوا في عقيدة السلف: الإمام أبو جعفر أحمد بن محمد بن سلامة الأزدي الطحاوي، من علماء القرن الثالث بمصر، وسمي بالطحاوي نسبة لبلدة في مصر، فكتب هذه العقيدة المختصرة النافعة المفيدة.

Among these *imāms* who wrote about the creed of the Salaf was al-Imām Abū Ja'far Aḥmad ibn Muḥammad ibn Salāmah al-Azdī al-Ṭaḥāwī, who was a scholar from the third century in Egypt. He was called 'al-Ṭaḥāwī' in relation to the town of his birth in Egypt. Al-Imām al-Ṭaḥāwī wrote this beneficial summarized creed.

وكتبت عليها شروح، حوالي سبعة شروح، ولكن لا تخلو من أخطاء؛ لأن الذين ألفوها كانوا على منهج المتأخرين، فلم تخل شروحهم من ملاحظات ومخالفة لما في عقيدة الطحاوي، إلا شرحاً واحداً فيما نعلم، وهو شرح العز بن أبي العز

رحمه الله، المشتهر بشرح الطحاوية، وهذا من تلاميذ ابن كثير فيما يظهر، وقد ضمن شرحه هذا منقولات من كتب شيخ الإسلام ابن تيمية، ومن كتب ابن القيم، ومن كتب الأئمة، فهو شرح حافل، وكان العلماء يعتمدون عليه ويعتنون به؛ لنقاوته وصحة معلوماته، فهو مرجع عظيم من مراجع العقيدة.

Around seven commentaries were written on it. However, these commentaries are not void of errors because the authors adhered to the methodologies of the later generations, so they are not free of views and observations that are contradictory to the creed of al-Ṭaḥāwī except for one—as far as we know—and that is the commentary of al-ʿIzz ibn Abi ʿl-ʿIzz,[3] which is popularly known as *The Commentary of al-Ṭaḥāwīyah*. He was one of the students of Ibn Kathīr, based on what is apparent. His commentary contains several citations from the literature of Shaykh al-Islām Ibn Taymiyyah and Ibn al-Qayyim, and also from the literature of the *imāms*, so it is a comprehensive commentary. The scholars have relied on it and paid special attention to it, because of its clarity and the correctness of the information in it. So it is a great reference point in creed.

والمؤلف - كما ذكر - ألف هذه العقيدة علىٰ مذهب أهل السنة عمومـًا، ومنهم الإمام أبو حنيفة النعمان بن ثابت الكوفي، فهو أقدم الأئمة الأربعة وأدرك التابعين وروىٰ عنهم. وكذلك صاحباه أبو يوسف، ومحمد الشيباني، وأئمة المذهب الحنفي.

Al-Ṭaḥāwī, as mentioned, wrote this creed according to the views of Ahl al-Sunnah in general, which includes al-Imām Abū Ḥanīfah al-Nuʿmān ibn Thābit al-Kūfī – who was the earliest of the four *imāms* and met the Tābiʿūn and related from them – as well as his two disciples: Abū Yūsuf and Muḥammad al-Shaybānī and the *imāms* of the Ḥanafī school of jurisprudence.

ذكر عقيدتهم، وأنها موافقة لمذهب أهل السنة والجماعة، وفي هذا ردٌّ علىٰ المنتسبين إلىٰ الحنفية في الوقت الحاضر أو في العصور المتأخرة، ينتسبون إلىٰ

3 He was the *imām* and great scholar, Ṣadr al-Dīn, Abu ʿl-Ḥasan ʿAlī ibn ʿAlāʾu ʿl-Dīn ʿAlī ibn Muḥammad ibn Abu ʿl-ʿIzz al-Ḥanafī al-Adhruʿī al-Ṣāliḥī. He came from a family of eminence and repute and was a student of al-Ḥāfiẓ Ibn Kathīr and supported the statements of Ibn Taymiyyah and Ibn al-Qayyim - may Allah have mercy on them.

الحنفية ويخالفون أبا حنيفة في العقيدة، فهم يمشون علىٰ مذهبه في الفقه فقط، ويخالفونه في العقيدة، فيأخذون عقيدة أهل الكلام والمنطق، وكذلك حدث في الشافعية المتأخرين منهم يخالفون الإمام الشافعي في العقيدة، وإنما ينتسبون إليه في الفقه، كذلك كثير من المالكية المتأخرين ليسوا علىٰ عقيدة الإمام مالك، لكنهم يأخذون من مذهب مالك في الفقه فقط، أما العقيدة فهم أصحاب طرق وأصحاب مذاهب متأخرة.

He states their creed and how it is in agreement with the views of Ahl al-Sunnah wa ʿl-Jamāʿah. This entails a refutation against those who associate themselves with the Ḥanafī school of *fiqh* in modern or later times: They associate themselves with the Ḥanafī school but contradict Abū Ḥanīfah in creed; rather they only follow his views in jurisprudence. They adopt the creed of those who profess *kalām* (theological dialectics) and the logicians. The same thing happened with the later Shāfiʿī scholars: they oppose al-Imām al-Shāfiʿī in creed and only associate themselves with him when it comes to jurisprudence. Similarly, many of the later Mālikī scholars do not follow the creed of al-Imām Mālik, but they adopt his views in jurisprudence only; as for creed, they follow [Ṣūfī] orders and the views of later generations.

ففي هذه العقدية ردٌّ علىٰ هؤلاء وأمثالهم ممن ينتسبون إلىٰ الأئمة، ويتمذهبون بمذاهب الأئمة الأربعة، ويخالفونهم في العقيدة، كالأشاعرة: ينتسبون إلىٰ الإمام أبي الحسن الأشعري في مذهبه الأول، ويتركون ما تقرر واستقر عليه أخيراً من مذهب أهل السنة والجماعة، فهذا انتساب غير صحيح؛ لأنهم لو كانوا علىٰ مذهب الأئمة لكانوا علىٰ عقيدتهم.

So this statement of creed entails a response to these people who associate themselves with the *imāms* and adopt their *madhāhib* (doctrines) in jurisprudence and oppose them in creed, such as the Ashʿarīs: they associate themselves with al-Imām Abu ʿl-Ḥasan al-Ashʿarī when it comes to his prior doctrines and leave the creed of Ahl al-Sunnah wa ʿl-Jamāʿah, which he adopted and settled upon later in life. Such an association is incorrect, because if they followed the doctrines of the *imāms*, they would have also followed their creed.

المتن

(٢) نَقُولُ فِي تَوْحِيدِ اللهِ -مُعْتَقِدِينَ بِتَوْفِيقِ اللهِ-: إِنَّ اللهَ واحِدٌ لا شَرِيكَ لَهُ.

(2) With the help of Allah, we say about *tawḥīd* (Oneness of Allah) – whilst believing in it: Allah is one and He has no partner.

الشرح

(نقول)، أي؛ نعتقد في توحيد الله عز وجل.

"With the help of Allah, we say…": I.e we believe regarding the oneness of Allah ﷻ.

والتوحيد لغة: مصدر وحّد: إذا جعل الشيء واحداً.

Linguistically, *"tawḥīd"* is the infinitive form of 'to take as one'.

وشرعاً: إفراد الله سبحانه وتعالىٰ بالعبادة، وترك عبادة ما سواه.

Technically, *tawḥīd* is to single out Allah ﷻ with worship and to leave the worship of anything else.

وأقسامه ثلاثة بالاستقراء من كتاب الله وسنة رسوله، صلىٰ الله عليه وسلم، وهذا ما تقرر عليه مذهب أهل السنة والجماعة، فمن زاد قسماً رابعاً أو خامساً فهو زيادة من عنده؛ لأن الأئمة قسّموا التوحيد إلىٰ أقسام ثلاثة من الكتاب والسنة. فكل آيات القرآن والأحاديث في العقيدة لا تخرج عن هذه الأقسام الثلاثة.

There are three categories of *tawḥīd*, as derived from the Book of Allah ﷻ and the Sunnah of the Messenger of Allah ﷺ. This is what has been adopted in the doctrine of Ahl al-Sunnah wa 'l-Jamā'ah; so if someone were to add a fourth or fifth category, it would be an addition from their own accord, because the *imāms* divided *tawḥīd* into three categories from the Qur'ān and Sunnah. All of the *āyāt* of the Qur'ān and ḥadīths concerning faith do not depart from these three categories.

الأول: توحيد الربوبية: وهو توحيد الله تعالىٰ وإفراده بأفعاله: كالخلق، والرزق، والإحياء والإماتة، وتدبير الكون، فليس هناك رب سواه سبحانه وتعالىٰ، رب العالمين.

The first category: *Tawḥīd al-Rubūbiyyah* (Oneness of Lordship), this is to take and single out Allah ﷻ as one in His actions, such as creating, providing, giving life, bringing death, and handling the affairs of the universe. There is no lord besides Him ﷻ, He is the Lord of the Worlds.

القسم الثاني: توحيد الألوهية أو توحيد العبادة؛ لأن الألوهية معناها عبادة الله عز وجل بمحبته وخوفه ورجائه، وطاعة أمره، وترك ما نهىٰ عنه فهو إفراد الله تعالىٰ بأفعال العباد التي شرعها لهم.

The second category: *Tawḥīd al-Ulūhiyyah* or *Tawḥīd al-'Ibādah* (Oneness of Worship), because *ulūhiyyah* means worshipping Allah ﷻ by loving Him, fearing Him and having hope in Him; as well as obeying His commands and leaving what He has forbidden. So, it is for someone to single Allah ﷻ out with the acts of worship that Allah ﷻ has sanctioned for them.

القسم الثالث: توحيد الأسماء والصفات: وهو إثبات ما أثبته الله لنفسه أو أثبته له رسوله صلىٰ الله عليه وسلم من الأسماء والصفات، وتنزيهه عما نزّه عنه نفسه، ونزّهه عنه رسوله صلىٰ الله عليه وسلم من العيوب والنقائص.

The third category: *Tawḥīd al-Asmā' wa 'l-Ṣifāt* (Oneness of Names and Attributes). It is to affirm the Names and Attributes that Allah ﷻ has affirmed for Himself and that His Messenger ﷺ affirmed for Him, and to deem Allah transcendent from that which he and His Messenger ﷺ have done so, from deficiencies and shortcomings.

فكل الآيات التي تتحدث عن أفعال الله فإنها في توحيد الربوبية، وكل الآيات التي تتحدث عن العبادة والأمر بها والدعوة إليها فإنها في توحيد الألوهية. وكل الآيات التي تتحدث عن الأسماء والصفات لله عز وجل فإنها في توحيد الأسماء والصفات.

All of the *āyāt* (verses) that talk about the acts of Allah ﷻ have to do with *Tawḥīd al-Rubūbiyyah* (Oneness of Lordship); and all of the *āyāt* that talk about commanding and advocating worship have to do with *Tawḥīd al-Ulūhiyah* (Oneness of Worship); and all of the *āyāt* that talk about the Names and Attributes of Allah the Almighty have to do with *Tawḥīd al-Asmā' wa 'l-Ṣifāt* (Oneness of the Names and Attributes).

وهذه الأقسام الثلاثة المطلوب منها هو توحيد الألوهية؛ لأنه هو الذي دعت إليه الرسل، ونزلت به الكتب، وقام من أجله الجهاد في سبيل الله، حتىٰ يُعبد الله وحده، وتُترك عبادة ما سواه.

The category sought after is *Tawḥīd al-Ulūhiyyah,* because this branch of *tawḥīd* is what the Messengers preached and the reason the Qur'ān was revealed, and *jihād* in the path of Allah has been prescribed for its sake, so that nothing would be worshipped besides Allah alone, and the worship of anything else besides Him would be left.

وأما توحيد الربوبية ومنه توحيد الأسماء والصفات فلم ينكره أحد من الخلق، وذكر الله سبحانه وتعالىٰ ذلك في آيات كثيرة، ذكر أن الكفار مُقرُّون بأن الله هو الخالق الرازق، المحيي المميت، والمدبر، فهم لا يخالفون فيه. وهذا النوع إذا اقتصر عليه الإنسان لا يدخله ذلك في الإسلام؛ لأن النبي، صلىٰ الله عليه وسلم، قاتل الناس وهم يقرون بتوحيد الربوبية، واستحل دمائهم وأموالهم.

As regards to *Tawḥīd al-Rubūbiyyah*, which includes *Tawḥīd al-Asmā' wa 'l-Ṣifāt*, no one denied it. Allah the Almighty mentions this in many *āyāt*, and He mentioned that the disbelievers acknowledge that Allah is the Creator and Provider, He who gives life, He who brings death, and He who has control; on this there is no opposition. A person does not accept Islām through the acceptance of *al-Rubūbiyyah* alone, because the Prophet ﷺ fought against people who acknowledged *Tawḥīd al-Rubūbiyyah*; he declared their blood and wealth as lawful.

ولو كان توحيد الربوبية كافياً لما قاتلهم الرسول عليه الصلاة والسلام، بل ما كان هناك حاجة إلىٰ بعثة الرسل، فدل علىٰ أن المقصود والمطلوب هو توحيد

الألوهية.

If *Tawḥīd al-Rubūbiyyah* sufficed, the Messenger ﷺ would not have fought them. In fact, there would be no need for the Messengers to be sent. This indicates that what is intended and desired is *Tawḥīd al-Ulūhiyyah.*

أما توحيد الربوبية فإنه دليل عليه، وآية له، ولذلك إذا أمر الله بعبادته ذكر خلقه للسموات والأرض، وقيامه سبحانه بشؤون خلقه، برهانـًا علىٰ توحيد الألوهية، وإلزامـًا للكفار والمشركين، الذين يعترفون بالربوبية وينكرون الألوهية، ولما قال لهم النبي صلىٰ الله عليه وسلم: «**قولوا: لا إله إلا الله**» قالوا: ﴿أَجَعَلَ الْآلِهَةَ إِلَٰهًا وَاحِدًا ۖ إِنَّ هَٰذَا لَشَيْءٌ عُجَابٌ﴾ [ص:٥].

Tawḥīd al-Rubūbiyyah, however, is an evidence and a sign for *Tawḥīd al-Ulūhiyyah*. Therefore, when Allah commands that He be worshipped, He mentions that He created the heavens and earth and handles the affairs of His creatures as a proof for the oneness of His worship and to present a compelling argument against the disbelievers and idolaters who acknowledge the lordship of Allah ﷻ but deny His worship. When the Prophet ﷺ commanded them to say 'There is no God but Allah', they said: **{Has he made the gods [only] one God? Indeed, this is a curious thing.}**[4] **[Qurʾān 38:5]**

وقال سبحانه وتعالىٰ: ﴿وَإِذَا ذُكِرَ اللَّهُ وَحْدَهُ اشْمَأَزَّتْ قُلُوبُ الَّذِينَ لَا يُؤْمِنُونَ

4 It is related that Ibn ʿAbbās ؓ said: "Abū Ṭālib fell sick, so some people from Quraysh came to visit him; and the Prophet ﷺ came to visit him as well. There was only enough space for one man to sit close to Abū Ṭālib. So, Abū Jahl stood up to stop the Prophet ﷺ from sitting there, and they complained to Abū Ṭālib about the Prophet ﷺ. So Abū Ṭālib said: 'O my nephew, what do you want from your people?' The Prophet ﷺ replied: 'I want them to say one word by which the Arabs will follow them and the non-Arabs will pay *jizyah* (a tax paid by non-Muslims who live under the protection of the Muslim state) to them.' Abū Ṭālib said: 'One word?' The Prophet ﷺ said: 'One word.' He said: 'O uncle, the word is that there is no God but Allah.' So, they said: 'One God! We have not heard this in the religion of the later days. This is not but a fabrication.'" He said: "And so the Qurʾān descended concerning them: ***{Ṣād. By the Qurʾān containing reminder...'* through *'This is not but a fabrication.'}*** Aḥmad, *Musnad:* 1/228; al-Tirmidhī, *Sunan: Kitāb al-tafsīr: wa min sūrat ṣād*, no. 3232; al-Tirmidhī said: '*ḥadīth ḥasan ṣaḥīḥ'*. Shaykh Aḥmad Shākir also said it was authentic (no. 2008).

بِالْآخِرَةِ ۖ وَإِذَا ذُكِرَ الَّذِينَ مِن دُونِهِ إِذَا هُمْ يَسْتَبْشِرُونَ﴾ [الزمر: ٤٥].

Allah the Almighty also says: **{And when Allah is mentioned alone, the hearts of those who do not believe in the Hereafter shrink with aversion, but when those [worshipped] other than Him are mentioned, immediately they rejoice.} [Qur'ān 39:45]**

وقال تعالىٰ: ﴿إِنَّهُمْ كَانُوا إِذَا قِيلَ لَهُمْ لَا إِلَٰهَ إِلَّا اللَّهُ يَسْتَكْبِرُونَ ﴿٣٥﴾ وَيَقُولُونَ أَئِنَّا لَتَارِكُوٓا۟ ءَالِهَتِنَا لِشَاعِرٍ مَّجْنُونٍ ﴿٣٦﴾﴾ [الصافات: ٣٥:٣٦]

Allah also says: **{Indeed they, when it was said to them, 'There is no Deity but Allah,' were arrogant, and were saying, 'Are we to leave our gods for a mad poet?'} [Qur'ān 37:35-36]**

فهم لا يريدون توحيد الألوهية، بل يريدون أن تكون الآلهة متعددة، وكلٌّ يعبد ما يريد.

Here, they do not want *Tawḥīd al-Ulūhiyyah* (Oneness of Worship) but rather multiple gods and that each person worships what he or she wants.

فيجب أن يُعلم هذا، فإن كل أصحاب الفرق الضالة الحديثة والقديمة، يركزون علىٰ توحيد الربوبية، فإنه إذا أقر العبد عندهم بأن الله هو الخالق الرازق، قالوا: هذا مسلم، وكتبوا بذلك عقائدهم، فكل عقائد المتكلمين لا تخرج عن تحقيق توحيد الربوبية والأدلة عليه

This has to be known, because the members of the deviant sects, new and old, focus on *Tawḥīd al-Rubūbiyyah.* According to their viewpoint, if someone acknowledges that Allah is the Creator and Provider, he is considered a Muslim. Also, they write such in their doctrines of creed. All of the doctrines of the *kalām* (theological dialectic) proponents establish *Tawḥīd al-Rubūbiyyah* and the evidence for it.

وهذا لا يكفي، بل لابد من الألوهية، قال تعالىٰ : ﴿وَلَقَدْ بَعَثْنَا فِي كُلِّ أُمَّةٍ رَّسُولًا أَنِ ٱعْبُدُوا۟ ٱللَّهَ وَٱجْتَنِبُوا۟ ٱلطَّٰغُوتَ﴾ [النحل: ٣٦] يأمرون الناس بعبادة الله وهي توحيد الألوهية.

This is not enough, but rather *Tawḥīd al-Ulūhīyyah* is needed. Allah ﷻ says: **{And We certainly sent into every nation a messenger, [saying], 'Worship Allah and avoid the Ṭāghūt.'} [Qur'ān 16:36]** The Messengers commanded people to worship Allah ﷻ, which is *Tawḥīd al-Ulūhīyyah.*

﴿وَمَآ أَرۡسَلۡنَا مِن قَبۡلِكَ مِن رَّسُولٍ إِلَّا نُوحِيٓ إِلَيۡهِ أَنَّهُۥ لَآ إِلَٰهَ إِلَّآ أَنَا۠ فَٱعۡبُدُونِ ٢٥﴾ [الأنبياء:٢٥]، ﴿وَٱعۡبُدُواْ ٱللَّهَ وَلَا تُشۡرِكُواْ بِهِۦ شَيۡـٔٗاۖ﴾ [النساء: ٣٦].

{And We sent not before you any messenger except that We revealed to him that, 'There is no deity except Me, so worship Me.'" [Qur'ān 21:25] {Worship Allah and associate nothing with Him.} [Qur'ān 4:36]

كل الآيات تأمر بتوحيد الألوهية وتدعو إليه، وجميع الرسل دعوا إلىٰ توحيد الألوهية وأمروا به أممهم، ونهوهم عن الشرك، هذا هو المطلوب والغاية والقصد من التوحيد، وأما توحيد الأسماء والصفات فأنكره المبتدعة من الجهمية والمعتزلة والأشاعرة، علىٰ تفاوت بينهم في ذلك.

All of these *āyāt* command and preach to the oneness of worship and all of the Messengers preached and enjoined it upon their people and they forbade them from polytheism. This is what is required and what is ultimately meant by *tawḥīd.* As regards to the oneness of Allah's Names and Attributes, it has been denied by heretics such as the Jahmites, the Muʿtazilites, and the Ashʿarites to varying extents.

وقوله (نقول): - أي يقول معشر أهل السنة والجماعة - **(في توحيد الله، معتقدين بتوفيق الله : إن الله واحد لا شريك له).**

"With the help of Allah, we say": 'We' denotes Ahl al-Sunnah wa 'l-Jamāʿah, **"about *tawḥīd* (Oneness of Allah) – whilst believing in it: Allah is one and He has no partner."**

العقيدة والتوحيد بمعنىٰ واحد. سواء سُميت عقيدة أو توحيداً أو إيماناً، فالمعنىٰ واحد وإن اختلفت الأسماء.

Creed and *tawḥīd* have the same meaning, regardless of whether it is called creed, or *tawḥīd*, or faith. It has one meaning, though given different names.

وقوله: (بتوفيق الله) هذا تسليم لله عز وجل، وتضرّع إلىٰ الله، وتبرؤ من الحول والقوة، فالإنسان لا يزكي نفسه، وإنما يقول: بتوفيق الله، بمشيئة الله، بحول الله، هذا أدب العلماء رحمهم الله.

"With the help of Allah...": This is an expression of submission and supplication to Allah, and a denouncement of one's own ability and strength. Rather, it is stated: "with Allah's help", "by Allah's will" or "by Allah's Might" [that a deed is performed.] This is the manner of the learned ones, may Allah have mercy on them.

(إن الله واحد لا شريك له) هذا هو التوحيد؛ واحد في ربوبيته، واحد في ألوهيته، وواحد في أسماءه وصفاته.

"Allah is one and He has no partner": This is *tawḥīd*. He is one in His Lordship, one in His Worship, and one in His Names and Attributes.

المتن

(٣) وَلا شَيْءَ مِثْلُهُ:

(3) There is nothing like Him.

الشرح

مأخوذ من قوله تعالىٰ: ﴿لَيْسَ كَمِثْلِهِۦ شَيْءٌ﴾ [الشورىٰ:١١]، وقوله تعالىٰ: ﴿وَلَمْ يَكُن لَّهُۥ كُفُوًا أَحَدٌۢ ۝٤﴾ [الإخلاص : ٤]، وقوله تعالىٰ: ﴿فَلَا تَجْعَلُواْ لِلَّهِ أَندَادًا﴾ [البقرة: ٢٢]، أي شبهاء ونظراء.

This is derived from the statement of Allah ﷻ: **{There is nothing like unto Him...} [Qur'ān 42:11]** And: **{Nor is there to Him any equivalent." [Qur'ān 112:4]** And also: **{So do not attribute to Allah equals while you know [that there is nothing similar to Him].} [Qur'ān**

2:22] I.e. likenesses and counterparts.

وقوله تعالىٰ: ﴿هَلۡ تَعۡلَمُ لَهُۥ سَمِيّٗا ٦٥﴾ [مريم: ٦٥]، أي: مماثل يساميه سبحانه وتعالىٰ، فالتمثيل والتشبيه منفيان عن الله عز وجل.

The Most High also says: **{Do you know of any similarity to Him?} [Qur'ān 19:65]** Meaning, nothing can vie with the Most Sublime. There are no similarities or likenesses to Allah ﷻ.

لا يشبهه أحد من خلقه، وهذا هو الواجب أن نثبت ما أثبته الله لنفسه ونعتقده ولا نشبهه بأحد من خلقه، ولا نمثّله بخلقه سبحانه وتعالىٰ، وهذا فيه رد علىٰ المشبهة الذين يعتقدون أن الله مثل خلقه، ولا يُفرقون بين الخالق والمخلوق، وهو مذهب باطل.

None of His creation is like Him. What is obligatory in regards to this is as follows: to affirm and believe whatever Allah has affirmed for Himself and not to assimilate Him to or liken Him with anything from His creation. This is a response to the Mushabbihah sect, who believe that Allah is like the creation and do not differentiate between the Creator and the created and this is evidently a false doctrine.

وفي مقابله مذهب المعطلة؛ الذين غلوا في التنزيه حتىٰ نفوا عن الله ما أثبته من الأسماء والصفات، فراراً من التشبيه بزعمهم.

Opposite to this deviant viewpoint is the doctrine of the Muʿaṭṭilah, who go to great excess in their sanctification of Allah's names, to the extent that they deny the Names and Attributes of Allah that He has affirmed, purportedly in order to avoid anthropomorphism.

فكلا الطائفتين غلت، المعطلة غلوا في التنزيه ونفي المماثلة، والمشبهة غلوا في الإثبات، وأهل السنة والجماعة توسّطوا؛ فأثبتوا ما أثبته الله لنفسه علىٰ ما يليق بجلاله، من غير تشبيه ولا تعطيل علىٰ حد قوله تعالىٰ ﴿لَيۡسَ كَمِثۡلِهِۦ شَيۡءٞۖ وَهُوَ ٱلسَّمِيعُ ٱلۡبَصِيرُ ١١﴾ [الشورىٰ:١١] فقوله: ﴿لَيۡسَ كَمِثۡلِهِۦ شَيۡءٞ﴾ نفي للتشبيه،

وقوله: ﴿وَهُوَ ٱلسَّمِيعُ ٱلْبَصِيرُ﴾ نفي للتعطيل، وهذا المذهب الذي يسير عليه أهل السنة والجماعة.

Both of these sects have gone to excess. The Muʿaṭṭilah have gone to excesses in the sanctification of Allah and negation of anthropomorphism, and the Mushabbihah have gone to excess in affirming Allah's Names and Attributes. Ahl al-Sunnah wa 'l-Jamāʿah take a middle course: they affirm what Allah has said about Himself in a manner that is in accord with His eminence, without comparing or negating, in accordance to His statement: **{There is nothing like unto Him, and He is the Hearing, the Seeing.} [Qur'ān 42:11]** His saying: **{There is nothing like unto Him}** negates all comparisons, and His saying: **{...and He is the Hearing, the Seeing}** negates the act of negation (*taʿṭīl*). This is the doctrine adopted by Ahl al-Sunnah wa 'l-Jamāʿah.

ولهذا يُقال: المعطل يعبد عدماً، والمشبه يعبد صنماً، والموحد يعبد إلهاً واحداً فرداً صمداً.

Hence it is said that a Muʿaṭṭil worships naught, a Mushabbih worships an idol, and a person of *tawḥīd* worships the One, the Unrivalled, the Refuge.

المتن

(٤) وَلا شَيْءَ يُعْجِزُهُ:

(4) There is nothing that can overwhelm Him.

الشرح

هذا إثبات لكمال قدرته: قال تعالىٰ : ﴿وَهُوَ عَلَىٰ كُلِّ شَىْءٍ قَدِيرٌ ١٢٠﴾ [المائدة: ١٢٠]. وقال تعالىٰ: ﴿وَكَانَ ٱللَّهُ عَلَىٰ كُلِّ شَىْءٍ مُّقْتَدِرًا ٤٥﴾ [الكهف : ٤٥]. وقال تعالىٰ : ﴿إِنَّهُۥ كَانَ عَلِيمًا قَدِيرًا ٤٤﴾ [فاطر: ٤٤].

This is to affirm the complete omnipotence of Allah. Allah says: **{And He**

is over all things able.} [Qur'ān 5:120] And: **{And Allah is ever, over all things, Perfect in Ability.} [Qur'ān 18:45]** And also: **{Indeed, He is ever Knowing and Competent.} [Qur'ān 35:44]**

والقدير معناه: المبالغ في القدرة، فقدرته سبحانه وتعالىٰ لا يعجزها شيء، إذا أراد شيئًا فإنما يقول له: كن فيكون.

The Omnipotent (al-Qadīr) means that He has the greatest extent of ability. Allah's ﷻ power cannot be rendered incapable by anything. If He wants something, He only says "be" and it is.

فهذا فيه إثبات قدرة الله عز وجل، وإثبات شمولها، وعمومها لكل شيء.

This is an affirmation of Allah's ﷻ omnipotence and affirmation of its totality and inclusive nature.

أما العبارة التي يقولها بعض المؤلفين: إنه علىٰ ما يشاء قدير. فهذه غلط؛ لأن الله لم يقيد قدرته بالمشيئة، بل قال: علىٰ كل شيء قدير، فقل ما قاله الله سبحانه وتعالىٰ. إنما هذه وردت في قوله تعالىٰ: ﴿وَهُوَ عَلَىٰ جَمْعِهِمْ إِذَا يَشَآءُ قَدِيرٌ ۝٢٩﴾ [الشورىٰ: ٢٩]؛ لأن الجمع له وقت محدد في المستقبل، وهو قادر علىٰ جمعهم في ذلك الوقت، أي أهل السماوات وأهل الأرض، قال تعالىٰ: ﴿وَمِنْ ءَايَٰتِهِۦ خَلْقُ ٱلسَّمَٰوَٰتِ وَٱلْأَرْضِ وَمَا بَثَّ فِيهِمَا مِن دَآبَّةٍۚ وَهُوَ عَلَىٰ جَمْعِهِمْ إِذَا يَشَآءُ قَدِيرٌ ۝٢٩﴾ [الشورىٰ:٢٩].

As regards to the statement of some authors that "He is able to do *as He wills*", it is a mistake, because Allah never limited His ability to His will, but rather said that He is able to do all things, therefore we should state the same as what Allah ﷻ has said about Himself. This is mentioned within the context of Allah's statement: **{And He, for gathering them when He wills, is competent.} [Qur'ān 42:29]** That is because the *gathering* has a specific time in the future, and He is able to gather them (the dwellers of heaven and earth) at that time. Allah ﷻ says: **{And of His signs is the creation of the heavens and earth and what He has dispersed throughout them of creatures. And He, for gathering them when He wills, is competent.} [Qur'ān 42:29]**

❁❁❁

المتن

(٥) وَلا إِلَهَ غَيْرُهُ.

(5) There is no God but Him.

الشرح

هذا هو توحيد الألوهية. **(لا إله)**، أي: لا معبود بحق غيره.

This is *Tawḥīd al-Ulūhiyyah*. **"There is no God..."** i.e. there is nothing rightfully worshipped besides him.

أما إذا قلت: لا معبود إلا هو؛ أو لا معبود سواه، فهذا باطل؛ لأن المعبودات كثيرة من دون الله عز وجل، فإذا قلت: لا معبود إلا الله، فقد جعلت كل المعبودات هي الله، وهذا مذهب أهل وحدة الوجود، فإذا كان قائل ذلك يعتقد هذا فهو من أصحاب أهل وحدة الوجود، وأما إن كان لا يعتقد هذا، إنما يقوله تقليداً أو سمعه من أحد، فهذا غلط، ويجب عليه تصحيح ذلك. وبعض الناس يستفتح بهذا في الصلاة فيقول: ولا معبود غيرك، والله معبود بحق، وما سواه فإنه معبود بالباطل، قال تعالى: ﴿ذَٰلِكَ بِأَنَّ ٱللَّهَ هُوَ ٱلْحَقُّ وَأَنَّ مَا يَدْعُونَ مِن دُونِهِۦ هُوَ ٱلْبَٰطِلُ وَأَنَّ ٱللَّهَ هُوَ ٱلْعَلِيُّ ٱلْكَبِيرُ ﴿٦٢﴾﴾ [الحج: ٦٢].

However if we say 'Nothing is worshipped except Him', it would be incorrect, because evidently there are many things that are worshipped besides Allah the Almighty. And if we say 'There is nothing worshipped but Allah', then that means that everything that is worshipped is Allah. This is the doctrine of the pantheists (proponents of *waḥdat al-wujūd*). If the person who says this actually believes in it, then he is a pantheist; but if he does not believe in it and only says it in imitation of others, then it is wrong and he has to rectify that. Some people [wrongly] commence their prayers with this, saying, 'There is nothing worshipped besides You.' However, Allah has the sole right to be worshipped, and the worship of all other things is in vain. Allah ﷻ says: **{That is because Allah is the Truth, and that which they**

call upon other than Him is falsehood, and because Allah is the Most High, the Grand." [Qur'ān 22:62]

المتن

(٦) قَدِيمٌ بِلا ابْتِداءٍ، دائِمٌ بِلا انْتِهاءٍ.

(6) He is eternal, without a beginning; Everlasting without an end.

الشرح

كما دل عليه قوله تعالىٰ: ﴿هُوَ ٱلْأَوَّلُ وَٱلْآخِرُ﴾ [الحديد:٣]، وقوله عليه الصلاة والسلام: «**أنت الأول فليس قبلك شيء، وأنت الآخر فليس بعدك شيء**».

As in His statement: **{He is the First and the Last.} [Qur'ān 57:3]** Also, the Prophet's ﷺ statement, **"You are the First, there is nothing before You; and You are the Last, there is nothing after You."**[5]

لكن كلمة (**قديم**) لا تُطلق علىٰ الله عز وجل إلا من باب الخبر، أما من جهة التسمية فليس من أسمائه: القديم، وإنما من أسمائه: الأول. والأول ليس مثل القديم؛ لأن القديم قد يكون قبله شيء، أما الأول فليس قبله شيء، قال عليه الصلاة والسلام: «**أنت الأول فليس قبلك شيء**».

However, the word 'eternal' (*qadīm*) does not denote Allah ﷻ unless it is only to inform about Him. When it comes to the names of Allah ﷻ, 'the eternal' (*al-qadīm*) is not one of His names. Rather, one of His names is the First (al-Awwal). The First is not the same as 'the eternal', because something eternal may have had something preceding it, but there is nothing before the First. The Prophet ﷺ said, **"You are the First, there is nothing before You."**

لكن المؤلف رحمه الله احتاط فقال: (**قديم بلا ابتداء**)، أما لو قال: (قديم)

5 Muslim, no. 2713.

وسكت، فهذا ليس بصحيح في المعنىٰ.

However, the author ﷺ took care by saying: "eternal without a beginning". If, however, he had only said 'eternal', then the meaning would not be correct.

المتن

(٧) لا يَفْنَىٰ وَلا يَبِيدُ.

(7) He neither perishes nor dies.

الشرح

الفناء والبيد بمعنىٰ واحد، فالله سبحانه وتعالىٰ موصوف بالحياة الباقية الدائمة، قال تعالىٰ: ﴿وَتَوَكَّلْ عَلَى ٱلْحَيِّ ٱلَّذِى لَا يَمُوتُ﴾ [الفرقان: ٥٨]. فالله لا يأتي عليه الفناء، قال سبحانه وتعالىٰ: ﴿كُلُّ شَىْءٍ هَالِكٌ إِلَّا وَجْهَهُۥ﴾ [القصص:٨٨]، وقال سبحانه وتعالىٰ: ﴿كُلُّ مَنْ عَلَيْهَا فَانٍ ﴿٢٦﴾ وَيَبْقَىٰ وَجْهُ رَبِّكَ ذُو ٱلْجَلَٰلِ وَٱلْإِكْرَامِ ﴿٢٧﴾﴾ [الرحمن:٢٦،٢٧].

'To perish' (*fanā'*) and 'to die' (*bayd*) have the same meaning. Allah ﷻ is described with everlasting life. Allah ﷻ says: **{And rely upon the Ever-Living who does not die...} [Qur'ān 25: 58]** So, Allah ﷻ does not perish. The Most High says: **{Everything will be destroyed except His Face.} [Qur'ān 28:88]** Allah ﷻ also says: **{Everyone upon the earth will perish, and there will remain the Face of your Lord, Owner of Majesty and Honour.} [Qur'ān 55:26-27]**

فله البقاء سبحانه وتعالىٰ، والخلق يموتون ثم يبعثون، وكانوا في الأول عدماً ثم خلقهم الله، ثم يموتون ثم يبعثهم الله عز وجل.

So, Allah ﷻ is everlasting, and created beings die and are then resurrected. They were non-existent until Allah ﷻ created them and Allah the Almighty will raise them from the dead.

فالله سبحانه وتعالىٰ ليس له بداية وليس له نهاية.

In short, Allah the Almighty has no beginning and no end.

المتن

(٨) وَلا يَكُونُ إِلّا ما يُرِيدُ.

(8) Nothing takes place except that which He wills.

الشرح

هذا فيه إثبات القدر وإثبات الإرادة، فلا يكون في ملكه ولا يحصل في خلقه من الحوادث والكائنات إلا ما أراده سبحانه وتعالىٰ بالإرادة الكونية: ﴿إِنَّمَآ أَمْرُهُۥٓ إِذَآ أَرَادَ شَيْـًٔا أَن يَقُولَ لَهُۥ كُن فَيَكُونُ ﴿٨٢﴾﴾ [يس:٨٢]

This is an affirmation of *Qadar* (predestination) and the will of Allah ﷻ. This means that nothing is present in His kingdom and no incident occurs or object arises in His creation unless Allah ﷻ wills so, as part of His universal will (*al-irādah al-kawnīyah*): **{His command is only when He intends a thing that He says to it, 'Be,' and it is.} [Qur'ān 36:82]**

فكل خير وكل شر فهو بإرادة الله الكونية، فلا يخرج عن إرادته شيء، وهذا فيه رد علىٰ القدرية الذين ينفون القدر، ويزعمون أن العبد هو الذي يخلق فعل نفسه ويوجد فعل نفسه، تعالىٰ الله عما يقولون، وهذا تعجيز لله، وأنه يكون في خلقه ما لا يريده سبحانه وتعالىٰ، فهذا وصف له بالنقص، فجميع ما يكون في الكون من خير وشر فإنه بإرادته، فيخلق الخير لحكمة، ويخلق الشر لحكمة، فهو من جهة خلقه له ليس بشر؛ لأنه لحكمة عظيمة، ولغاية عظيمة، وهي الابتلاء والامتحان، وتمييز الخبيث من الطيب، والجزاء علىٰ الأعمال الصالحة، والجزاء علىٰ الأعمال السيئة، له الحكمة في ذلك سبحانه وتعالىٰ، لم يخلق ذلك عبثًا.

Every good and bad thing is by the universal will of Allah ﷻ. Nothing is outside of His will. This is a response to the Qadarīyyah sect, who deny Allah's ﷻ predestination and contend that people themselves create their own actions and cause them to exist. Allah is transcendent of such a thing. This is attributing inability to Allah and insinuating that something He does not want exists in His creation, and is thus an ascription of deficiency to Him. Everything that exists, whether good or bad, its existence is because Allah ﷻ wanted it. Both good and bad are created out of his wisdom. We say about the bad, from the aspect that it is He who created it; it is not bad because it occurs due to a greater wisdom and purpose, namely, to test and try people, to separate the evil from the good, and to recompense for good deeds as well as bad deeds. The Most High is wise in doing so. He has not created in vain.

المتن

(٩) لا تَبْلُغُهُ الْأَوْهامُ، وَلا تُدْرِكُهُ الْأَفْهامُ.

(9) He cannot be perceived by the imagination nor comprehended by any understanding.

الشرح

فالله سبحانه وتعالىٰ لا يُحاط به، فالله أعظم من كل شيء سبحانه وتعالىٰ ﴿يَعْلَمُ مَا بَيْنَ أَيْدِيهِمْ وَمَا خَلْفَهُمْ وَلَا يُحِيطُونَ بِهِۦ عِلْمًا ﴿١١٠﴾﴾ [طه:١١٠]، فالله سبحانه يُعلم ولكن لا يُحاط به، فالله أعظم من كل شيء ، فلا يتخيله الفكر، ولا يجوز لإنسان أن يقول في الله إلا ما قاله سبحانه عن نفسه، أو قاله عنه رسوله عليه الصلاة والسلام .

Allah the Almighty cannot be [fully] comprehended. He is greater than everything. **{He knows what is in front of them and what is behind them, and they do not encompass Him in [their] knowledge." [Qur'ān 20:110]** Thus, Allah ﷻ is known, but not [fully] comprehended. Allah ﷻ is greater than all things, so thoughts cannot visualise Him, and it is not permissible for anyone to say something about Allah ﷻ besides what the Almighty has said about Himself or what His Messenger ﷺ said about Him.

المتن

(١٠) وَلا يُشْبِهُ الأَنَامَ.

(10) He does not resemble any created being (*anām*).

الشرح

هذه مثل العبارة التي مضت، ولا شيء مثله، والأنام معناه: الخلق، فالله سبحانه وتعالىٰ منزه عن مشابهة الخلق: ﴿لَيْسَ كَمِثْلِهِۦ شَىْءٌ ۖ وَهُوَ ٱلسَّمِيعُ ٱلْبَصِيرُ ﴿١١﴾﴾ [الشورىٰ:١١]، ﴿وَلَمْ يَكُن لَّهُۥ كُفُوًا أَحَدٌۢ ﴿٤﴾﴾ [الإخلاص:٤] فهو سبحانه منزه عن مشابهة خلقه، وإن كان له أسماء وصفات تشترك مع أسماء وصفات الخلق في اللفظ والمعنىٰ، لكن في الحقيقة والكيفية لا تشابه بينهما.

This is similar to the aforementioned statement, that there is nothing like Him. *Anām* means the creation. Allah ﷻ transcends resembling the creation: **{There is nothing like unto Him, and He is the Hearing, the Seeing.} [Qurʾān 42:11]** And: **{Nor is there to Him any equivalent.} [Qurʾān 112:4]** Allah ﷻ is transcendent and thus does not resemble the creation, although He has names and attributes that are common with the names and attributes of the creation in letters and meaning. However, as far as their reality and their exact nature, there is no similarity between them.

المتن

(١١) حَيٌّ لا يَمُوتُ.

(11) He is living and will never die;

الشرح

حياته كاملة لا يعتريها نقص ولا نوم ﴿ٱللَّهُ لَآ إِلَٰهَ إِلَّا هُوَ ٱلْحَىُّ ٱلْقَيُّومُ ۚ لَا تَأْخُذُهُۥ

سِنَةٌ وَلَا نَوْمٌ﴾ [البقرة:٢٥٥]، ﴿وَتَوَكَّلْ عَلَى ٱلْحَيِّ ٱلَّذِى لَا يَمُوتُ﴾ [الفرقان:٥٨] فنفىٰ عن نفسه السِّنة، وهي النوم الخفيف والنوم المستغرق، ونفىٰ عن نفسه الموت لكمال حياته سبحانه. والنوم والنعاس والموت نقص في الحياة، وهذه من صفة المخلوق، وحياة المخلوق ناقصة فهو ينام ويموت.

His existence is perfect, never subject to deficiency or sleep, **{Allah – there is no deity except Him, the Ever-Living, the Sustainer of [all] existence. Neither drowsiness overtakes Him nor sleep.} [Qur'ān 2:255] {And rely upon the Ever-Living who does not die...} [Qur'ān 25:58]** Here, He negates drowsiness for Himself, which is a light form of sleep, as well as deep sleep.[6] He also negates death for himself, due to the completeness of His life.[7] Sleep, drowsiness, and death detract from the totality of life. These are the qualities of created beings, and the life of created beings is deficient as they sleep and they die.

فالنوم كمال في حق المخلوق، نقص في حق الخالق؛ لأن المخلوق الذي لا ينام معتل الصحة، فهذا يدل علىٰ الفرق بين صفات الخالق وصفات المخلوق، والحي والقيوم: هاتان الصفتان مأخوذتان من قوله تعالىٰ: ﴿ٱللَّهُ لَآ إِلَٰهَ إِلَّا هُوَ ٱلْحَىُّ ٱلْقَيُّومُ﴾ الحي الذي له الحياة الكاملة، والقيوم صيغة مبالغة.

Sleep is perfection when it comes to created beings and a deficiency when it comes to the Creator, because a created being that does not sleep is lacking in health. This demonstrates the difference between the qualities of the Creator and those of the created. 'The Living (al-Ḥayy)' and 'the All-Sustaining (al-Qayyūm)': These are two qualities derived from the verse: **{Allah – there is no deity except Him, the Ever-Living, the Sustainer of [all] existence." [Qur'ān 2:255]** The Living is He who has absolute life, and the All-Sustaining (al-Qayyūm) is a form used for emphasis.

---

6 It is related that Abū Mūsā ﵁ said: "The Messenger of Allah ﷺ stood up amongst us and said five words: 'Allah the Almighty does not sleep and it does not befit Him to sleep...'" (Muslim, no. 179)

7 It is related from Ibn 'Abbās ﵄ that the Messenger of Allah ﷺ used to say: "O Allah, it is to You I surrender, in You I have faith, in You I trust, to You I repent, through You I fight my adversaries. O Allah, I take refuge in Your might – there is no god but You – from being led astray. You are the Living who does not die, and jinn and men die." Muslim, no. 2717.

المتن

(١٢) قَيُّومٌ لا يَنامُ.

(12) He is al-Qayyūm (the All-Sustaining) and does not sleep;

الشرح

القيوم هو: القائم بنفسه والمقيم لغيره، القائم بنفسه فلا يحتاج إلىٰ شيء، وغني عن كل شيء، المقيم لغيره، كل شيء فقير إليه يحتاج إلىٰ إقامته له سبحانه وتعالىٰ، فلولا إقامة الله للسموات والأرض والمخلوقات لتدمرت وفنيت، ولكن الله يقيمها ويحفظها ويمدها بما يصلحها.

The All-Sustaining (al-Qayyūm) is the one who is self-sustaining and who sustains everything else. He is self-sustaining and so is not in need of anything; and as He sustains everything else, everything is in need of Him. If it were not for the fact that Allah ﷻ sustains the heavens, the earth, and all created beings, they would be destroyed and would have perished. However, Allah ﷻ sustains and preserves them and provides them with what they need.

فجميع الخلق في حاجة إليه ﴿إِنَّ ٱللَّهَ يُمۡسِكُ ٱلسَّمَٰوَٰتِ وَٱلۡأَرۡضَ أَن تَزُولَاۚ وَلَئِن زَالَتَآ إِنۡ أَمۡسَكَهُمَا مِنۡ أَحَدٖ مِّنۢ بَعۡدِهِۦٓ﴾ [فاطر: ٤١].

All creation is in need of Him. **{Indeed, Allah holds the heavens and the earth, lest they cease. And if they should cease, no one could hold them [in place] after Him.} [Qurʾān 35: 41]**

المتن

(١٣) خالِقٌ بِلا حاجَةٍ، رازِقٌ بِلا مَؤُونَةٍ.

(13) He is the Creator without a need from His creation; a Provider

without subsistence;

الشرح

هو الذي خلق الخلق وهو ليس بحاجة إليهم، إنما خلقهم لعبادته ﴿وَمَا خَلَقْتُ ٱلْجِنَّ وَٱلْإِنسَ إِلَّا لِيَعْبُدُونِ ﴿٥٦﴾﴾ [الذاريات:٥٦].

It is He who created the creation without needing them; He created them only to worship Him: **{And I did not create the jinn and mankind except to worship Me.} [Qur'ān 51:56]**

فخلقهم لا لحاجة إليهم بأن ينصروه أو ليعينوه أو ليساعدوه - سبحانه - أو يحموه، إنما خلقهم لعبادته، وهم المحتاجون للعبادة؛ لتصلهم بالله وتربطهم بربهم، فالعبادة صلة بين العبد وربه، فتقربه من الله، ويحصل بها من الله على الثواب والجزاء، فالعبادة حاجة للخلق وليست بحاجة لله عز وجل ﴿إِن تَكْفُرُوٓا۟ أَنتُمْ وَمَن فِى ٱلْأَرْضِ جَمِيعًا فَإِنَّ ٱللَّهَ لَغَنِىٌّ حَمِيدٌ ﴿٨﴾﴾ [إبراهيم:٨] ﴿إِن تَكْفُرُوا۟ فَإِنَّ ٱللَّهَ غَنِىٌّ عَنكُمْ﴾ [الزمر:٧].

So, He created them not for any need of aid, help, protection or defence (Glorious is He). He created them only to worship Him, and they are the ones who are in need of worship to bring them closer to Allah and to connect them with their Lord. Worship is the link between people and their Lord, it draws them near to Allah ﷻ and they attain reward for it. So, worship is a need of the creation and not a need of Allah the Almighty. **{If you should disbelieve, you and whoever is on the earth entirely – indeed, Allah is Free of need and Praiseworthy.} [Qur'ān 14:8] {If you disbelieve – indeed, Allah is Free from need of you.} [Qur'ān 39:7]**

وقوله: (**رازق بلا مؤنة**) أي هو القائم بأرزاق عباده ولا ينقص ذلك مما عنده.

"A Provider without subsistence": He is the one who provides for His slaves, and that does not diminish anything from what He possesses.

المتن

(١٤) مُمِيتٌ بِلا مَخافَةٍ.

(14) He brings death without fear;

الشرح

أي: يميت الأحياء إذا كملت آجالهم ، لا لأنه خائف منهم ولكن ذلك لحكمته سبحانه وتعالىٰ؛ لأن الحياة في الدنيا لها نهاية، وأما الآخرة فليس للحياة فيها نهاية، فإماتتهم ليس خوفاً منهم أو ليستريح منهم، ولو كانوا يكفرون به فإنه لا يتضرر بكفرهم، وإنما يضرون أنفسهم، لكنه هو يفرح بتوبتهم؛ لأنه يحب - ويريد - لهم الخير، فهو يفرح بتوبتهم وهو ليس في حاجة إليهم، إنما ذلك من لطفه وإحسانه.

He brings death to the living when their terms are complete, not because He is afraid of them but rather out of His wisdom. This is because life in the world has an end, but there is no end to the life of the hereafter. So, He does not bring death to them due to fear of them or to get rid of them, even if they disbelieve in him, as He is not harmed by their disbelief; in fact, they only harm themselves. However, Allah rejoices over their repentance, because He loves and wants what is good for them, so he rejoices when they repent. He is not in need of them but rather that is only out of his grace and kindness.

المتن

(١٥) باعِثٌ بِلا مَشَقَّةٍ.

(15) He resurrects without difficulty.

الشرح

هذا من عجائب قدرته، أنه يميت الخلق ويفنيهم حتىٰ يتلاشوا ويصيروا ترابًا ورفاتًا. حتىٰ يقول الجاهل: لا يمكن أن يعودوا ولكن الله عز وجل يبعثهم من جديد ويعيد خلقهم من جديد، وليس عليه في ذلك مشقة، كما قال سبحانه وتعالىٰ: ﴿مَّا خَلْقُكُمْ وَلَا بَعْثُكُمْ إِلَّا كَنَفْسٍ وَاحِدَةٍ﴾ [لقمان:٢٨]. ﴿وَهُوَ ٱلَّذِى يَبْدَؤُا۟ ٱلْخَلْقَ ثُمَّ يُعِيدُهُۥ وَهُوَ أَهْوَنُ عَلَيْهِ ۚ وَلَهُ ٱلْمَثَلُ ٱلْأَعْلَىٰ فِى ٱلسَّمَٰوَٰتِ وَٱلْأَرْضِ ۚ وَهُوَ ٱلْعَزِيزُ ٱلْحَكِيمُ ﴿٢٧﴾﴾ [الروم:٢٧].

This is one of the wonders of His omnipotence: He brings death to His creatures and causes them to perish so that they decompose, becoming dust and residue, to the extent that the ignoramus would say that it is impossible to return them, rather Allah ﷿ resurrects them anew, creating them again. However, he has no difficulty in doing so. Allah ﷾ says: **{Your creation and your resurrection will not be but as that of a single soul.} [Qur'ān 31:28] {And it is He who begins creation; then He repeats it, and that is [even] easier for Him. To Him belongs the highest attribute in the heavens and earth. And He is The Exalted in Might, the Wise.} [Qur'ān 30:27]**

فالمشركون أنكروا البعث استبعاداً منهم كما ذكر الله ذلك عنهم: ﴿قَالَ مَن يُحْىِ ٱلْعِظَٰمَ وَهِىَ رَمِيمٌ ﴿٧٨﴾﴾ [يس:٧٨]، قال سبحانه وتعالىٰ: ﴿قُلْ يُحْيِيهَا ٱلَّذِىٓ أَنشَأَهَآ أَوَّلَ مَرَّةٍ﴾ [يس:٧٩].

Here, the polytheists denied resurrection because they found it implausible, as Allah ﷾ says about them: **{He says, 'Who will give life to bones while they are disintegrated?'} [Qur'ān 36:78]** Allah ﷾ says: **{Say, 'He will give them life who produced them the first time...'} [Qur'ān 36:79]**

أول مرة، ليس لها وجود أصلاً، فأوجدها من العدم سبحانه وتعالىٰ، فالذي خلقها من العدم: أليس بقادر علىٰ إعادتها من باب أولىٰ؟ هذا في نظر العقول، وإلا فإن الله سبحانه لا يُقاس بخلقه، إنما ذلك لضرب المثل: ﴿وَلَهُ ٱلْمَثَلُ ٱلْأَعْلَىٰ﴾ [الروم:٢٧].

The first time, the bones did not exist at all yet the Almighty brought them about from nothing. And so, is it not more apt that the one who created them from nothingness would be able to repeat it? This is an argument from the aspect of their reasoning. Otherwise, Allah ﷻ is not to be measured with His creation. This is only to offer a parable: **{And His is the Most Exalted example..." [Qur'ān 30:27]**

فهذا ردٌّ علىٰ هذا الجاحد، قال تعالىٰ: ﴿وَنَسِيَ خَلْقَهُۥ﴾ [يس:٧٨]، نسي أنه في الأول كان لا شيء ولا وجود له ﴿هَلْ أَتَىٰ عَلَى ٱلْإِنسَٰنِ حِينٌ مِّنَ ٱلدَّهْرِ لَمْ يَكُن شَيْـًٔا مَّذْكُورًا ۝١﴾ [الإنسان:١]، نسي أن الله أوجده من عدم.

This is a response to this disbeliever. Allah says: **{And he presents for Us an example and forgets his [own] creation.} [Qur'ān 36:78]** Meaning that he forgets that in the beginning he was nothing and did not exist at all. **{Has there [not] come upon man a period of time when he was not a thing [even] mentioned?} [Qur'ān 76:1]** He forgets that Allah ﷻ brought him about from nothing.

فهو يجمع هذه العظام المتفرقة، واللحوم الممزقة، والتراب الذي تحلل، وهذه الشعور المتبعثرة يعيدها كما كانت، ﴿وَمِنْ ءَايَٰتِهِۦٓ أَن تَقُومَ ٱلسَّمَآءُ وَٱلْأَرْضُ بِأَمْرِهِۦ ثُمَّ إِذَا دَعَاكُمْ دَعْوَةً مِّنَ ٱلْأَرْضِ إِذَآ أَنتُمْ تَخْرُجُونَ ۝٢٥﴾ [الروم:٢٥] ﴿وَنُفِخَ فِى ٱلصُّورِ فَصَعِقَ مَن فِى ٱلسَّمَٰوَٰتِ وَمَن فِى ٱلْأَرْضِ إِلَّا مَن شَآءَ ٱللَّهُ ثُمَّ نُفِخَ فِيهِ أُخْرَىٰ فَإِذَا هُمْ قِيَامٌ يَنظُرُونَ ۝٦٨﴾ [الزمر:٦٨]

He brings together those scattered bones, the torn flesh, the disintegrated dust, the scattered hair and returns it to how it was. **{And of His signs is that the heaven and earth remain by His command. Then when He calls you with a [single] call from the earth, immediately you will come forth.} [Qur'ān 30:25] {And the Horn will be blown, and whoever is in the heavens and whoever is on the earth will fall dead except whom Allah wills. Then it will be blown again, and at once they will be standing, looking on.} [Qur'ān 39:68]**

وهي نفخة البعث. فالأولىٰ نفخة الصعق والموت، والثانية نفخة البعث.

This is when the Horn blows for the Resurrection. The first blow is the blow of shock and death, and the second is the blow of resurrection.

﴿وَنُفِخَ فِي ٱلصُّورِ فَإِذَا هُم مِّنَ ٱلْأَجْدَاثِ﴾ [يس:٥١] أي : القبور: ﴿إِلَىٰ رَبِّهِمْ يَنسِلُونَ ۝٥١ قَالُوا۟ يَٰوَيْلَنَا مَنۢ بَعَثَنَا مِن مَّرْقَدِنَا ۜ هَٰذَا مَا وَعَدَ ٱلرَّحْمَٰنُ وَصَدَقَ ٱلْمُرْسَلُونَ ۝٥٢﴾ [يس:٥١:٥٢].

{And the Horn will be blown; and at once from the graves to their Lord they will hasten. They will say, 'O woe to us! Who has raised us up from our sleeping place?' [The reply will be], 'This is what the Most Merciful had promised, and the Messengers told the truth.'} [Qur'ān 36:51-52]

فالله قادر علىٰ كل شيء، وهذا رد علىٰ الكفار الذين يُعجزون الله عن إحياء الموتىٰ وإعادتهم كما كانوا.

Allah is able to do all things. This is a response to the disbelievers who challenge Allah's ability to bring the dead back to life and return them to how they were.

قال تعالىٰ: ﴿أَيَحْسَبُ ٱلْإِنسَٰنُ أَلَّن نَّجْمَعَ عِظَامَهُۥ ۝٣ بَلَىٰ قَٰدِرِينَ عَلَىٰٓ أَن نُّسَوِّىَ بَنَانَهُۥ ۝٤﴾ [القيامة:٣،٤]. ﴿يَوْمَ يَخْرُجُونَ مِنَ ٱلْأَجْدَاثِ سِرَاعًا كَأَنَّهُمْ إِلَىٰ نُصُبٍ يُوفِضُونَ ۝٤٣﴾ [المعارج:٤٣].

Allah says: **{Does man think that We will not assemble his bones? Yes. [We are] Able [even] to proportion his fingertips.} [Qur'ān 75:3-4] {The Day they will emerge from the graves rapidly as if they were, toward an erected idol, hastening.} [Qur'ān 70:43]**

هذه قدرة الله وإرادته ومشيئته، لا يعجزه شيء، لكن بعض المخلوقين يقيس الله بخلقه فيستبعد البعث؛ لأنه في نظره مستحيل، ولا ينظر إلىٰ قدرة الله، ولم يقدر الله حق قدره، وهذا من الجهل بالله عز وجل.

This is the omnipotence and will of Allah. There is nothing he is incapable of. Nevertheless, some people compare Allah to the creation and find the Resurrection implausible, because it is impossible according to their reasoning. They do not give consideration to Allah's ﷻ omnipotence and they do not have just appreciation for Allah's power. This is out of their ignorance about Allah ﷻ.

المتن

(١٦) ما زالَ بِصِفاتِهِ قَدِيمًا قَبْلَ خَلْقِهِ.

(16) He, along with His attributes, is eternal, existing before His creation.

الشرح

تقدم قول المصنف: **(قديم بلا ابتداء)**، فهو سبحانه وتعالىٰ ليس قبله شيء، ومعنىٰ ذلك: أنه متصف بصفات الكمال، فصفاته تكون أزلاً وأبداً، فكما أنه أول بلا بداية، فكذلك صفاته، فإنها تكون تابعة له سبحانه، فهي أولية بأولية الله سبحانه وتعالىٰ، فلم يكن أولاً بلا صفات ثم حدثت له الصفات بعد ذلك كما يقوله أهل الضلال، الذين يقولون: لم تكن له صفات في الأزل ثم كانت له صفات؛ لئلا يلزم علىٰ ذلك تعدد الآلهة - كما يزعمون - أو تعدد القدماء، وتكون الأسماء والصفات شريكة لله في أوليته. فنقول: يا سبحان الله! هذا يلزم عليه أن يكون الله ناقصاً - تعالىٰ الله- في فترة، ثم حدثت له الصفات وكمل بها، تعالىٰ عما يقولون، ولا يلزم من قدم الصفات قدم الأرباب؛ لأن الصفات ليست شيئاً غير الموصوف في الخارج، إنما هي معان قائمة بالموصوف، ليست شيئاً مستقلاً عن الموصوف، فإذا قلت مثلاً: «فلان سميع بصير، عالم فقيه، لغوي نحوي» فهل معنىٰ هذا أن الإنسان صار عدداً من الأشخاص، فلا يلزم من تعدد الصفات تعدد الموصوف، كما يقوله أصحاب الضلال.

The author said earlier: **"Eternal without beginning"**. Nothing came before the Most High. This means that Allah is described with attributes of perfection. His attributes are eternal, with neither a beginning nor an end. Just as He is the First, without beginning, so are His attributes, as they are intrinsic to Him. They are first, due to Allah ﷻ being First. He was not the First without attributes, with His attributes occurring later (as the people of misguidance say). They say that He did not possess His attributes from eternity, because they claim that would have a necessary consequence of multiple gods or multiple eternal beings, and the names and attributes sharing divinity with Allah ﷻ. We say in response: *Yā subḥān Allāh*! This dictates retraction from Allah's ﷻ transcendence for one period and that He then acquired attributes by which He would become transcendent. And Allah's eminence is above what they say. The fact that Allah's ﷻ attributes are eternal does not necessitate that created beings are also eternal, because Allah's ﷻ attributes are naught but external adjectives, they are attributes found in the described, not something separate from that being. If someone says, for example, that someone has hearing, sight, knowledge, and is also a jurist and a linguist, and grammarian, does that mean that this person is in fact several entities? Multiplicity of being is not a necessary consequence of multiplicity of attributes, as people of misguidance claim.

فالله سبحانه وتعالىٰ ليس لصفاته بداية كما أنه ليس لذاته بداية، فيوصف بأنه الخالق دائماً وأبداً.

The attributes of the Most High have no beginning just as Allah's essence has no beginning. Therefore, Allah has the attribute of being the Creator forever and always.

وأما أفعاله سبحانه، فهي قديمة النوع حادثة الآحاد.

Regarding His actions, they are eternal in kind and recur as instances.

فالله سبحانه وتعالىٰ متكلم قبل أن يصدر منه الكلام، وخالق قبل أن يصدر منه الخلق. وأما أنه يتكلم ويخلق، فهذه أفعال متجددة وهكذا.

Allah ﷻ had the attribute of speech before any instance of speaking, and He was the Creator before any instance of creating. His speech and creation are thus recurring actions and so on.

المتن

(١٧) لَمْ يَزْدَدْ بِكَوْنِهِمْ شَيْئًا لَمْ يَكُنْ قَبْلَهُمْ مِنْ صِفَتِهِ.

(17) Bringing the creation into existence did not add anything to His attributes that was not there already.

الشرح

أي : خلق الخلق. ولا نقول: لم يصر خالقاً إلا بعد أن خلقهم، بل هو يسمى خالقاً من الأزل، لا بداية لذلك، أما خلقه إنما هو متجدد.

I.e. creating the creation. We do not say that He became the Creator only after creating them but rather that His name was the Creator from eternity, without beginning. As for His creation, it is recurring.

المتن

(١٨) وَكَما كانَ بِصِفاتِهِ أَزَلِيًّا كَذَلِكَ لا يَزالُ عَلَيْها أَبَدِيًّا.

(18) Just as His attributes are eternal, they are also never ending.

الشرح

كما أنه موصوف بصفاته أزلياً، يعني: لا بداية لذلك، كذلك صفاته تلازمه - سبحانه - في المستقبل، فهو بصفاته أبدي لا نهاية له (أنت الآخر فلا بعدك شيء) باسمك وصفاتك، ولا يقال: إن هذه الصفات تنقطع عنه في المستقبل، بل هي ملازمة له سبحانه وتعالى.

As He is attributed with His attributes eternally i.e. they do not have a beginning, likewise His attributes are intrinsic to him in the future. With His attributes, Allah ﷻ is eternal without end. [The Prophet ﷺ said:] "You are the Last, nothing is after You", that goes for His names and attributes. It must not be said that these attributes will be separate from Him in the future. Rather, they are innate to Allah the Most High.

❁❁❁

المتن

(١٩) لَيْسَ مُنْذُ خَلَقَ الْخَلْقَ اسْتَفَادَ اسْمَ «الْخالِقِ».

(19) It was not only after the point of creation that He could be considered al-Khāliq (the Creator).

الشرح

هذا توضيح وتكرار لما سبق.

This is further explanation and repetition of the aforementioned.

❁❁❁

المتن

(٢٠) وَلا بِإِحْداثِه الْبَرِيَّةِ اسْتَفادَ اسْمَ «الْبارِي».

(20) Nor was it only after the point of origination that He could be considered al-Bārī (the Originator).

الشرح

من أسماء الله عز وجل: الباري، يعني: الخالق، برئ الخلق، يعني: خلقهم، فهو الباري، وهذا الاسم ملازم لذاته ليس له بداية.

One of Allah's ﷻ names is *al-Bārī*, i.e. the creator. To originate the creation (*bari'a*) means to create it, thus, Allah is *al-Bārī*. This name is intrinsic to the essence of Allah ﷻ, and has no beginning.

❁❁❁

المتن

(٢١) لَهُ مَعْنَىٰ الرُّبُوبِيَّةِ وَلا مَرْبُوب، وَمَعْنَىٰ الْخالِقِ وَلا مَخْلُوق.

(21) He was always al-Rabb (the Lord), even if there were no subjects; and always al-Khāliq (the Creator), even if there was no creation.

الشرح

كذلك هو رب قبل أن توجد المربوبات، والرب معناه: المالك والمتصرف والمصلح والسيد، وهذه الصفات لازمة لذاته، يوصف بالربوبية بلا بداية ولا نهاية، قبل وجود المربوبات وبعد فناء المربوبات.

In addition, He was the Lord before the presence of any subjects. The Lord *(Rabb)* means the king, disposer, keeper, and master. These attributes are intrinsic to Allah's essence. Allah has the attribute of Lordship without beginning or end, before the existence of any subjects and after the subjects perish.

المتن

(٢٢) وَكَما أَنَّهُ مُحْيِي الْمَوْتَىٰ بَعْدَما أَحْيَا، اسْتَحَقَّ هَذا الِاسْمَ قَبْلَ إِحْيائِهِمْ، كَذَلِكَ اسْتَحَقَّ اسْمَ الْخالِقِ قَبْلَ إِنْشائِهِمْ.

(22) As He is al-Muḥyī (the Giver of life) to the dead after having given them life, He possessed this name before giving life to anything; likewise He possessed the name al-Khāliq (the Creator) before He created them.

الشرح

كما أنه – سبحانه – يوصف بكونه محيي الموتىٰ في الأزل، وبأنه يحيي ويميت، ولا يكون هذا الوصف معدوماً حتىٰ يكون أحيا الموتىٰ، وإنما هذا له من القديم

والأزل، وأما إحياء الموتىٰ فهذا متجدد، أحيا ويحيي سبحانه إذا شاء.

Allah ﷻ has had the attribute of being the Giver of life to the dead from eternity, and that He gives life and brings death. Allah has had this attribute for eternity, so its existence is not conditional on His giving of life to the dead. Nonetheless, His giving of life to the dead is something that recurs, He gives life and lets live as He wills.

❁❁❁

المتن

(٢٣) ذَٰلِكَ بِأَنَّهُ عَلَىٰ كُلِّ شَيْءٍ قَدِيرٌ.

(23) This is because He is capable of doing all things;

الشرح

هذا وصف أزلي، لا يقال بأنه ما استفاد القدرة إلا بعد أن خلق وأوجد المخلوقات، بل القدرة صفة أزلية، وإنما كونه أوجد المخلوقات فهذا أثر ناتج من كونه علىٰ كل شيء قدير.

This is an eternal attribute. It should not be said that He acquired omnipotence only after creating the creation. Rather, omnipotence is an eternal attribute. The fact that He created all of the creation is a resulting effect of Him being able to do all things.

والله هو الذي وصف نفسه بأنه علىٰ كل شيء قدير من الموجودات ومن المعدومات، لم يقيد قدرته بشيء معين، لا يعجزه شيء، ولا يجوز التقييد بأنه قدير علىٰ كذا، ولا يقال: إنه علىٰ ما يشاء قدير، إنما هذا خاص بجمع الله سبحانه وتعالىٰ لأهل السموات والأرض: ﴿وَمِنْ ءَايَٰتِهِۦ خَلْقُ ٱلسَّمَٰوَٰتِ وَٱلْأَرْضِ وَمَا بَثَّ فِيهِمَا مِن دَآبَّةٍ وَهُوَ عَلَىٰ جَمْعِهِمْ إِذَا يَشَآءُ قَدِيرٌ ﴿٢٩﴾﴾ [الشورىٰ:٢٩] وهذه قضية معينة.

It is Allah Himself who has described Himself as being able to do all things, whether existent or non-existent. He has not restricted His omnipotence with any specific thing. He is incapable of nothing, and it is impermissible to restrict that by saying that He is able to do only certain things. Also it should not be said that He is able to do all that He wills only[8]. This phrase is specific to Allah's gathering of the dwellers of heaven and earth: **{And of his signs is the creation of the heavens and earth and what He has dispersed throughout them of creatures. And He, for gathering them when He wills, is competent.} [Qur'ān 42:29]** This is concerning a specific case.

المتن

(٢٤) وَكُلُّ شَيْءٍ إِلَيْهِ فَقِيرٌ.

(24) And all things are dependent on Him;

الشرح

لا شيء يمكن أن يستغني عن الله لا من الملائكة ولا السماوات والأرض ولا الجن ولا الإنس، ولا الجامدات من الجبال ولا البحار، كل شيء فقير إلىٰ الله: ﴿يَـٰٓأَيُّهَا ٱلنَّاسُ أَنتُمُ ٱلْفُقَرَآءُ إِلَى ٱللَّهِ ۖ وَٱللَّهُ هُوَ ٱلْغَنِىُّ ٱلْحَمِيدُ ۝١٥﴾ [فاطر:١٥].

Nothing can dispense with Allah, not the angels, the heavens, the earth, jinn, or man, and not any inanimate objects, such as the mountains and seas. Everything is in need of Allah: **{O mankind, you are those in need of Allah, while Allah is the Free of need, the Praiseworthy.} [Qur'ān 35:15]**

فكل شيء إليه فقير، لا الأولياء ولا السماوات، ومن يقول: إن الأولياء لهم قدرة غير البشر وإنهم يتصرفون في الكون، وإنهم ينفعون ويضرون من دون الله، فذلك من قول الكفرة والمشركين، فليس للأولياء والرسل والملائكة غنىً عن الله ولا

8 Because that would entail that He is not able to do what He did not will [Translator's Note].

تصرف من دونه .

All things are in need of Allah. Neither the saintly nor the heavens cease to be in need of Allah. Those who say that the saintly have non-human abilities and hold control in the universe and provide harm and benefit beside Allah, they are saying what disbelievers and idolaters say. Neither the saints, the Messengers, or the angels are free of the need of Allah ﷻ and they have no control besides from Him.

وهذا مما يبطل عبادة غير الله من الأصنام ونحوها، كيف تعبد أشياء فقيرة وتنسىٰ الذي بيده ملكوت كل شيء؟ ولهذا لما قال بعض علماء القبورية لعامي من أهل التوحيد: أنتم تقولون : إن الأولياء لا ينفعون ولا يضرون، قال: نقول: إنهم لا ينفعون ولا يضرون، قال: أليس الله تعالىٰ يقول: ﴿وَلَا تَحْسَبَنَّ ٱلَّذِينَ قُتِلُوا۟ فِى سَبِيلِ ٱللَّهِ أَمْوَٰتًۢا ۚ بَلْ أَحْيَآءٌ عِندَ رَبِّهِمْ يُرْزَقُونَ ﴿١٦٩﴾﴾ [آل عمران:١٦٩]. قال : وهل الله قال: يُرزقون، أو يَرزقون؟ قال: بل قال: (يُرزقون) بضم الياء، قال: إذن أنا أسأل الذي يرزقهم ولا أسألهم. فانخصم ذلك العالم بحجة العامي الذي هو علىٰ الفطرة.

This is why it is wrong to worship anything besides Allah, like idols or the like. How could someone worship something that is in need and neglect Him in whose Hand is the kingdom? In this regard, some scholars of the grave worshippers said to a layman from the adherents of *tawḥīd,* 'You say that the pious can neither benefit nor harm.' He said, 'We say that they can neither benefit nor harm.' He said, 'Does Allah the Almighty not say: **{And never think of those who have been killed in the cause of Allah as dead. Rather, they are alive with their Lord, receiving provision} [Qur'ān 3:169]?'** He replied, 'Did Allah say "*Yurzaqūn* (receiving provision)" or "*Yarzuqūn* (Giving provision)"?' He said, 'Indeed, He says, "*Yurzaqūn* (receiving provision) with a *ḍammah* on the *yā*.' He said, 'So I ask the one who provides and I do not ask them.' That scholar lost the debate due to the argument of that layman on the natural disposition of faith.

المتن

(٢٥) وَكُلُّ أَمْرٍ عَلَيْهِ يَسِيرٌ.

(25) And all things are easy for Him.

الشرح

﴿إِنَّمَآ أَمْرُهُۥٓ إِذَآ أَرَادَ شَيْـًٔا أَن يَقُولَ لَهُۥ كُن فَيَكُونُ ﴿٨٢﴾﴾ [يس:٨٢].

{His command is only when He intends a thing that He says to it, ‘Be,’ and it is.} [Qurʾān 36:82]

فهو يحيي ويميت، ويخلق ويرزق، ويعطي ويمنع، ويحيي الموتىٰ بعد فنائهم، وذلك يسير عليه سبحانه وتعالىٰ، لا يكلفه شيئًا ولا يشق عليه، خلاف المخلوق، فإنه يتكلف بفعل الأشياء، أو يعجز عنها، أما الله فليس شيء عليه صعبًا، ﴿مَّا خَلْقُكُمْ وَلَا بَعْثُكُمْ إِلَّا كَنَفْسٍ وَٰحِدَةٍ﴾ [لقمان :٢٨].

Allah ﷻ gives life and brings death, creates and provides, gives and prevents, and gives life to the dead after they perish. All of those things are easy for Him, the Most High. He incurs no burden from anything, nor does he bear difficulty. In contrast, created beings incur some kind of burden when doing things, or they can fail to do them. There is nothing, on the other hand, difficult for Allah: **{Your creation and your resurrection will not be but as that of a single soul.} [Qurʾān 31:28]**

المتن

(٢٦) لا يَحْتَاجُ إِلَىٰ شَيْءٍ.

(26) He is not in need of anything.

الشرح

الله سبحانه غني عن كل شيء، فالله ليس بحاجة إلىٰ الخلق؛ لأنه هو الغني، فهو

الذي يعطي الخلق سبحانه .

Allah ﷻ is free of need from anything. He is not in need of His creation, because He is al-Ghanī (the Self-Sufficient). He is the one who gives to His creatures.

المتن

(٢٧) ﴿لَيْسَ كَمِثْلِهِ شَيْءٌ وَهُوَ السَّمِيعُ البَصِيرُ﴾ [الشورى: ١١].

(27) {There is nothing like Him, and He is the All-Hearing, the All-Seeing.}

الشرح

هذا نفي للتشبيه عن الله سبحانه، والكاف لتأكيد النفي، مثل: ﴿وَكَفَىٰ بِٱللَّهِ عَلِيمًا ۝٧٠﴾ [النساء: ٧٠] الأصل : وكفى الله عليمـًا، ولكن جاءت الباء للتأكيد.

This is negation of *tashbīh* (anthropomorphism) for Allah ﷻ. The *kāf* [in '*laysa ka-mithlihi shay'un*' (there is nothing like unto Him)] is for emphasising the negation, like [the *bā'* in] '*kafā billāhi 'alīman*': **{And sufficient is Allah as Knower.} [Qur'ān 4:70]** In principle, it is said, '*wa kafā Allāh 'alīmā*'; however, the *bā'* brings emphasis.

وليس يشبهه شيء من الأشياء، لا الملائكة ولا الأنبياء والرسل ولا الأولياء ولا أي مخلوق ﴿وَهُوَ ٱلسَّمِيعُ ٱلْبَصِيرُ ۝١١﴾ [الشورى: ١١] فسمى نفسه السميع البصير.

There is nothing at all that resembles Allah ﷻ: neither the angels, Prophets, Messengers, saints, nor any other created being. **{...and He is the Hearing, the Seeing.} [Qur'ān 42:11]** He has named Himself al-Samī' (The All-Hearing), al-Baṣīr (The All-Seeing).

فالآية في أولها رد على المشبهة، وفي آخرها رد على المعطلة، ودلت على أنه لا يلزم من إثبات الأسماء والصفات التشبيه بالمخلوقات، فسمع وبصر

المخلوقات لا يشبه سمع ولا بصر الله عز وجل.

The first part of the verse contains a response to the proponents of *tashbīh* and the end of it contains a response to the proponents of *taʿṭīl* (divesting Allah ﷻ of his attributes). It indicates that *tashbīh* (anthropomorphism) is not a necessary consequence of *ithbāt* (affirming) the names and attributes of Allah ﷻ. In other words, created things hear and see but that does not resemble the hearing and sight of the Almighty.

المتن

(٢٨) خَلَقَ الْخَلْقَ بِعِلْمِهِ.

(28) He created the creation according to His divine knowledge.

الشرح

قال سبحانه: ﴿أَلَا يَعْلَمُ مَنْ خَلَقَ وَهُوَ ٱللَّطِيفُ ٱلْخَبِيرُ ۝١٤﴾ [تبارك: ١٤]. فخلقه دليل على علمه سبحانه وتعالى وقدرته كما قال تعالى ﴿وَمَا كَانَ ٱللَّهُ لِيُعْجِزَهُۥ مِن شَيْءٍ فِي ٱلسَّمَٰوَٰتِ وَلَا فِي ٱلْأَرْضِ إِنَّهُۥ كَانَ عَلِيمًا قَدِيرًا ۝٤٤﴾.

Allah ﷻ says: **{Does He who created not know, while He is the Subtle, the Acquainted?} [Qurʾān 67:14]** Thus, His creation is evidence of His omniscience and omnipotence. Allah ﷻ says: **{But Allah is not to be caused failure by anything in the heavens or on the earth. Indeed, He is ever Knowing and Competent.} [Qurʾān 35:44]**

المتن

(٢٩) وَقَدَّرَ لَهُمْ أَقْدارًا.

(29) And He ordained all things in due measure.

الشرح

قدر الله جل وعلا المقادير، ولم يوجد هذه الأشياء بدون تقدير ﴿وَإِن مِّن شَيْءٍ إِلَّا عِندَنَا خَزَآئِنُهُۥ وَمَا نُنَزِّلُهُۥٓ إِلَّا بِقَدَرٍ مَّعْلُومٍ ۝٢١﴾ [الحجر:٢١] فكل شيء قدره الله بمقادير وكيفيات لا تختلف ولا تتغير، فالإنسان قدر الله جسمه وحواسه وأعضاءه وتركيبه وأوزانه، حتىٰ صار إنسانًا معتدلاً يمشي ويقف ولو اختل شيء من أعضاء هذا الإنسان أو من تراكيبه اختل الجسم، وكذلك سائر الكائنات ﴿وَكُلُّ شَيْءٍ عِندَهُۥ بِمِقْدَارٍ ۝٨﴾ [الرعد:٨] فلكل شيء مقادير ينضبط بها، ولكل شيء مقادير تختلف عن مقادير الآخر.

Allah predestined the measures of all things, and He did not bring things into existence without measure. **{And there is not a thing but that with Us are its depositories, and We do not send it down except according to a known measure.} [Qur'ān 15:21]** So Allah ﷻ decreed all things according to certain measures and manners without inconsistency or change. Allah ﷻ decreed the bodies, senses, and limbs of man as well as their compositions and weights; and thus they become humans who have upright posture, walk, and stand. If some of the body parts or components of those humans were to fail, the whole body fails. Likewise for all other beings. **{And everything with Him is by due measure.} [Qur'ān 13:8]** So, everything has a predetermination by which it gets its order; and everything has a predetermination that differs from the predetermination of something else.

المتن

(٣٠) وَضَرَبَ لَهُمْ آجالًا.

(30) And set a fixed term for them.

الشرح

المخلوقات لها آجال ولها نهاية، قال سبحانه: ﴿كُلُّ مَنْ عَلَيْهَا فَانٍ ۝٢٦ وَيَبْقَىٰ وَجْهُ

رَبِّكَ ذُو ٱلْجَلَٰلِ وَٱلْإِكْرَامِ ﴿٢٧﴾ [الرحمن:٢٦-٢٧]، وقال سبحانه: ﴿كُلُّ شَىْءٍ هَالِكٌ إِلَّا وَجْهَهُۥ﴾ [القصص:٨٨].

Created things have a set span of existence and an end. Allah ﷻ says: **{Everyone upon the earth will perish, and there will remain the Face of your Lord, Owner of Majesty and Honour.} [Qurʾān 55:26-27]** Allah ﷻ also says: **{Everything will be destroyed except His Face.} [Qurʾān 28:88]**

كل شيء له عمر محدود، حدده الله - سبحانه - إما قصير وإما طويل، قال سبحانه: ﴿وَمَا يُعَمَّرُ مِن مُّعَمَّرٍ وَلَا يُنقَصُ مِنْ عُمُرِهِۦٓ إِلَّا فِى كِتَٰبٍ ۚ إِنَّ ذَٰلِكَ عَلَى ٱللَّهِ يَسِيرٌ ﴿١١﴾﴾ [فاطر:١١]، فالأعمار بيده سبحانه وتعالىٰ، وهذا يدل علىٰ كمال ربوبيته وكمال قدرته، فما شاء الله كان وما لم يشأ لم يكن.

Everything has a limited lifespan, set by Allah the Almighty, either short or long. Allah ﷻ said: **{And no aged person is granted [additional] life nor is his lifespan lessened but that it is in a register. Indeed, that for Allah is easy.} [Qurʾān 35:11]** So, everything's lifespan is in His Hand. This is evidence of the totality of His lordship and omnipotence. What He willed was and what He did not will was not.

المتن

(٣١) وَلَمْ يَخْفَ عَلَيْهِ شَيْءٌ قَبْلَ أَنْ يَخْلُقَهُمْ.

(31) Nothing was hidden from Him before He created it.

الشرح

بل هو عالم بالأشياء قبل أن توجد، لا أنه لا يعلمها إلا بعد أن وُجدت.

Rather, He knows everything before it exists, and does not only know it after it exists.

المتن

(٣٢) وَعَلِمَ ما هُمْ عامِلُونَ قَبْلَ أَنْ يَخْلُقَهُمْ.

(32) He knew what they would do before He created them.

الشرح

علم ما يعمل العباد قبل خلقهم، أن هذا من أهل الطاعة وهذا من أهل المعصية .

He knew what His servants would do before He created them; that so-and-so is from the obedient and so-and-so is from the sinful.

المتن

(٣٣) وَأَمَرَهُمْ بِطاعَتِهِ، وَنَهاهُمْ عَنْ مَعْصِيَتِهِ.

(33) He commanded them to obey Him and forbade them from disobeying Him.

الشرح

كما في قوله تعالىٰ: ﴿وَمَا خَلَقْتُ ٱلْجِنَّ وَٱلْإِنسَ إِلَّا لِيَعْبُدُونِ ﴿٥٦﴾﴾ [الذاريات:٥٦]، خلقهم أولاً، ثم أمرهم بعبادته سبحانه وتعالىٰ، فهو سبحانه أمرهم بطاعته وعبادته، مع أنه يعلم ما هم عاملون من قبل، ولكن الجزاء لا يترتب علىٰ العلم، وإنما الجزاء يترتب علىٰ العمل، فالله لا يعذب العبد بحسب العلم إلا إذا وقع منه الذنب، ولا يكرم المحسن حتىٰ يقع منه الفعل، فالجزاء مرتب علىٰ العمل، لا علىٰ العلم ولا علىٰ القدر، ففرق بين العلم وبين الجزاء، ولذلك أمرهم الله ونهاهم، فمن أطاع الأوامر وترك النواهي حصل علىٰ الثواب، ومن خالف الأوامر وارتكب النواهي حصل علىٰ العقاب بأفعاله هو لا بأفعال الله سبحانه، فالعبد هو المصلي والمزكي والحاج والمجاهد، فالأعمال تنسب إليه لا إلىٰ

الله، إلا من جهة الخلق والعلم والتقدير والتوفيق.

To this effect, Allah ﷻ says: **{And I did not create the jinn and mankind except to worship Me.} [Qur'ān 51:56]** First, He created them, and then, He commanded them to worship Him. So, He commanded them to obey and worship Him although He had known what they would do beforehand. Nonetheless, the recompense is not the result of Allah's ﷻ omniscience, but rather the result of people's actions. So Allah ﷻ does not punish anyone based on His knowledge unless they actually do the sin, and the goodly is not rewarded unless they actually do an act of good. So the recompense is the result of action not of Allah's knowledge nor predetermination. Thus, there is a differentiation between the knowledge and the recompense, which is why Allah commands and forbids. Those who obey the commands and leave what is forbidden receive the reward; and those who disobey the commands and commit what is forbidden have earned punishment by their actions and not by Allah's ﷻ actions. So the worshipper is the one who prays, pays the alms, performs the rites of *Ḥajj*, and fights in *jihād*. Actions are attributed to the person, not to Allah ﷻ, except from the aspect that He creates, knows, determines, and guides actions.

المتن

(٣٤) وَكُلُّ شَيْءٍ يَجْرِي بِتَقْدِيرِهِ وَمَشِيئَتِهِ.

(34) Everything happens according to His decree.

الشرح

لا شك أن كل شيء بتقديره لا يخرج عن تقدير الله من الخير والشر، والطاعة والمعصية، والكفر والإيمان، والمرض والصحة، والغنى والفقر، والعلم والجهل، كل شيء يجري بتقديره، وليس في ملكه شيء لم يقدره ولا يريده.

There is no doubt that everything is according to His decree. No good or bad thing, no act of obedience or sin, neither faith nor disbelief, neither sickness nor health, neither wealth nor poverty, and neither knowledge nor ignorance are outside of Allah's ﷻ decree. Everything happens according to

His predetermination. There is nothing in His kingdom that He did not decree or will.

المتن

(٣٥) وَكُلُّ شَيْءٍ يَجْرِي بِتَقْدِيرِهِ وَمَشِيئَتِهِ، وَمَشِيئَتُهُ تَنْفُذُ لا مَشِيئَةَ لِلْعِبادِ إلّا ما شاءَ لَهُمْ، فَما شاءَ لَهُمْ كانَ، وَما لَمْ يَشَأْ لَمْ يَكُنْ.

(35) His will always comes to pass; His slaves have no will except as He has willed for them; what He willed for them occurred, and what He did not will for them never took place.

الشرح

الله سبحانه وتعالىٰ له مشيئة، والعباد لهم مشيئة، ولكن مشيئة العباد مرتبة علىٰ مشيئة الله، وليست مستقلة، ولهذا قال سبحانه: ﴿وَمَا تَشَآءُونَ إِلَّآ أَن يَشَآءَ ٱللَّهُۚ إِنَّ ٱللَّهَ كَانَ عَلِيمًا حَكِيمًا ۝٣٠﴾ [الإنسان:٣٠] وقال سبحانه : ﴿وَمَا تَشَآءُونَ إِلَّآ أَن يَشَآءَ ٱللَّهُ رَبُّ ٱلْعَٰلَمِينَ ۝٢٩﴾ [التكوير:٢٩] فجعل لنفسه مشيئة هي من صفاته، وجعل لعباده مشيئة هي من صفاتهم، وربط مشيئتهم بمشيئته سبحانه، وفي هذا رد علىٰ القدرية والجبرية: فالقدرية ينفون مشيئة الله لأفعال العباد، ويجعلون للعبد مشيئة مطلقة، وأن العبد مستقل بأفعاله وإرادته ومشيئته، هذا مذهب القدرية من المعتزلة وغيرهم. والجبرية يقولون: العبد ليس له مشيئة، وإنما المشيئة لله فقط، والعبد يتحرك بدون اختياره ولا إرادته، مثل ما تحرك الآلة. فطائفة غلت في إثبات مشيئة الله وطائفة غلت في إثبات مشيئة العبد.

Allah ﷻ has a will, and humans have a will, but the will of human beings depends on the will of Allah ﷻ, therefore it is not independent. To this effect, Allah ﷻ says: **{And you do not will except that Allah wills. Indeed, Allah is ever Knowing and Wise.} [Qur'ān 76:30]** Allah ﷻ also says:

{And you do not will except that Allah wills – Lord of the worlds.} [Qur'ān 81:29] Allah ﷻ mentions a will for Himself, it is one of His attributes; and He mentioned a will for His slaves, it is one of their attributes; and He bound their will by His will. This entails a refutation against the Qadariyyah (adherents of 'free will' doctrine) and Jabriyyah (adherents of absolute fatalism) sects. The Qadariyyah deny the will of Allah ﷻ in the actions of people and say that people have an absolute will and are independent in their actions and wills. This is the doctrine of the Qadariyyah, from the Muʿtazilites and others. The Jabriyyah say that a person does not have a will, and that only Allah ﷻ has a will, and that people move without choice just like a tool is moved. One group is excessive in their affirmation of Allah's ﷻ will and the other is excessive in their affirmation of the free will of man.

وأما أهل السنة والجماعة: فأثبتوا المشيئتين، وجعلوا مشيئة العبد مربوطة بمشيئة الله، أخذاً من الآيتين السابقتين فقوله: ﴿وما تشاءون﴾ فيه إثبات مشيئة العباد، وقوله: ﴿إلا أن يشاء الله﴾ فيه إثبات مشيئة الله عز وجل، وفي الآية أن مشيئة العبد ليست مستقلة، وإنما هي مربوطة بمشيئة الله؛ لأنه خلق من خلق الله، خلقه وخلق مشيئته وخلق إرادته، ولهذا لما قال بعض الناس للنبي صلىٰ الله عليه وسلم: ما شاء الله وشئت، قال عليه الصلاة والسلام: «**أجعلتني لله نداً؟**» أي: شريكًا في المشيئة «**قل: ماشاء الله وحده**». ولما بلغ النبي صلىٰ الله عليه وسلم أن قومًا يقولون: ما شاء الله وشاء محمد، أنكر ذلك وقال: «**قولوا: ما شاء الله ثم شاء محمد**»، فجعل مشيئته مرتبة علىٰ مشيئة الله «بثم» التي تفيد الترتيب والتراخي، لا بالواو؛ لأنها تقتضي التشريك.

Ahl al-Sunnah wa 'l-Jamāʿah, on the other hand, affirm the will of both, and they say that the will of people is bound by the will of Allah ﷻ, as derived from the previous two verses. The saying of Allah ﷻ: **{And you do not will...}** includes affirmation of the will of people, [and His saying: **{...except that Allah wills – Lord of the worlds}**] includes affirmation of the will of Allah ﷻ. The verse entails that the will of people is not independent but rather bound by the will of Allah ﷻ because they are Allah's ﷻ creation. He created the people, and He created their will. In that regard, when some people said to the Prophet ﷺ, "As Allah and you will." The Prophet ﷺ said, **"Have you made me an equal to Allah?"** In other words, 'have you made me a partner in His will?' He said, **"Say: As Allah alone wills."** When the Prophet ﷺ heard that people were saying, "As Allah wills and as Muḥammad wills", he ﷺ disapproved and said, **"Say, 'As Allah wills, and then as Muḥammad wills.'"** And so He said that His will is bound by the will of Allah ﷻ using the word 'then' (*thumma*), which marks order and subsequence, instead of the word 'and' which denotes equality.[9]

المتن

(٣٦) يَهْدِي مَنْ يَشاءُ، وَيَعْصِمُ وَيُعافِي فَضْلًا، وَيُضِلُّ مَنْ يَشاءُ، وَيَخْذُلُ وَيَبْتَلِي عَدْلًا.

(36) He guides whom He wills, and protects and keeps them safe from harm out of His Grace; and He leads astray whom He wills, and abases and afflicts them out of justice.

الشرح

الله سبحانه يهدي من يشاء، ويضل من يشاء، وهذا بقضاء الله وقدره، ولكنه يهدي من يعلم أنه يصلح للهداية، ويهدي من يحرص على طلب الهداية ويُقبل عليها، فإن الله ييسره لليسرى، ويضل من يشاء بسبب إعراضه عن طلب الهداية والخير، فيضله الله عقوبة له على إعراضه وعدم رغبته في الخير، يوضح ذلك قوله تعالى: ﴿فَأَمَّا مَنْ أَعْطَىٰ وَاتَّقَىٰ ۝٥ وَصَدَّقَ بِالْحُسْنَىٰ ۝٦ فَسَنُيَسِّرُهُ لِلْيُسْرَىٰ ۝٧﴾ [الليل:٥-٧] فصار السبب من العبد، والقدر من جهة الله سبحانه: ﴿وَأَمَّا مَنْ بَخِلَ وَاسْتَغْنَىٰ ۝٨ وَكَذَّبَ بِالْحُسْنَىٰ ۝٩ فَسَنُيَسِّرُهُ لِلْعُسْرَىٰ ۝١٠﴾ [الليل:٨-١٠]

9 Aḥmad, 1/214, 224, 283 & 347; al-Bukhārī, *al-Adab al-Mufrad*, no. 783; Ibn Mājah, no. 2117; al-Nasā'ī, *'Amal al-Yawm wa 'l-Laylah*, no. 988.

فصار السبب من العبد والقدر من الله عز وجل، ولكن قدره الله عقوبة له.

Allah ﷻ guides whom He wills and He leads astray whom He wills, and this is according to His decree and predetermination. Nonetheless, Allah ﷻ guides those who are fit for guidance, who are keen on seeking it and accepting it. Allah ﷻ makes their path easy for them. And He leads astray whom He wills because of their aversion to seeking guidance and goodness. Thus, He leads them astray to punish them for their aversion and lack of desire for goodness. This is further explained by the statement of Allah ﷻ: **{As for he who gives and fears Allah and believes in the best [reward], We will ease him toward ease.} [Qur'ān 92:5-7]** Here, the cause is from the person, and the predetermination is from Allah ﷻ. **{But as for he who withholds and considers himself free of need and denies the best [reward], We will ease him toward difficulty.} [Qur'ān 92:8-10]** Here, the cause is from the person, and the predetermination is from Allah ﷻ. However, Allah ﷻ decrees that in order to punish him.

فقدر الله الهداية فضلاً من الله عز وجل، وتكرم علىٰ الشخص الذي يريد الخير ويريد الهداية، فييسره الله للخير ولفعله، وهذا لمصلحته، لا مصلحة لله عز وجل، وأما إضلال الضالين فعدل منه سبحانه وتعالىٰ، جزاءً لهم علىٰ إعراضهم وعدم إقبالهم علىٰ الخير وعلىٰ طاعة الله عز وجل، لم يظلمهم شيئًا، ولهذا نجد في الآيات ﴿وَٱللَّهُ لَا يَهۡدِي ٱلۡقَوۡمَ ٱلظَّٰلِمِينَ ۝٢٥٨﴾ [البقرة: ٢٥٨] ﴿وَٱللَّهُ لَا يَهۡدِي ٱلۡقَوۡمَ ٱلۡكَٰفِرِينَ ۝٢٦٤﴾ [البقرة: ٢٦٤]، ﴿وَٱللَّهُ لَا يَهۡدِي ٱلۡقَوۡمَ ٱلۡفَٰسِقِينَ ۝١٠٨﴾ [المائدة: ١٠٨] فجعل الظلم، والكفر، والفسق، أسباب لعدم الهداية، وهذه من أفعال العباد جازاهم عليها، عدلاً منه سبحانه وتعالىٰ لا ظلمًا ﴿وَمَا ظَلَمَهُمُ ٱللَّهُ وَلَٰكِن كَانُوٓاْ أَنفُسَهُمۡ يَظۡلِمُونَ ۝٣٣﴾ [النحل:٣٣]، فلا يليق به سبحانه أن يكرم من هذا وصفه وأيضًا لا يليق به سبحانه وتعالىٰ أن يُضيع عمل العاملين، قال سبحانه: ﴿أَمۡ حَسِبَ ٱلَّذِينَ ٱجۡتَرَحُواْ ٱلسَّيِّـَٔاتِ أَن نَّجۡعَلَهُمۡ كَٱلَّذِينَ ءَامَنُواْ وَعَمِلُواْ ٱلصَّٰلِحَٰتِ سَوَآءٗ مَّحۡيَاهُمۡ وَمَمَاتُهُمۡۚ سَآءَ مَا يَحۡكُمُونَ ۝٢١﴾ [الجاثية:٢١] ﴿وَخَلَقَ ٱللَّهُ ٱلسَّمَٰوَٰتِ وَٱلۡأَرۡضَ بِٱلۡحَقِّ وَلِتُجۡزَىٰ كُلُّ نَفۡسِۭ بِمَا كَسَبَتۡ وَهُمۡ لَا يُظۡلَمُونَ ۝٢٢﴾ [الجاثية:٢٢]، ﴿أَفَنَجۡعَلُ ٱلۡمُسۡلِمِينَ كَٱلۡمُجۡرِمِينَ ۝٣٥ مَا لَكُمۡ كَيۡفَ تَحۡكُمُونَ ۝٣٦﴾

[القلم:٣٥،٣٦] هذا جور ينزه الله عنه، ويقول سبحانه وتعالىٰ: ﴿أَمْ نَجْعَلُ ٱلَّذِينَ ءَامَنُواْ وَعَمِلُواْ ٱلصَّٰلِحَٰتِ كَٱلْمُفْسِدِينَ فِى ٱلْأَرْضِ أَمْ نَجْعَلُ ٱلْمُتَّقِينَ كَٱلْفُجَّارِ ﴿٢٨﴾﴾ [ص:٢٨].

Thus, Allah ﷻ ordains guidance out of grace and honour on His part for the person who wants good and guidance. Allah ﷻ makes his or her path to goodness and acts of goodness easy. This is for their interest, not for the interest of Allah the Almighty. As regards to Allah ﷻ leading misguided people astray, it is justice on His part. It is recompense for their aversion and lack of interest for good and obedience to Allah ﷻ. He does not wrong them. Due to this, we find that Allah ﷻ says in verses: **{...and Allah does not guide the wrongdoing people.} [Qur'ān 2:258] {And Allah does not guide the disbelieving people.} [Qur'ān 2:264] {...and Allah does not guide the defiantly disobedient people.} [Qur'ān 5:108]** Here, He says that oppression, disbelief, and *fisq* (defiant disobedience) are causes for not being guided. These are acts of people; Allah ﷻ recompenses them out of justice on His part, and not out of injustice. **{And Allah wronged them not, but they had been wronging themselves.} [Qur'ān 16:33]** It is not then befitting that Allah ﷻ honours someone who has such qualities, and it is also not befitting that Allah ﷻ lets the deeds of those who do good go to waste. Allah ﷻ says: **{Or do those who commit evils think We will make them like those who have believed and done righteous deeds – [make them] equal in their life and their death? Evil is that which they judge.} [Qur'ān 45:21] {And Allah created the heavens and earth in truth and so that every soul may be recompensed for what it has earned, and they will not be wronged.} [Qur'ān 45:22] {Then will We treat the Muslims like the criminals? What is [the matter] with you? How do you judge?} [Qur'ān 68:35-36]** This is injustice and Allah is transcendent of this. Allah ﷻ says: **{Or should we treat those who believe and do righteous deeds like corrupters in the land? Or should We treat those who fear Allah like the wicked?} [Qur'ān 38:28]**

فالله سبحانه وتعالىٰ لا يُضيع أجر من عمل صالحًا، ولا يجازي أحداً بغير فعله، وبغير كسبه ﴿وَمَا تُجْزَوْنَ إِلَّا مَا كُنتُمْ تَعْمَلُونَ ﴿٣٩﴾﴾ [الصافات:٣٩] فالعمل كله للعبد من الخير والشر، والمجازاة من الله فضلاً وعدلاً.

Allah ﷻ does not neglect the reward of those who do good, and He does not reward someone without action and without work. Allah ﷻ says: **{And you will not be recompensed except for what you used to do.} [Qur'ān 37:39]** All acts, whether good or bad, are attributed to the person, and the reward of either grace or justice is from Allah ﷻ.

المتن

(٣٧) وَكُلُّهُمْ يَتَقَلَّبُونَ فِي مَشِيئَتِهِ بَيْنَ فَضْلِهِ وَعَدْلِهِ.

(37) And all of them are subjugated by His will, between His grace and His justice.

الشرح

وكل العباد لا يخرجون عن التقلب في مشيئة الله بين فضلة على أهل الطاعة وأهل الخير، وعدله مع أهل الكفر والشرك، وهذا هو اللائق بحكمته وعظمته سبحانه، فلا يجمع بين المتضادات والمختلفات، بل ينزل الأشياء في منازلها، ولهذا من أسمائه: الحكيم، ومن صفاته: الحكمة، الحكيم الذي يضع الأشياء في مواضعها، فيضع الفضل في أهل الطاعة، ويضع العذاب في أهل الكفر والمعاصي، هذا فضله سبحانه وعدله.

None of Allah's ﷻ slaves are excluded from alternation within Allah's ﷻ will, alternation between grace for the people of obedience and goodness, and justice for the people of disbelief and idolatry. This is befitting of the wisdom and greatness of the Almighty. He does not make equal those who are opposite and different, but rather does everything in a manner befitting [each individual]. Hence one of Allah's ﷻ names is al-Ḥakīm (the Most Wise), and wisdom is one of His attributes. The Most Wise is He who 'puts all things in their right places'. Thus, He applies His grace with the people of obedience and His punishment with the people of disbelief and sin. This is grace and justice from Allah ﷻ.

المتن

(٣٨) وَهُوَ مُتَعالٍ عَنِ الأَضْدادِ والأَنْدادِ.

(38) He is transcendent of all opponents and peers.

الشرح

(متعال) أي: مرتفع بذاته وقدره وقهره عن الأضداد والأنداد، فالأنداد: هم الأمثال والشبهاء والنظراء، فالله سبحانه وتعالىٰ ليس له نظير، وليس له مثيل ولا شبيه، فلا أحد يشارك الله ولا يشابهه ولا يساويه جل وعلا، وهذا من علو قدره وقهره وهو العلي بذاته فوق مخلوقاته. أما الأضداد: فهم المعارضون له، فالله ليس له معارض، ولا يضاده أحد من خلقه، فإنه إذا أراد أمراً فلا يمكن لأحد أن يعترض ويمنع أمره سبحانه وتعالىٰ، وإذا أراد إعطاء فلا أحد يمنع، وإذا أراد منعاً لشيء فلا أحد يعطيه (لا مانع لما أعطيت، ولا معطي لما منعت).

Transcendent (*muta'ālin*) means His essence, His omnipotence, and His subjugation (*qahr*), is above all rivals. A rival (*nidd*) is an equal, similar being or a peer. There is nothing similar, equal, or comparable to Allah ﷻ. Nothing has a share of divinity, is equivalent to or resembles Allah the Most High. This is from Allah's ﷻ highness as it relates to His omnipotence and subjugation of all things. His essence is also high above His creations. As regards to 'opponents', it means any opposition. Allah ﷻ has no opposition, no one can oppose Him. If He wants something to be, no one can oppose or prevent His command. If He wants to give something, no one can withhold it, and if He wants to withhold something, no one can give it. "There is none to prevent what You have given, and none to give what you have prevented."[10]

10 It is related that Warrād, the scribe of al-Mughīrah ibn Shu'bah ؓ, said: Al-Mughīrah ibn Shu'bah dictated to me a letter to Mu'āwiyah ؓ, saying that the Prophet ﷺ said at the end of every obligatory prayer: "There is no God but Allah alone – He has no partner. His are the praise and kingdom, and He is able to do all things. O Allah, there is no one who can prevent what You have given, and no one who can give what You have withheld, nor does any fortune avail, from You is all fortune." [Al-Bukhārī,

قال تعالىٰ: ﴿مَّا يَفْتَحِ ٱللَّهُ لِلنَّاسِ مِن رَّحْمَةٍ فَلَا مُمْسِكَ لَهَا ۖ وَمَا يُمْسِكْ فَلَا مُرْسِلَ لَهُۥ مِنۢ بَعْدِهِۦ ۚ وَهُوَ ٱلْعَزِيزُ ٱلْحَكِيمُ ۝٢﴾ [فاطر:٢].

Allah ﷻ says: **{Whatever Allah grants to people of mercy – none can withhold it; and whatever He withholds – none can release it thereafter. And He is the Exalted in Might, the Wise.} [Qur'ān 35:2]**

فلا ند لله ولا ضد له فيما يأمر به وينهىٰ عنه، خلاف المخلوقين فيوجد من ينازعهم ويقف ضد تنفيذ أوامرهم، فالمخلوقات كلها لها مشارك، فالخلق يتشابهون في العلم والاسم وفي كل شيء، في الأجساد والصفات، ويشتركون في الأفعال والأملاك والله سبحانه لا يشبهه أحد ولا يشاركه أحد.

Thus, nothing can rival or oppose what Allah ﷻ commands and forbids, as opposed to created things, as there are those who contest them and stand in opposition to their commands. All created things have equals, who are comparable to them in knowledge, name, and everything else, physically or qualitatively. They have common actions and possessions. Allah, however, is not common with or partnered to anyone.

المتن

(٣٩) لا رادَّ لِقَضائِهِ، وَلا مُعَقِّبَ لِحُكْمِهِ، وَلا غالِبَ لِأَمْرِهِ.

(39) There is no one to prevent His decree, nor anyone to override His judgment, nor anyone to overpower His command.

الشرح

فالله ﴿إِذَا قَضَىٰٓ أَمْرًا فَإِنَّمَا يَقُولُ لَهُۥ كُن فَيَكُونُ ۝٣٥﴾ [مريم:٣٥] ﴿لَا مُعَقِّبَ لِحُكْمِهِۦ ۚ وَهُوَ سَرِيعُ ٱلْحِسَابِ ۝٤١﴾ [الرعد:٤١] فالله عز وجل إذا قضىٰ أمراً فلا يستطيع أحد أن ينقضه أو يرده، بخلاف المخلوق فقد يعطل تنفيذ حكمه وقد يُنقض.

no. 844; Muslim, no. 593.]

Allah says: **{When He decrees an affair, He only says to it, "Be," and it is.} [Qur'ān 19:35] {...there is no adjuster of His decision. And He is swift in account.} [Qur'ān 13:41]** If Allah ﷻ decrees something, no one is able to undo or reject it, as opposed to created things: the execution of their decrees can be suspended or undone.

(ولا غالب لأمره): وإذا أمر بالشيء لا أحد يغلب أوامره الكونية، أما أوامره الشرعية فقد تُعطل وقد تُخالف، وهذه للابتلاء والامتحان. ليترتب على ذلك الثواب أو العقاب.

"... Nor anyone to overpower His command": If He commands something, nothing can overpower His universal decree. The commands of His law, however, can be suspended or differed with. Those commands are trials and tests and the basis for reward and punishment.

❁❁❁

المتن

(٤٠) آمَنَّا بِذَلِكَ كُلِّهِ، وَأَيْقَنَّا أَنَّ كُلًّا مِنْ عِنْدِهِ.

(40) We believe in all of these things, and we are certain that all of it is from Him.

الشرح

كل ما سبق ذكره من أول العقيدة إلى آخرها، ندين لله به، وليس مجرد كلام بألسنتنا، بل هو من قلوبنا.

All of the aforementioned, from the beginning to the end of this creedal text is what we have adopted as our faith in Allah ﷻ. It is not only words on the tongue but it is also from our hearts.

❁❁❁

المتن

(٤١) وَإِنَّ مُحَمَّدًا عَبْدُهُ الْمُصْطَفَىٰ، وَنَبِيُّهُ الْمُجْتَبَىٰ، وَرَسُولُهُ الْمُرْتَضَىٰ.

(41) And Muḥammad ﷺ is His chosen slave, selected prophet, and messenger with whom He is pleased;

الشرح

لما بين الشيخ – رحمه الله – في أول كلامه – ما يجب من معرفة الله سبحانه، واعتقاد أنه الرب المستحق للعبادة دون ما سواه، وأنه متصف بصفات الكمال ونعوت الجلال التي هو متصف بها أزلاً وأبداً، لما بين هذا ووضحه، انتقل إلىٰ ما يجب اعتقاده في الرسول عليه الصلاة والسلام. وقوله: **(وإن محمداً عبده المصطفىٰ...)** هذا عطف علىٰ أول الكلام: **(نقول في توحيد الله، معتقدين بتوفيق الله إن الله واحد لا شريك له...)** إلىٰ آخره، ثم قال: **(وإن محمداً ...)** إلىٰ آخره، فلابد من اعتقاد هذا، كما نشهد لله بالألوهية، كذلك نشهد للرسول صلىٰ الله عليه وسلم بالرسالة، ولذلك فالشهادتان دائمـاً متلازمتان.

The *shaykh* ﵀ explained at the beginning of the discourse what is obligatory to know about Allah ﷻ, and that it is obligatory to believe that He is the Lord who is worthy of all worship to the exclusion of all other things, and that He has attributes of perfection and lofty characteristics, both eternally and infinitely. After explaining and clarifying this, he went on to explain what is obligatory to believe about the Messenger of Allah ﷺ. His statement, **"Muḥammad is His chosen slave..."** This is conjoined to the beginning of the discourse: **"With the help of Allah, we say about *Tawḥīd* (Oneness of Allah) – whilst believing in it: Allah is one: He has no partner..."** Then, he says: **"And that Muḥammad is..."** and so forth. We must have faith in this. Just as we have to attest to the right of worship of Allah, so we have to attest to the fact that Muḥammad ﷺ is the Messenger of Allah; and therefore, both testimonies of faith are always inseparable.

(وأن محمداً) هذا اسمه عليه الصلاة والسلام المشهور به، وقد جاء في القرآن:

﴿مَّا كَانَ مُحَمَّدٌ أَبَآ أَحَدٍ مِّن رِّجَالِكُمْ وَلَٰكِن رَّسُولَ ٱللَّهِ﴾ [الأحزاب:٤٠]، وفي قوله: ﴿وَءَامَنُوا۟ بِمَا نُزِّلَ عَلَىٰ مُحَمَّدٍ وَهُوَ ٱلْحَقُّ مِن رَّبِّهِمْ كَفَّرَ عَنْهُمْ سَيِّـَٔاتِهِمْ وَأَصْلَحَ بَالَهُمْ ۝٢﴾ [محمد :٢]، وفي قوله تعالىٰ ﴿مُّحَمَّدٌ رَّسُولُ ٱللَّهِ وَٱلَّذِينَ مَعَهُۥٓ﴾ [الفتح:٢٩]، وجاء أحمد في القرآن في قوله تعالىٰ عن عيسىٰ عليه السلام: ﴿يَٰبَنِىٓ إِسْرَٰٓءِيلَ إِنِّى رَسُولُ ٱللَّهِ إِلَيْكُم مُّصَدِّقًا لِّمَا بَيْنَ يَدَىَّ مِنَ ٱلتَّوْرَىٰةِ وَمُبَشِّرًۢا بِرَسُولٍ يَأْتِى مِنۢ بَعْدِى ٱسْمُهُۥٓ أَحْمَدُ﴾ [الصف:٦].

'Muḥammad' is the name that he is known by. Allah ﷻ said in the Qur'ān: **{Muḥammad is not the father of [any] one of your men, but [he is] the Messenger of Allah.} [Qur'ān 33:40]** Also: **{And those who believe and do righteous deeds and believe in what has been sent down upon Muḥammad – and it is the truth from their Lord – He will remove from them their misdeeds and amend their condition.} [Qur'ān 47:2]** And in the words of Allah ﷻ: **{Muḥammad is the Messenger of Allah; and those with him...} [Qur'ān 48:29]** The name 'Aḥmad' also appears in the Qur'ān as Allah ﷻ quotes 'Īsā ﵇ as saying: **{'O children of Israel, indeed I am the messenger of Allah to you confirming what came before me of the Torah and bringing good tidings of a messenger to come after me, whose name is Ahmad.'} [Qur'ān 61:6]**

وله أسماء جاءت في السنة، ذكرها ابن القيم في كتابه: «جلاء الأفهام».

He has other names that appear in the Sunnah as Ibn al-Qayyim mentioned in his book, *Jalā'u 'l-Afhām.*

والتعرف علىٰ الرسول صلىٰ الله عليه وسلم من واجبات الدين ومن أصول الإسلام، وقد قال الشيخ محمد بن عبد الوهاب في «ثلاثة الأصول» : «الأصل الأول: معرفة الله، والثاني: معرفة نبيه، والثالث: معرفة دين الإسلام بالأدلة»، كما يجب عليك معرفة الله، كذلك يجب عليك معرفة نبيه صلىٰ الله عليه وسلم، ومعرفة دين الإسلام بالأدلة. هذه أصول ثلاثة، وهي التي يسأل عنها الميت إذا وضع في قبره.

Learning about the Messenger of Allah ﷺ is a religious obligation and one of the fundamentals of Islam. Shaykh Muḥammad ibn ʿAbd al-Wahhāb said in *Thalāthat al-Uṣūl* (the *Three Fundamental Principles*): "The first principle: knowledge of Allah ﷻ; the second: knowledge of His Prophet; the third: knowledge of the religion of Islam with evidence." Just as you have to know about Allah ﷻ, you also have to know about His Prophet ﷺ and about the religion of Islām with evidence. These are the three fundamental principles that the dead will be asked about when placed in their graves.

وقوله: **(عبده)** فهو عبدالله عز وجل، وليس له من الألوهية شيء، ولا من الربوبية شيء، وإنما هو عبد الله ورسوله، مؤتمر بأوامره، منتهٍ عن نواهيه، مبلغ عن الله عز وجل، وهذا فيه رد علىٰ الغلو فيه عليه الصلاة والسلام؛ لأن هناك من يغلون في الرسول عليه الصلاة والسلام، ويجعلون له شيئًا من الربوبية أو الألوهية، ويدعونه مع الله، وهذا غلو - والعياذ بالله - كما غلت النصارىٰ في المسيح عيسىٰ ابن مريم، وقالوا إنه ابن الله أو الله أو ثالث ثلاثة.

"His slave": Muḥammad ﷺ is the slave of Allah ﷻ, and he has no share of divinity or lordship; rather he is no more than the slave and Messenger of Allah, who follows the commands and desists from doing what He has forbidden, and who delivers the word of Allah ﷻ. This contains a refutation of those who are excessive with regard to the Prophet ﷺ and ascribe some forms of lordship or worship to him and supplicate to him along with Allah. This is excess, and refuge is sought with Allah, it is similar to how the Christians are excessive with regard to the Messiah, ʿĪsā ibn Maryam ﷺ, and say that he is the son of Allah or part of a trinity.

ففي قوله: **(عبده المصطفىٰ)** فيه ردٌ للغلو، فهو عبد، وكل من في الأرض والسموات عبيد لله عز وجل، قال سبحانه ﴿إِن كُلُّ مَن فِي ٱلسَّمَٰوَٰتِ وَٱلْأَرْضِ إِلَّآ ءَاتِي ٱلرَّحْمَٰنِ عَبْدًا ﴿٩٣﴾﴾ [مريم:٩٣]، فالملائكة عبيد ﴿بَلْ عِبَادٌ مُّكْرَمُونَ ﴿٢٦﴾ لَا يَسْبِقُونَهُۥ بِٱلْقَوْلِ وَهُم بِأَمْرِهِۦ يَعْمَلُونَ ﴿٢٧﴾﴾ [الأنبيا:٢٦،٢٧]، والأنبياء والرسل عبيد كما قال سبحانه في نوح عليه السلام: ﴿كَانَ عَبْدًا شَكُورًا ﴿٣﴾﴾ [الإسراء:٣]، وقال عز وجل: ﴿فَكَذَّبُواْ عَبْدَنَا﴾ [القمر:٩]، وقال في داود: ﴿وَٱذْكُرْ عَبْدَنَا دَاوُۥدَ ذَا ٱلْأَيْدِۖ إِنَّهُۥٓ أَوَّابٌ ﴿١٧﴾﴾ [ص:١٧]، وقال في سليمان: ﴿نِعْمَ ٱلْعَبْدُ إِنَّهُۥٓ أَوَّابٌ ﴿٣٠﴾﴾

[ص:٣٠]، وقال في أيوب: ﴿وَٱذۡكُرۡ عَبۡدَنَآ أَيُّوبَ﴾ [ص:٤١]، وقال في عيسىٰ: ﴿إِنۡ هُوَ إِلَّا عَبۡدٌ أَنۡعَمۡنَا عَلَيۡهِ وَجَعَلۡنَٰهُ مَثَلٗا لِّبَنِيٓ إِسۡرَٰٓءِيلَ ٥٩﴾ [الزخرف: ٥٩]، فإذا كان الأنبياء والرسل والملائكة عبيد لله، وهم أشرف الخلق، فغيرهم من الأولياء والصالحين من باب أولىٰ.

"...His chosen slave": This entails a response to that excessiveness, as he is a slave, as everyone in the heavens and on earth is a slave to Allah ﷻ. Allah says: **{There is no one in the heavens and earth but that he comes to the Most Merciful as a slave.} [Qur'ān 19:93]** The angels are also slaves. Allah ﷻ says: **{Rather, they are [but] honoured slaves. They cannot precede Him in word, and they act by His command.} [Qur'ān 21:26-27]** The Prophets and Messengers are also slaves of Allah, as Allah ﷻ says about Nūh (Noah) ؑ: **{Indeed, he was a grateful slave.} [Qur'ān 17:3]** Allah ﷻ also says: **"...And they denied Our slave..." [Qur'ān 54:9]** He says about Dāwūd (David) ؑ: **{...And remember Our slave, David, the possessor of strength; indeed, he was one who repeatedly turned back [to Allah].} [Qur'ān 38:17]** And He says about Sulaymān (Solomon) ؑ: **{An excellent slave, indeed he was one repeatedly turning back [to Allah]." [Qur'ān 38:30]** And He says about Ayyūb (Job) ؑ: **{And remember Our slave Job...} [Qur'ān 38:41]** And He says about 'Īsā (Jesus) ؑ: **{Jesus was not but a slave upon whom We bestowed favour, and We made him an example for the Children of Israel.} [Qur'ān 43:59]** If the Prophets, Messengers and angels (being the most distinguished creatures) are slaves of Allah ﷻ, then others, such as the saints and righteous, have to be so with even more certainty.

وأفضلهم محمد صلىٰ الله عليه وسلم، وهو آخر الأنبياء، وسماه الله عبداً في قوله: ﴿وَإِن كُنتُمۡ فِي رَيۡبٖ مِّمَّا نَزَّلۡنَا عَلَىٰ عَبۡدِنَا﴾ [البقرة: ٢٣] يعني: رسول الله صلىٰ الله عليه وسلم، وقال تعالىٰ: ﴿تَبَارَكَ ٱلَّذِي نَزَّلَ ٱلۡفُرۡقَانَ عَلَىٰ عَبۡدِهِۦ﴾ [الفرقان: ١] ﴿سُبۡحَٰنَ ٱلَّذِيٓ أَسۡرَىٰ بِعَبۡدِهِۦ﴾ [الإسراء: ١]، ومقام العبودية هو أعلىٰ المقامات، ولا شيء أشرف من العبودية لله عز وجل.

Muḥammad ﷺ is superior to all of them, and He is the final prophet. Allah ﷻ named him a 'slave' as He says: **{And if you are in doubt about what**

We have sent down upon Our slave [Muḥammad]...} [Qur'ān 2:23] I.e. what we sent to the Messenger of Allah ﷺ. Allah ﷻ also says: **{Blessed is He who sent down the Criterion upon His slave...} [Qur'ān 25:1] {Exalted is He who took His slave by night...} [Qur'ān 17:1]** The status of being the slave of Allah ﷻ has the highest possible standing; there is nothing more honourable than servitude to Allah ﷻ.

قال عليه الصلاة والسلام: «**لا تطروني كما أطرت النصارىٰ عيسىٰ ابن مريم، إنما أنا عبد، فقولوا: عبد الله ورسوله**».

The Prophet ﷺ said, "Do not exceed in praising me as the Christians praised the son of Mary, for I am only a slave, so call me the slave and messenger of Allah."[11]

ومعنىٰ المصطفىٰ: المختار، من الاصطفاء، وهو الاختيار، قال تعالىٰ: ﴿ وَٱذْكُرْ عِبَٰدَنَآ إِبْرَٰهِيمَ وَإِسْحَٰقَ وَيَعْقُوبَ أُو۟لِى ٱلْأَيْدِى وَٱلْأَبْصَٰرِ ﴿٤٥﴾ إِنَّآ أَخْلَصْنَٰهُم بِخَالِصَةٍ ذِكْرَى ٱلدَّارِ ﴿٤٦﴾ وَإِنَّهُمْ عِندَنَا لَمِنَ ٱلْمُصْطَفَيْنَ ٱلْأَخْيَارِ ﴿٤٧﴾﴾ [ص:٤٥-٤٧] المصطفين: جمع مصطفىٰ، وهو المختار، أصله مصتفىٰ، ثم أُبدلت التاء طاء فصارت مصطفىٰ؛ ليسهل النطق بها.

Muṣṭafā means the chosen one. Allah ﷻ says: **{And remember Our slaves, Abraham, Isaac and Jacob – those of strength and [religious] vision. Indeed, We chose them for an exclusive quality: remembrance of the home [of the Hereafter]. And indeed they are, to Us, among the chosen...} [Qur'ān 38:45-47]** 'The chosen' *(al-muṣṭafayn)* is the plural form of 'one who is chosen' *(muṣṭafā)*. Its root is *mustafā* then the *tā'* was switched for a *ṭā'* and it became *muṣṭafā*, so that it would be easier to pronounce.

فالمصطفىٰ هو المختار؛ لأن الله سبحانه اختار محمداً عليه الصلاة والسلام للرسالة من بين قومه، والله أعلم حيث يجعل رسالته، فلا يختار إلا من يعلم أنه يستحق الاختيار، وأنه يقوم بالمهمة؛ لأن هذه المهمة صعبة وعظيمة، فلا

11 Al-Bukhārī, no. 3445.

يختار الله إلا من هو لها أهل، قال سبحانه: ﴿ٱللَّهُ أَعْلَمُ حَيْثُ يَجْعَلُ رِسَالَتَهُۥ﴾ [الأنعام:١٢٤].

Thus, *al-muṣṭafā* is the chosen one, as out of all his people, Allah ﷻ chose Muḥammad ﷺ for the message (of Islām), and Allah ﷻ knows best whom to give the message to. He chooses only the right people who are worthy of being chosen and who can fulfil this difficult and great task. Thus Allah only selects the competent: **{Allah is most knowing of where He places His message.} [Qur'ān 6:124]**

و(**المجتبىٰ**) بمعنىٰ المصطفىٰ.

"Al-Mujtabā": Means *al-muṣṭafā* (the chosen one).

والنبي: من أوحىٰ إليه الله بشرع ولم يُؤمر بتبليغه، والرسول: من أوحي إليه بشرع وأمر بتبليغه، وهذا أشهر ما قيل في الفرق بين النبي والرسول، ومعنىٰ: أمر بتبليغه، أي : أمر بإلزام الناس وأن يقاتلهم علىٰ ما جاء به.

"Al-nabī" is someone who receives divine revelation but has not been commanded to deliver the message. *"Al-rasūl"* is someone who receives divine revelation and has been commanded to deliver the message. This is the most popular opinion on the difference between a prophet and a messenger. 'To deliver the message' means a command to make people follow, and to fight for the sake of the divine revelation.

وكذلك النبي، يُوحىٰ إليه ويدعو إلىٰ الله عز وجل، ولكن يتبع من قبله من الأنبياء ويمشي علىٰ طريق من قبله، ولا ينفرد بشريعة خاصة، مثل أنبياء بني إسرائيل، جاءوا بالتوراة ودعوا إلىٰ التوراة التي أنزلها الله علىٰ موسىٰ عليه السلام.

Accordingly, a prophet receives divine revelation and preaches the word of Allah ﷻ; however, a prophet follows previous prophets and treads the same path as them and does not have a unique law, as is the case with the prophets of the Children of Israel. They received and preached the Torah which was sent down to Mūsā (Moses) ﷺ.

و(**المرتضىٰ**) بمعنىٰ المجتبىٰ والمصطفىٰ، فالمرتضىٰ بمعنىٰ: أن الله ارتضاه.

"...With whom He is pleased": *Al-murtaḍā* means *al-muṣṭafā* and *al-mujtabā* (the chosen one). The definition of *'al-murtaḍā'* is that Allah ﷻ is pleased with him.

❁❁❁

المتن

(٤١) وَإِنَّهُ خاتَمُ الْأَنْبِياءِ، وَإِمامُ الْأَتْقِياءِ، وَسَيِّدُ الْمُرْسَلِينَ، وَحَبِيبُ رَبِّ الْعالَمِينَ.

(41) And that he ﷺ is the final Prophet (*khātim al-anbiyā'*), the leader of the pious, the chief of the Messengers, and the beloved of the Lord of the Worlds.

الشرح

هذه من صفاته عليه الصلاة والسلام.

These are from the characteristics of the Prophet ﷺ.

خاتم الأنبياء، ومعنىٰ **(خاتم)** الذي لا يأتي بعده نبي، وختام الشيء هو: الذي يُجعل عليه حتىٰ لا يزاد عليه ولا ينقص منه، فالله ختم الرسالات بمحمد صلىٰ الله عليه وسلم، قال جل في علاه: ﴿مَّا كَانَ مُحَمَّدٌ أَبَآ أَحَدٍ مِّن رِّجَالِكُمْ وَلَٰكِن رَّسُولَ ٱللَّهِ وَخَاتَمَ ٱلنَّبِيِّـۧنَ﴾ [الأحزاب:٤٠]، فلا حاجة لمجيء نبي بعده؛ لأن القرآن موجود، والسنة النبوية موجودة، والعلماء الربانيون موجودون، يدعون إلىٰ الله ويبصرون الناس؛ فدين محمد باقٍ إلىٰ قيام الساعة لا يبدل ولا ينسخ ولا يغير؛ لأن الله سبحانه جعله صالحـًا لكل زمان ولكل مكان، أما شرائع الأنبياء السابقين فتكون مؤقتة لأممهم في فترة من الفترات، ثم ينسخ الله تلك الشريعة بشريعة أخرىٰ تتناسب مع الأمة الأخرىٰ ﴿لِكُلٍّ جَعَلْنَا مِنكُمْ شِرْعَةً وَمِنْهَاجًا﴾ [المائدة:٤٨]. كما قال تعالىٰ: ﴿لِكُلِّ أَجَلٍ كِتَابٌ ٣٨﴾ أي لكل كتاب أجل.

He is *khātim al-anbiyā'*. What *khātim* (seal) means is that no prophet is to come after him. The 'seal' of something is what is placed upon it so that it does not increase or diminish. Thus, Allah ﷻ has sealed all messages with Muḥammad ﷺ. Allah ﷻ says: **{Muhammad is not the father of [any] one of your men, but [he is] the Messenger of Allah and last of the prophets.} [Qur'ān 33:40]** So there is no need for any prophet after him because the Qur'ān is present and the Prophetic Sunnah is present, and the learned teachers who preach Allah's ﷻ word and give sight to people are present. So the religion of Muḥammad ﷺ remains until the coming of the Hour and is not changed, abolished or amended, because Allah ﷻ made it suitable for every time and place. The laws of previous prophets, on the other hand, were limited to their people of a certain period. Then, Allah ﷻ replaced these laws with other laws that were more suitable for the later people. **{To each of you We prescribed a law and a method.} [Qur'ān 5:48]** Similarly, Allah ﷻ says: **{For every term is a decree.} [Qur'ān 13:38]** This means that every book has a term and appointed time.

فدين الإسلام كامل لا يحتاج بعد محمد صلىٰ الله عليه وسلم إلىٰ رسول، والعلماء ورثة الأنبياء، فمن اعتقد أنه يأتي بعد محمد صلىٰ الله عليه وسلم نبي فهو كافر بالله خارج من الملة، وقد أخبر النبي صلىٰ الله عليه وسلم أنه يأتي كذبة يدعون النبوة من بعده، قال عليه الصلاة والسلام: **«سيأتي بعدي كذابون ثلاثون، كلهم يدعي أنه نبي، وأنا خاتم الأنبياء لا نبي بعدي»**.

The religion of Islām is complete and is not in need of any messenger after Muḥammad ﷺ. And the scholars are the heirs of the Prophets. If anyone believes that a prophet is to come after Muḥammad ﷺ he has disbelieved in Allah and exited the religion. The Prophet ﷺ told us that liars will appear, claiming that they are prophets after him. The Prophet ﷺ said, "After me, there will come thirty liars, all of whom will claim that they are prophets. And I am the seal of the Prophets. There is no prophet after me."[12]

فمن ادعىٰ النبوة أو ادعيت له النبوة ومن اتبعهم، فكلهم كفرة، وقد قاتلهم

---

12 It is related that Abū Hurayrah ﷺ said: The Prophet ﷺ said: "The Hour will not come until two parties fight, and there will be a great number of casualties among them. Their claim is the same. And the Hour will not come until the *dajjāls* are sent forth. They are around thirty. Each one claims to be a messenger of Allah." [Al-Bukhārī, no. 3609; Muslim, no. 157/84 (*Kitāb al-fitan*)]

المسلمون وكفّروهم، وآخر من ادعىٰ النبوة في الوقت الحاضر: القادياني الباكستاني الذي ادّعىٰ النبوة له أتباعه القاديانية، ويُسمون بالأحمدية نسبة إلىٰ اسمه؛ لأن اسمه أحمد القادياني، وقد كفره العلماء وطردوه من البلاد الإسلامية، وكفَّروا أتباعه؛ لأن هذا تكذيب لله ولرسوله، وتكفيرهم بإجماع المسلمين، لم يخالف في هذا أحد.

So anyone who claims to be a prophet, or if it is claimed that anyone is a prophet and they are followed, all of them are disbelievers. The Muslims have fought them and declared them disbelievers. The most recent person to claim to be a prophet in modern times is the Pakistani[13] man, al-Qādiyānī. He claimed to be a prophet, and his followers are the Qādiyānīs. They are also called Aḥmadīs in relation to his name, as his name is Aḥmad al-Qādiyānī. Scholars declared him a disbeliever and drove him out of the Muslim lands, and they declared his followers disbelievers as well, because they reject what Allah ﷻ and His Messenger ﷺ have said. In fact, they are disbelievers according to the unanimous agreement of the Muslim community, without disagreement from anyone.

فلابد للمسلم أن يعتقد أنه عليه الصلاة والسلام خاتم الأنبياء والمرسلين، وإمام الأتقياء؛ يعني القدوة الوحيد للأتقياء الذين يتقون الله عز وجل: ﴿لَّقَدْ كَانَ لَكُمْ فِى رَسُولِ ٱللَّهِ أُسْوَةٌ حَسَنَةٌ لِّمَن كَانَ يَرْجُواْ ٱللَّهَ وَٱلْيَوْمَ ٱلْآخِرَ﴾ [الأحزاب:٢١]

A Muslim has to believe that Muḥammad ﷺ was the seal of the prophets and messengers, and the leader (*imām*) of the pious, more so, he is the unrivalled example for the pious (those who are conscious of Allah ﷻ). Allah ﷻ says: **{There has certainly been for you in the Messenger of Allah an excellent pattern for anyone whose hope is in Allah and the Last Day and [who] remembers Allah often.} [Qur'ān 33:21]**

أما غير النبي صلىٰ الله عليه وسلم فيقتدىٰ به إن كان يقتدي بالنبي صلىٰ الله عليه وسلم، أما من خالف الرسول عليه الصلاة والسلام فلا يجوز الاقتداء به: ﴿قُلْ إِن كُنتُمْ تُحِبُّونَ ٱللَّهَ فَٱتَّبِعُونِى يُحْبِبْكُمُ ٱللَّهُ وَيَغْفِرْ لَكُمْ ذُنُوبَكُمْ﴾ [آل

13 [T] He was Indian, and his city is located in the Punjab region.

عمران:٣١]، فلا طريق إلىٰ الله إلا باتباع الرسول عليه الصلاة والسلام والاقتداء به.

On the other hand, the example of anyone besides the Prophet ﷺ is to be followed only if they follow the example of the Prophet ﷺ. In contrast, it is impermissible to follow anyone who acts contrarily to the Messenger of Allah ﷺ. Allah ﷻ says: **{Say, [O Muḥammad], 'If you should love Allah, then follow me, [so] Allah will love you and forgive you your sins.'} [Qur'ān 3:31]** So the only path to Allah ﷻ is via following the Messenger of Allah ﷺ and to take him as an example.

(وسيد المرسلين) هو عليه الصلاة والسلام سيد ولد آدم، كما قال عليه الصلاة والسلام: «**أنا سيد ولد آدم ولا فخر**» أخبر الأمة بذلك من باب الشكر لله عز وجل، ولتشكر الأمة ربها عز وجل علىٰ هذه النعمة: أن جعل رسولها سيد الرسل.

"The chief *(sayyid)* of the Messengers" is the Prophet ﷺ, the chief of Ādam's عليه السلام descendants. Similarly, the Prophet ﷺ said, "I am the chief of the sons of Ādam, I say so without boasting." He informed his nation of this out of thanks to Allah ﷻ, and in order that his Ummah give thanks to their Lord for the blessing that He made their messenger the chief of the Messengers.[14]

و**(سيد)** معناه: المقدم والإمام، فهو أفضل الرسل عليه الصلاة والسلام، وإمامهم ومقدمهم .

Sayyid (chief) means someone who is foremost or who is a leader. Thus, he is the most superior of all Messengers, he is their leader and chieftain.

و**(حبيب رب العالمين)** هذه العبارة فيها مؤاخذة؛ لأنه لا يكفي قوله: حبيب، بل هو خليل رب العالمين؛ والخلة أفضل من مطلق المحبة؛ فالمحبة درجات،

14 Al-Tirmidhī, no 3624; Aḥmad, no 3/144-145; al-Tirmidhī said: "This ḥadīth is *ḥasan ṣaḥīḥ.*" It is supported by another ḥadīth as related from Abū Hurayrah رضي الله عنه: "I am the chief of the people (*qawm*) on the Judgment Day;" and with another wording: "I am the chief of man (*nās*) on Judgment Day." [Al-Bukhārī, no. 3340, 4712; Muslim, no. 194, 2278.]

أعلاها الخلة، وهي خالص المحبة، ولم تحصل هذه المرتبة إلا لاثنين من الخلق إبراهيم عليه الصلاة والسلام ﴿وَٱتَّخَذَ ٱللَّهُ إِبْرَٰهِيمَ خَلِيلًا ﴿١٢٥﴾﴾ [النسا:١٢٥]، ونبينا عليه الصلاة والسلام، فقد أخبر بذلك فقال: «**إن الله اتخذني خليلاً كما اتخذ إبراهيم خليلاً**». فلا يقال: حبيب الله؛ لأن هذا يصلح لكل مؤمن، فلا يكون للنبي صلىٰ الله عليه وسلم في هذا ميزة، أما الخلة فلا أحد يلحقه فيها.

"...the Beloved *(ḥabīb)* of the Lord of the Worlds": There is an objection to be made about the phrase used here, because it does not suffice to say *ḥabīb*, but rather he is the *khalīl* (intimate friend) of the Lord of the Worlds. *Khullah* (intimate friendship) is superior to love in the absolute sense of the latter. Love is of different levels, and *khullah* is pure love. Only two people have ever attained this rank: Ibrāhīm (Abraham) ﷺ, as Allah ﷻ says: **{And Allah took Abraham as an intimate friend *(khalīl)*.} [Qur'ān 4:125]** And our Prophet ﷺ, as he has told us, "Allah has taken me as a *khalīl* as He has taken Ibrāhīm as a *khalīl*." So *ḥabībullāh* (Allah's beloved) should not be said, as this is befitting of every believer, so there would not thereby be any distinction for the Prophet ﷺ; *khullah* (intimate friendship), on the other hand, is not jointly attributed to anyone else.[15]

❁❁❁

المتن

(٤٣) وَكُلُّ دَعْوَىٰ النُّبُوَّةِ بَعْدَهُ فَغَيٌّ وَهَوًىٰ.

(43) Every claim to prophecy after him is false and [based on] whims and desires.

الشرح

هذا سبق في معنىٰ أنه خاتم النبيين، فكل دعوىٰ للنبوة بعده فباطله وكفر؛ لأنه لا يأتي بعد نبينا عليه الصلاة والسلام نبي، وعيسىٰ عليه الصلاة والسلام لما ينزل

15 Muslim no. 532. It is also related that Ibn Masʿūd ؓ said: The Prophet ﷺ said: "If I were to take anyone as a *khalīl*, I would have taken the son of Abū Quḥāfah as a *khalīl*, but your companion is the *khalīl* of Allah." Meaning himself ﷺ. Muslim, no. 2383; al-Bukhārī's wording has: "However, there is the brotherhood and affection of Islam."

آخر الزمان فإنه لا يأتي علىٰ أنه نبي ورسول أو يأتي بشريعة جديدة، إنما يأتي علىٰ أنه مجدد لدين رسول الله صلىٰ الله عليه وسلم، ومتبع لرسول الله صلىٰ الله عليه وسلم، ويحكم بالشريعة الإسلامية.

This was already mentioned in the discussion related to the fact that he is the seal of the prophets. Every claim to prophecy after him is both false and a form of disbelief, because there is no prophet after our Prophet ﷺ. When ʿĪsā عليه السلام comes in the end of times, he will not return as a prophet and messenger and he will not bring a new law; he will come as a reviver of the religion of the Messenger of Allah ﷺ and as his follower; and he will judge according to the Islamic law.

المتن

(٤٤) وَهُوَ الْمَبْعُوثُ إِلَىٰ عامَّةِ الْجِنِّ، وَكافَّةِ الْوَرَىٰ، بِالْحَقِّ والْهُدَىٰ، وَبِالنُّورِ والضِّياءِ.

(44) He was sent to all of the jinn and all of mankind with truth, guidance, light, and illumination.

الشرح

كذلك، هذا ما يجب اعتقاده في النبي صلىٰ الله عليه وسلم، لا يكفي أن نعتقد أنه رسول الله فقط، بل أنه رسول إلىٰ الناس عامة، بل إلىٰ الجن والإنس، قال سبحانه: ﴿وَمَآ أَرۡسَلۡنَٰكَ إِلَّا كَآفَّةً لِّلنَّاسِ بَشِيرًا وَنَذِيرًا﴾ [سبأ:٢٨]، وقال له: ﴿قُلۡ يَٰٓأَيُّهَا ٱلنَّاسُ إِنِّي رَسُولُ ٱللَّهِ إِلَيۡكُمۡ جَمِيعًا﴾ [الأعراف: ١٥٨] فرسالته إلىٰ الناس عامة، وهذا من خصائصه عليه الصلاة والسلام، فهو رسول للناس عامة، ووجبت طاعته علىٰ جميع الخلق، عربهم وعجمهم، وأسودهم وأبيضهم، وإنسهم وجنهم، فكل من بلغته دعوة الرسول عليه الصلاة والسلام وجب أن يطيعه وأن يتبعه، فمن أقر أنه رسول الله للعرب خاصة، كما يقوله طائفة من

النصارىٰ، أنه رسول الله للعرب خاصة، وينكرون نبوته لغيرهم، فهذا كفر بالله عز وجل، وتكذيب لله عز وجل ولرسوله، فالله يقول: ﴿وَمَآ أَرۡسَلۡنَٰكَ إِلَّا كَآفَّةٗ لِّلنَّاسِ بَشِيرٗا وَنَذِيرٗا﴾ [سبأ:٢٨]، ويقول سبحانه : ﴿تَبَارَكَ ٱلَّذِي نَزَّلَ ٱلۡفُرۡقَانَ عَلَىٰ عَبۡدِهِۦ لِيَكُونَ لِلۡعَٰلَمِينَ نَذِيرًا ۝١﴾ [الفرقان:١] فرسالته عالمية.

This also has to be asserted as belief about the Prophet ﷺ. It does not suffice to believe that he is the Messenger of Allah, but there must be conviction that he is a messenger to all of mankind; rather, to both jinn and mankind. Allah ﷻ says: **{And We have not sent you except comprehensively to mankind as a bringer of good tidings and a warner.} [Qurʾān 34:28]** And Allah ﷻ said to him: **{Say, [O Muḥammad], 'O mankind, indeed I am the Messenger of Allah to you all.'} [Qurʾān 7:158]** So his message is to all of mankind. This is one of his distinguishing features (*khaṣāʾiṣ*): He is the Messenger of Allah to all of mankind, and it is obligatory for everyone, whether Arab or non-Arab, black or white, jinn or human, to obey him. It is obligatory upon anyone who learns of the message of the Messenger of Allah ﷺ to obey and follow him. If someone acknowledges that he is the Messenger of Allah to Arabs only (as a group of Christians say that he is the Messenger of Allah to Arabs only and deny that he is a prophet for anyone else), then this is disbelief in Allah ﷻ and His Messenger ﷺ. Allah ﷻ says: **{And We have not sent you except comprehensively to mankind as a bringer of good tidings and a warner.} [Qurʾān 34:28]** And Allah ﷻ says: **{Blessed is He who sent down the Criterion upon His servant that he may be to the worlds a warner.} [Qurʾān 25:1]** His message is thus universal.

وقال عليه الصلاة والسلام: «**كان النبي يُبعث إلىٰ قومه خاصة، وبعثت إلىٰ الناس عامة**». وكاتب رسول الله صلىٰ الله عليه وسلم ملوك الأرض يدعوهم إلىٰ الإسلام، فدل علىٰ أنه مرسل إلىٰ أهل الأرض كلهم، وأمر بالجهاد حتىٰ يدخل الناس في الإسلام، فدل علىٰ عموم رسالته عليه الصلاة والسلام، فيجب اعتقاد هذا.

And the Prophet ﷺ said, "The Prophets were sent to their people only, but I was sent to all mankind." The Messenger of Allah ﷺ sent letters to the kings of the world and called on them to accept Islām, so it is evidence that he was sent to all people on earth. He also commanded to strive until people accepted Islām, which evidences the generality of his message, and it is obligatory to believe that.[16]

فتجب في حقه هذه الاعتقادات:

With regard to the Messenger ﷺ, the following is obligatory to believe:

أولاً: أنه عبد الله ورسوله.

ثانيـاً: أنه خاتم النبيين لا نبي بعده.

ثالثـاً: أن رسالته عامة للإنس والجن.

1. He is the slave of Allah and His Messenger.
2. He is the seal of the Prophets, and that there is no prophet after him.
3. His message is general to both mankind and jinn.

ودليل عمومها للإنس: كما سبق من الآيات ومكاتبة النبي صلىٰ الله عليه وسلم.

The evidence that his message is general to mankind is all of the aforementioned verses from the Qur'ān and the letters of the Prophet ﷺ.

وأما عمومها للجن: فلقوله تعالىٰ: ﴿وَإِذْ صَرَفْنَآ إِلَيْكَ نَفَرًا مِّنَ ٱلْجِنِّ يَسْتَمِعُونَ ٱلْقُرْءَانَ فَلَمَّا حَضَرُوهُ قَالُوٓا۟ أَنصِتُوا۟ ۖ فَلَمَّا قُضِىَ وَلَّوْا۟ إِلَىٰ قَوْمِهِم مُّنذِرِينَ ﴿٢٩﴾ قَالُوا۟ يَٰقَوْمَنَآ إِنَّا سَمِعْنَا كِتَٰبًا أُنزِلَ مِنۢ بَعْدِ مُوسَىٰ مُصَدِّقًا لِّمَا بَيْنَ يَدَيْهِ يَهْدِىٓ إِلَى ٱلْحَقِّ وَإِلَىٰ طَرِيقٍ مُّسْتَقِيمٍ ﴿٣٠﴾ يَٰقَوْمَنَآ أَجِيبُوا۟ دَاعِىَ ٱللَّهِ﴾ [الأحقاف:٢٩-٣١] يعنون: محمداً عليه الصلاة والسلام.

The evidence for the generality of his message for the jinn is the saying of Allah ﷻ: **{And [mention, O Muḥammad], when We directed to you a few of the jinn, listening to the Qur'ān. And when they attended**

16 Al-Bukhārī, no. 335 & 438; Muslim: "...and I was sent to both the red and the black." (no. 521).

it, they said, 'Listen quietly.' And when it was concluded, they went back to their people as warners. They said, 'O our people, indeed we have heard a [recited] Book revealed after Moses confirming what was before it which guides to the truth and to a straight path. O our people, respond to the Messenger of Allah and believe in him; Allah will forgive for you your sins and protect you from a painful punishment.} [Qurʾān 46:29-31] Here, they are speaking about Muḥammad ﷺ.

وفي قوله تعالىٰ: ﴿قُلْ أُوحِىَ إِلَىَّ أَنَّهُ ٱسْتَمَعَ نَفَرٌ مِّنَ ٱلْجِنِّ فَقَالُوٓا۟ إِنَّا سَمِعْنَا قُرْءَانًا عَجَبًا ۝١ يَهْدِىٓ إِلَى ٱلرُّشْدِ فَـَٔامَنَّا بِهِۦ﴾ [الجن: ١-٢]، فدل علىٰ عموم رسالته للجن، فالنبي صلىٰ الله عليه وسلم بعث لأهل الأرض كلهم، إنسهم وجنهم، فمن آمن به دخل الجنة، ومن لم يؤمن به دخل النار، من الإنس والجن.

Allah ﷻ also says: **{Say, [O Muḥammad], 'It has been revealed to me that a group of the jinn listened and said, "Indeed, we have heard an amazing Qurʾān. It guides to the right course, and we have believed in it."'} [Qurʾān 72:1-2]** This indicates that his message is general for all jinn. Thus, the Prophet ﷺ was sent to all people on earth, both jinn and mankind. Those who believe in him will enter Paradise, and those who do not believe in him will enter the fire of Hell (both jinn and man).

وقوله: **(وبالنور والضياء)** هما بمعنىٰ واحد وقد بعث النبي صلىٰ الله عليه وسلم بهما. قال تعالىٰ: ﴿يَـٰٓأَيُّهَا ٱلنَّبِىُّ إِنَّآ أَرْسَلْنَـٰكَ شَـٰهِدًا وَمُبَشِّرًا وَنَذِيرًا ۝٤٥ وَدَاعِيًا إِلَى ٱللَّهِ بِإِذْنِهِۦ وَسِرَاجًا مُّنِيرًا ۝٤٦﴾ [الأحزاب: ٤٥،٤٦].

"...Light, and illumination": They have the same meaning. The Prophet ﷺ was sent with both of them. Allah ﷻ says: **{O Prophet, indeed We have sent you as a witness and a bringer of good tidings and a warner. And one who invites to Allah, by His permission, and an illuminating lamp.} [Qurʾān 33: 45-46]**

المتن

(٤٥) وَأَنَّ الْقُرْآنَ كَلامُ اللهِ،

(45) And [we believe] that the Qur'ān is the speech of Allah;

الشرح

بعد أن تؤمن بالله عز وجل، وتؤمن برسوله صلىٰ الله عليه وسلم، تؤمن أن القرآن كلام الله؛ لأن هذا هو الذي جاء به الرسول صلىٰ الله عليه وسلم، وأنزل الله عليه القرآن، وهذا القرآن ليس من كلام محمد صلىٰ الله عليه وسلم ولا من كلام جبريل، إنما هو كلام الله عز وجل، تكلم الله به، وتلقاه جبريل من الله، وتلقاه النبي عليه الصلاة والسلام من جبريل عليه السلام، وتلقته الأمة من النبي صلىٰ الله عليه وسلم.

After you believe in Allah ﷻ and you believe in the Messenger of Allah ﷺ, you have to believe that the Qur'ān is the speech of Allah ﷻ, because it is what the Messenger of Allah ﷺ brought to us. Allah ﷻ revealed the Qur'ān to him. The Qur'ān is not from the speech of Muḥammad ﷺ and not from the speech of Jibrīl عليه السلام, but rather it is the speech of Allah ﷻ. Allah ﷻ spoke it, Jibrīl took it from Allah ﷻ, the Prophet ﷺ took it from Jibrīl عليه السلام, and the Muslims took it from the Prophet ﷺ.

فهو كلام الله، منه بدأ سبحانه، لم يأخذه جبريل من اللوح المحفوظ كما يقوله أهل الضلال، ولم يكن من كلام جبريل ولا محمد، إنما هو من كلام رب العالمين. وأما جبريل ومحمد عليهما الصلاة والسلام فهما مبلغان عن الله عز وجل، فالكلام إنما يقال ويضاف لمن قاله مبتدأ، لا من قاله مبلغاً ومؤدياً.

It is the speech of Allah ﷻ; it originated from Him. Jibrīl عليه السلام did not take it from al-Lawḥ al-Maḥfūẓ (the Preserved Tablet) as some deviant people say. It is not from the speech of Jibrīl or Muḥammad, rather, it is the speech of the Lord of the Worlds. A point that must be noted is that Jibrīl عليه السلام and Muḥammad ﷺ only deliver the speech from Allah ﷻ. Speech is only ascribed to whoever said it in origin and not to anyone who transmitted or quoted it.

فمن قال: إن جبريل أخذه من اللوح المحفوظ، أو : إن الله خلقه في شيء وأخذه جبريل من ذلك الشيء، فهو كافر بالله عز وجل كفراً مخرجاً من الملة، كما تقوله الجهمية والمعتزلة ومن نحا نحوهم، فهو كلام الله، حروفه ومعانيه، تكلم الله به كيف شاء، فنحن نصف الله بأنه يتكلم، والكلام من صفاته الفعلية، والكيفية التي تكلم بها نقول: الله أعلم بها، هذه كسائر صفاته، نؤمن بها ولا نعلم كيفيتها، فالمعنىٰ معروف، وأما الكيفية فهي مجهولة لنا.

Whoever says that Jibrīl ﷵ took it from the Preserved Tablet, or that Allah ﷻ created it within something and Jibrīl ﷵ took it from that thing has disbelieved in Allah ﷻ and left the religion of Islām. This is the claim of the Jahmīs, the Muʿtazilites and the like. It is the speech of Allah, its letters and meanings. Allah ﷻ spoke in whatever manner He so willed. We confirm that Allah ﷻ has the attribute of speech, and this speech is an attribute of action. As regards to the manner in which Allah ﷻ spoke it, we say, Allah ﷻ knows best. It is like all of the other attributes: we believe in them but we do not know the manner. The meaning is known but the manner is unknown to us.

المتن

(٤٦) مِنْهُ بَدا بِلا كَيْفِيَّةٍ قَوْلًا، وَأَنْزَلَهُ عَلَىٰ رَسُولِهِ وَحْيًا.

(46) It began as a word from Him, in a manner that we do not know; and He sent it down to His Messenger as Revelation (*waḥī*).

الشرح

أي : أن القرآن نزل من الله، تكلم الله به وأنزله، لم ينزل من غيره ولم يبدأ من غيره، ليس كما يقولون: إنه بدأ من جبريل، أو من اللوح، أو من الهواء، إنما بدايته من الله، وسمعه جبريل وبلغه إلىٰ النبي صلىٰ الله عليه وسلم وحياً،

والنبي عليه الصلاة والسلام بلغه للناس، ولو كان هذا القرآن من كلام البشر لاستطاع أحد من الناس أن يأتي بسورة من مثله، فلما عجزوا عن ذلك دل علىٰ أنه من كلام الله عز وجل، قال تعالىٰ: ﴿وَإِن كُنتُمْ فِى رَيْبٍ مِّمَّا نَزَّلْنَا عَلَىٰ عَبْدِنَا فَأْتُوا۟ بِسُورَةٍ مِّن مِّثْلِهِۦ وَٱدْعُوا۟ شُهَدَآءَكُم مِّن دُونِ ٱللَّهِ إِن كُنتُمْ صَٰدِقِينَ ﴿٢٣﴾﴾ [البقرة:٢٣]، وقال سبحانه وتعالىٰ: ﴿أَمْ يَقُولُونَ ٱفْتَرَىٰهُ ۖ قُلْ فَأْتُوا۟ بِعَشْرِ سُوَرٍ مِّثْلِهِۦ مُفْتَرَيَٰتٍ﴾ [هود: ١٣]

The meaning of this statement is that the Qur'ān came down from Allah ﷻ. Allah ﷻ spoke and revealed it, and it did not descend from anyone else. It did not begin from Jibrīl ﵇ (as some say) or from the Tablet, or from the air. Its origin is with Allah ﷻ, and Jibrīl ﵇ heard it and delivered it to the Prophet ﷺ as divine revelation. The Prophet ﷺ subsequently delivered it to the people. If the Qur'ān was the word of a human, someone would have been able to create a *sūrah* of its like. The fact that they were unable to do so is evidence that it is the word of Allah ﷻ. Allah ﷻ says: **{And if you are in doubt about what We have sent down upon Our servant [Muḥammad], then produce a *sūrah* the like thereof and call upon your witnesses other than Allah, if you should be truthful.} [Qur'ān 2:23]** Allah ﷻ also says: **{Or do they say, 'He invented it'? Say, 'Then bring ten *sūrahs* like it that have been invented...'} [Qur'ān 11:13]**

فعجزهم الله بذلك، مع أنهم عرب فصحاء، والقرآن بلغة العرب، وبالحروف التي يتكلمون بها، وهم يحرصون علىٰ معاندة الرسول صلىٰ الله عليه وسلم، ولو كان باستطاعتهم أن يعارضوا هذا القرآن، لما ادخروا وسعًا في ذلك، فلما عجزوا عن ذلك دل علىٰ أنه كلام الله الذي لا يأتيه الباطل من بين يديه ولا من خلفه.

Allah ﷻ challenged them to that and they were not able to do so, even though they were eloquent speakers of Arabic, and the Qur'ān is in the Arabic tongue, in the same letters that they used to speak, and they were adamant in their opposition to the Messenger of Allah ﷺ. If they were afforded any chance to raise an objection to the Qur'ān, they would have not spared a moment to do so, and the fact that they failed to do so is evidence that it is the word of Allah ﷻ which nothing can falsify from before or after.

المتن

(٤٧) وَصَدَّقَهُ الْمُؤْمِنُونَ عَلَىٰ ذَلِكَ حَقًّا.

(47) The believers attest to it being absolute truth;

الشرح

فالمؤمنون بالله ورسوله يصدقون بأن القرآن كلام الله عز وجل، وأن محمداً صلىٰ الله عليه وسلم إنما هو مبلغ عن الله.

Those who believe in Allah and His Messenger ﷺ attest to the Qur'ān being the word of Allah ﷻ, and that Muḥammad ﷺ delivered it from Allah.

وأما قول الله عز وجل: ﴿إِنَّهُۥ لَقَوْلُ رَسُولٍ كَرِيمٍ ۝١٩ ذِى قُوَّةٍ عِندَ ذِى ٱلْعَرْشِ مَكِينٍ ۝٢٠﴾ [التكوير: ١٩-٢٠] فالمراد بإسناده إلىٰ جبريل هو من باب التبليغ؛ لأنه لا يمكن أن يكون القرآن من كلام الله ومن كلام جبريل، الكلام لا يكون إلا من واحد، فلا يمكن وصفه بأنه كلام أكثر من واحد، ونسبته إلىٰ الله حقيقية، وأما نسبته لجبريل فمن باب التبليغ. وفي الآية الأخرىٰ: ﴿إِنَّهُۥ لَقَوْلُ رَسُولٍ كَرِيمٍ ۝٤٠ وَمَا هُوَ بِقَوْلِ شَاعِرٍ ۚ قَلِيلًا مَّا تُؤْمِنُونَ ۝٤١﴾ [الحاقة: ٤٠-٤١]

Nonetheless, Allah ﷻ says: **{[That] indeed, the Qur'ān is a word [conveyed by] a noble messenger, owner of power, and high rank with (Allah) the Lord of the Throne.} [Qur'ān 81:19-20]** The reason why it was attributed to Jibrīl ﷺ is from the aspect of him delivering it, as it is impossible to be both the word of Allah ﷻ and the word of Jibrīl ﷺ. It can only be from one of them, and it cannot be the word of more than one. The attribution to Allah ﷻ is literal, and the attribution to Jibrīl ﷺ is from the aspect that he delivered it. In another verse, Allah ﷻ says: **{[That] indeed, the Qur'ān is the word of a noble Messenger. And it is not the word of a poet; little do you believe.} [Qur'ān 69:40-41]**

يعني : محمداً صلىٰ الله عليه وسلم، فالإضافة إليه إضافة تبليغ. وقد أضافة

سبحانه تارة إلىٰ نفسه وتارة إلىٰ جبريل وتارة إلىٰ محمداً، والكلام الواحد لا يمكن أن يتكلم به أكثر من واحد. فتكون إضافته إلىٰ الله إضافة ابتداء وهو كلامه وإضافته إلىٰ جبريل ومحمد إضافة تبليغ.

This refers to Muḥammad ﷺ. It is attributed to him because he delivered it. Sometimes Allah ﷻ attributes it to Himself, and sometimes to Jibrīl عليه السلام, and sometimes to Muḥammad ﷺ; yet the speech is one and the same. It is not possible that more than one had spoken it. The attribution to Allah ﷻ is because of its origin, it is His speech. And the attribution to Jibrīl عليه السلام and Muḥammad ﷺ is because they delivered it.

المتن

(٤٨) وَأَيْقَنُوا أَنَّهُ كَلَامُ اللهِ تَعالَىٰ بِالْحَقِيقَةِ.

(48) And they are certain that it is truly the word of Allah.

الشرح

ليس بالمجاز كما يقوله الجهمية والمعتزلة، هم يقولون: كلام الله، ولكن نسبته إلىٰ الله مجاز؛ لأن الله خالقه، فإضافته إلىٰ الله إضافة مخلوق إلىٰ خالقه.

This is not in a figurative sense, as the Jahmīs and Muʿtazilites say. They say that it is the speech of Allah ﷻ, but the attribution to Allah ﷻ is figurative, and that its attribution to Allah ﷻ is an attribution of a created thing to its creator.

فنقول: كذبتم؛ لأن الإضافة إلىٰ الله علىٰ نوعين: إضافة معانٍ، وإضافة أعيان:

We say in response that this is wrong because there are two types of attributions to Allah ﷻ: the attribution of meanings and the attribution of objects.

النوع الأول: إضافة المعاني إلىٰ الله مثل الكلام، فإضافة المعاني إلىٰ الله إضافة

صفة إلىٰ موصوف، فالكلام والسمع والبصر والقدرة والإرادة إضافة صفة إلىٰ موصوف؛ لأن هذه معانٍ لا تقوم بنفسها وإنما تقوم بالموصوف بها.

The first type: The attribution of meanings to Allah, such as speech. The attribution of meanings to Allah ﷻ is an attribution of attributes to the entity. So speech, hearing, sight, omnipotence and will are all attributes of the described entity, as these meanings do not exist by themselves but rather with the described entity.

النوع الثاني: إضافة أعيان، مثل: بيت الله، ناقة الله، عبد الله. هذه إضافة مخلوق إلىٰ خالقه، وفائدة الإضافة هنا التشريف والتكريم.

The second type: The attribution of objects, such as the house of Allah, the camel of Allah, and the slave of Allah. This is the attribution of created beings to their creator. The benefit of their attribution here is to denote honouring and nobility.

المتن

(٤٩) لَيْسَ بِمَخْلُوقٍ كَكَلَامِ الْبَرِيَّةِ.

(49) It is not created like the speech of human beings.

الشرح

أي كلام الله ليس بمخلوق. رداً علىٰ الجهمية والمعتزلة الذين يقولون: إن القرآن مخلوق؛ لأن الله عندهم لا يتكلم، علىٰ منهجهم في نفي الصفات كلها، فراراً - بزعمهم - من التشبيه؛ لأنهم لم يفرقوا بين صفات الخالق وصفات المخلوق ففروا من التشبيه الموهوم ووقعوا في التعطيل المذموم وهو شر منه، كالمستجير من الرمضاء بالنار.

So, it is said that the speech of Allah ﷻ is not created. This is a refutation of the Jahmīs and Muʿtazilites who say that the Qurʾān is created, because, according to them, Allah ﷻ does not speak, according to their doctrine of negating all of Allah's ﷻ attributes in order to avoid *tashbīh* (anthropomorphism), as they claim. This is because they do not differentiate between the attributes of the Creator and those of created beings, so they try to avoid their imagined *tashbīh* but instead commit *ta'ṭīl* (divesting Allah ﷻ of His attributes), which is even more reprehensible, like someone escaping heat by entering a fire.

ولو أنهم أثبتوا ما أثبته الله لنفسه، وعرفوا أن هناك فرقًا بين صفات الخالق وصفات المخلوق، لأصابوا عين الحق واستراحوا وأراحوا الناس، ولكنهم في ضلال.

If only they affirmed what Allah ﷻ affirms about Himself, and understood that there is a difference between the attributes of the Creator and those of created things, they would have reached the truth and been relieved, and relieved others. Instead, they remain in error.

المتن

(٥٠) فَمَنْ سَمِعَهُ فَزَعَمَ أَنَّهُ كَلامُ الْبَشَرِ فَقَدْ كَفَرَ.

(50) Whoever hears it and says that it is the speech of man has disbelieved.

الشرح

فمن سمع كلام الله وزعم أنه كلام البشر فقد كفر؛ لأنه جحد كلام الله عز وجل، فإذا لم يكن لله كلام ينزله علىٰ عباده فبم تقوم الحجة عليهم؟ فقصدهم بقولهم هذا هدم الشرائع، فإذا كان ليس في الكون كلام لله لا في التوراة ولا في الإنجيل ولا القرآن، فمعنىٰ ذلك أنه ما قامت علىٰ الناس الحجة من الله، وهذا من أعظم الكفر وأعظم الضلال.

If someone hears the speech of Allah ﷻ and claims that it is the word of a human, that person is then a disbeliever, because he has rejected the speech of Allah the Almighty. If Allah ﷻ did not have speech that He sent down to His slaves, how would the arguments be placed against them? Their intent in saying such a thing is demolishing the divine revelations. If there were no speech of Allah ﷻ in the universe, not in the Torah or the Injīl (Gospel), or the Qurʾān, it would have meant that Allah ﷻ has not set up any arguments against people. This is the greatest form of disbelief and misguidance.

المتن

(٥١) وَقَدْ ذَمَّهُ اللهُ وَعابَهُ، وَأَوْعَدَهُ بِسَقَرَ، حَيْثُ قالَ تَعالَىٰ: ﴿سَأُصْلِيهِ سَقَرَ﴾ [المدثر: ٢٦].

(51) Allah has warned, censured and threatened him with Hellfire (*Saqar*); wherein the Most High has said: *"I will cast him into Hellfire." [Qurʾān 74: 26]*

الشرح

وقد ذم الله عز وجل من قال هذه المقالة، فجعل القرآن كلام البشر، كما قال الوليد بن المغيرة المخزومي، وهو من أكابر كفار مكة ومن عظمائهم وكانوا يسمونه: زهرة مكة؛ لشرفه فيهم، فلما سمع القرآن من الرسول صلىٰ الله عليه وسلم أعجبه وعلم أنه ليس من كلام البشر، ومدح القرآن فقال: ليس بالشعر وليس بالسحر، أنا أعرف ضروب الشعر، وأعرف أنواع السحر، وأعرف الكهانة، وأعرف وأعرف ... فليس القرآن من هذه الأمور. فعند ذلك توجه إليه قومه الكفار بالتوبيخ والتعنيف؛ لأن معنىٰ هذا أنه اعترف للرسول عليه الصلاة والسلام بالرسالة، فلما رأىٰ ذلك انحرف – والعياذ بالله – بالكلام فقال: ﴿إِنْ هَٰذَآ إِلَّا قَوْلُ ٱلْبَشَرِ ۝٢٥﴾ [المدثر: ٢٥] فأنزل الله عز وجل: ﴿إِنَّهُۥ فَكَّرَ وَقَدَّرَ ۝١٨ فَقُتِلَ كَيْفَ قَدَّرَ ۝١٩ ثُمَّ قُتِلَ كَيْفَ قَدَّرَ ۝٢٠ ثُمَّ نَظَرَ ۝٢١ ثُمَّ عَبَسَ وَبَسَرَ ۝٢٢ ثُمَّ أَدْبَرَ وَٱسْتَكْبَرَ ۝٢٣ فَقَالَ إِنْ هَٰذَآ إِلَّا سِحْرٌ يُؤْثَرُ ۝٢٤ إِنْ هَٰذَآ إِلَّا قَوْلُ ٱلْبَشَرِ ۝٢٥﴾

[المدثر:١٨-٢٥] قال عز وجل: ﴿سَأُصْلِيهِ سَقَرَ ﴿٢٦﴾﴾ [المدثر:٢٦]، وهي النار.

Allah ﷻ has condemned those who say such a statement, which is tantamount to [saying] the Qur'ān is human speech, like al-Walīd ibn al-Mughīrah al-Makhzūmī. He was one of the people at the forefront amongst the disbelievers of Makkah. They called him *zahrat Makkah* (the flower of Makkah) because of his status among the Makkans. When he heard the Qur'ān from the Messenger ﷺ, he had a liking for it and knew that it was not the speech of a human. He praised the Qur'ān, saying, 'It is not poetry, and not sorcery. I know the different types of poetry and sorcery, and the ways of the diviners, and so on. The Qur'ān is not one of those things.' When he said that, his people censured him because it meant that he acknowledged the message of the Messenger of Allah ﷺ. When he saw that, he changed his discourse and Allah ﷻ is our refuge. He said: **{This is nothing but the word of a human being!} [Qur'ān 74:26]** So Allah ﷻ revealed: **{Indeed, he thought and deliberated. So may he be destroyed [for] how he deliberated. Then may he be destroyed [for] how he deliberated. Then he considered [again]; then he frowned and scowled; then he turned back and was arrogant and said, 'This is not but magic imitated [from others]. This is not but the word of a human being.'} [Qur'ān 74:18-25]** Allah ﷻ says: **{I will drive him into Saqar.} [Qur'ān 74:26]** *Saqar* is the Fire.

❁❁❁

المتن

(٥٢) فَلَمّا أَوْعَدَ اللهُ بِسَقَرَ لِمَنْ قالَ ﴿إِنْ هَذا إِلّا قَوْلُ الْبَشَرِ﴾ [المدثر: ٢٥]، عَلِمْنا وَأَيْقَنّا أَنَّهُ قَوْلُ خالِقِ الْبَشَرِ.

(52) Because Allah has promised Hell for those who say *{This is nothing but the word of a human being!} [Qur'ān 74: 25]*, we know and are certain that it is the word of the Creator of human beings.

الشرح

فمن قال: إن القرآن ليس كلام الله وإنه كلام البشر، أو الملك، فهو مثل الوليد بن

المغيرة، فما الفرق بين هذا وهذا إلا أنه ادعىٰ الإسلام والوليد لم يدع الإسلام؟ فدعوىٰ الإسلام لا تكفي، فإنه إن كفر بالقرآن لم ينفعه ادعاء الإسلام؛ لأن هذا ردة – والعياذ بالله –. فتبين بهذا أنه لابد من الاعتراف بأن القرآن كلام الله حقيقة.

Whoever says that the Qurʾān is not the word of Allah ﷻ but the word of a human or an angel is similar to al-Walīd ibn al-Mughīrah. What is the difference between them besides the fact that one claims to be Muslim and al-Walīd did not claim so? It does not suffice to claim to be Muslim, because if someone disbelieves in the Qurʾān, then any claim to be Muslim is to no avail, as that is a form of apostasy. So it is clear that the Qurʾān has to be recognised as the word of Allah ﷻ in the most literal sense.

المتن

(٥٣) وَلا يُشْبِهُ قَوْلَ الْبَشَرِ.

(53) And it does not resemble the speech of humans.

الشرح

لو كان الكلام من كلام الرسول صلىٰ الله عليه وسلم فلا لوم علىٰ الوليد ابن المغيرة إن قال إن القرآن من كلام محمد صلىٰ الله عليه وسلم، فكيف يتوعده الله بهذا الوعيد الشديد؟ فدل علىٰ أنه قال مقاله عظيمة وفظيعة – حيث نسب القرآن لغير الله، وكل من سار علىٰ هذا المذهب وهذا المنهج فإنه مثل الوليد بن المغيرة، يكون في النار خالداً فيها.

If the Qurʾān were from the speech of the Messenger of Allah ﷺ there would have been no blame on al-Walīd ibn al-Mughīrah for saying that the Qurʾān is the word of Muhammad ﷺ. So why did Allah ﷻ make such stern threats against him? This demonstrates that he said something significant and abhorrent insofar as he attributed the Qurʾān to someone other than Allah ﷻ. Anyone who has the same view or follows along the same course is just like al-Walīd ibn al-Mughīrah and they will abide in the Fire forever.

المتن

(٥٤) وَمَنْ وَصَفَ اللهَ بِمَعْنًى مِنْ مَعانِي الْبَشَرِ فَقَدْ كَفَرَ.

(54) Whoever ascribes to Allah an attribute of humans has disbelieved.

الشرح

يعني: من شبه الله بمعنىٰ من معاني البشر فقد كفر لأنه تنقص الله عز وجل.

That is to say that anyone who likens Allah ﷻ with a quality associated with humans has disbelieved, because he declares a shortcoming to Allah the Most High.

المتن

(٥٥) فَمَنْ أَبْصَرَ هَذا اعْتَبَرَ،

(55) He who understands this will take heed;

الشرح

لأن هناك فرقاً واضحاً بين صفات الخالق وصفات المخلوق، وإن اشتركت في الاسم والمعنىٰ، ولكن تختلف في الحقيقة وتختلف في الواقع والخارج، فلا تشابه بين كلام الله وكلام البشر، ولا تشابه بين سمع الله وسمع البشر، ولا تشابه بين بصر الله وبصر البشر، ولا علم الله وعلم البشر، ولا مشيئة وإرادة الله ومشيئة وإرادة البشر. ففرق بين صفات الله وصفات المخلوق، فمن لم يفرق بينهما صار كافراً.

This is because there is a clear difference between the characteristics of the Creator and the characteristics of created things, even if they have a common name and meaning. Nonetheless, the actual nature is different in reality and appearance. There is no resemblance between the speech of Allah ﷻ and the speech of man, and there is no resemblance between the hearing of Allah ﷻ and the hearing of man, and there is no resemblance between the sight of Allah ﷻ and the sight of man, and between the knowledge of Allah ﷻ and the knowledge of man, and between the will of Allah ﷻ and the will of man. There is a difference between the attributes of Allah ﷻ and the attributes of man, and anyone who does not differentiate between them is a disbeliever.

المتن

(٥٦) وَعَنْ مِثْلِ قَوْلِ الْكُفَّارِ انْزَجَرَ.

(56) And will refrain from saying such things as the disbelievers say.

الشرح

من تدبر الآيات القرآنية التي أنزلها الله في الوليد بن المغيرة، من تدبرها عرف بطلان أقوال هذه الفرق الضالة في كلام الله عز وجل.

If you reflect on the Qur'ānic verses that Allah ﷻ revealed about al-Walīd ibn al-Mughīrah, you will ascertain that the views of these deviant sects on Allah's speech are incorrect.

المتن

(٥٧) عَلِمَ أَنَّهُ بِصِفَاتِهِ لَيْسَ كَالْبَشَرِ.

(57) And will know that His attributes are not like that of man.

الشرح

وصفاته من الكلام وغيره ليست كصفات البشر للفرق بين صفات الخالق وصفات المخلوق.

His characteristics, such as speech or anything else, are not like the characteristics of humans because of the difference between the characteristics of the Creator and those of created beings.

المتن

(٥٨) والرُّؤْيَةُ حَقٌّ لِأَهْلِ الْجَنَّةِ بِغَيْرِ إِحاطَةٍ وَلا كَيْفِيَّةٍ.

(58) It is true that the people of Paradise will see Allah, without encompassing Him and in a manner that is unknown to us.

الشرح

الرؤية: أي: رؤية المؤمنين لربهم سبحانه وتعالىٰ، فإن المؤمنين يرون ربهم سبحانه وتعالىٰ في الآخرة، يرونه عيانـًا بأبصارهم كما يرون القمر ليلة البدر، وكما يرون الشمس صحواً ليس دونها سحاب، كما أخبر المصطفىٰ صلىٰ الله عليه وسلم بذلك في الأحاديث الصحيحة المتواترة عنه عليه الصلاة والسلام، ولذلك قال المصنف: الرؤية حق، أي : ثابتة بالكتاب والسنة وإجماع أهل السنة والجماعة من السلف والخلف، ولم يخالف فيها إلا المبتدعة وأصحاب المذاهب المنحرفة.

The *Ru'yah* (vision) refers to believers seeing their Lord the Most High. The believers will see their Lord in the afterlife in plain view with their sight, like they see the moon on the night of a full moon, and like they see the sun in a clear sky without clouds, as the Muṣṭafā ﷺ has told about in authentic and successive (*mutawātir*) ḥadīths reported from him. Accordingly, the author said: "The *Ru'yah* (Vision) ... is true": that is, it is well-established in the Qur'ān, the Sunnah, and unanimous agreement of the predecessors (*salaf*) and successors (*khalaf*) of *Ahl al-Sunnah wa 'l-Jamā'ah*.[17] No one

17 It is related that Jarīr ibn 'Abdullāh al-Bajalī ﷺ said: "We were with the Prophet ﷺ

has disagreed on that, other than the innovators and followers of fallacious doctrines.

فالمؤمنون يرون ربهم سبحانه وتعالىٰ كما قال سبحانه: ﴿وُجُوهٌ يَوْمَئِذٍ نَّاضِرَةٌ ۝٢٢ إِلَىٰ رَبِّهَا نَاظِرَةٌ ۝٢٣﴾ [القيامة: ٢٢،٢٣]، وهي وجوه المؤمنين ﴿نَّاضِرَةٌ ۝٢٢﴾ يعني من النضرة وهي: البهاء والحسن ﴿تَعْرِفُ فِي وُجُوهِهِمْ نَضْرَةَ ٱلنَّعِيمِ ۝٢٤﴾ [المطففين: ٢٤] وأما ﴿نَاظِرَةٌ ۝٢٣﴾ فمعناها: المعاينة بالأبصار، تقول: نظرت إلىٰ كذا، أي: أبصرته، فالنظر له استعمالات في كتاب الله عز وجل، إذا عُدّي بـ(إلىٰ) فمعناه المعاينة بالأبصار، ﴿أَفَلَا يَنظُرُونَ إِلَى ٱلْإِبِلِ كَيْفَ خُلِقَتْ ۝١٧ وَإِلَى ٱلسَّمَآءِ كَيْفَ رُفِعَتْ ۝١٨ ...﴾ [الغاشية: ١٧-١٨]، أي: ألم ينظروا بأبصارهم إلىٰ هذه المخلوقات العجيبة الدالة علىٰ قدرة الله عز وجل. وفي هذه الآية: ﴿إِلَىٰ رَبِّهَا نَاظِرَةٌ ۝٢٣﴾ [القيامة: ٢٣] معداة بـ(إلىٰ).

Thus, the believers will see their Lord, as Allah ﷻ says: **{[Some] faces, that Day, will be radiant, looking at their Lord.} [Qurʾān 75:22-23]** Those are the faces of the believers. 'Radiant' (*nāḍirah*) means that they will be spectacular and beautiful. Allah ﷻ says: **{You will recognise in their faces the radiance of pleasure.} [Qurʾān 83:24]** *'Nāẓirah'* means to watch something with sight. It is said, *'naẓartu ilā kadhā'* (I looked at something); that is to say 'I saw it', from sight. The word *"naẓar"* has different uses in the Qurʾān. If it is transitive by way of the preposition *ilā* (to/at), then it denotes vision and sight. Allah ﷻ says: **{Then do they not look *(yanẓurūn)* at the camels – how they are created? And at the sky – how it is raised?} [Qurʾān 88:17-18]** Meaning: Do they not see those wonderful creations that demonstrate Allah's ﷻ omnipotence with their sight?! In this verse: **{Looking at their Lord} [Qurʾān 75:22-23]** *"naẓar"* is transitive by way of the preposition *ilā*.

وإذا عُدي النظر بنفسه وبدون واسطة فمعناه التوقف والانتظار: ﴿يَوْمَ يَقُولُ ٱلْمُنَٰفِقُونَ وَٱلْمُنَٰفِقَٰتُ لِلَّذِينَ ءَامَنُوا ٱنظُرُونَا نَقْتَبِسْ مِن نُّورِكُمْ﴾ [الحديد: ١٣]،

---

and he looked at the moon on the night of a full moon and said: 'Verily, you will see your Lord as you see this moon. You will have no trouble seeing Him.'" [al-Bukhārī, no. 8; Muslim, no. 16]

﴿انْظُرُونَا﴾ أي : انتظرونا من أجل أن نستضيء بنوركم؛ لأن المنافقين ينطفئ نورهم والعياذ بالله، فيبقون في ظلمة، فيطلبون من المؤمنين أن ينتظروهم حتىٰ يقتبسوا من نورهم. وقوله تعالىٰ: ﴿هَلْ يَنظُرُونَ إِلَّآ أَن يَأْتِيَهُمُ ٱللَّهُ﴾ [البقرة: ٢١٠] أي: ما ينتظرون إلا مجيء الرب يوم القيامة لفصل القضاء بين عباده.

If the verb *"naẓar"* is transitive without a preposition, then it means to stop and wait. Allah ﷻ says: **{On the [same] Day the hypocrite men and hypocrite women will say to those who believed, 'Wait for us *(unẓurūnā)* that we may acquire some of your light.'} [Qur'ān 57:13]** This means 'wait for us so that we can take some of your light', as the lights of the hypocrites will be extinguished (and Allah ﷻ is our refuge) and they will remain in darkness and ask the believers to wait for them so that they can draw from their light. The Most High also says: **{Do they await but that Allah should come to them...} [Qur'ān 2:210]** Meaning that they are only waiting for the coming of the Lord on Judgment Day to judge between His slaves.

وإذا عُدي النظر بفي فمعناه التفكر والاعتبار، كما قال تعالىٰ: ﴿أَوَلَمْ يَنظُرُواْ فِى مَلَكُوتِ ٱلسَّمَٰوَٰتِ وَٱلْأَرْضِ﴾ [الأعراف: ١٨٥]، أي: يتفكروا في مخلوقات الله العلوية والسفلية، ويستدلون بها علىٰ قدرة الله الخالق سبحانه وتعالىٰ واستحقاقه للعبادة.

Whenever *"naẓar"* is transitive by way of the preposition *fī* (in), it denotes thought and reflection, like when Allah ﷻ says: **{Do they not reflect on *(yanẓurūn fī)* the realm of the heavens and the earth and everything that Allah has created and [think] that perhaps their appointed time has come near?} [Qur'ān 7:185]** That is, think about the creations of Allah ﷻ high and low, and infer the omnipotence of the Creator and His worthiness to be worshipped.

الحاصل: أن النظر هنا عُدي بـ(إلىٰ) ومعناه: الرؤية والمعاينة.

To sum up, whenever *"naẓar"* is transitive by way of *ilā,* it denotes sight and vision.

وقال سبحانه وتعالىٰ: ﴿لِّلَّذِينَ أَحْسَنُوا۟ ٱلْحُسْنَىٰ وَزِيَادَةٌ﴾ [يونس:٢٦] فسر النبي صلىٰ الله عليه وسلم (الحسنىٰ) بأنها الجنة، وفسر (الزيادة) بأنها النظر إلىٰ وجه الله الكريم، وهذا في صحيح مسلم.

Allah ﷻ says: **{For them who have done good is the best [reward] and extra.} [Qurʾān 10:26]** The Prophet ﷺ explained that 'the best reward' (*al-ḥusnā*) is Jannah and that the 'extra' (*ziyādah*) is to see Allah's ﷻ Face, as related in the *Ṣaḥīḥ* of Muslim.[18]

وقال تعالىٰ: ﴿لَهُم مَّا يَشَآءُونَ فِيهَا وَلَدَيْنَا مَزِيدٌ ﴿٣٥﴾﴾ [ق:٣٥] المزيد: هو النظر إلىٰ وجه الله الكريم.

Allah ﷻ also says: **{They will have whatever they wish therein, and with Us is more.} [Qurʾān 50:35]** 'More' (*mazīd*) is to see the Face of Allah ﷻ.

وقال تعالىٰ عن الكفار: ﴿كَلَّآ إِنَّهُمْ عَن رَّبِّهِمْ يَوْمَئِذٍ لَّمَحْجُوبُونَ ﴿١٥﴾﴾ [المطففين:١٥] فإذا كان الكفار محجوبون عن الله، أي: لا يرونه؛ لأنهم كفروا به في الدنيا فهم محجوبون عن النظر إليه يوم القيامة، وهذا أعظم حرمان وأعظم عذاب، والعياذ بالله، فدلت الآية علىٰ أن المؤمنين ليسوا محجوبين عن الله يوم القيامة، وأنهم يرونه بالنظر إليه في الآخرة؛ لأنهم آمنوا به في الدنيا ولم يروه، وإنما استدلوا عليه سبحانه بآياته ورسالاته، فالله أكرمهم بالنظر إليه يوم القيامة.

Allah ﷻ says about the disbelievers: **{No! Indeed, from their Lord, that Day, they will be partitioned.} [Qurʾān 83:15]** In other words, they are partitioned from Allah ﷻ, that is, they will not be able to see Him, because they disbelieved in Him on earth, so they are veiled from seeing Him on the Day of Judgment. This is the greatest deprivation and punishment (Allah ﷻ is our refuge). These verses indicate that the believers are not veiled from Allah ﷻ on the Day of Judgment, and that they see Him in the afterlife because they believe in Him in this world though they do not see Him, but rather look to His signs and messages as evidence; and so Allah ﷻ will honour them by allowing them to see Him on the Day of Resurrection.

---

18 Muslim, no. 181; al-Tirmidhī, no. 2557.

والنظر إلىٰ وجه الله عز وجل أعظم نعيم في الجنة.

To see Allah's ﷻ Face is the greatest blessing in Jannah.

هذا مذهب أهل السنة والجماعة، وهذه بعض أدلتهم من القرآن.

This is the doctrine of *Ahl al-Sunnah wa 'l-Jamā'ah*, and this is some of their evidence from the Qur'ān.

وأما أدلتهم من السنة فكثيرة جداً بلغت حد التواتر، كما قال العلامة ابن القيم في كتابه القيم «حادي الأرواح إلىٰ بلاد الأفراح»، وساق الأحاديث الواردة في الرؤية وقد بلغت حد التواتر.

There is also so much evidence from the Sunnah that it is to the level of mass-transmission (*tawātur*), as al-'Allāmah Ibn al-Qayyim states in his precious book, *Ḥādī al-Arwāḥ ilā Bilād al-Afrāḥ*. There he cites ḥadīths mentioning the *Ru'yah*, and they are so many that they have reached the degree of *tawātur*.

منها: قوله عليه الصلاة والسلام: «**إنكم سترون ربكم يوم القيامة، كما ترون القمر ليلة البدر، وكما ترون الشمس صحواً ليس دونها سحاب، لا تُضامون في رؤيته - أو: لا تَضامُّون في رؤيته -**». يعني: لا تزدحمون علىٰ رؤية الله عز وجل؛ لأن كل واحد يرىٰ الرب وهو في مكانه من غير زحام كما أن الناس يرون الشمس والقمر من غير زحام؛ لأن العادة إذا كان الشيء في الأرض وخفي يزدحمون علىٰ رؤيته ولكن إذا كان الشيء مرتفعاً كالشمس والقمر فإنهم لا يزدحمون علىٰ رؤيته، كلٌ يراه وهو في مكانه، إذا كان هذا في المخلوق الشمس والقمر، فكيف في الخالق سبحانه وتعالىٰ؟

One of those ḥadīths is the following: The Prophet ﷺ said: "You will see your Lord on the Day of Judgment as you see the moon on the night of a full moon, and as you see the sun clearly without clouds. You will have no difficulty (*tuḍamūn*) seeing Him or you will be in unison (*taḍāmmūn*) when seeing Him." I.e. they do not crowd (*tazdaḥimūn*) each other to see Allah ﷻ, because everyone sees their Lord from their position without crowding, just as people see the sun and moon without crowding. Usually, if something is on earth and is somewhat hidden, people crowd each other to see it. But if something is up high, like the sun or moon, they do not crowd each other to see it. Everyone sees it from the places they are in. Since this is true for created things in the sun and the moon, then with even more certainty it is true for the Creator.[19]

ولم ينكر الرؤية إلا أهل البدع كالجهمية والمعتزلة الذين ينفون الرؤية، يقولون: يلزم من إثبات الرؤية أن يكون الله في جهة، والله عندهم ليس في جهة، وهو عندهم لا داخل العالم ولا خارجه، ولا فوق ولا تحت، ولا يمنه ولا يسرة، ليس في جهة، وهذا معناه أنه معدوم، تعالىٰ الله عما يقولون ، فنفوا الرؤية من أجل هذا الرأي الباطل.

No one has denied the *Ru'yah* besides some heretical groups, such as the Jahmīs and Muʿtazilites, who reject the *Ru'yah*, saying that Allah ﷻ being in a certain direction is a necessary consequence of the affirmation (*ithbāt*) of the *Ru'yah*. For them, Allah ﷻ is neither within nor outside of the universe, and He is neither above nor below, neither to the right nor to the left; he is in no specific direction. This means that Allah ﷻ would have to be non-existent. Far be it from Allah ﷻ what they say about Him. They reject the *Ru'yah* because of this false reasoning.

وأما الأشاعرة: لما لم يمكنهم إنكار الأدلة من الكتاب والسنة أثبوا الرؤية وقالوا: يُرىٰ ولكن ليس في جهة، وهذا من التناقض العجيب! ليس هناك شيء يُرىٰ وهو ليس في جهة، ولذلك رد عليهم المعتزلة؛ لأن هذا من المستحيل. وأهل السنة يقولون: يُرىٰ سبحانه وتعالىٰ وهو في جهة العلو من فوقهم، فالجهة إن أريد بها الجهة المخلوقة فالله ليس في جهة؛ لأنه ليس بحال في خلقه سبحانه وتعالىٰ.

As for the Ashʿarīs, because they are not able to deny the evidence from the Qur'ān and Sunnah, they affirm the *Ru'yah* but say that Allah ﷻ is seen but not in any specific direction. This is a startling contradiction! There is noth-

19 Al-Bukhārī, no. 554, 806 & 7434; Muslim, no. 182: "*...tuḍārrūn...*"

ing that is seen but is not in a certain direction. On this basis, the Mu'tazilites responded to them because of that being impossible. *Ahl al-Sunnah* say that Allah ﷻ is seen while He is high above them. So if what is meant by a 'direction' is the created direction, then Allah does not have a direction, because He is under no circumstances within His creation.

وإن أريد بها العلو فوق المخلوقات فهذا ثابت لله عز وجل، فالله في العلو فوق السماوات، فالجهة لم يرد إثباتها أو نفيها في كتاب الله، ولكن يقال فيها على التفصيل السابق.

If what is meant is highness above all creation, then this is something that is affirmed about Allah ﷻ. Allah ﷻ is high above the heavens. Direction is neither affirmed nor denied in the Qur'ān; however, the aforementioned details can be said about it.

ومعنى: (**بغير إحاطة ولا كيفية**) أنهم لا يحيطون بالله عز وجل، ويرونه سبحانه بغير إحاطة، والله عظيم لا يمكن الإحاطة به، قال سبحانه: ﴿وَلَا يُحِيطُونَ بِهِۦ عِلْمًا ۝١١٠﴾ [طه:١١٠]، وقال جل وعلا: ﴿لَّا تُدْرِكُهُ ٱلْأَبْصَٰرُ﴾ [الأنعام:١٠٣] يعني: لا تحيط به، وليس معناه: لا تراه؛ لأن الله سبحانه وتعالى لم يقل: لا تراه الأبصار، إنما قال: ﴿لَّا تُدْرِكُهُ ٱلْأَبْصَٰرُ﴾ فالإدراك شيء والرؤية شيء آخر، فهي تراه سبحانه بدون إحاطة، وفي هذا رد على من استدل بهذه الآية على نفي الرؤية وقال: الرؤية لا تمكن؛ لأن الله قال: ﴿لَّا تُدْرِكُهُ ٱلْأَبْصَٰرُ﴾. فنقول لهم: أنتم لا تعرفون معنى ﴿لَّا تُدْرِكُهُ ٱلْأَبْصَٰرُ وَهُوَ يُدْرِكُ ٱلْأَبْصَٰرَ﴾.

"Without encompassing Him and in a manner that is unknown": It means that they do not fully encompass Allah ﷻ. They see him but do not encompass Him. Allah ﷻ is great and cannot be encompassed. Allah ﷻ says: **{...But they do not encompass Him in knowledge.} [Qur'ān 20:110]** Allah ﷻ also says: **{Vision perceives Him not.} [Qur'ān 6:103]** In other words, He is not encompassed by sight. It does not mean that He cannot be seen. Allah ﷻ did not say that He cannot be seen by sight but rather that 'vision does not encompass Him'. Encompassment is one thing and seeing is something else. This is also a response to those who deduce the non-occurrence of the *Ru'yah* from this verse, those who say that the *Ru'yah* is impossible because Allah ﷻ said that He is not comprehended by sight (*lā tudrikuhu al-abṣār*). We say to them 'you do not know the meaning of *"Vision perceives Him not, but He perceives [all] vision"*'.

﴿لَّا تُدْرِكُهُ ٱلْأَبْصَٰرُ وَهُوَ يُدْرِكُ ٱلْأَبْصَٰرَ﴾، معناها: لا تحيط به، وليس معناه: لا تراه، ولم يقل سبحانه: لا تراه الأبصار.

"Vision perceives Him not, but He perceives [all] vision" means that He is not encompassed by sight. It does not mean that He cannot be seen by sight. Allah ﷻ has not said that He is not seen by sight.

واستدلوا أيضاً فقالوا: موسىٰ عليه السلام قال: ﴿رَبِّ أَرِنِىٓ أَنظُرْ إِلَيْكَ ۚ قَالَ لَن تَرَىٰنِى﴾ [الأعراف:١٤٣] هذا دليل علىٰ نفي الرؤية.

They also cited as evidence the fact that Mūsā ﵇ said: **{'My Lord, show me [Yourself] that I may look at You.' [Allah] said, 'You will not see Me.'} [Qur'ān 7:143]** This is their evidence for denying the Vision.

نقول لهم: هذا في الدنيا، لأن موسىٰ سأل ذلك في الدنيا، ولا أحد يرىٰ الله في الدنيا لا الأنبياء ولا غيرهم، وأما في الآخرة فيرىٰ المؤمنون ربهم، وحال الدنيا ليست كحال الآخرة، فالناس في الدنيا ضعاف في أجسامهم وفي مداركهم، لا تستطيع أن ترىٰ الله عز وجل، وأما في الآخرة فإن الله يعطيهم قوة يستطيعون بها أن يروا ربهم - جل وعلا - إكراماً لهم.

We say to them: This is on earth, because Mūsā ﵇ asked that when he was on earth and no one sees Allah on earth, not the Prophets and not anyone else. In the afterlife, however, the believers will see their Lord, and the situation on earth is not like the situation in the afterlife. On earth, people have weak bodies and senses, and they are not able to see Allah ﷻ. In the afterlife, however, Allah ﷻ gives them the strength to be able to see their Lord, out of honour for them.

ولهذا لما سأل موسىٰ ربه في هذه الآية: ﴿قَالَ لَن تَرَىٰنِى وَلَٰكِنِ ٱنظُرْ إِلَى ٱلْجَبَلِ فَإِنِ

ٱسْتَقَرَّ مَكَانَهُۥ فَسَوْفَ تَرَىٰنِىۚ فَلَمَّا تَجَلَّىٰ رَبُّهُۥ لِلْجَبَلِ جَعَلَهُۥ دَكًّا﴾ [الأعراف:١٤٣] الجبل اندك وصار ترابًا، والجبل أصم صلب، فكيف بالمخلوق المكون من لحم ودم وعظام؟ فهو لا يستطيع رؤية الله في الدنيا.

That is why when Mūsā ﷺ asked his Lord in this verse, Allah ﷻ said: **{'You will not see Me, but look at the mountain; if it should remain in place, then you will see Me.' But when his Lord appeared to the mountain, He rendered it level...} [Qur'ān 7:143]** The mountain crumbled to dust, yet a mountain cannot hear and is solid, so what would happen to a created being that is made from flesh, blood, and bones? He could not see Allah ﷻ in this world.

وسؤال موسىٰ رؤية الله دليل علىٰ جواز الرؤية وإمكانها؛ لأن موسىٰ لا يسأل ربه شيئًا لا يجوز، إنما سأله شيئًا يجوز، ولكن لا يكون هذا في الدنيا، فالله سبحانه قال: ﴿لَنْ تَرَانِي﴾ ولم يقل: إني لا أرىٰ.

The fact that Mūsā ﷺ asked for the sight of Allah is evidence that it is plausible and possible, because Mūsā ﷺ would not ask his Lord for something impossible; rather, he asked Him about something that is possible. It will not, however, happen in this world. Allah ﷻ says: ***{You will not see Me...}*** but He did not say, I am not to be seen.

فالله يُرىٰ في الآخرة، وأولىٰ الناس بهذه الرؤية الأنبياء.

Allah ﷻ will thus be seen in the afterlife. And the most worthy people of seeing Him are the Prophets.[20]

وقوله: **(ولا كيفية)** أي: لا يقال: كيف يرون الله؟ لأن هذا كسائر صفات الله عز وجل لا نعرف كيفيتها، فنحن نؤمن بها ونعرف معناها ونثبتها، ولكن الكيفية مجهولة ولا نعرفها، فالله أعلم بها سبحانه.

"And in a manner unknown": One should not say, 'How do they see

20 It is related that Abū Mūsā al-Ashʿarī ؓ said: The Messenger of Allah ﷺ said: "There are two gardens, and the vessels and all that is in them are made of silver; and there are two gardens, and the vessels and all that is in them are made of gold, and nothing comes between the people seeing their Lord but the clothing of *kibr* on His Face in the Garden of Eden." [al-Bukhārī, no. 4878, 4880; Muslim, no. 180]

Allah ﷻ?' Because like all other attributes of Allah the Almighty, we do not know the exact nature; so we believe in it and we know what it means and we affirm it; however, the modality is unknown, and we do not know it. Only Allah ﷻ knows it.

❁❁❁

المتن

(٥٩) كَما نَطَقَ بِهِ كِتابُ رَبِّنا ﴿وُجُوهٌ يَوْمَئِذٍ ناضِرَةٌ ۝ إِلَىٰ رَبِّها ناظِرَةٌ﴾ [القيامة: ٢٢-٢٣]

(59) As the Book of our Lord has told: *{Some faces that Day will be radiant, Looking at their Lord.}* [Qur'ān 75:22-23]

الشرح

هذا صريح أنه نظر إلىٰ الله بالأبصار حيث عُدّي بإلىٰ، فمعناه الرؤية بالأبصار، قالت المعتزلة: ﴿إِلَىٰ رَبِّهَا﴾ (إلىٰ) جمع بمعنىٰ: نِعَم. أي إلىٰ نِعَم ربها ناظرة. وهذا تخريف يضحك منه العقلاء، لأن الحرف لا يحول إلىٰ جمع.

This clearly shows that it is to see Allah ﷻ with sight as the verb is transitive by way of the preposition *ilā,* which then means to see with sight. The Muʿtazilites say that *ilā* in "*ilā Rabbihim*" (at their Lord) is a plural form of 'favours'. In other words, they are 'waiting (*nāzirah*) for the favours (*ilā*) of their Lord'. Anyone who possesses reason would laugh at a fallacy such as this, as a preposition cannot change into a plural form.

❁❁❁

المتن

(٦٠) وَتَفْسِيرُهُ عَلَىٰ ما أَرادَهُ اللهُ تَعالَىٰ وَعَلِمَهُ.

(60) The explanation of this is only as Allah knows and wills.

الشرح

أي تفسير ﴿إِلَىٰ رَبِّهَا نَاظِرَةٌ ﴿٢٣﴾﴾ [القيامة: ٢٣] أي : علىٰ ما أراده الله جل وعلا، وهو المعاينة بالأبصار، لا علىٰ ما أراده المبتدعة.

This means that the explanation of **{*Looking at their Lord.*}** **[Qur'ān 75:23]** is only as Allah ﷻ intended, that is, to see Him with sight, not as the innovators intend.

المتن

(٦١) وَكُلُّ ما جاءَ فِي ذَلِكَ مِنَ الْحَدِيثِ الصَّحِيحِ عَنِ الرَّسُولِ ﷺ فَهُوَ كَما قالَ.

(61) Everything that is related in a *ṣaḥīḥ* (authentic) *ḥadīth* from the Messenger ﷺ regarding this is [exactly] how he said.

الشرح

كل ما جاء عن الرسول عليه الصلاة والسلام في إثبات الرؤية فهو حق علىٰ حقيقته، مثل ما جاء في القرآن سواء، يجب الإيمان به؛ لأن كلام الرسول صلىٰ الله عليه وسلم وحي من الله ﴿وَمَا يَنطِقُ عَنِ ٱلْهَوَىٰٓ ﴿٣﴾ إِنْ هُوَ إِلَّا وَحْيٌ يُوحَىٰ ﴿٤﴾﴾ [النجم:٣-٤]

Everything that the Messenger of Allah ﷺ said regarding the affirmation of the *Ru'yah* is true and literal, just as what is found in the Qur'ān. It is obligatory to believe in it because the word of the Messenger of Allah ﷺ is divine revelation from Allah ﷻ. Allah ﷻ says: **{Nor does he speak from [his own] inclination. It is not but a revelation revealed.} [Qur'ān 53:3-4]**

ويسمىٰ بالوحي الثاني، ولقد أخبر النبي صلىٰ الله عليه وسلم في أحاديث كثيرة متواترة أن المؤمنين يرون ربهم يوم القيامة، فيجب الإيمان بذلك من غير تحريف ولا تعطيل ومن غير تمثيل ولا تكييف.

It is called '*al-waḥy al-thānī*' (the second divine revelation), and the Prophet ﷺ stated in many ḥadīths that have *mutawātir isnāds* (concurrent chains of transmission) that the believers see their Lord on the Day of Judgment, so it is obligatory to have faith in that without *taḥrīf* (distorting the meaning), *taʿṭīl* (depriving it of its meaning), *tamthīl* (likening it to the creation), or *takyīf* (assigning an outright qualitative designation).

❁❁❁

المتن

(٦٢) وَمَعْناهُ عَلَىٰ ما أَرادَ.

(62) It means what he intended.

الشرح

أي ما أراد الرسول صلىٰ الله عليه وسلم، لا علىٰ ما أراده المبتدعة والمحرفة.

I.e. it means what the Messenger of Allah ﷺ intended, not what the innovators and those who distort the meaning intend.

❁❁❁

المتن

(٦٣) لا نَدْخُلُ فِي ذَلِكَ مُتَأَوِّلِينَ بِآرائِنا، وَلا مُتَوَهِّمِينَ بِأَهْوائِنا.

(63) We do not interpret it according to our own opinions or base our conceptions upon our whims and inclinations;

الشرح

كما يفعله الجهمية والمعتزلة ومن تتلمذ عليهم وأخذ برأيهم من التأويل الباطل.

As is done by the Jahmīs, Muʿtazilites, and those who learn from them and adopt their reasoning, utilising invalid interpretations.

بل الواجب علينا أن نتبع الكتاب والسنة، ولا نتدخل بعقولنا وأفكارنا ونحكمها علىٰ ما جاء في الكتاب والسنة، الواجب أن الكتاب والسنة يحكمان علىٰ العقول والأفكار.

Rather, what is obligatory upon us is to follow the Qur'ān and Sunnah, and not allowing our minds and thoughts to interfere and judge over what is stated therein. Instead, it is obligatory to make the Qur'ān and Sunnah judge over our minds and thoughts.[21]

المتن

(٦٤) فَإِنَّهُ ما سَلِمَ فِي دِينِهِ إِلَّا مَنْ سَلَّمَ لِلَّهِ عز وجل وَلِرَسُولِهِ ﷺ.

(64) Because no one is safe in his religion except the one who surrenders himself completely to Allah and His Messenger ﷺ;

الشرح

ومعنىٰ (سلَّم) أي: قَبِلَ ما جاء عن الله، وعن رسوله صلىٰ الله عليه وسلم وآمن به علىٰ ما جاء، من غير أن يتدخل بتحريفه وتأويله، هذا معنىٰ التسليم.

'Surrender' means to accept whatever Allah ﷻ and His Messenger ﷺ say, and to have faith in that accordingly, without intervening via *taḥrīf* (distortion) or *taʿwīl* (interpretation). This is what it means to submit (*taslīm*).

قال الإمام الشافعي رحمه الله تعالىٰ: «آمنت بالله وبما جاء في كتاب الله علىٰ مراد الله، وآمنت برسول الله وبما جاء عن رسول الله علىٰ مراد رسول الله صلىٰ الله عليه وسلم» أي: لا علىٰ الهوىٰ والتحريف وأقوال الناس.

Al-Imām al-Shāfiʿī ؒ said: "I believe in Allah and what has come in the Book of Allah according to the intent of Allah ﷻ; and I believe in the Mes-

21 It is related that ʿĀʾishah ؓ related that the Prophet ﷺ said: "The most hated men to Allah are those who are most vehement in their disputes." Al-Bukhārī, no. 2457; Muslim, no. 2668

senger of Allah, and what has come from the Messenger of Allah, according to the intent of the Messenger of Allah ﷺ." In other words, not according to *hawā* (desires), distortions, or upon the opinions of men.[22]

من سَلَّم وانقاد وردّ ما اشتبه عليه، ولم يعرف معناه أو لم يعرف كيفيته، رده إلىٰ عالمه، وهو الله، سبحانه وتعالىٰ، فالذي يشكل عليه شيء يرجع إلىٰ أهل العلم وفوق كل ذي علم عليم، فإن لم يكن عند العلماء علم بهذا فإنه يجب تفويضه إلىٰ الله جل وعلا.

One has to accept, submit and refer anything unclear (in terms of meaning or nature) back to someone who knows, namely, to Allah the Most High. If something is problematic for someone, they should refer it back to those who have knowledge, and there is always someone with higher knowledge. If those who have knowledge (scholars) do not know about that thing, then the matter should be entrusted to Allah the Almighty.

المتن

(٦٥) وَرَدَّ عِلْمَ ما اشْتَبَهَ عَلَيْهِ إِلَىٰ عالِمِهِ.

(65) And refers to those who know for the knowledge of matters unclear to him.

الشرح

ولذلك كان النبي صلىٰ الله عليه وسلم إذا سأل أصحابه عن بعض الأشياء التي لا يعرفونها قالوا: الله ورسوله أعلم. فلا يدخلون في المتاهات ويتخرصون.

This is why when the Prophet ﷺ asked his companions about things they

22 Abu ʿAbdullāh Muḥammad ibn ʿUmar al-Rāzī said:

Feats of the mind end in restraint, and the works of men are ultimately in error.
And our souls are in isolation of our bodies, and the outcome of worldly ways is harm and plague.
And we did not gain anything from our life-long search besides he said and they said.

See *Ṭabaqāt al-Shāfiʿīyyah*, 8/96.

did not know, they would say, 'Allah and His Messenger know best'. They did not delve into enigmas or conjecture.

فإن وجدت عالمـًا موثوقـًا يبين لك فالحمد لله، وإلا فابق علىٰ تسليمك واعتقادك أنه حق وأن له معنىٰ، ولكن لم يتبين لك.

Therefore if you find a reliable person with knowledge to explain something unclear to you, then that is good—praise be to Allah; otherwise, continue to accept it and believe that it is true and that it does have a meaning, though the meaning is not clear to you.

المتن

(٦٦) وَلا تَثْبُتُ قَدَمُ الْإِسْلامِ إِلّا عَلَىٰ ظَهْرِ التَّسْلِيمِ والِاسْتِسْلامِ.

(66) One's Islām is not secure unless it is based on acceptance and submission.

الشرح

لا يثبت الإسلام الصحيح إلا بالتسليم لله عز وجل، قال سبحانه: ﴿فَلَا وَرَبِّكَ لَا يُؤْمِنُونَ حَتَّىٰ يُحَكِّمُوكَ فِيمَا شَجَرَ بَيْنَهُمْ ثُمَّ لَا يَجِدُواْ فِيٓ أَنفُسِهِمْ حَرَجًا مِّمَّا قَضَيْتَ وَيُسَلِّمُواْ تَسْلِيمًا ﴿٦٥﴾﴾ [النساء:٦٥].

The correct belief in Islām is based only on submission to Allah ﷻ. Allah ﷻ says: **{But no, by your Lord, they will not [truly] believe until they make you, [O Muḥammad], judge concerning that over which they dispute among themselves and then find within themselves no discomfort from what you have judged and submit in [full, willing] submission.} [Qur'ān 4:65]**

والاستسلام هو: الانقياد والطاعة لما جاء عن الله ورسوله صلىٰ الله عليه وسلم.

'Submission' is acceptance and obedience to whatever Allah and His Messenger ﷺ say.

المتن

(٦٧) فَمَنْ رامَ عِلْمَ ما حُظِرَ عَنْهُ عِلْمُهُ، وَلَمْ يَقْنَعْ بِالتَّسْلِيمِ فَهْمُهُ، حَجَبَهُ مَرامُهُ عَنْ خالِصِ التَّوْحِيدِ، وَصافِي الْمَعْرِفَةِ، وَصَحِيحِ الإِيمانِ.

(67) He who seeks the knowledge of what is beyond his capacity to know, and whose intellect is not content with surrender, his search will veil him from true faith in Allah's oneness (*tawḥīd*), clear knowledge, and from correct faith.

الشرح

من لم يؤمن بما حجب عنه علمه، مثل علم الكيفية، فالواجب علينا الإيمان بها وردها، أي: رد علمها إلىٰ الله عز وجل ﴿فَأَمَّا ٱلَّذِينَ ءَامَنُواْ فَيَعۡلَمُونَ أَنَّهُ ٱلۡحَقُّ مِن رَّبِّهِمۡۖ وَأَمَّا ٱلَّذِينَ كَفَرُواْ فَيَقُولُونَ مَاذَآ أَرَادَ ٱللَّهُ بِهَٰذَا مَثَلٗاۘ﴾ [البقرة:٢٦].

In regards to asserting faith in things that are impossible to know, such as the nature (*kayfiyyah*) [of Allah's attributes], it is obligatory to believe in these things and refer knowledge of them back to Allah ﷻ. **{And those who have believed know that it is the truth from their Lord. But as for those who disbelieve, they say, 'What did Allah intend by this as an example?'} [Qur'ān 2:26]**

وقال عز وجل: ﴿هُوَ ٱلَّذِيٓ أَنزَلَ عَلَيۡكَ ٱلۡكِتَٰبَ مِنۡهُ ءَايَٰتٞ مُّحۡكَمَٰتٌ هُنَّ أُمُّ ٱلۡكِتَٰبِ وَأُخَرُ مُتَشَٰبِهَٰتٞۖ فَأَمَّا ٱلَّذِينَ فِي قُلُوبِهِمۡ زَيۡغٞ فَيَتَّبِعُونَ مَا تَشَٰبَهَ مِنۡهُ ٱبۡتِغَآءَ ٱلۡفِتۡنَةِ وَٱبۡتِغَآءَ تَأۡوِيلِهِۦۗ وَمَا يَعۡلَمُ تَأۡوِيلَهُۥٓ إِلَّا ٱللَّهُۗ﴾ [آل عمران:٧].

Allah ﷻ says: **{It is He who has sent down to you the Book; in it are verses [that are] clear – they are the foundation of the Book – and others not entirely clear. As for those in whose hearts is deviation [from truth], they will follow that of it which is not entirely clear, seeking discord and seeking an interpretation [suitable to them]. And no one knows its [true] interpretation except Allah.} [Qur'ān 3:7]**

حجب الله علمه عن الخلق فلا تتعب نفسك، ثم قال: ﴿وَٱلرَّٰسِخُونَ فِى ٱلْعِلْمِ
يَقُولُونَ ءَامَنَّا بِهِۦ كُلٌّ مِّنْ عِندِ رَبِّنَا﴾ [آل عمران:٧]. يسلّمون ويستسلمون، ولا
يمنعهم عدم معرفة معناه من الإيمان به والتسليم له. أو أن المعنىٰ أنهم يردون
المتشابه من كتاب الله إلىٰ المحكم منه ليفسروه ويتضح معناه ويقولون: ﴿كُلٌّ
مِّنْ عِندِ رَبِّنَا﴾.

Allah ﷻ has kept some knowledge hidden from created beings, so do not tire yourself [in this.] Then He said: **{But those firm in knowledge say, 'We believe in it. All [of it] is from our Lord.'}** **[Qur'ān 3:7]** They submit and accept, and the fact that they do not know what it means does not keep them from having faith in it and accepting it. Or it could mean that they refer the ambiguous parts *(mutashābih)* of the Book of Allah back to the clear, unambiguous parts *(muḥkam)* for the interpretation of them and to get a clear meaning of them; and they say, 'All of it is from our Lord'.

المتن

(٦٨) فَيَتَذَبْذَبُ بَيْنَ الْكُفْرِ وَالْإِيمَانِ، وَالتَّصْدِيقِ وَالتَّكْذِيبِ، وَالْإِقْرَارِ وَالْإِنْكَارِ.

(68) He will find himself wavering between disbelief and faith, belief and denial, acceptance and rejection;

الشرح

من لم يُسلِّم لله ولا إلىٰ الرسول، فإنه يحجب عن معرفة الله ومعرفة الحق،
فيكون في متاهات وضلالات.

Knowledge of Allah ﷻ and the truth is obscured from those who do not submit to Allah ﷻ or the Prophet ﷺ. They become entangled in labyrinths/enigmas and deviations.[23]

---

23 Abdullāh ibn Masʿūd ؓ said: The Messenger of Allah ﷺ said: "The *mutanaṭṭiʿūn* are doomed." He said that three times. (Muslim, no. 2670). "The *mutanaṭṭiʿūn* are those who go into things too deeply and are excessive in speech. Those who speak from the depths of their throats. It is derived from *naṭʿ*, the hard palate of the mouth, and

وهذه حال المنافقين الذين يتذبذبون، تارة مع المسلمين وتارة مع المنافقين، وتارة يصدقون وتارة يكذبون ﴿كُلَّمَآ أَضَآءَ لَهُم مَّشَوْاْ فِيهِ وَإِذَآ أَظْلَمَ عَلَيْهِمْ قَامُواْ﴾ [البقر:٢٠]. أما أهل الإيمان فما عرفوا قالوا به، وما لم يعرفوا وكلوا علمه إلىٰ الله جل وعلا، ولا يكلفون أنفسهم شيئًا لا يعرفونه، أو يقولون علىٰ الله ما لا يعلمون - فالقول علىٰ الله بغير علم هو عديل الشرك، بل هو أعظم من الشرك، قال تعالىٰ: ﴿قُلْ إِنَّمَا حَرَّمَ رَبِّيَ ٱلْفَوَٰحِشَ مَا ظَهَرَ مِنْهَا وَمَا بَطَنَ وَٱلْإِثْمَ وَٱلْبَغْيَ بِغَيْرِ ٱلْحَقِّ وَأَن تُشْرِكُواْ بِٱللَّهِ مَا لَمْ يُنَزِّلْ بِهِۦ سُلْطَٰنًا وَأَن تَقُولُواْ عَلَى ٱللَّهِ مَا لَا تَعْلَمُونَ ۝٣٣﴾ [الأعراف:٣٣]. فجعل القول علىٰ الله بغير علم فوق الشرك بالله، مما يدل علىٰ خطورة القول علىٰ الله بغير علم.

This is the condition of the hypocrites, those who waver in faith and are sometimes with the Muslims and sometimes with the hypocrites and who sometimes believe and sometimes disbelieve. **{Every time it lights [the way] for them, they walk therein; but when darkness comes over them, they stand [still].} [Qur'ān 2:20]** Those who have faith, on the other hand, talk about what they know, and what they do not know they entrust the knowledge of it to Allah ﷻ, and they do not take it upon themselves to do something they do not know or say something about Allah ﷻ that they do not know. To speak about Allah ﷻ without knowledge is akin to polytheism, nay it is even greater than it. Allah ﷻ says: **{Say, 'My Lord has only forbidden immoralities – what is apparent of them and what is concealed – and sin, and oppression without right, and that you associate with Allah that for which He has not sent down authority, and that you say about Allah that which you do not know.'} [Qur'ān 7:33]** Here, speaking about Allah ﷻ without knowledge is placed above polytheism, which demonstrates the seriousness of speaking about Allah ﷻ without knowledge.

المتن

---

it is further used for going deeply into any word or act." (Ibn al-Athīr, *al-Nihāyah*, 5/74).

(٦٩) مُوَسْوَسًا تائِهًا، زائِغًا شاكًّا، لا مُؤْمِنًا مُصَدِّقًا، وَلا جاحِدًا مُكَذِّبًا.

(69) Subject to satanic whispers, lost and in doubt, being neither a true believer nor an obstinate denier.

الشرح

هذه حالة أهل التردد والنفاق، دائماً شاكين ، دائماً مترددين ومتذبذبين؛ لأنه ما ثبتت قدم أحدهم في الإسلام ولم يسلم لله ولا إلىٰ رسول الله صلىٰ الله عليه وسلم.

This is the state of those who waver in faith and are hypocrites, they are always in doubt. They also waver in faith, because they are not strong in Islām and have not submitted to Allah ﷻ or to the Messenger of Allah ﷺ.

كما ذكر الله عن المنافقين أنهم ﴿مُّذَبْذَبِينَ بَيْنَ ذَٰلِكَ لَآ إِلَىٰ هَٰٓؤُلَآءِ وَلَآ إِلَىٰ هَٰٓؤُلَآءِ﴾ [النساء:١٤٣]، ﴿وَإِذَا لَقُوا۟ ٱلَّذِينَ ءَامَنُوا۟ قَالُوٓا۟ ءَامَنَّا وَإِذَا خَلَوْا۟ إِلَىٰ شَيَٰطِينِهِمْ قَالُوٓا۟ إِنَّا مَعَكُمْ إِنَّمَا نَحْنُ مُسْتَهْزِءُونَ ﴿١٤﴾ ٱللَّهُ يَسْتَهْزِئُ بِهِمْ وَيَمُدُّهُمْ فِى طُغْيَٰنِهِمْ يَعْمَهُونَ ﴿١٥﴾﴾ [البقرة:١٤-١٥].

Accordingly, Allah ﷻ says about the hypocrites: **{Wavering between them, [belonging] neither to the believers nor to the disbelievers.} [Qur'ān 4:143] {And when they meet those who believe, they say, 'We believe'; but when they are alone with their evil ones, they say, 'Indeed, we are with you; we were only mockers.' [But] Allah mocks them and prolongs them in their transgression [while] they wander blindly.} [Qur'ān 2:14-15]**

المتن

(٧٠) وَلا يَصِحُّ الْإيمانُ بِالرُّؤْيَةِ لِأَهْلِ دارِ السَّلامِ لِمَنِ اعْتَبَرَها مِنْهُمْ بِوَهْمٍ، أَوْ تَأَوَّلَها بِفَهْمٍ.

(70) One has not correctly believed in the *Ru'yah* of the people of Dār al-Salām (Jannah), if he tries to imagine what it will be like or interprets it according to his intellect;

الشرح

دار السلام هي الجنة، فلا يصح الإيمان بالرؤية أي رؤية الله فيها لمن يتوهم ويتأول فيها وينفي حقيقتها، ولم يسلم لله ولا إلىٰ رسوله صلىٰ الله عليه وسلم، ويتدخل فيها بفكره وفهمه.

Dār al-Salām is Jannah. One has not correctly believed in the *Ru'yah*, namely, seeing Allah ﷻ in Jannah, if he interprets it or denies the reality of it and does not submit to Allah ﷻ and the Messenger of Allah ﷺ and intervenes with his own ideas or whims.

المتن

(٧١) إِذْ كانَ تَأْوِيلُ الرُّؤْيَةِ وَتَأْوِيلُ كُلِّ مَعْنًىٰ يُضافُ إِلَىٰ الرُّبُوبِيَّةِ تَرْكِ التَّأْوِيلِ وَلُزُومِ التَّسْلِيمِ.

(71) Because the interpretation of this *Ru'yah*, and the interpretation of every attribute associated with the Lordship (*Rubūbiyyah*) is by avoiding one's personal interpretations and committing to strict acceptance.

الشرح

كل هذا تأكيد لما سبق في أنه يجب التسليم لما جاء عن الله وعن رسول الله صلىٰ الله عليه وسلم، ومن ذلك الرؤية، لا نتدخل فيها كما تدخل أهل البدع، بل نثبتها كما جاءت ونؤمن بها، ونثبت أن المؤمنين يرون ربهم في عرصات يوم القيامة قبل دخول الجنة، وبعد دخولهم الجنة يرونه أيضـًا، إكرامـًا لهم حيث آمنوا به في الدنيا ولم يروه.

Everything here emphasises the aforementioned, namely that it is obligatory to accept everything that Allah ﷻ and the Messenger of Allah ﷺ have said, which includes the *Ru'yah*. We do not involve ourselves in it like the followers of innovations, rather we affirm it and believe in it as it is. We affirm that the believers see their Lord in the *'araṣāt* (the place where Judgment will take place) on the Day of Judgment before they enter Jannah. They also see Him after entering Jannah as an honour for them for having believed in Him in the worldly life without seeing Him.

المتن

(٧٢) وَعَلَيْهِ دِينُ الْمُسْلِمِينَ.

(72) The religion of the Muslims is according to this.

الشرح

وهذا الأمر عليه دين المسلمين، وهو الإيمان والتسليم لما جاء عن الله ورسوله، وعدم التدخل في ذلك بالأفهام والأوهام والتأويلات الباطلة، والتحريفات الضالة، هذا دين الإسلام، بخلاف غير المسلمين، فإنهم يتدخلون فيما جاء عن الله وعن رسوله عليه الصلاة والسلام، ويحرفون الكلم عن مواضعه.

The religion of the Muslims is in accordance with these beliefs, namely faith and acceptance of everything that Allah ﷻ and the Messenger of Allah ﷺ have said, and not to interfere in this with one's own understanding, conceptions, false interpretations, and deviant distortions. This is the religion of Islām, unlike non-Muslims: they interfere in what Allah ﷻ and the Messenger of Allah ﷺ have said and distort the proper usages of the words.

المتن

(٧٣) وَمَنْ لَمْ يَتَوَقَّ النَّفْيَ والتَّشْبِيهَ زَلَّ وَلَمْ يُصِبِ التَّنْزِيهَ.

(73) He who does not take caution against *nafy* (negating Allah's ﷻ attributes) and *tashbīh* (declaring that Allah's ﷻ attributes resemble that of the creation), has erred and not properly affirmed Allah's transcendence;

الشرح

لابد كما سبق من الوسط بين التعطيل وبين التشبيه، فلا يبالغ ويغلو في تنزيه الله حتىٰ يعطل الله من صفاته كما فعل المعطلة، ولا يُثبت إثباتـًا فيه غلو حتىٰ يشبه الله بخلقه، بل يعتدل فيُثبت لله ما ثبته لنفسه وأثبته له رسوله، من غير تشبيه ولا تمثيل، ومن غير تعطيل ولا تكييف، هذا هو الصراط المستقيم المعتدل. فالله سبحانه وتعالىٰ لا شبيه له، ولا مثيل ولا عديل له، سبحانه وتعالىٰ.

As mentioned, there is a necessary middle course between *taʿṭīl* (divesting Allah ﷻ of His attributes) and *tashbīh* (assimilation). One should not be so excessive in asserting Allah's transcendence as to divest Allah ﷻ of His attributes as the Muʿaṭṭilah do; and also not excessive in affirmation (*ithbāt*) so as to declare that He resembles His creation. Rather, one should be moderate and affirm what Allah ﷻ asserted about Himself and what His Messenger ﷺ asserted about Him, without *tashbīh* (asserting resemblances), *tamthīl* (asserting equality), *taʿṭīl* (divesting Allah ﷻ of His attributes), and without *takyīf* (asserting a specific nature/mannerism). This is because there is nothing like Allah ﷻ, nothing resembles Him, and He has no equal.

المتن

(٧٤) فَإِنَّ رَبَّنا جَلَّ وَعَلا مَوْصُوفٌ بِصِفاتِ الْوَحْدانِيَّةِ،

(74) For our Lord, the Most High possesses the attributes of oneness (*waḥdānīyah*);

الشرح

صفات الوحدانية بأن الله واحد لا شريك له، لا في ربوبيته ولا في ألوهيته، ولا في أسمائه وصفاته، فهو واحد في كل هذه الحقائق.

The attributes of oneness, in the sense that Allah ﷻ is One and does not share His *Rubūbiyyah* (lordship), His *Ulūhiyyah* (worship), and names and attributes with anyone. Thus, He is One in all of these realities.

❁❁❁

المتن

(٧٥) مَنْعُوتٌ بِنُعُوتِ الْفَرْدانِيَّةِ، لَيْسَ فِي مَعْناهُ أَحَدٌ مِنَ الْبَرِيَّةِ.

(75) He possesses the qualities of uniqueness (*fardānīyah*). No created being shares the reality [of those attributes].

الشرح

منعوت، أي: موصوف بصفات الكمال، ونعوت الجلال، التي لا يشبهه فيها أحد من خلقه، بل أسماؤه وصفاته خاصة به ولائقة به، وصفات المخلوقين وأسماء المخلوقين خاصة بهم ولائقة بهم، وبهذا يتضح لك الحق والصواب، وتبرأ من طريقة المعطلة ومن طريقة المشبهة.

"Man'ūt" (attributed) i.e. he is described with the attributes of perfection and qualities of majesty, which do not resemble anything in His creation. In fact, His names and attributes are exclusively His and they are befitting of Him. Similarly, the characteristics and names of created things are specific to and appropriate for them. Knowing the truth and dissociating oneself from the ways of the Mu'aṭṭilah and the Mushabbihah are based on this.

❁❁❁

المتن

(٧٦) وَتَعالَىٰ عَنِ الْحُدُودِ والْغاياتِ والْأَرْكانِ والْأَعْضاءِ والْأَدَواتِ.

(76) He is beyond having limits, ends, parts, limbs, and instruments.

الشرح

هذا فيه إجمال: إن كان يريد الحدود المخلوقة فالله منزه عن الحدود والحلول في المخلوقات، وإن كان يريد بالحدود: الحدود غير المخلوقة، وهي جهة العلو، فهذا ثابت لله جل وعلا وتعالىٰ، فالله لا ينزه عن العلو، لأنه حق، فليس هذا من باب الحدود ولا من باب الجهات المخلوقة.

This contains an element of generality: If he means created limits, then Allah transcends limits and entrance *(ḥulūl)* in any of His creation. If he considered 'limits' to be non-created limits, namely the direction of highness, then this is something affirmed about Allah ﷻ. Allah ﷻ does not transcend highness because that is the truth, so it is not a matter of limits or a matter of created direction.

والغايات فيها إجمال أيضـًا، فهي تحتمل حقـًا وتحتمل باطلاً، فإن كان المراد بالغاية: الحكمة من خلق المخلوقات، وأنه خلقها لحكمة، فهذا حق، ولكن يقال: حكمة، لا يقال: غاية، قال تعالىٰ: ﴿وَمَا خَلَقْتُ ٱلْجِنَّ وَٱلْإِنسَ إِلَّا لِيَعْبُدُونِ ۝٥٦﴾ [الذاريات:٥٦].

There is also generality in 'ends' (*ghāyāt*). It can be interpreted correctly or incorrectly. If what is meant by *ghāyāt* is wisdom in creating all creations, and that He created them with wisdom, then that is true. However, it should be said 'wisdom' and not 'end' (*ghāyah*). Allah ﷻ says: **{And I did not create the jinn and mankind except to worship Me.} [Qur'ān 51:56]**

وإن أريد بالغاية: الحاجة إلىٰ المخلوقات، فنعم، هذا نفي صحيح، فالله عز وجل لم يخلق الخلق لحاجته وفقره إليهم، فإنه غني عن العالمين.

If what is meant by *ghāyāt* is the need for creations, then, yes, it is correct to deny this. Allah ﷻ did not create the creation for some need of them, as Allah ﷻ is free from need of everyone.

(والأركان، والأعضاء، والأدوات) فيها إجمال أيضـًا، إن أُريد بالأركان

والأعضاء والأدوات: الصفات الذاتية مثل الوجه، واليدين، فهذا حق، ونفيه باطل. وإن أُريد نفي الأعضاء التي تشابه أعضاء المخلوقين وأدوات المخلوقين فالله سبحانه منزه عن ذلك، فالأبعاض والأعضاء فالحاصل أن هذا فيه تفصيل:

"...Parts, limbs, and instruments": There is also generality here. If what is meant by 'parts, limbs, and instruments' is the attributes of Allah's ﷻ essence (*dhāt*), such as the Face and Hands, then those are true, and it is wrong to deny them. And if what is meant is to deny limbs that share similarities with the limbs and instruments of created things, then Allah ﷻ transcends that. As relating to parts and limbs, in short, it requires further elaboration:

أولاً: إذا أُريد بذلك نفي الصفات الذاتية عن الله تعالىٰ من الوجه واليدين، وما ثبت له سبحانه وتعالىٰ من صفاته الذاتية، فهذا باطل.

First: If what is meant is to deny the attributes of Allah's ﷻ essence (*dhāt*), such as the Face or Hands, and the other attributes of His essence (*al-ṣifāt al-dhāt*) that have been affirmed, then it is incorrect.

ثانياً: أما إن أُريد بذلك أن الله منزه عن مشابهة أبعاض المخلوقين وأعضاء المخلوقين وأدوات المخلوقين، فنعم، الله منزه عن ذلك؛ لأنه لا يشبهه أحد من خلقه، لا في ذاته ولا في أسمائه ولا في صفاته.

Second: If what is meant, on the other hand, is that Allah ﷻ transcends having the parts, limbs, and instruments of created things, then yes, Allah ﷻ transcends that, as none of His creations are like Him – neither in His essence, His names, nor His attributes.

الحاصل: أن هذه الألفاظ التي ساقها المصنف فيها إجمال ولكن يحمل كلامه علىٰ الحق؛ لأنه – رحمه الله تعالىٰ- من أهل السنة والجماعة، ولأنه من أئمة المحدثين، فلا يمكن أن يقصد المعاني السيئة، ولكنه يقصد المعاني الصحيحة،وليته فصّل ذلك وبيّنه ولم يجمل هذا الإجمال .

To sum up, the language put forth by the author has an element of generality, nevertheless it should be interpreted correctly because he رحمه الله was an adherent of the Sunnah and *Jamā'ah*. Furthermore, he was an *imām* of the ḥadīth masters, so he could not have meant anything wrong, rather he intended the correct meanings. If only he elaborated and clarified this, and did not leave it so ambiguous.

المتن

(٧٧) لا تَحْوِيهِ الْجِهاتُ السِّتُّ كَسائِرِ الْمُبْتَدَعاتِ.

(77) He is not bound by the six directions of space like all created beings are.

الشرح

نقول: هذا فيه إجمال، إن أُريد الجهات المخلوقة، فالله منزّه عن ذلك، لا يحويه شيء من مخلوقاته، وإن أُريد جهة العلو وأنه فوق المخلوقات كلها، فهذا حق ونفيه باطل، ولعل قصد المؤلف بالجهات الست، أي: الجهات المخلوقة؛ لا جهة العلو لأنه مثبت للعلو - رحمه الله -، ومثبت للاستواء.

This is somewhat general. If what is meant is the directions of created beings, then Allah ﷻ transcends that as nothing of His creation contains Him; and if what is meant is the direction of highness and that He is above all created things, then this is true and it is wrong to deny it. Perhaps the author means by the 'six directions' created directions, and not the direction of highness, because the author ؒ affirms Allah's ﷻ highness, and he also confirms the *istiwāʾ* (Allah rising above the Throne [*al-ʿArsh*]).

المتن

(٧٨) والْمِعْراجُ حَقٌّ، وَقَدْ أُسْرِيَ بِالنَّبِيِّ ﷺ.

(78) And the *Miʿrāj* (Ascension) is true. The Prophet ﷺ was taken on the journey by night;

الشرح

معنىٰ الإسراء هو السير ليلاً، فقد أُسري بالنبي صلىٰ الله عليه وسلم من المسجد الحرام إلىٰ المسجد الأقصىٰ في ليلة واحدة.

Isrā' means to 'travel by night', and the Prophet ﷺ was taken by night on a journey from al-Masjid al-Ḥarām (the Sacred Mosque) to al-Masjid al-Aqṣā in a single night.

أسرىٰ به جبريل بأمر من الله تعالىٰ قال تعالىٰ ﴿سُبْحَـٰنَ ٱلَّذِىٓ أَسْرَىٰ بِعَبْدِهِۦ لَيْلًا مِّنَ ٱلْمَسْجِدِ ٱلْحَرَامِ إِلَى ٱلْمَسْجِدِ ٱلْأَقْصَا﴾ [الإسراء:١].

It was Jibrīl عليه السلام who took him by the command of Allah سبحانه وتعالى. Allah سبحانه وتعالى says: **{Exalted is He who took His slave by night from al-Masjid al-Ḥarām to al-Masjid al-Aqṣā...} [Qur'ān 17:1]**

وهذا من معجزاته عليه الصلاة والسلام؛ لأن هذه المسافة كانت تقطع في شهر أو أكثر، وقطعها النبي صلىٰ الله عليه وسلم في ليلة واحدة.

This was one of the miracles of the Prophet ﷺ, because such a distance could only be travelled in a month or more, and the Prophet ﷺ travelled it in one night.

وأما المعراج: فهو آله الصعود وعرج، يعني صعد ﴿تَعْرُجُ ٱلْمَلَـٰٓئِكَةُ وَٱلرُّوحُ إِلَيْهِ﴾ [المعارج:٤]. يعني : تصعد، فالعروج معناه: الصعود، والمعراج آلة الصعود التي يصعد بها.

The *Mi'rāj* (Ascension) is the means of ascension. And *'araja* means 'to ascend' (*ṣa'ada*). Allah سبحانه وتعالى says: **{The angels and the Spirit will *ta'ruju* to Him...} [Qur'ān 70:4]** I.e. they ascend. Thus, *'urūj* has the same meaning as *ṣu'ūd*. And *al-mi'rāj* is the means of ascension.

وكلاهما ثابت للنبي صلىٰ الله عليه وسلم.

Both have been affirmed for the Prophet ﷺ.[24]

---

24 The ḥadīth of the *Isrā'* (Night Journey) and *Mi'rāj* (Ascension) is related by al-

فالإسراء من المسجد الحرام إلىٰ المسجد الأقصىٰ، وأما المعراج فمن الأرض إلىٰ السماء، وكل هذا حصل في ليلة واحدة، أُسري به إلىٰ بيت المقدس وصلىٰ فيه بالأنبياء، ثم عرج به إلىٰ السماء وجاوز السبع الطباق، وأراه الله من آياته ما أراه من آياته الكبرىٰ، ثم نزل إلىٰ الأرض، ثم جاء به جبريل إلىٰ المكان الذي أُسري به منه في ليلة واحدة.

The *Isrāʾ* (Night Journey) was undertaken from the Sacred Mosque to the al-Aqsa Mosque, and the *Miʿrāj* from earth to the heavens. All of this happened in one night: He was taken by night on a journey to Bayt al-Maqdis where he led the Prophets in prayer, and then he ascended to the heavens and went past the seventh level, and Allah ﷻ presented to him from the great signs that He showed him. Then, he descended to earth, and Jibrīl ﵇ brought him back to the place where he had first taken him for the journey, in one night.

فالإسراء مذكور في سورة الإسراء، والمعراج مذكور في سورة النجم ﴿وَٱلنَّجۡمِ إِذَا هَوَىٰ ۝١ مَا ضَلَّ صَاحِبُكُمۡ وَمَا غَوَىٰ ۝٢ وَمَا يَنطِقُ عَنِ ٱلۡهَوَىٰٓ ۝٣ إِنۡ هُوَ إِلَّا وَحۡيٞ يُوحَىٰ ۝٤ عَلَّمَهُۥ شَدِيدُ ٱلۡقُوَىٰ ۝٥﴾ [النجم:١-٥] يعني: جبريل ﴿ذُو مِرَّةٖ فَٱسۡتَوَىٰ ۝٦ وَهُوَ بِٱلۡأُفُقِ ٱلۡأَعۡلَىٰ ۝٧﴾ [النجم: ٦-٧] هذا العروج، ﴿ثُمَّ دَنَا﴾ من ربه سبحانه وتعالىٰ أو أن جبريل دنا من الرسول صلىٰ الله عليه وسلم: ﴿ ثُمَّ دَنَا فَتَدَلَّىٰ ۝٨ فَكَانَ قَابَ قَوۡسَيۡنِ أَوۡ أَدۡنَىٰ ۝٩ فَأَوۡحَىٰٓ إِلَىٰ عَبۡدِهِۦ مَآ أَوۡحَىٰ ۝١٠﴾ [النجم:٨-١٠].

The *Isrāʾ* is mentioned in Sūrat al-Isrāʾ and the *Miʿrāj* is mentioned in Sūrat al-Najm. **{By the star when it descends, your companion has not strayed, nor has he erred, nor does he speak from [his own] inclination. It is not but a revelation revealed, Taught to him by one intense in strength..."**—meaning Jibrīl ﵇—**{One of soundness. And he rose to [his] true form while he was in the higher [part of the] horizon.} [Qurʾān 53:1-7]** This is the *ʿUrūj*. **{Then he approached...}** His Lord, or it means that Jibrīl approached the Messenger of Allah ﷺ: **{...and descended and was at a distance of two bow lengths or nearer. And he**

Bukhārī, no. 3207 & 7517, and Muslim, no. 162.

revealed to His slave what he revealed." [Qur'ān 53:8-10]

فالإسراء والمعراج حق، ومن أنكرهما واستبعدهما فهو كافر بالله عز وجل، ومن تأولهما فهو ضال، ولم ينكره إلا المشركون، فمن يقول: أُسري بروحه دون جسده، أو كان ذلك منامـًا لا يقظة، فهذا ضلال؛ لأن الله قال: ﴿أَسْرَىٰ بِعَبْدِهِ﴾ والعبد اسم للروح والبدن، لا يقال للروح إنها عبد، وكان الإسراء في حال اليقظة ولم يكن منامـًا؛ لأن المنام ليس فيه عبرة، كل الناس يرون الرؤيا ويرون عجائب، وليست خاصة بالنبي صلىٰ الله عليه وسلم.

The *Isrā'* and the *Mi'rāj* are both true. Anyone who denies them or considers them implausible has disbelieved in Allah ﷻ, and anyone who assigns an interpretation to them has gone astray. It was none other than the polytheists who denied those events. If anyone says that it was his soul that travelled and not his body, or that it was a dream and not when he was awake, then he is astray, because Allah ﷻ said that He took His slave on a journey by night (*asrā bi-'abdih*), and *'abd* (slave) denotes both soul and body. It is not said that a soul (*rūḥ*) is a 'slave'. The Night Journey happened in a state of wakefulness and was not a dream, because dreams are not given [such] consideration. All people have dreams and see amazing things, and this is not something specific to the Prophet ﷺ.

❁❁❁

المتن

(٧٩) وَعُرِجَ بِشَخْصِهِ فِي الْيَقَظَةِ إِلَىٰ السَّماءِ.

(79) And he ascended in his bodily form to the heavens while awake;

الشرح

عرج بشخصه، رد علىٰ الذين يقولون: عرج بروحه، بل عرج بشخصه - والشخص اسم للروح والجسم، والله يقول: ﴿أَسْرَىٰ بِعَبْدِهِ﴾.

"He ascended in his bodily form" is a refutation to those who say that he ascended in spirit. Rather, he ascended in person, as 'bodily form' denotes both spirit and body, and Allah ﷻ says that He *asrā bi-ʿabdihī* (took His slave on a journey by night).

المتن

(٨٠) ثُمَّ إِلَىٰ حَيْثُ شاءَ اللهُ مِنَ الْعُلا، وَأَكْرَمَهُ اللهُ بِما شاءَ،

(80) And then to whatever high places Allah willed. Allah honoured him as He so willed.

الشرح

هذا المعراج إلىٰ السماء.

This is the Ascension to the heavens.

المتن

(٨١) وَأَوْحَىٰ إِلَيْهِ ما أَوْحَىٰ ﴿ما كَذَبَ الْفُؤادُ ما رَأَى﴾ [النجم: ١١].

(81) And He revealed to him what he revealed. *{The heart did not lie [about] what it saw.}* [Qur'ān 53:11]

الشرح

أوحىٰ الله إليه بذلك المكان ما أوحىٰ ، وكلمه الله سبحانه ولم ير الله؛ لأن الله لا يُرىٰ في الدنيا.

Allah divinely inspired to him at that place what He divinely inspired, and Allah ﷻ spoke to him, but he did not see Allah because Allah ﷻ is not seen in this worldly life.

هذا المعراج المذكور في سورة النجم.

This is the Ascension mentioned in Sūrat al-Najm (Qur'ān 53).

المتن

(٨٢) فَصَلَّىٰ اللهُ عَلَيْهِ وَسَلَّمَ فِي الْآخِرَةِ والْأُولَىٰ.

(82) May Allah give him peace and blessings in this life and the next.

الشرح

هذا من حقوقه عليه الصلاة والسلام: أن يصلىٰ عليه ويسلم عند ذكره ﴿إِنَّ ٱللَّهَ وَمَلَٰٓئِكَتَهُۥ يُصَلُّونَ عَلَى ٱلنَّبِيِّۚ يَٰٓأَيُّهَا ٱلَّذِينَ ءَامَنُواْ صَلُّواْ عَلَيۡهِ وَسَلِّمُواْ تَسۡلِيمًا ٥٦﴾ [الأحزاب:٥٦].

This is one of the rights of the Prophet ﷺ, to pray for blessings and peace for Him when he is mentioned. Allah ﷻ states: **{Indeed, Allah confers blessing upon the Prophet, and His angels [ask Him to do so]. O you who have believed, ask [Allah to confer] blessing upon him and ask [Allah to grant him] peace.} [Qur'ān 33:56]**

ولما أصبح النبي صلىٰ الله عليه وسلم في مكة وأخبر المشركين بهذه الحادثة اشتد كفرهم وتكذيبهم بهذه المناسبة؛ من أجل أن يشوهوا الرسول صلىٰ الله عليه وسلم. ويقولون: نحن نمشي إلىٰ فلسطين مدة شهر فأكثر، وهو يقول: في ليلة واحدة! فارتد بعض ضعاف الإيمان بسبب هذه الحادثة، وأما أهل الإيمان الصحيح فثبتوا وصدقوا، ولهذا لما قالوا لأبي بكر رضي الله عنه: أما ترىٰ صاحبك كيف يقول؟ قال: وماذا يقول؟ قالوا: إنه يقول: إنه ذهب إلىٰ بيت المقدس وجاء في ليلة واحدة، قال: فإن كان قاله فهو كما قال. لأنه لا ينطق عن الهوىٰ. وقال: أنا أصدقه بخبر السماء – أي الوحي – أفلا أصدقه في هذا!؟ هذا هو الإيمان الثابت الراسخ الذي لا يتزعزع.

By morning, when the Prophet ﷺ told the idolaters of Makkah about this incident, it intensified their disbelief and they used it to discredit the Messenger of Allah ﷺ. They said, "We travel to Palestine in a month or longer and he says he travelled in one night!" Some people, who were weak in faith, abandoned their faith because of this incident. Those who had true faith, however, remained steadfast and believed in it. To this effect, when it was said to Abū Bakr ﷺ, "What do you think about what your companion has said?" He replied, "What has he said?" They said, "He says that he went to Bayt al-Maqdis and came back in one night." He replied, "If he said so, then it is as he said because he does not speak of his own accord." And He said, "I believe in what he tells of the heavens (i.e. the divine revelation), so should I not believe him in this?" This is strong, firm faith that is unwavering.

المتن

(٨٣) والْحَوْضُ الَّذِي أَكْرَمَهُ اللهُ تَعالَىٰ بِهِ غِياثًا لِأُمَّتِهِ حَقٌّ.

(83) The *Ḥawḍ* (pool) with which Allah has honoured him, to quench the thirst of his Ummah [on the Day of Judgement], is real.

الشرح

من جملة ما يعتقده أهل السنة والجماعة ما صح فيه الخبر عن رسول الله صلىٰ الله عليه وسلم من أمور يوم القيامة، وما يحدث في يوم القيامة من أمور، فمن ذلك: الحوض: فإن النبي صلىٰ الله عليه وسلم أخبرنا أن له حوضاً في يوم القيامة في المحشر يرده أتباعه الذين آمنوا به واتبعوه، فيشربون منه، فإذا شربوا منه شربة واحدة لم يظمؤوا بعدها أبداً، وذلك لأن يوم القيامة يوم شديد وعصيب وفيه حر شديد.

Among the beliefs of *Ahl al-Sunnah wa 'l-Jamā'ah* is what has been authentically reported from the Messenger of Allah ﷺ as relates to the Day of Judgment, and the things that take place on that Day, such as the *Ḥawḍ*.

The Prophet ﷺ said that he will have a pool[25] on the Day of Judgment at the place of Resurrection and that he will give it to his followers (those who believe in him and follow him) to drink from. After drinking from it just once, they will never face thirst thereafter. This is because the Day of Judgment will be severe and difficult, and it will be extremely hot.

فيحصل الظمأ الشديد، فجعل الله هذا الحوض غياثاً لأمة محمد صلىٰ الله عليه وسلم يغيثهم به، ومعلوم أن الغيث الذي ينزله الله من السماء تحيا به الأرض وتحيا به النفوس، فكذلك الحوض فإنه غياثٌ يغيث الله به العباد عند شدة حاجتهم إلىٰ الماء.

So there will be extreme thirst, and Allah ﷻ made this pool to quench the thirst of the Ummah of Muḥammad ﷺ. It is known that both the earth and living things gain life from the rain that Allah ﷻ sends down from the heavens. The same goes for the *Ḥawḍ*. It is water that Allah ﷻ provides to quench the thirst of people during their severe need for water.

والحوض هو مجمع الماء، وقد وصفه عليه الصلاة والسلام بأنه حوض عظيم طوله شهر وعرضه شهر، وآنيته عدد نجوم السماء، وأن من يشرب منه شربة لا يظمأ بعدها أبداً، ماؤه أبيض من اللبن وأحلىٰ من العسل.

A *ḥawḍ* is a pool of water. The Prophet ﷺ described it as being a great pool: the length of which is one month's travel and the width of which is one month's travel. Its vessels are as many as the stars of the heavens, and whoever drinks from it will never face thirst thereafter. Its water is whiter than milk and sweeter than honey.[26]

وأخبر عليه الصلاة والسلام أنه يرده أقوامٌ ثم يذادون ويمنعون من الشرب منه، فيقول الرسول صلىٰ الله عليه وسلم: «يارب، أمتي، أمتي» فيقول الله عز وجل:

25 It is related that Anas ibn Mālik ﷺ said that the Messenger of Allah ﷺ said: "The size of my *Ḥawḍ* is like what is between Aylah and San'ā' in Yemen, and it has jugs like the number of stars in the heavens." Al-Bukhārī, no. 6580; Muslim, no. 2303

26 It is related that 'Abdullāh ibn 'Amr ﷺ said: "The Prophet ﷺ said: 'My pool is one month's travel, its water is whiter than milk, its scent sweeter than musk, and its vessels are many as the stars in the heavens. Whoever drinks from it shall never thirst again.'" Al-Bukhārī, no. 6579; Muslim, no. 2292

«إنك لا تدري ما أحدثوا بعدك» فيقول عليه الصلاة والسلام: **«سُحقًا وبُعداً لمن بدّل وغير»**، ويمنع من وروده أهل البدع المضلة المخالفون لرسول الله صلىٰ الله عليه وسلم الذين كفروا وارتدوا علىٰ أعقابهم، تاركين السنة، وذاهبين بأهوائهم وآرائهم المذاهب المنحرفة، هؤلاء يمنعون من حوض النبي صلىٰ الله عليه وسلم؛ لأنهم بدلوا وغيروا من هدي النبي صلىٰ الله عليه وسلم، ولا يرده إلا من كان متبعـًا لسنة رسول الله صلىٰ الله عليه وسلم قولاً وعملاً واعتقاداً.

The Prophet ﷺ also said that some people will come to it and then be driven away and prevented from drinking from it. The Messenger of Allah ﷺ will say, "O Lord, my Ummah! My Ummah!" And Allah ﷻ will say, "You do not know what they have innovated after you." So the Prophet ﷺ will say, "Away with those who shifted and altered."[27] He will thus prevent the misguided people of innovation, those who opposed the Messenger of Allah ﷺ, who committed disbelief, turned back on their heels and abandoned the Sunnah and who instead adopted their own desires, opinions and deviant schools of thought. Those people will be prevented from the *Ḥawḍ* of the Prophet ﷺ because they have changed and altered the guidance of the Prophet ﷺ and no one will come to it besides those who follow the Sunnah of the Messenger of Allah ﷺ in word, action, and belief.

وبعض العلماء يرىٰ أن الكوثر المذكور في قوله تعالىٰ: ﴿إِنَّآ أَعۡطَيۡنَٰكَ ٱلۡكَوۡثَرَ ١﴾ [الكوثر:١] هو الحوض، وبعض العلماء يرىٰ أن معنىٰ الكوثر: الخير الكثير، ولا شك أن الحوض يدخل في هذا الخير الكثير؛ لأنه خير لهذه الأمة، فهذا هو حوض النبي صلىٰ الله عليه وسلم، فيجب الإيمان به واعتقاده، وأن يتمسك الإنسان بالسنة، حتىٰ يرد هذا الحوض، ولا يُردّ عنه يوم القيامة.

Some scholars of Islām hold that the *kawthar* mentioned in the statement of Allah ﷻ: **{Indeed, We have granted you, [O Muḥammad], al-Kawthar;} [Qurʾān 108:1]** is the *Ḥawḍ,* while others hold that *kawthar* means 'much good'. Undoubtedly, the *Ḥawḍ* is included among those good things as it is a good thing for the Ummah.[28] This is the *Ḥawḍ* of the Prophet ﷺ

---

27 Al-Bukhārī, no. 6582, 6584 & 70518; Muslim, no. 2291, 2304.

28 It is related that Saʿīd ibn Jubayr related that he heard Ibn ʿAbbās ﷺ saying about *kawthar* that it is "the good that Allah gave him." Abū Bishr said: "I said to Saʿīd ibn

and it is necessary to believe in it and to hold fast to the Sunnah, in order to come to the *Ḥawḍ* and not be driven away from it on the Day of Judgment.

المتن

(٨٤) والشَّفاعَةُ الَّتِي ادَّخَرَها لَهُمْ حَقٌّ، كَما رُوِيَ فِي الأَخْبارِ.

(84) The *Shafāʿah* (intercession) allocated to his followers is real, as related in the narrations.

الشرح

الشفاعة أيضـًا من مسائل العقيدة المهمة؛ لأنه قد ضل في إثباتها أناس، وغلا في إثباتها أناس، وتوسط فيها أناس.

The *shafāʿah* (intercession) is also an important matter of creed,[29] because some people have gone astray with regards to affirming it. Some people have gone to excess in affirming it, while others followed a middle course.

فالشفاعة يوم القيامة الناس فيها على ثلاثة أقسام:

Regarding intercession on the Day of Judgment, the people fall into three categories:

Jubayr: 'People say that it is a river in Jannah.' Saʿīd replied: 'The river in Jannah is among the good that Allah has given him.'" Al-Bukhārī, no. 4966, 6578. It is related that Anas ibn Mālik ﷺ said: "One day, when the Messenger of Allah ﷺ was among us, he fell asleep and then lifted his head with a smile, so we said: 'What makes you laugh, O Messenger of Allah?' He said: 'A *sūrah* was sent down to me just now.' He read: **{Indeed, We have granted you, [O Muḥammad], al-Kawthar.}** Then, he said: 'Do you know what *kawthar* is?' We said: 'Allah and His Messenger know best'. He said: 'It is a river my Lord has promised me. There is much good in it. And it is a pool that my ummah will come to on the Day of Judgment.'" Muslim, no. 400.

29 The ḥadīth of the Intercession has been recorded by al-Bukhārī (no. 3340, 4712 & 7510), and Muslim (no. 193 & 194). It states: "....'Go to the Prophet', and they will come to me and I will fall in prostration below the Throne, and it will be said, 'O Muḥammad, raise your head and intercede and your intercession will be granted, ask and you will be given.'"

قوم غلوا في إثباتها حتىٰ طلبوها من الأموات ومن القبور ومن الأصنام والأشجار والأحجار ﴿وَيَعْبُدُونَ مِن دُونِ ٱللَّهِ مَا لَا يَضُرُّهُمْ وَلَا يَنفَعُهُمْ وَيَقُولُونَ هَٰٓؤُلَآءِ شُفَعَٰٓؤُنَا عِندَ ٱللَّهِ﴾ [يونس:١٨]، ﴿مَا نَعْبُدُهُمْ إِلَّا لِيُقَرِّبُونَآ إِلَى ٱللَّهِ زُلْفَىٰٓ﴾ [الزمر:٣].

[i] People who are excessive in affirming it, thereby seeking intercession from the dead, the graves, idols, trees and stones. Allah ﷻ says: **{And they worship other than Allah that which neither harms them nor benefits them, and they say, 'These are our intercessors with Allah.'} [Qurʾān 10:18]** Allah also says: **{And those who take protectors besides Him [say], 'We only worship them that they may bring us nearer to Allah in position.'} [Qurʾān 39:3]**

وطائفة غلت في نفي الشفاعة كالمعتزلة والخوارج، فإنهم نفوا الشفاعة في أهل الكبائر، وخالفوا ما تواترت به الأدلة من الكتاب والسنة في إثبات الشفاعة.

[ii] People who are excessive in their denial of the intercession. Among these sects are the Muʿtazilites and the Khārijites as they deny any intercession for those who commit major sins (*kabāʾir*). Thus they contradicted concurrent (*mutawātir*) pieces of evidence from the Qurʾān and Sunnah that confirm the Intercession.

وأهل السنة والجماعة توسطوا فأثبتوا الشفاعة علىٰ الوجه الذي ذكره الله ورسوله، وآمنوا بها من غير إفراط ولا تفريط.

[iii] *Ahl al-Sunnah wa ʾl Jamāʿah* steer a middle course and affirm the intercession in the manner that Allah and His Messenger have mentioned and they believe in it, without excess nor abandonment.

والشفاعة في اللغة مأخوذة من الشفع، وهو ضد الوتر، فالوتر هو الفرد الواحد. والشفع هو أكثر من واحد، اثنين أو أربعة أو ستة، وهو ما يسمىٰ بالعدد الزوجي.

Linguistically speaking, the word *shafāʿah* is derived from *shafʿ* (even, or pair), which is the opposite of *witr* (odd, or singular). *Witr* is a single unit. *Shafʿ* is greater than one (two, four, six...). It is what is known as even numbers.

وشرعـًا: الوساطة في قضاء الحاجات، وساطة بين من عنده الحاجة وصاحب الحاجة، وهي على قسمين: شفاعة عند الله، وشفاعة عند الخلق.

Technically, intercession means mediation to fulfil certain needs. It is mediation between anyone who has a need and someone who can furnish that need. This is of two kinds: intercession with Allah, and intercession with the creation.

فالشفاعة عند الخلق على قسمين:

Intercession with people is of two kinds:

شفاعة حسنة، وهي في الأمور الحسنة النافعة المباحة، تتوسط عند من عنده حاجات الناس من أجل أن يقضيها لهم، قال سبحانه: ﴿مَّن يَشْفَعْ شَفَٰعَةً حَسَنَةً يَكُن لَّهُۥ نَصِيبٌ مِّنْهَا﴾ [النساء:٨٥]، وقال عليه الصلاة والسلام: «**اشفعوا تؤجروا، ويقضي الله على لسان رسوله ما شاء**».

[i] To intercede in a good cause (*shafā'ah ḥasanah*), which is that you mediate with someone who is able to provide the good, beneficial, and permissible needs of people. Allah ﷻ says: **{Whoever intercedes for a good cause will have a reward therefrom.} [Qur'ān 4:85]** The Prophet ﷺ said, "Intercede and you will be rewarded, and Allah fulfils what He permitted on the tongue of His Messenger."[30]

هذه شفاعة حسنة وفيها أجر؛ لأن فيها نفعـًا للمسلمين في قضاء حاجاتهم وحصولهم على مطلوبهم الذي فيه نفع لهم، وليس فيها تعدّ على أحد أو ظلمٌ لأحد.

This is intercession in a good cause. It entails a reward because it is a benefit to Muslims and gets their needs fulfilled and provides for the things that they desire and that are of benefit to them, and it does not involve any offense or injustices against anyone.

والقسم الثاني: شفاعة سيئة، وهي التوسط في أمور محرمة، كالشفاعة في إسقاط

30 Al-Bukhārī, no. 1432; Muslim, no. 2627.

الحدود إذا وجبت، وهذا يدخل فيمن لعنه النبي صلىٰ الله عليه وسلم في قوله: «**لعن الله من آوىٰ محدثًا**». والشفاعة أيضًا في أخذ حقوق الآخرين وإعطائها لغير مستحقها، قال تعالىٰ: ﴿وَمَن يَشْفَعْ شَفَٰعَةً حَسَنَةً يَكُن لَّهُۥ نَصِيبٌ مِّنْهَا﴾ [النساء:٨٥].

[ii] To intercede in a bad cause, which is to mediate in forbidden matters, such as interceding to have someone exempted from a *ḥadd* penalty, if a *ḥadd* penalty is obligated. This is included among those who the Prophet ﷺ cursed in his saying, "Allah cursed one who shelters an offender."[31] Intercession can also be used to infringe upon the rights of others and transfer property to the wrong people. Allah ﷻ says: **{...And whoever intercedes for an evil cause will have a burden therefrom.} [Qurʾān 4:85]**

أما الشفاعة عند الله فليست كالشفاعة عند المخلوق، فالشفاعة عند الخالق: أن يكرم الله جل وعلا بعض عباده في أن يدعو لأحد المسلمين المستحقين للعذاب بسبب كبيرة ارتكبها، فيشفع عنده الشافع في أن يعفو عنه ولا يعذبه؛ لأنه مؤمن موحد، فيشفع الشافع عند الله جل وعلا بأن يعفو عنه، أو فيمن دخل النار في معصية فيشفع الشافع عند الله في أن يخرج ويرفع عنه العذاب، وهي ما تسمىٰ بالشفاعة في أهل الكبائر.

Intercession with Allah ﷻ, on the other hand, is not like intercession with created beings. Intercession with the Creator is that Allah ﷻ honours some of His slaves to supplicate for one of the Muslims who deserve punishment due to committing major sins. The intercessor intercedes with Him to pardon them and not punish them because of them being faithful believers in Allah's oneness. The intercessor intercedes with Allah ﷻ to pardon such people or for someone who enters the Fire because of sin – the intercessor intercedes with Allah ﷻ to have him brought out and relieved of the punishment. This is what is termed as intercession for those who commit major sins.

---

31 It is related that ʿAli ؓ said: "We have nothing but the Book of Allah and this parchment from the Prophet ﷺ: 'Madīnah is a sanctuary from ʿĀʾir Mountain to such and such a place, and whoever commits a sin there, or shelters an offender is cursed by Allah, the angels, and all the people, and no exchange or ransom will be accepted from him.'" Al-Bukhārī, no. 1870; Muslim, no. 1370

لكن الشفاعة عند الله يشترط لها شرطان:

Notwithstanding, there are two prerequisites for intercession with Allah ﷻ:

الشرط الأول: أن تكون بإذن الله، فلا أحد يشفع عند الله إلا بإذن، فهو الذي يأذن للشافع أن يشفع، أما من قبل أن يأذن فلا أحد يتقدم إلىٰ الله عز وجل: ﴿مَن ذَا ٱلَّذِى يَشْفَعُ عِندَهُۥٓ إِلَّا بِإِذْنِهِۦ﴾ [البقرة: ٢٥٥]، وليس كالمخلوق الذي يتقدم الناس للشفاعة عنده وإن لم يأذن، فالله جل وعلا لا يشفع أحد عنده إلا بإذنه.

(i) Allah ﷻ has to permit this intercession. None can intercede with Allah except with his permission. He is the one who gives permission to the interceder to intercede. Before His permission, no one can approach Allah the Almighty. **{Who is it that can intercede with Him except by His permission?} [Qur'ān 2:255]** It is not like created beings where people approach to intercede with them, even if they do not permit. None can intercede with Allah except with his permission.

الشرط الثاني: أن يكون المشفوع فيه من أهل التوحيد وأهل الإيمان، ممن يرضىٰ الله عنهم قولهم وعملهم، ﴿وَلَا يَشْفَعُونَ إِلَّا لِمَنِ ٱرْتَضَىٰ﴾ [الأنبياء:٢٨]، أي: رضي الله قوله وعمله، وجاء الشرطان في قوله تعالىٰ: ﴿إِلَّا مِنۢ بَعْدِ أَن يَأْذَنَ ٱللَّهُ لِمَن يَشَآءُ وَيَرْضَىٰٓ ﴿٢٦﴾﴾ [النجم:٢٦]. أن يأذن الله هذا الشرط الأول، ويرضىٰ هذا الشرط الثاني.

(ii) The second prerequisite is that the person who the intercession is for is someone who is from the people of *tawḥīd* (Allah's oneness), *īmān* (has faith), and whom Allah ﷻ is pleased with in terms of his speech and actions. Allah ﷻ says: **{...And they cannot intercede except on behalf of one whom He approves.} [Qur'ān 21:28]** Meaning those whom Allah ﷻ is pleased with in regards to their speech and actions. Both of these preconditions are mentioned in the statement of Allah ﷻ: **{And how many angels there are in the heavens whose intercession will not avail at all except [only] after Allah has permitted [it] to whom He wills and approves.} [Qur'ān 53:26]** [To summarize:] the first prerequisite for *shafāʿah* is that Allah permits it, and the second is that Allah ﷻ approves of the person.

أما الكافر فإنه لا تنفعه الشفاعة ﴿فَمَا تَنفَعُهُمْ شَفَٰعَةُ ٱلشَّٰفِعِينَ ﴿٤٨﴾﴾ [المدثر:٤٨]، ﴿مَا لِلظَّٰلِمِينَ مِنْ حَمِيمٍ وَلَا شَفِيعٍ يُطَاعُ ﴿١٨﴾﴾ [غافر:١٨] فالشفاعة في القرآن شفاعتان؛ شفاعة منفية وهي التي انتفت شروطها، وشفاعة مثبتة وهي التي تحققت شروطها.

On the other hand, intercession is of no benefit to a disbeliever. **{So it will not benefit them the intercession of [any] intercessors.} [Qur'ān 74:48] {For the wrongdoers there will be no devoted friend and no intercessor [who is] obeyed.} [Qur'ān 40:18]** Therefore, there are two kinds of intercession in the Qur'ān: (i) A denied intercession, which is an intercession that does not meet the conditions. (ii) A confirmed intercession, whose conditions are fulfilled.

فالكافر لا تنفعه الشفاعة؛ لو شفع فيه أهل السماوات وأهل الأرض ما قبل الله فيه شفاعتهم؛ لأنه مشرك كافر بالله عز وجل، لا يرضىٰ الله قوله ولا عمله، إلا ما جاء في شفاعة النبي صلىٰ الله عليه وسلم في عمه أبي طالب، فهي شفاعة خاصة، وأيضـًا ليست شفاعة من أجل خروجه من النار، إنما هي شفاعة من أجل تخفيف العذاب عن هذا الرجل؛ لما حصل منه من مؤازرة النبي صلىٰ الله عليه وسلم وحمايته له - عليه الصلاة والسلام - والمدافعة عنه، فالنبي صلىٰ الله عليه وسلم يشفع في تخفيف العذاب عنه فقط.

Intercession is of no benefit to a disbeliever. If those in the heavens and on earth were to intercede on the behalf of a disbeliever, Allah ﷻ would not accept any intercession for him, because he is an idolater and a disbeliever in Allah ﷻ, and Allah ﷻ is not pleased with his speech and actions. An exception to that is the intercession of the Prophet ﷺ for his uncle, Abū Ṭālib. This is a special type of intercession, and it is not an intercession for him to be brought out of the Fire but rather for the punishment of that man to be lessened because of the aid, protection, and defence he provided for the Prophet ﷺ. So the Prophet ﷺ will only intercede for his punishment to be lessened.

هذه هي الشفاعة الثابتة بشروطها ، وهي أنواع:

These are the confirmed intercessions with their conditions, and they are of several types:

منها أنواع خاصة بالنبي صلىٰ الله عليه وسلم، وأنواع مشتركة بينه وبين غيره من الأنبياء، والملائكة والصالحين والأفراط الذين ماتوا قبل البلوغ، كل هؤلاء يشفعون عند الله سبحانه وتعالىٰ.

Some of these types are exclusively for the Prophet ﷺ and some of them are common to both him and all other Prophets, angels, righteous people and those who die before maturity. All of these people intercede with Allah the Almighty.

وأما الشفاعة الخاصة بالنبي صلىٰ الله عليه وسلم فهي أنواع:

The intercession that is exclusively for the Prophet ﷺ is also of several types:

أولها: شفاعته عليه الصلاة والسلام في أهل الموقف إذا طال الموقف يوم القيامة، واشتد الكرب، واشتد الزحام، ودنت الشمس من الرؤوس، وحصل الكرب العظيم، أهل المحشر يريدون من يشفع لهم لفصل القضاء بينهم وصرفهم من هذا الموقف: إما إلىٰ جنة وإما إلىٰ نار؛

(i) His intercession for the people at the place of gathering. As their standing on the Day of Judgment becomes lengthy, as their distress and crowding intensifies, the sun draws near to their heads, and great anguish abounds, the people at the place of resurrection seek someone to intercede for them for the Judgment to begin and to be removed from that place of standstill, either to Jannah or to the Fire.

فيذهبون إلىٰ آدم عليه السلام فيعتذر لهيبة المقام وجلالته، ثم يذهبون إلىٰ نوح عليه السلام أول الرسل فيعتذر، ثم يذهبون إلىٰ موسىٰ كليم الله فيعتذر، ثم يذهبون إلىٰ عيسىٰ عليه السلام فيعتذر أيضـًا، ثم يذهبون إلىٰ محمد صلىٰ الله عليه وسلم فيقول: «**أنا لها، أنا لها**» ثم يأتي فيخر ساجداً بين يدي الله عز وجل، ويحمده ويثني عليه ويدعوه حتىٰ يقال له: «**ارفع رأسك، وسل تُعطه،**

واشفع تشفع» بعد الدعاء والاستئذان، لا يشفع مباشرة، بل يسجد ويدعو ويثني

على الله ويتوسل إليه بأسمائه وصفاته، ثم يؤذن له بالشفاعة، ثم يشفع للفصل

بين الخلائق فيقبل الله شفاعته، ويأتي سبحانه وتعالى لفصل القضاء بين عباده،

قال سبحانه : ﴿كَلَّا إِذَا دُكَّتِ ٱلْأَرْضُ دَكًّا دَكًّا ۝ وَجَآءَ رَبُّكَ وَٱلْمَلَكُ صَفًّا

صَفًّا ۝﴾ [الفجر:٢١،٢٢] وقال سبحانه: ﴿هَلْ يَنظُرُونَ إِلَّآ أَن يَأْتِيَهُمُ ٱللَّهُ فِى ظُلَلٍ

مِّنَ ٱلْغَمَامِ وَٱلْمَلَٰٓئِكَةُ وَقُضِىَ ٱلْأَمْرُ﴾ [البقرة:٢١٠].

So, they turn to Ādam ﷺ but he declines to do so out of reverence for such a position and for the majesty of Allah. Then, they turn to Nūḥ ﷺ who was the first messenger of Allah, but he declines. Then, they turn to Mūsā ﷺ, to whom Allah ﷻ spoke, but he declines. Then, they turn to ʿĪsā ﷺ but he declines as well. Then, they turn to Muḥammad ﷺ and he says: "It is for me, it is for me." Then, he comes and falls in prostration before Allah the Almighty, and he praises Him and prays until it is said to him, "Raise your head, ask and you shall be given, intercede and your intercession will be heard."[32] After supplicating and seeking permission, he does not intercede directly, but rather prostrates himself, supplicates, praises Allah and appeals to Him through His names and attributes. Then, he is given permission to intercede, and then he intercedes for the judgment of the creation to begin. Allah ﷻ accepts his intercession and comes to judge His slaves. Allah ﷻ says: {No! When the earth has been levelled – pounded and crushed – And your Lord has come and the angels, rank upon rank.} [Qurʾān 89:21-22] Allah also says: {Do they await but that Allah should come to them in covers of clouds and the angels [as well] and the matter is [then] decided?} [Qurʾān 2:210]

هذه شفاعته عليه الصلاة والسلام في الفصل بين الخلائق، وهي مقام عظيم شرّف

الله به النبي صلى الله عليه وسلم، وهي المقام المحمود الذي قال الله سبحانه

فيه: ﴿وَمِنَ ٱلَّيْلِ فَتَهَجَّدْ بِهِۦ نَافِلَةً لَّكَ عَسَىٰٓ أَن يَبْعَثَكَ رَبُّكَ مَقَامًا مَّحْمُودًا ۝﴾

[الإسراء:٧٩]؛ لأنه يحمده عليه الأولون والآخرون، ويظهر فضله عليه الصلاة

والسلام في هذا الموقف العظيم.

This is the intercession of the Prophet ﷺ to begin the judgment of the cre-

---

32 Al-Bukhārī, no. 3340, 4712, 7510; Muslim, no. 193-194.

ation. It is an immense honour given to the Prophet ﷺ, the highest honour of praise about which Allah ﷻ says: **{And from [part of] the night, pray with it as additional [worship] for you; it is expected that your Lord will resurrect you to a praised station.} [Qur'ān 17:79]** Because the first and the last [generations] praise him over it, and his virtue is shown at that great place.

الشفاعة الثانية: الخاصة بالنبي صلىٰ الله عليه وسلم: شفاعته في أهل الجنة أن يدخلوا الجنة، فأول من يستفتح باب الجنة هو محمد صلىٰ الله عليه وسلم، وهو أول من يدخلها، وأول من يدخلها من الأمم أمته عليه الصلاة والسلام.

(ii) His intercession on behalf of the people of Jannah to be brought to Jannah.[33] The first person whom the gate of Jannah will be opened to is Muḥammad ﷺ and he will be the first to enter.[34] And the first of the communities of believers to enter it will be his Ummah.

الشفاعة الثالثة: الخاصة بالنبي صلىٰ الله عليه وسلم: شفاعته لأهل الجنة بأن يرفع الله منازلهم ودرجاتهم، فيشفع في أناس في أن يرفع الله درجاتهم في الجنة، فيرفعهم الله بشفاعته عليه الصلاة والسلام.

(iii) His intercession with Allah ﷻ to raise the ranks and degrees (*darajāt*) of the people of Jannah. He will intercede for people in order that Allah ﷻ raises their degrees in Jannah, and Allah will do so after his intercession.

الشفاعة الرابعة: - وهي مشتركة - الشفاعة في أهل الكبائر من المؤمنين فيمن استحق دخول النار أن لا يدخلها، وفي من دخلها أن يخرج منها، وهذه هي محط الخلاف بين الفرق؛ فالجهمية والخوارج وأضرابهم أنكروها وقالوا: من دخل النار لا يخرج منها، وأهل السنة والجماعة أثبتوها كما جاءت واعتقدوها،

---

33 It is related that Anas ibn Mālik ؓ said that the Messenger of Allah ﷺ said: "I am the first intercessor in Jannah." Muslim, no. 196.

34 It is related that Anas ibn Mālik ؓ said: "The Messenger of Allah ﷺ said: 'I will come to the gate of Jannah on the Day of Resurrection, and the gatekeeper will say, 'Who are you?' and I will say, 'Muḥammad.' Then, he will say, 'I was commanded not to open it for anyone before you.'" Muslim, no. 197.

ويجب علىٰ المسلم أن يعتقدها ويؤمن بها، وأن يسأل الله أن يُشفع فيه نبيه عليه الصلاة والسلام؛ لأنه بحاجة إليها.

(iv) The fourth intercession (which is general), is the intercession for the people of major sins (*kabāʾir*) among the Muslims, for those who deserve to enter the Fire to not enter it, and for those who have entered it to be brought out of it. This has been a focus of dispute among different sects. The Jahmīs and Khārijites, and those like them, deny it and say that those who enter the Fire do not come out of it. Ahl al-Sunnah wa 'l-Jamāʿah affirm and believe in it as it is related in the texts. It is imperative that a Muslim believes and has faith in that and asks Allah ﷻ that the Prophet ﷺ intercedes on his behalf, because he is in need of that.

الشفاعة الخامسة: وهي خاصة بالنبي صلىٰ الله عليه وسلم، وهي شفاعته في عمه أبي طالب، أبو طالب مات علىٰ الشرك وعلىٰ دين عبد المطلب المشرك، قال: هو علىٰ ملة عبد المطلب، ومات علىٰ ذلك، فصار من أهل النار الخالدين فيها. ولكن الله عز وجل يشفع رسوله عليه الصلاة والسلام في تخفيف العذاب عنه، فيكون في ضحضاح من نار، ما يرىٰ أن أحداً أشد منه عذاباً، مع أنه أهون أهل النار عذاباً.

(v) His intercession on behalf of his uncle, Abū Ṭālib, who died an idolater and a follower of the religion of ʿAbd al-Muṭṭalib, the idolater. He said that he followed the religion of ʿAbd al-Muṭṭalib and he died upon that, thus he is one of those who will abide in the Fire forever. However, Allah the Almighty accepts the intercession of His Messenger ﷺ for his punishment to be lessened, so he will be in a shallow part of the Fire. It will be thought that no one is receiving punishment worse than him, although he is to receive the lightest punishment of those in the Fire.[35]

والشفاعة في أهل الكبائر مشتركة، فالملائكة يشفعون، والأنبياء يشفعون، والأولياء والصالحون يشفعون، والأفراط يشفعون لآبائهم.

---

35 It is related that al-ʿAbbās ibn ʿAbd al-Muṭṭalib ؓ said to the Prophet ﷺ: "What have you availed your uncle, for he used to protect you and stand up for you?" He said: "He is in a shallow part of the Fire, and if it were not my sake, he would have been in the lowest depths of the Fire." [al-Bukhārī, no. 3883; Muslim, no. 209]

The intercession on behalf of the people of major sins is common to different groups: the angels, the Prophets, the saintly, and the pious all intercede[36], and children who die early will intercede for their parents.

المتن

(٨٥) والْمِيثاقُ الَّذِي أَخَذَهُ اللهُ تَعالَىٰ مِنْ آدَمَ وَذُرِّيَّتِهِ حَقٌّ.

(85) The Covenant (*mīthāq*) that Allah made with Ādam ﷺ and his descendants is real.

الشرح

الميثاق الذي أخذه الله تعالىٰ من آدم وذريته أن يعبدوه ولا يشركوا به شيئًا حق، كما جاء في الحديث أن النبي صلىٰ الله عليه وسلم أخبرنا أن الله استخرج ذرية آدم من ظهره كأمثال الذر، وأشهدهم علىٰ أنفسهم بالوحدانية، وأخذ عليهم الميثاق أن يعبدوه ولا يشركوا به شيئًا، فنحن نؤمن بذلك، وهذا العهد والميثاق لا يكفي، بل لابد معه من إرسال الرسل، ولذلك أرسل الله الرسل، ولو كان هذا يكفي وحده لما أرسل الله الرسل، ولكن أرسل الرسل من أجل أن تذكر به وتدعو الناس إلىٰ ما تضمنه.

The Covenant (*mīthāq*) that Allah ﷻ made with Ādam ﷺ and his descendants, namely that they worship Him and do not associate anything as partners with Him, is real. This is according to what has been related in a ḥadīth in which the Prophet ﷺ told us that Allah ﷻ brought forth the descendants of Ādam ﷺ from his loin (*ẓahrihī*) in the form of very small particles (*dharr*), and He called them as witnesses to testify against themselves

---

36 It is related that Abū Saʿīd ؓ said, as attributed to the Prophet ﷺ: "Allah says: '... The angels have interceded, the Prophets have interceded, and the believers have interceded, and no one remains but the Most Merciful of the merciful.' He will then take a handful from the Fire and bring out of it people who never did any good and who had been turned into charcoal, and He will cast them into a river called the River of Life..." Muslim, no. 183.

that Allah ﷻ is one. He made a covenant with them to worship Him and not worship anything alongside Him[37]. We believe in that. This pledge and covenant did not suffice, but rather it was also necessary to send messengers in order to serve as a reminder and to preach what it entails.

وأما قوله تعالىٰ: ﴿وَإِذۡ أَخَذَ رَبُّكَ مِنۢ بَنِيٓ ءَادَمَ مِن ظُهُورِهِمۡ ذُرِّيَّتَهُمۡ﴾ [الأعراف:١٧٢] فذهب بعض المفسرين إلىٰ أن هذا هو العهد الذي أخذه الله علىٰ ذرية آدم والميثاق، وليس كذلك، بل هذا شيء آخر، والله يقول: ﴿مِن ظُهُورِهِمۡ﴾ ولم يقل: من ظهر آدم، وتكملة الآية: ﴿وَأَشۡهَدَهُمۡ عَلَىٰٓ أَنفُسِهِمۡ أَلَسۡتُ بِرَبِّكُمۡۖ قَالُواْ بَلَىٰ﴾، وقال بعض العلماء: معنىٰ ذلك: الفطرة التي فطرهم الله عليها، والآيات الكونية التي نصبها الله لهم؛ ليعرفوا منها ربهم.

As regards to the statement of Allah ﷻ: **{And [mention] when your Lord took from the children of Adam – from their loins – their descendants...} [Qurʾān 7:172]** Some of the scholars of Qurʾānic interpretation (*tafsīr*) are upon the view that this is the pledge and covenant that Allah ﷻ made with the descendants of Ādam, but it is not so. Rather, this is something else. Allah ﷻ says: **{from their loins}** and not *'from the loins' (ẓahr)* of Ādam ؑ. The verse goes on to say: **{and made them testify of themselves, [saying to them], 'Am I not your Lord?' They said, 'Yes...'}** Some scholars said that this is in relation to the natural disposition of faith (*fiṭrah*) that Allah ﷻ has created in mankind and the natural signs that Allah ﷻ has set up for them to know their Lord.

فالله سبحانه فطرهم علىٰ التوحيد وعلىٰ الإسلام ﴿فَأَقِمۡ وَجۡهَكَ لِلدِّينِ حَنِيفٗاۚ فِطۡرَتَ ٱللَّهِ ٱلَّتِي فَطَرَ ٱلنَّاسَ عَلَيۡهَاۚ﴾ [الروم: ٣٠] وهي دين الإسلام ودين التوحيد، فالإسلام معناه التوحيد الذي جاءت به الرسل، ومعناه: عبادة الله

---

37 It is related that Ibn ʿAbbās ؓ said that the Prophet ﷺ said: "Verily, Allah made the covenant with the loins of Ādam at Nuʿmān [i.e. ʿArafah], and He brought forth from his spine every seed that he would sow, and He scattered them before him and then He spoke to them as they stood in front Him, saying, 'Am I not your Lord,' and they said, 'Yes, we confess... what the falsifiers have done.' Aḥmad, no. 1/272; al-Ḥākim, 2/544. Al-Ḥākim said it is authentic (*ṣaḥīḥ*) and al-Dhahabī concurred with him. Al-Haythamī states in *Majmaʿ al-Zawāʾid (7/25)*: Aḥmad related it and its men are those of *al-ṣaḥīḥ*. Shākir said it was authentic in his edition of the *Musnad* of Aḥmad, no 2455.

وحده لا شريك له، هذا هو الدين القيم.

Allah ﷻ has thus created them with a natural disposition of the recognition of Allah's ﷻ oneness *(tawḥīd)* and submission *(islām)*[38]. **{So direct your face toward the religion, inclining to truth. [Adhere to] the *fiṭrah* of Allah upon which He has created [all] people.} [Qur'ān 30:30]** It is the religion of Islām and the religion of *tawḥīd*. Islām means the kind of *tawḥīd* that was brought by the Messengers. It means to worship Allah alone without partners. This is the correct religion.

ومع هذا نصب الأدلة علىٰ ربوبيته فيما يشاهدونه في أنفسهم من خلقهم العجيب، وما فيهم من الآيات العجيبة التي تدل علىٰ الخالق سبحانه وتعالىٰ، وكذلك ما نصبه أمامهم من السماوات والأرض والمخلوقات التي تدل علىٰ الخالق، إن هذه المخلوقات لابد لها من خالق، لم توجد صدفة أو توجد بدون خالق ﴿أَمْ خُلِقُوا مِنْ غَيْرِ شَيْءٍ أَمْ هُمُ الْخَالِقُونَ ۝٣٥ أَمْ خَلَقُوا السَّمَاوَاتِ وَالْأَرْضَ ۚ بَل لَّا يُوقِنُونَ ۝٣٦﴾ [الطور: ٣٥، ٣٦].

Nonetheless, He has set up evidence of His *Rubūbiyyah* (lordship) in what they observe in the wonderful form and wonderful signs within themselves that point to the Creator. He has also set up the heavens, earth, and creations that point to the Creator. Those created things necessarily have a creator. They did not come about by chance or without a creator. **{Or were they created by nothing, or were they the creators [of themselves]? Or did they create the heavens and the earth? Rather, they are not certain.} [Qur'ān 52:35-36]**

فيا عجباً كيف يعصىٰ الإله   أم كيف يجحده الجاحد
وفي كل شيء له آيــة   تدل علىٰ أنه واحــد

So it is indeed amazing how Allah is disobeyed, and how those who disbelieve deny Him.

38 It is related that Abū Hurayrah ؓ said: "The Prophet ﷺ said: 'Every child is born with *fiṭrah* and it is his parents who make him a Jew or a Naṣrānī (Christian) or a Majūsī (Magian). Just as a camel is born whole – do you perceive any severed limb?'" Then, Abū Hurayrah recited: **{[Adhere to] the *fiṭrah* of Allah upon which He has created [all] people...}**

There are signs in everything that point to Allah being One.

كل ما أمامك يدل على وحدانية الله، ويشهد لله بالانفراد في خلق هذه المخلوقات ﴿إِنَّ ٱلَّذِينَ تَدۡعُونَ مِن دُونِ ٱللَّهِ لَن يَخۡلُقُواْ ذُبَابٗا وَلَوِ ٱجۡتَمَعُواْ لَهُۥ﴾ [الحج:٧٣]

Everything in front of you points to the Oneness of Allah ﷻ, and testifies to the fact that it is Allah alone who created all of those things. **{Indeed, those you invoke besides Allah will never create [as much as] a fly, even if they gathered together for that purpose.} [Qurʾān 22:73]**

فالخالق الله سبحانه، ولا أحد يخلق معه، فكيف يُعبد غيره ممن لا يخلق ولا يرزق ولا يملك لنفسه نفعاً ولا ضراً؟! فمعنى الآية ﴿وَإِذۡ أَخَذَ رَبُّكَ... ﴾ [الأعراف: ١٧٢] شهادة الفطرة وشهادة الكائنات على وحدانية الله سبحانه وتعالى، وليس لأحد أن يعتذر يوم القيامة ويقول: ﴿إِنَّا كُنَّا عَنۡ هَٰذَا غَٰفِلِينَ ١٧٢﴾ [الأعراف:١٧٢].

Therefore, the Creator is Allah and there is no one who creates alongside Him. Thus, how can other things that neither create nor provide and are unable to help or harm themselves be worshipped?! What the verse **{And [mention] when your Lord took...}** means is that the natural disposition of faith *(fiṭrah)* and all objects attest to the Oneness of Allah and no one is to put forth an excuse on the Day of Judgment and say: **{Indeed, we were of this unaware.} [Qurʾān 7:172]**

فالاحتجاج بالتقليد لا يصلح أمام البراهين القاطعة والأدلة الساطعة.

So, to put forth the argument of blind-following is not appropriate against that decisive proof and clear evidence.

المتن

(٨٦) وَقَدْ عَلِمَ اللهُ تعالَىٰ فِيما لَمْ يَزَلْ عَدَدَ مَنْ يَدْخُلُ الْجَنَّةَ، وَعَدَدَ مَنْ يَدْخُلُ النَّارَ جُمْلَةً واحِدَةً، فَلا يُزادُ فِي ذَلِكَ الْعَدَدُ وَلا يُنْقُصُ مِنْهُ.

(86) Allah knew, before the existence of time, the exact number of those who will enter *Jannah* (Paradise) and the exact number of those who will enter the Fire. This number shall neither be greater nor smaller.

الشرح

هذا الكلام وما بعده من كلام الشيخ - رحمه الله - كله في موضوع القضاء والقدر.

The *shaykh*'s ﷺ discourse from here onwards has to do with *qadar* (predestination) and *qaḍā'* (preordainment).

والإيمان بالقضاء والقدر هو أحد أركان الإيمان الستة، كما قال عليه الصلاة والسلام: «**الإيمان أن تؤمن بالله وملائكته وكتبه ورسله واليوم الآخر وتؤمن بالقدر خيره وشره**»، وفي القرآن قوله جل وعلا: ﴿إِنَّا كُلَّ شَيْءٍ خَلَقْنَٰهُ بِقَدَرٍ ۝٤٩﴾ [القمر:٤٩] وقوله: ﴿وَخَلَقَ كُلَّ شَيْءٍ فَقَدَّرَهُۥ تَقْدِيرًا ۝٢﴾ [الفرقان:٢].

Faith in predestination and preordainment is one of the six pillars of faith (*īmān*), as the Prophet ﷺ said, "Faith is to believe in Allah, His Angels, His Books, His Messengers, the Last Day, and to believe in *Qadar*, whether good or bad."[39] In the Qur'ān, Allah ﷻ says: **{Indeed, all things We created with predestination.} [Qur'ān 54:49]** And His statement: **{...And has created each thing and determined it with [precise] predetermination.} [Qur'ān 25:2]**

فليس هناك شيء بدون تقدير، أو أن هناك أشياء تقع صدفة، أو أن الأمر أُنف؛ إن كل شيء يحدث فإنه مقدر ومكتوب.

There is nothing that was not predestined and nothing that happens by chance or without intervention. Everything that happens is predestined and written.

والإيمان بالقضاء والقدر يتضمن أربع درجات، نلخصها فيما يلي:

39 Al-Bukhārī, no. 50; Muslim, no. 10.

Faith in *qaḍā'* and *qadar* involves four levels, summed up as follows:

المرتبة الأولىٰ: الإيمان بعلم الله الشامل المحيط بكل شيء، وأن الله علم الأشياء أزلاً، علم ما كان وما يكون وما لم يكن لو كان كيف يكون ، لا يخفىٰ علىٰ علمه شيء سبحانه وتعالىٰ.

(i) To have faith in the omniscience of Allah ﷻ, which comprehends all things, and that Allah ﷻ knew everything beforehand from eternity. He knew what was and what would be and what would not be, and how those things would have been. Nothing is hidden from His knowledge, Glorified be He.

المرتبة الثانية: أن الله جلا وعلا كتب في اللوح المحفوظ مقادير الخلائق، بعد أن علمها سبحانه.

(ii) That Allah ﷻ wrote in *al-Lawḥ al-Maḥfūẓ* (the Preserved Tablet) the predetermined measures of all created things after having known that.

وهي الكتابة العامة الشاملة لكل شيء، وفي الحديث: «**إن أول ما خلق الله القلم، قال: أكتب، قال : ما أكتب؟ قال: أكتب ما هو كائن إلىٰ يوم القيامة**» فجرىٰ القلم بما هو كائن إلىٰ يوم القيامة.

This is the general "Writing" (*kitābah*) that encompasses all things. It states in a narration, "The first thing that Allah ﷻ created was the Pen. He said, 'Write.' It said, 'What should I write?' He said, 'Write all that is to be until the Day of Judgment[40].'" So the Pen wrote all that is to be until the Day of Judgment.

المرتبة الثالثة: مرتبة المشيئة، لا يكون في هذا الكون شيء إلا بإرادة الله ومشيئته مما هو في اللوح المحفوظ، وفي علمه سبحانه وتعالىٰ، لا يحدث شيء بدون إرادته، ولا يكون في ملكه ما لا يريد سبحانه، ﴿إِنَّ ٱللَّهَ يَفۡعَلُ مَا يُرِيدُ ١٤﴾

40 Abū Yaʿlā, no. 2329, as ascribed to the Prophet (*marfūʿ*); al-Bayhaqī, *al-Sunan al-Kubrā,* as ascribed to Ibn ʿAbbās (*mawqūf*), 9/3. Abū Dāwūd, no. 4700; al-Tirmidhī, no. 2160.

[الحج:١٤]، ﴿كَذَٰلِكَ ٱللَّهُ يَفۡعَلُ مَا يَشَآءُ ۝٤٠﴾ [آل عمران:٤٠]، فما يحدث في هذا الكون من حياة وموت، وغنىً وفقر، وإيمان وكفر، كل ذلك شاءه الله وأراده، شاء الخير وشاء الشر، وشاء الإيمان وشاء الكفر، فدخل في مشيئته كل شيء، ما شاء كان وما لم يشأ لم يكن.

(iii) The level of the divine will. Nothing happens in the universe except what Allah ﷻ wills and wants, as written on the Preserved Tablet, and according to His omniscience. Nothing happens outside of His will, and there is nothing inside of His kingdom that He does not want. **{Indeed, Allah does what He intends.} [Qur'ān 22:14] {Such is Allah; He does what He wills.} [Qur'ān 3:40]** All of what occurs in this universe of life and death, wealth and poverty, faith and disbelief are things that Allah ﷻ has willed. He wills both good and bad. He wills both faith and disbelief. So everything is included in the will of Allah ﷻ. What He wills is, and what He does not will is not.

المرتبة الرابعة: مرتبة الخلق والإيجاد، فما شاءه وأراده فإنه يوجده ويخلقه ﴿ٱللَّهُ خَٰلِقُ كُلِّ شَيۡءٖۖ وَهُوَ عَلَىٰ كُلِّ شَيۡءٖ وَكِيلٞ ۝٦٢﴾ [الزمر:٦٢] ﴿أَلَا لَهُ ٱلۡخَلۡقُ وَٱلۡأَمۡرُ﴾ [الأعراف:٥٤]، ﴿مَآ أَصَابَ مِن مُّصِيبَةٖ فِي ٱلۡأَرۡضِ وَلَا فِيٓ أَنفُسِكُمۡ إِلَّا فِي كِتَٰبٖ مِّن قَبۡلِ أَن نَّبۡرَأَهَآۚ﴾ [الحديد: ٢٢].

(iv) The level of creation and origination. What Allah ﷻ wills and wants, He brings into existence and creates. **{Allah is the Creator of all things, and He is, over all things, Disposer of affairs.} [Qur'ān 39:62] {His is the creation and the command.} [Qur'ān 7:54] {No disaster strikes upon the earth or among yourselves except that it is in a register before We bring it into being...} [Qur'ān 57: 22]**

وأدلة العلم أدلة كثيرة جداً.

There is much revealed evidence for the omniscience of Allah ﷻ.

ومن جملة الذي وصف الله به نفسه، العلم، فإنه سبحانه وتعالىٰ يعلم عدد من يدخل الجنة ومن يدخل النار، وذلك في علمه الأزلي.

One of the attributes that Allah ﷻ ascribes to Himself is omniscience, or knowledge (*ʿilm*). Allah ﷻ knows how many people will enter Jannah and how many will enter the Fire. That is part of His eternal knowledge.

وأن ما قدره الله تعالىٰ، لا يزاد فيه ولا ينقص، ومن ذلك: أنه يعلم أهل الجنة وأهل النار، ويعلم ما هم عاملون، نؤمن بذلك ونتجه إلىٰ العمل، ولا نتناقش في القضاء والقدر: كيف؟ ولماذا؟ وكيف يُحاسبُ علىٰ شيء قد قدره؟ إلىٰ آخر الهذيانات وإضاعة الأوقات، والاعتراض علىٰ الله عز وجل.

Whatever Allah ﷻ has predetermined does not increase or decrease. Among those things is that He knows the people of Jannah and the people of the Fire; He knows what they do. We believe in that and in accordance with it we act; not discussing *qadar* and *qaḍāʾ*. For example: asking 'how?', 'why?' or 'how can someone be held accountable for something that was predetermined?' and other forms of nonsense, time wasting, and argumentation against Allah ﷻ.

الواجب عليك فعل الطاعات واجتناب المعاصي، فليس شأن العبد التفتيش في سر الله عز وجل ومخاصمة الرب جل وعلا، إنما شأنه العمل، ولذلك لما أخبر النبي صلىٰ الله عليه وسلم أصحابه أن ما منهم من أحد إلا مكتوب مقعده من الجنة أو مقعده من النار، قالوا: يا رسول الله، ألا نتكل علىٰ كتابنا ونترك العمل؟ قال: «**لا، اعملوا فكل ميسر لما خُلق له**»، قال تعالىٰ: ﴿إِنَّ سَعْيَكُمْ لَشَتَّىٰ ۝٤ فَأَمَّا مَنْ أَعْطَىٰ وَاتَّقَىٰ ۝٥ وَصَدَّقَ بِالْحُسْنَىٰ ۝٦ فَسَنُيَسِّرُهُ لِلْيُسْرَىٰ ۝٧﴾ [الليل:٤-٧] السبب من العبد نفسه، إما أن يسعد وإما أن يشقىٰ ﴿وَأَمَّا مَنْ بَخِلَ وَاسْتَغْنَىٰ ۝٨ وَكَذَّبَ بِالْحُسْنَىٰ ۝٩ فَسَنُيَسِّرُهُ لِلْعُسْرَىٰ ۝١٠﴾ [الليل:٨-١٠] فالمطلوب منا العمل الصالح وترك العمل السيئ.

What one is obliged to do is to perform good deeds and abstain from sins, and it is not a person's business to investigate the mysteries of Allah ﷻ and to wrangle with Him, rather his task is to work. To this effect, when the Prophet ﷺ told his companions that there is not a single one of them whose place in Jannah or the Fire is not written, they said: "O Messenger of Allah, should we not rely on what was written and abandon deeds?" He said, "No. Do good deeds, for the path of each has been made easy for them.[41]" Allah ﷻ says: **{Indeed, your efforts are diverse. As for he who gives and fears Allah and believes in the best [reward], We will ease him towards ease.} [Qur'ān 92:4-7]** The cause emanates from the person himself. He is either going to be one of the blessed, or one of the wretched. **{But as for he who withholds and considers himself free of need and denies the best [reward], We will ease him toward difficulty.} [Qur'ān 92:8-10]** What is required of us is to do good deeds and leave bad ones.

أما الاحتجاج بالقضاء والقدر فليس بعذر، فإن الله عز وجل قد بين لنا الخير والشر فليس هناك عذر، فالناس يقعون في مشاكل بسبب دخولهم في أشياء ليست من اختصاصهم، فيقول: إن كان الله قد كتب لي أن أدخل الجنة دخلتها، وإن كان قد كتب لي أن أدخل النار دخلتها، ولا يعمل شيئًا.

Advancing *qaḍā'* and *qadar* as a pretext is not a sound excuse, because Allah ﷻ has made clear what is good and what is bad, so there are no excuses. People fall into trouble because of delving into matters that do not concern them. They say, for example, 'If Allah ﷻ has written that I will enter Jannah, I am going to enter it, and if He has written that I will enter the Fire, then I am going to enter it', and then they do not do any good deeds.

فيقال له: أنت لا تقول بهذا في نفسك، هل تقعد في البيت وتترك طلب الرزق وتقول: إن كان الله قد كتب لي رزقًا فسييسره لي؟ أو تخرج وتسعىٰ وتطلب الرزق؟ البهائم والطيور لا تقعد في أوكارها، بل تخرج وتطلب الرزق، وجاء في الحديث: «**لو أنكم تتوكلون علىٰ الله حق توكله لرزقكم كما يرزق الطير، تغدو خماصًا وتروح بطانًا**» فالله فطرها علىٰ طلب الرزق، وعلىٰ فعل الأسباب، وهي بهائم، وأنت رجل عاقل!.

It should be said to them, "You would not say so when it comes to your everyday life. Do you sit at home and leave seeking sustenance and say, 'If Allah ﷻ has written that I will receive sustenance, then He will make that easy for me', or would you go out to work and seek livelihood? Animals and

41 Al-Bukhārī, no. 6605; Muslim, no. 2647.

birds do not sit in their dens and nests but go out and seek sustenance". It has been related in a ḥadīth: "If only you placed due trust in Allah ﷻ, He would provide for you as He provides for birds, they go out hungry in the morning and come back with full bellies in the evening."[42] Allah has created birds in a way that they take the means and seek sustenance. Those are animals, and you are a rational human being!

وأيضـًا : لو أن أحداً سرق منك شيئـًا، هل تقول: هذا قضاء وقدر، أم تشتكيه؟ بل تشتكيه وتطلب وتخاصم، ولا تحتج بالقضاء والقدر!

Furthermore, if someone stole something from you, would you say, "This was predestined and preordained" or would you report it? Of course, you would report it and file a claim, and you would not advance predetermination as an argument.

المتن

(٨٧) وَكَذَلِكَ أَفْعالُهُمْ فِيما عَلِمَ مِنْهُمْ أَنْ يَفْعَلُوهُ.

(87) The same applies to the actions of people, as He knew what they would do.

الشرح

أي : علم أفعالهم في الأزل.

That is, He knew what they would do from eternity.

المتن

42 Aḥmad, *al-Musnad,* 1/30, 52; 'Abd ibn Ḥumayd, no. 10; al-Tirmidhī, no. 2344; Ibn Mājah, no. 4169. Al-Tirmidhī said: This ḥadīth is *ḥasan ṣaḥīḥ*. Shākir said that it is authentic in his edition of the *Musnad* of Aḥmad, no. 205, 370, 373.

(٨٨) وَكُلٌّ مُيَسَّرٌ لِما خُلِقَ لَهُ.

(88) The path of each shall be made easy for him.

الشرح

قال تعالىٰ: ﴿فَأَمَّا مَنْ أَعْطَىٰ وَٱتَّقَىٰ ۝ وَصَدَّقَ بِٱلْحُسْنَىٰ ۝ فَسَنُيَسِّرُهُۥ لِلْيُسْرَىٰ ۝ وَأَمَّا مَنۢ بَخِلَ وَٱسْتَغْنَىٰ ۝ وَكَذَّبَ بِٱلْحُسْنَىٰ ۝ فَسَنُيَسِّرُهُۥ لِلْعُسْرَىٰ ۝﴾ [الليل: ٥-١٠].

Allah the Most High says: **{As for he who gives and fears Allah and believes in the best [reward], We will ease him toward ease. But as for he who withholds and considers himself free of need and denies the best [reward], We will ease him toward difficulty.} [Qur'ān 92:5-10]**

المتن

(٨٩) والْأَعْمالُ بِالْخَواتِيمِ.

(89) It is the final deeds that dictate one's fate.

الشرح

(والأعمال بالخواتيم): الإنسان لا يغتر بعمله وإن كان أصلح الصالحين، بل يخاف من سوء العاقبة، ولا يحكم علىٰ أحد بأنه من أهل النار بموجب أفعاله؛ لأنه لا يدري بماذا يختم له، ويوضح ذلك حديث النبي صلىٰ الله عليه وسلم من حديث ابن مسعود: «**إن أحدكم ليجمع خلقه في بطن أمه أربعين يومـًا نطفة، ثم يكون علقة مثل ذلك، ثم يكون مضغة مثل ذلك، ثم يرسل إليه الملك فينفخ فيه الروح، ويؤمر بأربع كلمات: بكتب رزقه وأجله وعمله وشقي أو سعيد، وإن أحدكم ليعمل بعمل أهل الجنة حتىٰ ما يكون بينه وبينها إلا ذراع فيسبق عليه الكتاب فيعمل بعمل أهل النار فيدخلها، وإن أحدكم ليعمل بعمل أهل النار**

حتىٰ ما يكون بينه وبينها إلا ذراع فيعمل بعمل أهل الجنة فيدخلها».

It is the final deeds (*al-khawātīm*) that dictate one's fate. People should not be deceived by their good deeds, even if they are the most righteous of people. Rather, they should fear a bad ending, and no one is judged to be one of the people of the Fire based on their deeds, because their final deeds are not known. To clarify, it is related that Ibn Mas'ūd ﷺ related that the Prophet ﷺ said, "Each one of you is gathered in his mother's womb in the form of a drop for forty days. Then, he becomes an *'alaqah* for the same. Then, he becomes a piece of flesh for the same. Then, the angel is sent to him and breathes the spirit into him, and it is commanded to write four things: it writes his sustenance, his term, his deeds, and whether he is to be blessed or wretched. Verily, one of you keeps doing the deeds of the people of Jannah until there is nothing between him and it but a cubit, and so what was written comes to pass, and he does the deeds of the people of the Fire and enters it. And, verily, one of you keeps doing the deeds of the people of the Fire until there is nothing between him and it but a cubit, and so he does the deeds of the people of Jannah and enters it."[43]

فالإنسان يخاف من سوء الخاتمة، ولا يحكم علىٰ أحد بسوء الخاتمة؛ لأنه لا يدري بما يختم له. فالتوبة تجبُّ ما قبلها: ﴿قُل لِّلَّذِينَ كَفَرُوٓاْ إِن يَنتَهُواْ يُغۡفَرۡ لَهُم مَّا قَدۡ سَلَفَ ...﴾ [الأنفال: ٣٨].

So people should fear having a bad ending to life (*khātimah*), and no one should be judged as having had a bad ending because what their life concluded upon is not known. Repentance wipes out everything before it: **{Say to those who have disbelieved [that] if they cease, what has previously occurred will be forgiven for them.} [Qur'ān 8: 38]**

فالأعمال بالخواتيم، ولكن من لطف الله عز وجل بعباده أن من عاش علىٰ الخير فإنه يختم له بالخير، ومن عاش علىٰ الشر فإنه يختم له بالشر، فالإنسان يعمل الأسباب ويحسن الظن بالله عز وجل.

So it is the final deeds that dictate one's fate. However, out of Allah's ﷻ grace, those who live a good life are given a good ending, and those who live a bad life are given a bad ending. A person should take the necessary meas-

43 Al-Bukhārī, no. 8023; Muslim, no. 3462.

ures and think and expect good from Allah ﷻ.

وبعض الناس يقول: أتوب قبل الموت، فنقول له: وهل تدري متى تموت؟ يمكن أن تموت في لحظة لا يمكن معها التوبة، ولا تدري هل التوبة مقبولة أم لا؛ لأن التوبة لها شروط.

Some people say, "I will repent before death". We say to them, "Do you know when you are going to die? You could die at a moment when repentance is not possible, and you do not know whether your repentance will be accepted or not, because there are conditions for repentance."

المتن

(٩٠) والسَّعِيدُ مَنْ سَعِدَ بِقَضاءِ اللهِ، والشَّقِيُّ مَنْ شَقِيَ بِقَضاءِ اللهِ.

(90) The fortunate are those who are fortunate by Allah's decree, and the wretched are those who are wretched by Allah's decree.

الشرح

لا يشقى بقضاء الله عز وجل، إنما يشقى بعمله الذي قدره الله له. من قدر الله أنه يشقى أو يسعد فسييسره له.

A person is not wretched by Allah's ﷻ decree but rather by his deeds which Allah has decreed for him. If Allah decrees anyone to be either fortunate (*sa'īd*) or wretched (*shaqīy*), He makes that path easy for them.

المتن

(٩١) وَأَصْلُ الْقَدَرِ سِرُّ اللهِ تَعالَىٰ فِي خَلْقِهِ.

(91) Allah has kept the exact nature of the *qadar* (predestination)

hidden from His creation;

الشرح

أي: لن تصل إلىٰ سره، مهما حاولت التفتيش في القضاء والقدر. فلا تكلف نفسك، ولكن آمن بالقضاء والقدر، واعمل الأعمال الصالحة واجتنب الأعمال السيئة، وأما أن تبحث عن أسرار القدر فهذا ليس من اختصاصك، ولا هو من شأنك، وما كلفت به.

I.e. no one can solve its mystery, no matter how hard they tried to study *qadar*, so do not burden yourself trying to do so. Instead, have faith in it and do good deeds and abstain from bad deeds. Searching for the mysteries of *qadar*, on the other hand, is none of your concern or business, and you are not commanded to do so.

المتن

(٩٢) لَمْ يَطَّلِعْ عَلَىٰ ذَلِكَ مَلَكٌ مُقَرَّبٌ، وَلا نَبِيٌّ مُرْسَلٌ.

(92) Neither a high-ranking angel nor a messenger sent to man has been given knowledge of it.

الشرح

هذا من شأن الله عز وجل، ومن الغيب الذي لا يعلمه إلا الله، ولا يعلمه غيره، لا الملائكة ولا الأنبياء ولا غيرهم، وأفضل الرسل يقول: ﴿وَلَوْ كُنتُ أَعْلَمُ ٱلْغَيْبَ لَأَسْتَكْثَرْتُ مِنَ ٱلْخَيْرِ﴾ [الأعراف:١٨٨].

This is Allah's ﷻ affair, and a matter of the unseen which no one (neither the angels, nor the Prophets, nor anyone else) knows but Allah ﷻ. In fact, the most superior of all Messengers ﷺ said:**{And if I knew the unseen, I could have acquired much wealth...} [Qur'ān 7:188]**

المتن

(٩٣) والتَّعَمُّقُ والنَّظَرُ فِي ذَلِكَ ذَرِيعَةُ الْخِذْلانِ، وَسُلَّمُ الْحِرْمانِ، وَدَرَجَةُ الطُّغْيانِ.

(93) Delving into this and reflecting too much upon it is only a means to disappointment, a ladder of non-attainment, and a class of transgression.

الشرح

هذا كلام عظيم، أي التعمق في القضاء والقدر ومسائله، وإشغال الوقت والنفس والقلب، مما يورث الشكوك ويخذل عن العمل، فهذا من اللعب والخذلان.

These are great words. That is to say, 'scrutiny' about *qaḍā'* and *qadar*, and about the issues associated with them, and occupying one's time, energy, and heart is amongst that which inherently causes doubts and diminishes deeds, all of this is in vain and leads to disappointment.

إذا خذل الله العبد شغله في هذه الأمور، وإذا أكرم الله العبد شغله في طاعته، واغتنام وقته.

When Allah ﷻ forsakes His slaves, He keeps them occupied with such matters, and when He honours His slaves, He keeps them occupied with obedience and allows them to take advantage of their time.

فنحن لنا حدود لا نتعداها، فالله ما كلفنا بالبحث في القضاء والقدر، ولكن كلفنا باعتقاد ذلك بالعمل الصالح وترك العمل السيئ.

We have limits that we should not transgress. Allah ﷻ has not commanded us to study *qaḍā'* and *qadar*, but He has commanded us to believe in them, to do righteous deeds, and to refrain from bad deeds.

المتن

(٩٤) فالْحَذَرَ كُلَّ الْحَذَرِ مِنْ ذَلِكَ نَظَرًا وَفِكْرًا وَوَسْوَسَةً.

(94) So be very careful of over-analysing and over-thinking about it, or allowing satanic whispers to assail you;

الشرح

أي احذر من هذه الأمور، والنظر في هذه الأمور، والتفكير فيها، والوسوسة وهي: التردد والشك، اترك هذه الأمور، وسد هذا الباب أصلاً.

I.e. beware of such matters, and beware of speculating about such matters, and also of devilish whispers, in other words, indecisiveness and doubts. Leave those things and put an end to them at their roots.

❀❀❀

المتن

(٩٥) فَإِنَّ اللهَ تَعالَىٰ طَوَىٰ عِلْمَ الْقَدَرِ عَنْ أَنامِهِ،

(95) Because Allah has kept the knowledge of *qadar* hidden from mankind;

الشرح

هذا تأكيد لما سبق (**القدر سر الله تعالىٰ**) ومعنىٰ طوىٰ: أخفىٰ، فطوىٰ الله هذه المعلومات عن خلقه؛ لأنه ليس لهم فيها مصلحة.

This emphasises the aforementioned, namely that Allah ﷻ has kept the exact nature of *qadar* hidden from His creation. This is because it is not of any benefit to them.

❀❀❀

المتن

(٩٦) وَنَهاهُمْ عَنْ مَرامِهِ.

(96) And He forbade them from seeking it;

الشرح

عن مرام القدر أن يبحثوا فيه، والنبي صلىٰ الله عليه وسلم غضب لما رأىٰ الصحابة يتساءلون في هذا فقال: «أبهذا أُمرتم؟ أم لهذا خُلقتم؟».

That is, from the desire to study *qadar*. The Prophet ﷺ was angered when he saw some of the Companions posing questions to each other about *qadar*, and he said: "Is this what you were commanded to do?" or, "Is this what you were created for?"[44]

المتن

(٩٧) كَمَا قَالَ اللهُ تَعَالَىٰ فِي كِتَابِهِ ﴿لَا يُسْأَلُ عَمَّا يَفْعَلُ وَهُمْ يُسْأَلُونَ﴾ [الأنبياء: ٢٣]،

(97) As the Most High has said in His Book: *"He is not questioned about what He does, but they will be questioned."*

الشرح

أنت لا تسأل الله ولا تناقشه عن أفعاله وعن قضائه وقدره، تأدب مع الله؛ لأنك عبد، فلا تتدخل في شؤونه جل وعلا، فالله لا يسأل عما يفعل؛ لأن الله لا يفعل شيئًا إلا لحكمة، والحكمة قد تظهر وقد تخفىٰ علينا، فنؤمن بأن الله لا يفعل شيئًا عبثًا؛ إنما يفعله لحكمة، سواءً ظهرت لنا أو لم تظهر.

---

44 It is related that ʿAmr ibn Shuʿayb related that his father related that his grandfather said: "The Messenger of Allah ﷺ came out one day and people were speaking about *qadar*, and it was as if pomegranate seeds had burst on his face because of anger. He said: 'Why do you use one part of the Book of Allah against another? This is what led to the doom of the nations who came before you.'" ʿAbdullāh ibn ʿAmr ؓ said: "I was never so happy to have missed a gathering with the Messenger of Allah ﷺ as I was to have missed that gathering." Aḥmad, 2/178, 181, 185 & 195; Ibn Mājah, no. 85. Aḥmad Shākir said that it is authentic (*ṣaḥīḥ*) in his edition of *al-Musnad* by Aḥmad (no. 6668).

You should not question Allah about or raise any objections to His actions or what He has preordained and predestined. Behave properly with Allah, as you are a slave, so you should not get involved in His affairs. Allah is not to be questioned over what He does, as Allah ﷻ does not do anything without wisdom, but this wisdom could be either apparent or hidden from us.

فالإنسان مسؤول عن عمله، ليس مسؤولاً عن أعمال الله عز وجل، فاعتن بما أنت مسؤول عنه يوم القيامة، وهو عملك، فعلى العبد التسليم لله.

People are responsible for their actions and not the actions of Allah ﷻ, so have concern for what you will be questioned about on the Day of Judgment. It is imperative for people to submit to Allah ﷻ.

المتن

(٩٨) فَمَنْ سَأَلَ: لِمَ فَعَلَ؟ فَقَدْ رَدَّ حُكْمَ الْكِتَابِ.

(98) So, whoever asks, 'Why did He do so?' He has indeed rejected a judgment of the Book.

الشرح

أي قال: لم فعل الله كذا؟ لم قدّر الله كذا وكذا؟ فمن قال هذا، فقد رد حكم الكتاب؛ لأن الله يقول: ﴿لَا يُسْـَٔلُ عَمَّا يَفْعَلُ﴾ [الأنبياء:٢٣].

That is, if anyone asks, "Why has Allah done so?" or "Why has Allah predetermined so?" then they have indeed rejected the judgment of the Book, because Allah ﷻ has said: **{He is not questioned about what He does.} [Qurʾān 21:23]**

المتن

(٩٩) وَمَنْ رَدَّ حُكْمَ الْكِتابِ كانَ مِنَ الْكافِرِينَ.

(99) And whoever rejects a judgment of the Book is among the disbelievers.

الشرح

فمن رد حكم الكتاب والسنة، واعترض على ذلك، وذهب إلى العقل والتفكير صار من الكافرين؛ لأن الإيمان بالكتاب والسنة هما ركنان من أركان الإيمان.

Anyone who rejects the judgment of the Qur'ān and Sunnah, objects to it and instead turns to the intellect and thoughts is among the disbelievers[45], because belief in the Qur'ān and Sunnah are two pillars of faith.

المتن

(١٠٠) فَهَذا جُمْلَةُ ما يَحْتاجُ إِلَيْهِ مَنْ هُوَ مُنَوَّرٌ قَلْبُهُ مِنْ أَوْلِياءِ اللهِ تَعالَى،

(100) This is a summary of what is needed by one whose heart has been given light, one who is among the *awliyā'* (allies) of Allah, the Most High.

الشرح

أي يحتاجه في أمور القضاء والقدر، فأنت تؤمن بالقدر ومراتبه الأربع؛ تؤمن بتفاصيلها التي جاءت في الكتاب والسنة، ولا تدخل في المناقشات والاعتراضات، بل تعمل العمل الصالح والأسباب المناسبة.

That is, what is needed in matters of *qaḍā'* and *qadar*. So, you should believe in *qadar* and the four levels of it, and you should believe in its details related in the Qur'ān and Sunnah, and you should not pose any objections or advance any arguments but instead do righteous deeds and seek the proper causes.

45 'Ā'ishah ﵂ related that the Prophet ﷺ said: "The most hated men to Allah are those who are most vehement in their disputes." Al-Bukhārī, no. 2457; Muslim, no. 2668.

المتن

(١٠١) وَهِيَ دَرَجَةُ الرَّاسِخِينَ فِي الْعِلْمِ.

(101) And this is what constitutes the level of those firmly grounded in knowledge;

الشرح

الراسخون، يعني: الثابتين في العلم، الذين عندهم علم راسخ، وليس عندهم شكوك ولا جهل، فهم يؤمنون بالقضاء والقدر، ويعملون الأعمال الصالحة، ويتركون الأعمال السيئة، ولا يتدخلون مع الله في سر من أسراره، ولا يناقشونه ويعترضون عليه، هذا شأن الراسخين في العلم، وأما الجهّال فيدخلون في ضلالات وأمور ابتدعوها.

Firmly grounded (*rāsikhūn*) means having strong, unwavering knowledge – those whose knowledge is firm, and who don't have doubts or ignorance. They are those who believe in *qaḍā'* and *qadar*, and do righteous deeds and refrain from doing bad ones. They do not get involved in matters that Allah ﷻ has kept hidden, nor raise objections or advance arguments against Him. The ignorant, on the other hand, fall into error and matters that they innovate.

المتن

(١٠٢) لِأَنَّ الْعِلْمَ عِلْمانِ: عِلْمٌ فِي الْخَلْقِ مَوْجُودٌ، وَعِلْمٌ فِي الْخَلْقِ مَفْقُودٌ.

(102) As knowledge is of two types: knowledge that is clear to the creation and knowledge that has been kept hidden from them.

الشرح

العلم علمان:

There are two kinds of knowledge:

علم استأثر به الله، فلا يعلمه إلا هو سبحانه وتعالىٰ، وهو علم الغيب.

Knowledge that Allah ﷻ alone possesses, with the exclusion of others; namely knowledge of the unseen (*'ilm al-ghayb*).

وعلم في الخلق موجود، علّمهم الله إياه، وهو ما لهم فيه مصلحة وذلك بما أنزل الله من الكتاب، وما أرسل به الرسول ﴿وَيُعَلِّمُهُمُ ٱلْكِتَٰبَ وَٱلْحِكْمَةَ﴾ [البقر:١٢٩] الكتاب: القرآن، والحكمة: السنة، وقيل: الفقه في دين الله فالله علمنا والرسول علمنا ﴿وَيُعَلِّمُكُم مَّا لَمْ تَكُونُوا۟ تَعْلَمُونَ ﴿١٥١﴾﴾ [البقر:١٥١].

Knowledge which Allah ﷻ has taught created beings. This is the knowledge that is to their benefit. He taught them by sending down the Book and sending the Messengers. Allah ﷻ says: **{And teach them the Book and wisdom.} [Qur'ān 2:129]** The 'Book' is the Qur'ān, and 'wisdom' is the Sunnah, but it has also been said that 'wisdom' is to have understanding of Allah's religion. Allah has taught us and the Messenger of Allah ﷺ has taught us: **{And teaching you that which you did not know.}" [Qur'ān 2:151]**

❁❁❁

المتن

(١٠٣) فَإِنْكارُ الْعِلْمِ الْمَوْجُودِ كُفْرٌ، وادِّعاءُ الْعِلْمِ الْمَفْقُودِ كُفْرٌ.

(103) To deny the knowledge that Allah taught us is disbelief, and to claim possession of the knowledge that He kept hidden from us is also disbelief.

الشرح

إنكار العلم الشرعي وما فيه من الأمر والنهي والإخبار عن الماضي والمستقبل،

إنكاره كفر.

To reject prescribed knowledge, which includes what is commanded and forbidden, and what has been told about past and future events, is disbelief.

وادعاء علم الغيب كفر ﴿قُل لَّا يَعْلَمُ مَن فِي ٱلسَّمَٰوَٰتِ وَٱلْأَرْضِ ٱلْغَيْبَ إِلَّا ٱللَّهُ﴾ [النمل:٦٥]، وأكمل الخلق عليه الصلاة والسلام يقول: ﴿وَلَوْ كُنتُ أَعْلَمُ ٱلْغَيْبَ لَٱسْتَكْثَرْتُ مِنَ ٱلْخَيْرِ﴾ [الأعراف:١٨٨] فالنبي عليه الصلاة والسلام لا يعلم الغيب إلا ما علمه الله ﴿وَلَا يُحِيطُونَ بِشَيْءٍ مِّنْ عِلْمِهِۦٓ إِلَّا بِمَا شَآءَ﴾ [البقرة:٢٥٥].

To claim to have knowledge of the unseen is disbelief: **{Say, 'None in the heavens and earth knows the unseen except Allah, and they do not perceive when they will be resurrected.'} [Qurʾān 27:65]** The most perfect of all creation ﷺ said: **{And if I knew the unseen, I could have acquired much wealth.} [Qurʾān 7:188]** Thus, the Prophet ﷺ does not know anything from the unseen besides what Allah taught him. Allah says: **{And they encompass not a thing of His knowledge except for what He wills.} [Qurʾān 2:255]**

المتن

(١٠٤) وَلا يَثْبُتُ الإِيمانُ إِلّا بِقَبُولِ الْعِلْمِ الْمَوْجُودِ، وَتَرْكِ طَلَبِ الْعِلْمِ الْمَفْقُودِ.

(104) Faith is only affirmed by accepting the knowledge that Allah taught us and not seeking the knowledge that He kept hidden from us.

الشرح

لا يثبت الإيمان إلا بقبول العلم الموجود، وهو علم الكتاب والسنة، وترك علم الغيب لله ﴿فَقُلْ إِنَّمَا ٱلْغَيْبُ لِلَّهِ﴾

Faith is only affirmed by accepting the knowledge Allah taught us, namely the knowledge of the Book and the Sunnah, and leaving the knowledge of the unseen to Allah. Allah says: **{The unseen is only for Allah [to admin-**

ister].}

المتن

(١٠٥) وَنُؤْمِنُ بِاللَّوْحِ والْقَلَمِ، وَبِجَمِيعِ ما فِيهِ قَدْ رُقِمَ.

(105) We believe in the *Lawḥ* (Tablet) and the *Qalam* (Pen) and all that was written on it.

الشرح

هذا تابع لما سبق من الكلام عن القضاء والقدر، وقد سبق أن من مراتب الإيمان بالقضاء والقدر: الإيمان بما كتب في اللوح المحفوظ، وأن الله لما علم كل شيء كتب ذلك في اللوح المحفوظ، وذلك أن الله خلق الخلق، وأول ما خلق القلم، فقال له: «اكتب»، قال: ما أكتب؟ قال: «أكتب ما هو كائن إلىٰ يوم القيامة»، فجرىٰ القلم بأمر الله بكتابة ما هو كائن إلىٰ يوم القيامة، كما جاء في الحديث.

This is a continuation of the discussion about *qaḍāʾ* and *qadar*. As mentioned earlier, among the levels of faith in *qadar* is faith in what was written in *al-Lawḥ al-Maḥfūẓ* (the Preserved Tablet) and faith in the fact that after knowing all things, Allah ﷻ wrote them on *al-Lawḥ al-Maḥfūẓ*. In other words, Allah ﷻ created the creations and the first thing He created was the Pen. He said to it, "Write." It said, "What should I write?" He said, "Write all that will be until the Day of Judgment." And so, by the command of Allah ﷻ, the Pen wrote all that will be until the Day of Judgment, as related in the *ḥadīth*.[46]

ولا يعلم كيفية اللوح والقلم إلا الله، وهما مخلوقان من مخلوقات الله عز وجل، نؤمن بذلك، ولذلك قال المؤلف: (نؤمن باللوح والقلم وبما فيه قد رقم)؛ يعني

46 Abū Dāwūd, no 4700; al-Tirmidhī, no. 2160; Abū Yaʿlā, no. 2329, as attributed to the Messenger of Allah ﷺ; al-Bayhaqī, *al-Sunan;* 9/3, as attributed to one of the Companions, but it is effectively attributed to the Messenger of Allah ﷺ.

اللوح المحفوظ، والكتابة فيه.

No one knows the exact nature of *al-Lawḥ al-Maḥfūẓ* and the Pen besides Allah. They are both created things and are two of Allah's ﷻ creations. We believe in that. To that effect, the author said: "We believe in the *Lawḥ* (Tablet) and the *Qalam* (Pen) and all that was written on it", that is, the Preserved Tablet, and the writing on it.

وهذه هي المرتبة الثانية من مراتب الإيمان بالقضاء والقدر، وهي: الإيمان بالكتابة في اللوح المحفوظ.

This is the second level of belief in *qaḍāʾ* and *qadar*, namely belief in what is written in the Preserved Tablet.

المتن

(١٠٦) فَلَوِ اجْتَمَعَ الْخَلْقُ كُلُّهُمْ عَلَىٰ شَيْءٍ كَتَبَهُ اللهُ تَعالَىٰ فِيهِ أَنَّهُ كائِنٌ؛ لِيَجْعَلُوهُ غَيْرَ كائِنٍ لَمْ يَقْدِرُوا عَلَيْهِ، وَلَوِ اجْتَمَعُوا كُلُّهُمْ عَلَىٰ شَيْءٍ لَمْ يَكْتُبْهُ اللهُ تَعالَىٰ فِيهِ؛ لِيَجْعَلُوهُ كائِنًا لَمْ يَقْدِرُوا عَلَيْهِ.

(106) So, if the entire creation got together to prevent something occurring that Allah the Most High has written would occur, they would not be able to do so. And if they got together to make something occur that Allah had not written would occur, they would not be able to do so.

الشرح

الكتابة التي كتبها الله تعالىٰ في اللوح المحفوظ لا يقدر أحد علىٰ تغييرها، فلو اجتمع الخلق علىٰ أن يغيروا شيئًا كتبه الله لما استطاعوا، ولو اجتمعوا علىٰ أن يوجدوا شيئًا لم يكتبه الله في اللوح المحفوظ لم يوجدوه، كما جاء ذلك في حديث ابن عباس لما قال له النبي صلىٰ الله عليه وسلم: «**واعلم أن الخلق**

لو اجتمعوا علىٰ أن ينفعوك بشيء لم ينفعوك إلا بشيء قد كتبه الله لك، ولو اجتمعوا علىٰ أن يضروك بشيء لم يضروك إلا بشيء قد كتبه الله عليك، رفعت الأقلام وجفت الصحف».

No one is able to change what is written in *al-Lawḥ al-Maḥfūẓ*, so if all of creation got together to change something that Allah ﷻ has written, they would not be able to do so. Similarly, if they got together to bring something about that Allah has not written in *al-Lawḥ al-Maḥfūẓ*, they would not bring it about. It is related in a *ḥadīth* of Ibn 'Abbās that the Prophet ﷺ said to him, "And know that if the creation were to come together to cause you benefit, they would not benefit you unless Allah had already written so, and if they were to come together to cause you harm, they would not harm you unless Allah had already written so. The pens have been lifted, and the pages have dried."[47]

فلا تغيير ولا تبديل لما كتبه الله جلا وعلا في اللوح المحفوظ.

So there is no possibility of going against what Allah ﷻ has written in the Preserved Tablet.

المتن

(١٠٧) جَفَّ الْقَلَمُ بِما هُوَ كائِنٌ إِلَىٰ يَوْمِ الْقِيامَةِ، وَما أَخْطَأَ الْعَبْدَ لَمْ يَكُنْ لِيُصِيبَهُ، وَما أَصابَهُ لَمْ يَكُنْ لِيُخْطِئَهُ.

(107) The Pen has dried, having written down all that will take place until the Day of Judgment. What someone did not receive was not meant for him, and what has come to him would never have passed him by.

الشرح

47 Al-Tirmidhī, no. 2521; Aḥmad, 1/293; al-Ḥākim, 3/541. Al-Tirmidhī said, "*ḥadīth ḥasan ṣaḥīḥ*." Al-Ḥākim said, "This *ḥadīth* is *'ālī*." [T] *'Ālī* usually means a short line of transmission to the Prophet ﷺ.

هذا معنىٰ الإيمان بالقضاء والقدر، أن تعلم أنه لن يصيبك إلا ما كتبه الله عليك، وما أصابك لم يكن ليخطئك، وما أخطأك لم يكن ليصيبك.

This is what it means to believe in *qaḍāʾ* and *qadar*: that you know that nothing happens to you except what Allah has written for you, and that anything that happens to you was not to pass you by, and what passes you by was not to happen to you.

فإذا أصابتك مصيبة مما تكره، فإنك تعلم أن هذا مكتوب في اللوح المحفوظ، ولابد أن يقع، فتتسلىٰ بذلك عن الجزع والسخط، وتؤمن بالله عز وجل.

If some misfortune that you dislike happens to you, then you know that it is written in *al-Lawḥ al-Maḥfūẓ*, and that it is inevitable. Thus you find comfort in that and you neither grieve nor become discontented; you just have faith in Allah the Almighty.

وما أخطأك لم يكن ليصيبك، لو حرصت علىٰ طلب شيء وبذلت كل وسعك وجهدك فلن تحصل عليه، فإذا فعلت السبب وبذلت كل شيء ولم تحصل عليه، فإنك تسلم وتؤمن بالقضاء والقدر، ولا تنزعج ويكون عندك هواجس وهموم، فالنبي صلىٰ الله عليه وسلم يقول: «**احرص علىٰ ما ينفعك، واستعن بالله ولا تعجزن، فإن أصابك شيء فلا تقل: لو أنّي فعلت كذا وكذا لكان كذا وكذا، ولكن قل : قدّر الله وما شاء فعل، فإن (لو) تفتح عمل الشيطان**».

And whatever passes you by was not meant to happen to you. Even if you were keen on getting something, and you put forth all of your energy and resources, you would not attain it. So, if you took the means and put forth your utmost effort and did not attain it, you should accept that and have faith in *qadar*. You should not feel disturbed and have concerns and worries, as the Prophet ﷺ said: "Strive for what benefits you, seek help from Allah, and do not be weakened. If something happens to you, do not say, 'if only I did such and such, then such and such would have happened'. Rather, say, 'Allah has destined (it), and He does what He wills', for 'if' makes way for the work of the devil."[48]

48 Muslim, no. 2664.

إذا علمت هذا هان عليك الأمر، ولا يحصل منك جزع، ولا تحسر، الأمور بيده سبحانه، نعم أنت تفعل الأسباب وتحرص علىٰ ما ينفعك، ولكن النتائج من لدن الله عز وجل، وما تدري ما الخيرة؟ فلا يعطيك الله عز وجل ذلك الشيء؛ لأنك لو حصلت عليه يكون عليك منه ضرر، فالله يعلم، وأنت لا تعلم، عليك أن ترضىٰ بقضاء الله وقدره.

If you know this, then matters become easy for you, and you do not grieve or regret. All matters are in Allah's ﷻ hands. Indeed, you should take the means and strive after what benefits you, but the results are from Allah ﷻ, and you do not know what is to your best interest. Allah ﷻ may not have given you that thing, because you might have been harmed if you had got it. Allah knows, and you do not, so you have to be content with what Allah has decreed and destined.

وفي القرآن الكريم يقول الله لنبيه صلىٰ الله عليه وسلم: ﴿قُل لَّن يُصِيبَنَآ إِلَّا مَا كَتَبَ ٱللَّهُ لَنَا هُوَ مَوْلَىٰنَا وَعَلَى ٱللَّهِ فَلْيَتَوَكَّلِ ٱلْمُؤْمِنُونَ ٥١﴾ [التوبة:٥١].

In the Noble Qur'ān, Allah says to His Prophet ﷺ: **{Say, 'Never will we be struck except by what Allah has decreed for us; He is our protector.' And upon Allah let the believers rely.}** [Qur'ān 9:51]

ويقول رداً علىٰ الكفار لما قالوا في شأن الذين قتلوا في يوم أحد: ﴿لَّوْ كَانُواْ عِندَنَا مَا مَاتُواْ وَمَا قُتِلُواْ﴾ [آل عمران:١٥٦]، قال عز وجل: ﴿قُل لَّوْ كُنتُمْ فِى بُيُوتِكُمْ لَبَرَزَ ٱلَّذِينَ كُتِبَ عَلَيْهِمُ ٱلْقَتْلُ إِلَىٰ مَضَاجِعِهِمْ﴾ [آل عمران:١٥٤].

He said in response to what the disbelievers said about those who were killed in the Battle of Uḥud: **{If they had been with us, they would not have died or have been killed.}** [Qur'ān 3:156] Allah ﷻ says: **{Say, 'Even if you had been inside your houses, those decreed to be killed would have come out to their death beds.'}** [Qur'ān 3:154]

فما كُتب علىٰ الإنسان لابد من نفاذه فيه، ولو تحرز وتحصن وعمل من الاحتياطات ما عمل، لم يمنعه ذلك من قضاء الله وقدره، قال تعالىٰ: ﴿أَيْنَمَا تَكُونُواْ يُدْرِككُّمُ ٱلْمَوْتُ وَلَوْ كُنتُمْ فِى بُرُوجٍ مُّشَيَّدَةٍ﴾ [النساء:٧٨].

Whatever is written for someone must come to pass for them. No matter how many protective measures they take, it will not prevent them from the decree and *qadar* of Allah. Allah ﷻ says: **{Wherever you may be, death will overtake you, even if you should be within towers of lofty construction.} [Qur'ān 4:78]**

المتن

(١٠٨) وَعَلَىٰ الْعَبْدِ أَنْ يَعْلَمَ أَنَّ اللهَ قَدْ سَبَقَ عِلْمُهُ فِي كُلِّ كائِنٍ مِنْ خَلْقِهِ.

(108) Allah's slaves must know that He already knows everything that will happen in His creation.

الشرح

هذه هي المرتبة الأولىٰ من مراتب الإيمان بالقضاء والقدر: علىٰ العبد أن يؤمن ويعتقد أن الله علم ما كان وما لم يكن بعلمه الأزلي، الذي هو موصوف به أبداً وأزلاً، علم الأشياء كلها بعلمه المحيط قبل وقوعها، فلابد من اعتقاد ذلك.

This is the first level of faith in *qadar*, namely to affirm faith in and believe that Allah ﷻ knows what will take place and what will not with His eternal omniscience, with which He is attributed eternally and infinitely. He knew all things with His all-encompassing knowledge even before they happen. It is necessary to believe in this.

المتن

(١٠٩) فَقَدَّرَ ذَلِكَ تَقْدِيرًا مُحْكَمًا مُبْرَمًا.

(109) He decreed it precisely and decisively.

الشرح

عَلِمَهُ سبحانه وتعالىٰ وقدّره ﴿وَخَلَقَ كُلَّ شَيْءٍ فَقَدَّرَهُۥ تَقْدِيرًا ۝﴾ [الفرقان:٢].

He knew it and destined it. Allah ﷻ says: **{...and has created each thing and determined it with [precise] determination.} [Qur'ān 25:2]**

فالأمور ليست فوضىٰ أو ليست لها ضوابط، كلها مرتبة ومنضبطة بقضاء الله وقدره وكتابته، والله منزه عن الفوضىٰ والعبث.

Thus, matters are neither chaotic nor without control. Everything is arranged and controlled by the decree and determination of Allah ﷻ, and is written by Him. Allah ﷻ transcends any kind of chaos and frivolity.

المتن

(١١٠) لَيْسَ فِيهِ نَاقِضٌ وَلا مُعَقِّبٌ، وَلا مُزِيلٌ وَلا مُغَيِّرٌ، وَلا نَاقِصٌ وَلا زَائِدٌ مِنْ خَلْقِهِ فِي سَماواتِهِ وَأَرْضِهِ.

(110) None from His creation on either the heavens or the earth can undo it, overturn it, remove it, change it, take from it, or add to it.

الشرح

لا أحد يتصرف، فيغير ما قضاه الله وقدّره، لا راد لقضائه ولا معقب لحكمه ﴿وَٱللَّهُ يَحْكُمُ لَا مُعَقِّبَ لِحُكْمِهِۦ﴾ [الرعد:٤١]. فلا أحد ينقص شيئًا من قضاء الله، ولا يزيد شيئًا أبدًا، هذا شيء قضي منه وانتهىٰ منه.

No one can do anything to change what Allah ﷻ has decreed and determined. No one can deny His decree or overturn His judgment. **{And Allah decides; there is no adjuster of His decision.} [Qur'ān 13:41]** No one can ever take away from or add to anything that Allah ﷻ has decreed. It is something that Allah has already decided and it is finalized.

إذا اعتقد المسلم ذلك أراحه من كثير من الشكوك والأوهام، ولكن ليس معنىٰ ذلك أنه يتكل علىٰ القضاء والقدر والكتاب، ويترك العمل، هو مأمور بالعمل

وطلب الرزق وفعل الأسباب، هذا من ناحية العمل، وأما من ناحية النتائج فهي بيد الله عز وجل.

If a Muslim believes in the aforementioned, then he will be relieved of much doubts and misconceptions. However, this does not mean that someone should rely on *qadar* and what was written and abandon action.[49] Rather a Muslim is commanded to take action, seek sustenance and take the means. This is as far as action is concerned. All results, on the other hand, are in Allah's ﷻ hands.

المتن

(١١١) وَذَٰلِكَ مِنْ عَقْدِ الْإِيمانِ، وَأُصُولِ الْمَعْرِفَةِ،

(111) This is one of the tenets of faith and a principle of knowledge [of Allah];

الشرح

هذه العقيدة، عقيدة القضاء والقدر، من عقيدة الإيمان بالله سبحانه وتعالى، فالذي لا يكون مؤمناً بالقضاء والقدر لا يكون مؤمناً بالله جل وعلا، بل كان متنقصاً لله عز وجل، فالإيمان به من العقيدة وليس من الأشياء الثانوية أو الفرعية، فالإيمان بالقضاء والقدر من صميم العقيدة، وهو ركن من أركان الإيمان، كما قال عليه الصلاة والسلام: «**الإيمان أن تؤمن بالله وملائكته وكتبه**

49 It is related that 'Alī ﷺ said: "We were at a funeral in Baqī' al-Gharqad, and the Prophet ﷺ came to us and sat, and we sat around him, and he had a small stick, and he lowered his head and began scraping the ground with his stick. Then, he said: 'There is not one among you, nor any soul that has been breathed, whose place in Jannah and the Fire has not been written, and who has not been written as blessed or wretched.' One man said: 'O Messenger of Allah, should we not then rely on what was written and stop doing deeds? Those of us who are among the blessed are destined to do the deeds of the blessed, and those of us who are among the wretched are destined to have the deeds of the wretched.' He said: 'The deeds of the blessed have been made easy for them, and the deeds of the wretched have been made easy for them.' Then, he read: ***{As for he who gives and fears Allah...}*** [al-Bukhārī, no. 1362; Muslim, no. 2647]

ورسله واليوم الآخر، وتؤمن بالقدر خيره وشره».

This doctrine, the doctrine of *qaḍā'* and *qadar*, is one of the tenets of faith in Allah ﷻ. If someone is not a believer in *qadar*, then he is not a believer in Allah ﷻ and is in fact undervaluing Allah, Glorified be He. Belief in that is one of the fundamentals of creed, rather than a secondary or subsidiary matter. Faith in *qaḍā'* and *qadar* lies at the core of the faith and is one of its pillars, as the Prophet ﷺ said: "Faith is to believe in Allah, His angels, His books, His Messengers, the Last Day, and in *qadar*, its good and bad."[50]

المتن

(١١٢) والاعْتِرافِ بِتَوْحِيدِ اللهِ تَعالَىٰ وَرُبُوبِيَّتِهِ، كَما قالَ تَعالَىٰ فِي كِتابِهِ ﴿وَخَلَقَ كُلَّ شَيْءٍ فَقَدَّرَهُ تَقْدِيرًا﴾ [الفرقان: ٢]، وَقالَ تَعالَىٰ ﴿وَكانَ أَمْرُ اللهِ قَدَرًا مَقْدُورًا﴾ [الأحزاب: ٣٨].

(112) And it is part of acknowledging the *tawḥīd* (Oneness) and *rubūbiyyah* (Lordship) of Allah; as the Most High says in His Book: *{...and [He] has created each thing and determined it with [precise] determination.}* [Qur'ān 25:2] Allah also says: *{And ever is the command of Allah a destiny decreed.}* [Qur'ān 33:38]

الشرح

الإيمان بالقضاء والقدر يدخل في توحيد الربوبية؛ لأنه من أفعال الله جل وعلا، فمن جحد القضاء والقدر لم يكن مؤمنًا بتوحيد الربوبية.

Faith in *qaḍā'* and *qadar* is a part of the belief in *tawḥīd al-rubūbiyyah* (Oneness of Lordship), because it has to do with the actions of Allah ﷻ. Therefore, if someone rejects predetermination then he is not a believer in *tawḥīd al-rubūbiyyah*.

﴿وَخَلَقَ كُلَّ شَيْءٍ فَقَدَّرَهُۥ تَقْدِيرًا ۝٢﴾ [الفرقان:٢] ﴿وَكَانَ أَمْرُ ٱللَّهِ قَدَرًا مَّقْدُورًا ۝٣٨﴾

---

50 Al-Bukhārī, no. 50; Muslim, no. 10.

[الأحزاب: ٣٨]، ﴿إِنَّا كُلَّ شَيْءٍ خَلَقْنَٰهُ بِقَدَرٍ﴾ [القمر:٤٩]، هذه الآيات الثلاث مع غيرها من الآيات تدل على الإيمان بالقضاء والقدر ﴿مَآ أَصَابَ مِن مُّصِيبَةٍ إِلَّا بِإِذْنِ ٱللَّهِ﴾ [التغابن:١١]، ﴿مَآ أَصَابَ مِن مُّصِيبَةٍ فِى ٱلْأَرْضِ وَلَا فِىٓ أَنفُسِكُمْ إِلَّا فِى كِتَٰبٍ﴾ [الحديد:٢٢]. يعني اللوح المحفوظ.

Allah ﷻ says: **{And [He] has created each thing and determined it with [precise] determination.} [Qurʾān 25:2]** Allah ﷻ also says: **{And ever is the command of Allah a destiny decreed.} [Qurʾān 33:38]** And: **{Indeed, all things We created with predestination.} [Qurʾān 54:49]** These three verses and other verses point to faith in *qaḍāʾ* and *qadar*. And: **{No disaster strikes except by the permission of Allah.} [Qurʾān 64:11]** And: **{No disaster strikes upon the earth or among yourselves except that it is in a register.} [Qurʾān 57:22]** Meaning that it is in the Preserved Tablet.

المتن

(١١٣) فَوَيْلٌ لِمَنْ صارَ لِلَّهِ تَعالَىٰ فِي الْقَدَرِ خَصِيمًا.

(113) So woe to those who dispute with Allah's decree;

الشرح

الذي يدخل في أمور القضاء ويشكك فيه خصيم الله، ولا يصح الإيمان إلا بالإيمان بالقضاء والقدر بمراتبه الأربع، حسب ما جاء في الكتاب والسنة، ولا تتدخل في السؤالات والإشكالات والشكوك والأوهام، فإن هذا معناه مخاصمة الله عز وجل، فالذين تدخلوا في القضاء والقدر لم يتوصلوا إلىٰ شيء، بل وقعوا في حيرة واضطراب وإفساد للعقيدة.

Anyone who delves into and questions matters of *qadar* is an adversary to Allah ﷻ. Faith is only correct when there is faith in *qaḍāʾ* and *qadar* according to their four levels, based on what is found in the Qurʾān and Sunnah.

Therefore we should not get involved in questioning or problematizing, in doubts or misconceptions, because all of this is tantamount to raising objections to Allah ﷻ. Those who delve into matters of *qaḍā'* and *qadar* have never arrived at anything but they have instead fallen into confusion, perplexity, and corruption of faith.

❁❁❁

المتن

(١١٤) وَأَحْضَرَ لِلنَّظَرِ فِيهِ قَلْبًا سَقِيمًا.

(114) And who study it with a sick heart;

الشرح

فأمور القضاء والقدر وشؤون الله عز وجل لا يدركها النظر والتفكير والعقل، فلا تكلف عقلك شيئًا لا يستطيعه، فالعقل محدود، لا يمكنه أن يدرك كل شيء، فلا تدخله في متاهات وأمور لا يطيقها.

Matters of *qaḍā'* and *qadar*, and all other matters of Allah ﷻ, are not comprehended through speculation, intellect, and reason, so do not burden your mind with something which it is not able to do. The mind is limited, and it is not able to comprehend everything, so don't get it involved in enigmas and matters that it cannot handle.

❁❁❁

المتن

(١١٥) لَقَدِ الْتَمَسَ بِوَهَمِهِ فِي فَحْصِ الْغَيْبِ سِرًّا كَتِيمًا،

(115) They have sought to uncover an un-discoverable matter with their vain and deluded attempts at examining the unseen;

الشرح

لأن القضاء والقدر سر الله جل وعلا في خلقه، فلا تبحث عنه، ولا تُكلف بذلك، إنما كُلفت بالعمل والطاعة والامتثال.

Because Allah ﷻ has kept *qaḍā'* and *qadar* hidden from His creation, we should not search for it. It is not our responsibility to do so; rather our responsibility is to do good deeds, be obedient, and be compliant.

المتن

(١١٦) وَعادَ بِما قالَ فِيهِ أَفّاكًا أَثِيمًا.

(116) Instead becoming sinful and liars due to what they say about it.

الشرح

أي يكون كل كلامه وكل بحثه إفكًا، يعني: كذبًا وإثمًا - والعياذ بالله- لأنه فعل ما لم يؤمر به، وتدخل فيما ليس من شأنه.

Everything they say and search for is sinful lies and falsehoods (*ifk*)—And Allah ﷻ is our refuge. This is because they do what they are not commanded and they get involved in matters that do not concern them.

المتن

(١١٧) والْعَرْشُ والْكُرْسِيُّ حَقٌّ.

(117) The *ʿArsh* (Throne) and the *Kursī* (Footstool) are true.

الشرح

الله سبحانه وتعالىٰ خلق السماوات، وخلق الأرض، وخلق الكرسي، وخلق العرش، كلها مخلوقات لله عز وجل، السماوات فوق الأرض، وفوق السماوات

البحر، وفوق البحر الكرسي، وفوق الكرسي العرش، فهو أعلىٰ المخلوقات، وذلك كما جاء في الحديث: «**إن السماوات السبع بالنسبة للكرسي كسبع دراهم ألقيت في ترس**»، يعني: السماوات السبع وعظمها وما فيها - مقارنة بالكرسي - كسبعة دراهم ألقيت في مثل الصحن الذي يتترس به المقاتل، فما نسبة سبعة دراهم في ترس مستدير؟ نسبتها قليلة، وفي ذلك قوله تعالىٰ: ﴿وَسِعَ كُرۡسِيُّهُ ٱلسَّمَٰوَٰتِ وَٱلۡأَرۡضَۖ﴾ [البقرة:٢٥٥]، والعرش أعظم من الكرسي، فالكرسي بالنسبة إلىٰ العرش كحلقة ملقاة في أرض فلاة، كما جاء في الحديث، فلو ألقيت حلقة في أرض واسعة فما نسبتها إلىٰ هذه الفلاة؟ لا شيء.

Allah the Almighty created the heavens, He created the earth, He created the *Kursī* (footstool), and He created the *'Arsh* (Throne) – all of these are creations of Allah ﷻ. The heavens are above the earth, and above the heavens is the sea, and above the sea is the *kursī,* and above the *kursī* is the Throne, so it is the highest of all creations. This is according to the *ḥadīth*: "Verily, the seven heavens compared to the *kursī* are like seven dirhams thrown into a shield," – i.e. the seven heavens in all their greatness and with all they contain (as compared to the *kursī*) are like seven dirhams cast into the like of a disc that is taken as a shield by a soldier. What are seven dirhams compared to a round shield? They are minor in proportion. In that regard, Allah ﷻ says: **{His *kursī* extends over the heavens and the earth.} [Qur'ān 2:255]** Yet the *'Arsh* (Throne) is even greater than the footstool. The *kursī*, compared to the Throne, is like a ring cast into a desert, as related in a *ḥadīth*. If you were to cast a ring into a vast piece of land, how would it compare to that piece of land? It would be nothing at all.

هذه مخلوقات عظيمة وواسعة لا يعلمها إلا الله سبحانه وتعالىٰ.

These creations are great and vast and none knows about them except Allah, the Most High.

فالعرش أعلىٰ المخلوقات، والله سبحانه عالٍ فوق عرشه فوق مخلوقاته.

The Throne is the highest of all creations, and Allah is the Most High above His Throne and above His creations.

والكرسي تحت العرش، وجاء في الأثر أنه موضع القدمين، فالكرسي مخلوق، وليس المقصود به العلم، كما نسب ذلك لابن عباس رضي الله عنه، أنه قال في قوله: ﴿وَسِعَ كُرْسِيُّهُ﴾ أي: علمه، أي: وسع علمه السماوات والأرض. المعنىٰ صحيح، ولكن ليس هذا المقصود من الآية، فالكرسي مخلوق، والعلم صفة من صفات الله عز وجل ليست من مخلوقاته، فيجب الإيمان بالعرش وبالكرسي، هذا حق علىٰ حقيقته، وليس العرش كما يقوله الأشاعرة - ومن نحا نحوهم- إن العرش هو الملك، فيقولون في قوله تعالىٰ : ﴿ٱسْتَوَىٰ عَلَى ٱلْعَرْشِ﴾ [الأعراف:٥٤]، أي: استولىٰ علىٰ الملك، وهذا ضلال، فالعرش مخلوق: ﴿وَكَانَ عَرْشُهُۥ عَلَى ٱلْمَآءِ﴾ [هود:٧]، فالعرش تحته الكرسي، والكرسي تحته السماوات، والأرض تحت السموات . في الحديث: «**فإذا سألتم الله الجنة فاسألوه الفردوس الأعلىٰ، فإنه وسط الجنة وأعلىٰ الجنة، وفوقه عرش الرحمن**» فالفردوس هو أعلىٰ الجنان وفوقه عرش الرحمن.

The *kursī,* which is the place for the feet, or *footstool,* as related in one report, is under the Throne. So, the *kursī* is a created thing, and what is meant by it is not knowledge, as has been attributed to Ibn ʿAbbās ﷺ. It has been attributed to him that he said with regard to the saying of Allah: **{His *kursī* extends over the heavens and the earth}** that *kursī* means His knowledge, meaning that His knowledge encompasses the heavens and earth. The meaning is correct; however, that is not what is meant by the verse. The *kursī* is a created thing, and knowledge is one of Allah's ﷻ attributes, not of one of His creations. So, it is obligatory to have faith in the Throne and the *kursī.* This is the truth according to the literal sense. The Throne is not 'the Kingdom' as the Ashʿarites and those with the same tendencies believe. They say with regard to the saying of Allah ﷻ: **{And then He rose above (*istawā*) the Throne} [Qurʾān 7:54]** - that it means that He seized (*istawlā*) the kingdom. This is misguidance, because the Throne is something created. Allah ﷻ says: **{And His Throne had been upon water.} [Qurʾān 11:7]** Thus, under the Throne is the *kursī,* and under the *kursī* are the heavens, and the earth is under the heavens. It is related in a *ḥadīth*: "If you ask Allah, then ask Him for the Highest Firdaws, as it is in the middle and highest place of Jannah, and above it is the Throne of the All-Merciful."[51] Firdaws is the highest garden of Jannah, and above it is the Throne of the All-Merciful.

فعرشه مخلوق وله حملة، وهم طائفة من الملائكة: ﴿وَيَحۡمِلُ عَرۡشَ رَبِّكَ فَوۡقَهُمۡ يَوۡمَئِذٖ ثَمَٰنِيَةٞ ١٧﴾ [الحاقة:١٧] قبل يوم القيامة يحمله أربعة، فإذا جاء يوم القيامة تضاعفوا وصاروا ثمانية، فكل واحد من الملائكة لا يُتصور خلقه وعظمته وقوته.

The Throne is created, and it has bearers, who are namely a group of angels. **{And they will bear the Throne of your Lord above them, that Day, eight [of them].} [Qur'ān 69:17]** Before the Day of Judgment, there are four angels that carry it. When the Day of Judgment comes, they are doubled, becoming eight, and each one of those angels has unimaginable form, greatness, and strength.

وهل يقال: إذا قيل إن العرش هو الملك. إن المُلك تحمله الملائكة؟

Would it be said then, that if the Throne was the kingdom, that the kingdom is borne by angels?

❁❁❁

المتن

(١١٨) وَهُوَ مُسْتَغْنٍ عَنِ الْعَرْشِ وَما دُونَهُ.

(118) He is not in need of the Throne or that which is beneath it.

الشرح

لا تتصور أن معنىٰ قوله تعالىٰ: ﴿ثُمَّ ٱسۡتَوَىٰ عَلَى ٱلۡعَرۡشِ﴾ [الأعراف:٥٤] أنه محتاج إلىٰ العرش كاستواء المخلوق علىٰ المخلوق، بل الله عز وجل مستوٍ علىٰ العرش، وهو غني عن العرش وما دون العرش.

51 Al-Bukhārī, no. 2790, 7423.

It should not be imagined that the saying of Allah ﷻ: **{And then He rose above the Throne} [Qurʾān 7:54]** means that He is in need of the Throne, like when a created thing mounts another created thing. Rather, Allah ﷻ is above the Throne, and He has no need of the Throne or anything that is beneath it.

جميع المخلوقات محتاجة إلىٰ الله ﴿إِنَّ ٱللَّهَ يُمۡسِكُ ٱلسَّمَٰوَٰتِ وَٱلۡأَرۡضَ أَن تَزُولَاۚ وَلَئِن زَالَتَآ إِنۡ أَمۡسَكَهُمَا مِنۡ أَحَدٖ مِّنۢ بَعۡدِهِۦٓۚ﴾ [فاطر:٤١] فهو الذي يمسك العرش، ويمسك السماوات، ويمسك الأرض والمخلوقات، بقدرته وعزته، فهي المحتاجة إليه، وهو غني عنها سبحانه وتعالىٰ.

All created things are in need of Allah ﷻ. **{Indeed, Allah holds the heavens and the earth, lest they cease. And if they should cease, no one could hold them [in place] after Him.} [Qurʾān 35:41]** It is Allah ﷻ who holds the Throne, the earth and all other created things by His omnipotence and might. Those things are in need of Him, and He is not in need of them.

ولا يلزم من كون الشيء فوق الشيء أن يكون الأعلىٰ محتاجاً إلىٰ ما تحته، فالسماوات فوق الأرض وليست محتاجة إلىٰ الأرض.

It does not necessarily follow that if something is above something else, that the higher thing is in need of what is beneath it. The heavens, for instance, are above the earth, and they are not in need of it.

المتن

(١١٩) مُحِيطٌ بِكُلِّ شَيْءٍ وَفَوْقَهُ.

(119) He encompasses all things and is above them.

الشرح

محيط علمه بكل شيء، وهو فوق المخلوقات، فعلمه محيط بكل شيء ﴿إِنَّ

ٱللَّهَ لَا يَخۡفَىٰ عَلَيۡهِ شَيۡءٞ فِي ٱلۡأَرۡضِ وَلَا فِي ٱلسَّمَآءِ ۝٥﴾ [آل عمران:٥] وإحاطته بالأشياء: علمه بها، وإلا فالله عز وجل في جهة العلو.

His knowledge encompasses everything. He is above the creation, and His knowledge encompasses all things. **{Indeed, from Allah nothing is hidden in the earth nor in the heaven.} [Qur'ān 3:5]** His encompassing of things is His knowledge of them. Otherwise, Allah ﷻ is in the direction of Highness.

المتن

(١٢٠) وَقَدْ أَعْجَزَ عَنِ الإِحاطَةِ خَلْقَهُ.

(120) Yet His creations are unable to encompass Him.

الشرح

فالله سبحانه وتعالىٰ يعلم ما بين أيديهم وما خلفهم ولا يحيطون به علماً، قال الله عز وجل: ﴿وَلَا يُحِيطُونَ بِشَيۡءٖ مِّنۡ عِلۡمِهِۦٓ إِلَّا بِمَا شَآءَۚ وَسِعَ كُرۡسِيُّهُ ٱلسَّمَٰوَٰتِ وَٱلۡأَرۡضَۖ﴾ [البقرة:٢٥٥] فالله محيط بكل شيء علماً ﴿لِتَعۡلَمُوٓاْ أَنَّ ٱللَّهَ عَلَىٰ كُلِّ شَيۡءٖ قَدِيرٞ وَأَنَّ ٱللَّهَ قَدۡ أَحَاطَ بِكُلِّ شَيۡءٍ عِلۡمَۢا ۝١٢﴾ [الطلاق:١٢].

Allah the Almighty knows what lays before them and behind them, and their knowledge does not encompass Him. Allah ﷻ says: **{And they encompass not a thing of His knowledge except for what He wills. His Kursī extends over the heavens and the earth.} [Qur'ān 2:255]** Thus, Allah's ﷻ knowledge encompasses everything. **{So you may know that Allah is over all things competent and that Allah has encompassed all things in knowledge.} [Qur'ān 65:12]**

المتن

(١٢١) وَنقُولُ: إِنَّ اللهَ اتَّخَذَ إِبْراهِيمَ خَلِيلًا، وَكَلَّمَ اللهُ مُوسَىٰ تَكْلِيمًا، إِيمانًا وَتَصْدِيقًا وَتَسْلِيمًا.

(121) And we say with faith, belief, and acceptance, that Allah took Ibrāhīm (Abraham) as His *Khalīl* (Beloved) and spoke directly to Mūsā (Moses).

الشرح

من عقيدة المسلمين أن الرسل أفضل الخلق وأن الرسل يتفاضلون فهم يعتقدون أن الله اتخذ إبراهيم خليلاً، كما قال الله تعالىٰ: ﴿وَٱتَّخَذَ ٱللَّهُ إِبْرَٰهِيمَ خَلِيلًا ﴿١٢٥﴾﴾ [النساء:١٢٥] والخلة هي أعلىٰ درجات المحبة، فالله جل وعلا يحب عباده المؤمنين والمتقين والمحسنين، ويحب التوابين ويحب المتطهرين، ولكن الخلة لم يحصل عليها إلا اثنان من العالم: إبراهيم ومحمد عليهما الصلاة والسلام، وقد قال عليه الصلاة والسلام: **«إن الله اتخذني خليلاً كما اتخذ إبراهيم خليلاً»**.

One of the beliefs of the Muslims is that the Messengers are the best of all created beings, and that the Messengers themselves vary in virtue. Muslims believe that Allah ﷻ took Ibrāhīm عليه السلام as a close friend (*khalīl*), as Allah ﷻ says: **{And Allah took Abraham as an intimate friend.} [Qurʾān 4:125]** *Khullah* (from *khalīl*) is the highest degree of love. Allah ﷻ loves His faithful, pious and goodly slaves, and He loves those who repent and those who purify themselves. However, *khullah* was only achieved by two people in the universe: Ibrāhīm and Muḥammad عليهما السلام. The Prophet ﷺ said, "Allah has taken me as a *khalīl* as He has taken Ibrāhīm as a *khalīl*."[52]

﴿وَكَلَّمَ ٱللَّهُ مُوسَىٰ تَكْلِيمًا ﴿١٦٤﴾﴾ [النساء:١٦٤] ففضل بعض النبيين علىٰ بعض، وإن كانوا كلهم بالمرتبة العليا، لكن الله جل وعلا فضل بعضهم علىٰ بعض ﴿تِلْكَ ٱلرُّسُلُ فَضَّلْنَا بَعْضَهُمْ عَلَىٰ بَعْضٍ مِّنْهُم مَّن كَلَّمَ ٱللَّهُ وَرَفَعَ بَعْضَهُمْ دَرَجَٰتٍ﴾ [البقرة:٢٥٣] فكل نبي يعطيه الله عز وجل تفضيلاً خاصاً به، فضل إبراهيم

52 Muslim, no. 532; al-Bukhārī related similar versions (no. 466, 467). See the earlier citation.

ومحمداً عليهما الصلاة والسلام بالخلة، وفضل موسىٰ بأنه كلمه تكليماً بدون واسطة الملك، وسمع موسىٰ كلامه، ناداه سبحانه وناجاه؛ والمناداة: الصوت المرتفع، والمناجاة: الصوت الخفي، كل هذا حصل لموسىٰ عليه الصلاة والسلام، وهذه فضيلة لم يحصل عليها غيره، وقال: ﴿تَكْلِيمًا﴾ للتأكيد، حتىٰ لا يقول أحد: إن هذا مجاز، فلما أكده بالمصدر، دل علىٰ أنه تكليم حقيقي من الله عز وجل، وهذا فيه إثبات الكلام لله عز وجل، وفيه إثبات الفضيلة لموسىٰ عليه الصلاة والسلام علىٰ غيره من النبيين في هذه الخصلة، ولا يلزم إذا كان عند نبي من الأنبياء ميزة خاصة أن يكون أفضل من غيره علىٰ الإطلاق، بل هو أفضل من غيره من الأنبياء في هذه الخصلة.

{And Allah spoke to Moses with [direct] speech.} [Qur'ān 4:164] Allah ﷻ favoured some of the Prophets over others, although all of them are in the highest rank. Nonetheless, Allah ﷻ favoured some of them over others. **{Those messengers – some of them We caused to exceed others. Among them were those to whom Allah spoke, and He raised some of them in degree.} [Qur'ān 2:253]** Allah favoured each prophet with something special. He favoured Ibrāhīm and Muḥammad ﷺ with *khullah*. He favoured Mūsā by speaking directly to him without an angel as an intermediary. Mūsā heard His speech, He called on him (*nādāhu*), and He spoke softly with him (*nājāhu*). The former (*munādāh*) is to speak loudly and the latter (*munājāh*) is to speak softly. All of this happened with Mūsā عليه السلام. This is a virtue that no one else was given. Allah ﷻ said that He spoke to him *directly* (*kallamahū taklīman*) for emphasis, so that no one would be able to say that it is a figure of speech. As He emphasizes the verb with the infinitive form (*taklīman*), it indicates that He literally spoke to him. This entails affirmation (*ithbāt*) of speech for Allah ﷻ, and it also entails affirmation of the superiority of Mūsā عليه السلام to other prophets as it pertains to this characteristic. But one prophet being distinguished from the other prophets in regards to a certain characteristic does not necessarily mean that he is superior in all respects. Rather, he is superior to the other prophets in that characteristic only.

المتن

(١٢٢) وَنُؤْمِنُ بِالْمَلائِكَةِ والنَّبِيِّينَ.

(122) And we believe in the Angels and the Prophets.

الشرح

هذا من أركان الإيمان، التي أولها: الإيمان بالله، وثانياً: الإيمان بالملائكة، وهم عالم من عالم الغيب لا يعلمه إلا الله سبحانه وتعالىٰ، خلقهم الله تعالىٰ من النور؛ لعبادته وتنفيذ أوامره في مخلوقاته، أوكل إليهم أعمالاً يقومون بها وينفذونها في مخلوقاته، منهم الموكل بالوحي، ومنهم الموكل بالقطر والنبات، ومنهم الموكل بقبض الأرواح، ومنهم الموكل بالنفخ في الصور، ومنهم الموكل بحفظ أعمال بني آدم، ومنهم الموكل بالجبال، ومنهم الموكل بالأجنّة في بطون الحوامل، كما في حديث ابن مسعود (ثم يرسل إليه الملك فيكتب رزقه وأجله وعمله وشقي أو سعيد).

This is amongst the pillars of faith, the first of which is faith in Allah ﷻ, and the second is faith in the angels. Angels make up a kingdom of the kingdoms of the unseen, which no one knows except Allah ﷻ. Allah created them from light in order that they worship Him and execute His commands with respect to His creations. He entrusted them with tasks that they carry out and execute on Allah's creations. Among them is the angel entrusted with the divine revelation, those that are entrusted with the rain and vegetation, taking away the souls, blowing into the horn, keeping a record of the deeds of the children of Ādam, the mountains, and the foetuses inside of the wombs. This [last task] is mentioned in a *ḥadīth* as related from Ibn Masʿūd ؓ: "Then He sends the angel to it and it writes down its sustenance, its term, its deeds, and whether it is blessed or wretched."[53]

فهم موكلون بأعمال يقومون بها كما أمر الله تعالىٰ بها: ﴿لَا يَسْبِقُونَهُۥ بِٱلْقَوْلِ وَهُم بِأَمْرِهِۦ يَعْمَلُونَ ﴿٢٧﴾﴾ [الأنبياء:٢٧]، ﴿يُسَبِّحُونَ ٱلَّيْلَ وَٱلنَّهَارَ لَا يَفْتُرُونَ ﴿٢٠﴾﴾

53 Al-Bukhārī, no. 3208; Muslim, no. 2643.

[الأنبياء:٢٠].

They are assigned tasks that they carry out as Allah ﷻ has commanded: **{They cannot precede Him in word, and they act by His command.} [Qur'ān 21:27] {They exalt [Him] night and day [and] do not slacken.} [Qur'ān 21:20]**

فهم يعبدون الله عبادة متواصلة ومع ذلك يقومون بما أوكل إليهم من تنفيذ الأوامر في المخلوقات ولهم مهام عظيمة، وخلقتهم لا يعلمها إلا الله سبحانه وتعالىٰ، تختلف عن خلقة بني آدم ﴿جَاعِلِ ٱلْمَلَـٰٓئِكَةِ رُسُلًا أُو۟لِىٓ أَجْنِحَةٍ مَّثْنَىٰ وَثُلَـٰثَ وَرُبَـٰعَ﴾ [فاطر:١] ولبعضهم أكثر من ذلك ﴿يَزِيدُ فِى ٱلْخَلْقِ مَا يَشَآءُ﴾ [فاطر:١]

They worship Allah ﷻ continuously and simultaneously carry out the commands they were assigned with respect to the creation. They have great tasks, and their forms are only known by Allah.[54] They have different forms than the children of Ādam, **{[Who] made the angels messengers having wings, two or three or four.} [Qur'ān 35:1]** Some of them have more than that: **{He increases in creation what He wills.} [Qur'ān 35:1]**

فجبريل عليه السلام له ستمائة جناح، كل جناح منها سد الأفق، فلا يعلم خلقتها ولا كيفيتها إلا الله. أما البشر فلا يستطيعون رؤية الملك علىٰ صورته، وإنما يأتي الملك في صورة إنسان كما كان جبريل يأتي إلىٰ النبي صلىٰ الله عليه وسلم في صورة إنسان، ويجلس إليه ويكلمه، ولم يره النبي صلىٰ الله عليه وسلم علىٰ صورته الملكية إلا مرتين، مرة وهو في بطحاء مكة رآه في الأفق، ومرة عند سدرة المنتهىٰ في ليلة الإسراء والمعراج، وما عدا هاتين المرتين فإن جبريل يأتي النبي صلىٰ الله عليه وسلم في صورة إنسان، وكثيراً ما يأتي في صورة دحية الكلبي رضي

54 It is related that Abū Dharr ؓ said: "The Messenger of Allah ﷺ said: 'I see what you do not see, and I hear what you do not hear. The heavens creak and it is only right that they creak. There is not a space of four fingers without an angel prostrating its forehead before Allah." Aḥmad, 5/173; al-Tirmidhī, no. 2317; Ibn Mājah, no 4190; al-Ḥākim, *al-Mustadrak,* 2/510-551. Al-Ḥākim said: "The transmission (*isnād*) of this *ḥadīth* is sound (*ṣaḥīḥ*) and [al-Bukhārī and Muslim] did not cite it."

الله عنه.

Jibrīl ﷺ has six-hundred wings, and each wing fills the horizon, so no one knows their exact nature but Allah. Humans, however, cannot see the angels in their proper form. But an angel can come in the form of a human, as Jibrīl ﷺ used to come to the Prophet ﷺ in the form of a human and sit with him and speak to him. The Prophet ﷺ did not see him in his angelic form except for twice: once in a valley of Makkah, and once at the Lote Tree at the Utmost Boundary (*sidrat al-muntahā*) during the night of the Isrāʾ and the Ascension. Apart from those two instances, Jibrīl ﷺ always came to the Prophet ﷺ in the form of a human, and he often came in the form of Diḥyah al-Kalbī ﷺ.

وقوله: **(والنبيين)** النبيين جمع نبي وهو من أوحي إليه بشرع ولم يؤمر بتبليغه، والرسول: من أوحي إليه بشرع وأمر بتبليغه ويجب الإيمان بجميع الأنبياء والمرسلين ومن آمن ببعضهم وكفر ببعضهم فهو كافر بالجميع ﴿لَا نُفَرِّقُ بَيْنَ أَحَدٍ مِّن رُّسُلِهِۦ﴾

The author says: **"the Prophets"** which is the plural of prophet, who is someone to which was revealed a prescribed law but who was not commanded to deliver the message. A 'messenger' refers to one who received revelation of a prescribed law and was commanded to deliver the message. It is obligatory to believe in all of the Prophets and Messengers. Whoever believes in some of them and disbelieves in others is a disbeliever in all of them. **{We make no distinction between any of His Messengers.} [Qur'ān 2:285]**

المتن

(١٢٣) وَالْكُتُبِ الْمُنَزَّلَةِ عَلَىٰ الْمُرْسَلِينَ، وَنَشْهَدُ أَنَّهُمْ كَانُوا عَلَىٰ الْحَقِّ الْمُبِينِ.

(123) And the Books revealed to the Messengers; and we testify that they were upon the clear truth.

الشرح

من أصول الإيمان وأركانه: الإيمان بالكتب التي أنزلها الله علىٰ الرسل لهداية الخلق؛ فالله تعالىٰ أنزل الكتب علىٰ الرسل من كلامه ووحيه وتشريعه، أنزلها علىٰ الرسل ليبلغوها إلىٰ أممهم، فيها الأوامر وفيها النواهي، وفيها شرع الله جل وعلا.

Among the foundations and pillars of faith is belief in the Books that were revealed by Allah to the Messengers to guide people. Allah ﷻ sent down the Books to the Messengers with His speech, divine revelations (*waḥy*), and His prescriptions. He revealed them to the Messengers to convey them to their people. They contain what is commanded, what is forbidden and the prescribed laws of Allah ﷻ.

منها ما سماه الله في القرآن ومنها ما لم يسمه، ونحن نؤمن بجميع الكتب، ما سماه لنا وما لم يسمه، كالتوراة التي أنزلها علىٰ موسىٰ، والإنجيل الذي أنزله علىٰ عيسىٰ، والقرآن الذي أنزله علىٰ محمد صلىٰ الله عليه وسلم، والزبور الذي أنزله علىٰ داود ﴿وَءَاتَيْنَا دَاوُۥدَ زَبُورًا ﴾ [النساء:١٦٣] وصحف إبراهيم عليه الصلاة والسلام.

Among them are those that Allah ﷻ named in the Qur'ān, and among them are those that Allah ﷻ did not name. We believe in all of the Books, those that He has named and those that He has not, such as the Torah, which He sent down to Mūsā ﷺ, and the Injīl, which He sent down to ʿĪsā ﷺ, and the Qur'ān, which He sent down to Muḥammad ﷺ, and the Psalms (*zabūr*), which He sent down to Dāwūd ﷺ, **{And to David We gave the book [of Psalms],}** [Qur'ān 4:163] and the scriptures (*ṣuḥuf*) of Ibrāhīm ﷺ.

فنؤمن بها كلها وأنها في مصلحة الخلق وهداية الخلق وإقامة الحجة، فمن آمن ببعض الكتب وكفر ببعضها فهو كافر بالجميع؛ لأنها كلها من كلام الله فلا يجوز الإيمان ببعضها والكفر بالبعض الآخر، قال تعالىٰ: ﴿أَفَتُؤْمِنُونَ بِبَعْضِ ٱلْكِتَٰبِ وَتَكْفُرُونَ بِبَعْضٍ ۚ فَمَا جَزَآءُ مَن يَفْعَلُ ذَٰلِكَ مِنكُمْ إِلَّا خِزْىٌ فِى ٱلْحَيَوٰةِ ٱلدُّنْيَا ۖ﴾ [البقرة:٨٥].

We believe in all of them, and we believe that they are for the benefit and guidance of people, and also to put forth the proper arguments against them. If someone believes in just some of the Books and disbelieves in some, he is a disbeliever in all of them, because all of them are part of the word of Allah, so it is not permissible to have faith in some of them and disbelieve in the others. Allah ﷻ says: **{So do you believe in part of the Scripture and disbelieve in part? Then what is the recompense for those who do that among you except disgrace in the worldly life.} [Qurʾān 2:85]**

وكذلك الكتاب الواحد يجب الإيمان به كله والعمل به كله، فلا نأخذ ما يوافق شهواتنا وندع ما يخالفها.

Similarly, it is obligatory to believe in and act in accordance with the entirety of any given book, so we don't accept only that which is in accordance with our desires and reject what goes against them.

فمن جحد كتاباً من كتب الله، أو بعضاً من الكتاب، أو كلمة من الكتاب، أو حرفاً من الكتاب، فهو كافر بالله عز وجل.

Therefore, anyone who rejects one of Allah's Books or a part of one of them, or a word from one of them, or a letter from one of them, is a disbeliever in Allah.

المتن

(١٢٤) وَنُسَمِّي أَهْلَ قِبْلَتِنا مُسْلِمِينَ مُؤْمِنِينَ.

(123) We call those who share our *qiblah* (prayer direction) believing Muslims.

الشرح

هذا من العقيدة، أنه من نطق بالشهادتين واستقام عليهما فإنه مسلم، ولو صدر منه بعض المعاصي، ولو كانت من الكبائر، وما دامت المعاصي دون الشرك، ولكن

يكون مسلماً ناقص الإسلام وناقص الإيمان وفاسقاً، ولكنه لا يُحكم بكفره إن كانت معاصيه دون الشرك، هذه عقيدة أهل السنة والجماعة، لا يُكفِّرون بالمعاصي التي هي دون الشرك، ولكن ينقص بها الإيمان، وصاحبها يفسق بها الفسق الأصغر الذي لا يخرج من الملة. خلافاً للخوارج الذين يُكفّرون بالكبائر ويخرجون بها من الملة، ويخلدون صاحبها في النار. وخلافاً للمعتزلة الذين يُخرِجون صاحب الكبيرة من الإسلام، ولكن لا يدخلونه في الكفر، ويقولون: هو في منزلة بين المنزلتين، ولكن لو ماتوا على الكبيرة فالمعتزلة مثل الخوارج في الحكم عليهم، وخلاف عقيدة المرجئة الذين يقولون: إنه لا يضر مع الإيمان معصية، من صدق بالله عز وجل فإنه يكون مؤمناً، وإن فعل ما فعل، ولو ترك جميع أركان الإسلام عندهم لا يكون كافراً، المهم التصديق والاعتقاد، أما الأعمال فلا تزيد في الإيمان ولا تنقصه وليست منه، فهو مؤمن تام الإيمان ما دام مصدقاً. هذا مذهب المرجئة، وهو مذهب ضال.

It is a matter of faith to believe that anyone who utters and upholds the Two Testimonies of Faith is a Muslim. Even if they happened to sin and even if those were major sins, as long as they are less than polytheism (*shirk*). However, the faith and Islām of such a Muslim are deficient, and he is a sinner (*fāsiq*). Nonetheless, he is not to be judged a disbeliever if his sins are less than idolatry. This is the creed of Ahl al-Sunnah wa 'l-Jamā'ah, they do not declare anyone a disbeliever over sins that are less than idolatry. However, such sins detract from someone's faith and the one who commits them is a minor sinful person (commits *fisq aṣghar*), and this does not emit him from the sphere of the religion. Contrarily, the Khārijites declare those who commit *kabā'ir (*major sins) to be disbelievers, and that they leave the religion of Islām by that and will abide in the Fire forever. This is also in contrast to the Muʿtazilites: they say that those who commit major sins leave the religion, but they do not say that they are disbelievers. They say that they have a status between those two (*manzilah bayna 'l-manzilatayn*). However, if those people die committing major sins, then the Muʿtazilites are like the Khārijites in their judgement of them. This is in contrast to the belief of the Murji'ites: they say that faith is not affected by sin. For them, anyone who believes in Allah ﷻ is a believer, no matter what they do, even if they abandon all of the pillars of Islām. For them, they are not disbelievers as what matters is the belief and conviction in the heart. They also believe that faith does not increase or decrease in accordance with actions, and actions are not even a part of faith. They are perfect believers as long as they believe. This is the doctrine of the Murji'ites, and it is a misguided doctrine.

فهم مع الخوارج علىٰ طرفي نقيض؛ قوم تشددوا، وهم الخوارج، وقوم ذابوا وماعوا وقالوا: إن هذه المعاصي لا تضر، وهم المرجئة، وأما أهل السنة والجماعة فتوسطوا، ومذهبهم مأخوذ من الكتاب والسنة، وهو العدل، وفيه الجمع بين الأدلة. أما الخوارج والمعتزلة فأخذوا نصوص الوعيد وتركوا نصوص الوعد، وأما المرجئة فأخذوا بنصوص الوعد وتركوا نصوص الوعيد، لكن أهل السنة والجماعة أخذوا بنصوص الوعد وبنصوص الوعيد، وجمعوا بينها، وهذا الحق ﴿وَٱلرَّٰسِخُونَ فِى ٱلْعِلْمِ يَقُولُونَ ءَامَنَّا بِهِۦ كُلٌّ مِّنْ عِندِ رَبِّنَا﴾ [آل عمران:٧] فيردون هذا إلىٰ هذا، ولا يأخذون بطرف ويتركون الطرف الآخر كما هو مذهب أهل الزيغ ﴿فَأَمَّا ٱلَّذِينَ فِى قُلُوبِهِمْ زَيْغٌ فَيَتَّبِعُونَ مَا تَشَٰبَهَ مِنْهُ﴾ [آل عمران:٧] يأخذون بالمتشابه ويتركون المحكم الذي يفسر المتشابه.

Thus, they are on the opposite side of the Khārijites. One party (the Khārijites) is too vehement, and the other party is too passive and lenient and says that sin has no effect on faith, and they are the Murji'ites. Ahl al-Sunnah wa 'l-Jamāʿah, on the other hand, steer a middle course. Their doctrine is derived from the Qur'ān and Sunnah. It is just and brings unity to all of the evidence. The Khārijites and Muʿtazilities, however, hold fast to the passages where there is the threat of punishment and leave those where there is a promise of reward. The Murji'ites hold fast to the passages with the promise of reward and desert those with threat of punishment. Nonetheless, Ahl al-Sunnah wa 'l-Jamāʿah hold fast to both types and unite those passages, which is the correct methodology: **{But those firm in knowledge say, 'We believe in it. All [of it] is from our Lord.'} [Qur'ān 3:7]** They refer one to the other, and they do not adopt one side and leave another, as is the case with the doctrines of the deviant sects. **{As for those in whose hearts is deviation [from truth], they will follow that of it which is unspecific.} [Qur'ān 3:7]** They hold fast to the parts that are ambiguous (*mutashābih*) and abandon the parts that have a clear meaning (*muḥkam*), by which the ambiguous parts gain interpretation.

وقول المصنف: (**مسلمين مؤمنين**) ليس علىٰ إطلاقه؛ لأنهم قد يكونون ناقصين في الإسلام والإيمان، ومتوعدين من الله عز وجل.

The author says: **"believing Muslims"**, but this is not in the most absolute sense, because they may be lacking in faith and adherence to Islām and thus, fall under the threat of Allah the Almighty.

المتن

(١٢٥) ما دامُوا بِما جاءَ بِهِ النَّبِيُّ ﷺ مُعْتَرِفِينَ، وَلَهُ بِكُلِّ ما قالَهُ وَأَخْبَرَ مُصَدِّقِينَ..

(125) As long as they acknowledge what the Prophet ﷺ taught and believe in what he said and reported.

الشرح

أما لو جحدوا شيئًا مما جاء به النبي صلىٰ الله عليه وسلم ولم يعترفوا، صاروا كفاراً، ولو آمنوا ببعض ما جاء به، فإن جحدوا بعضه فهم كافرون بجميع ما جاء به، فالواجب الإيمان به كله، سواء وافق أهواءنا أو خالفها؛ لأنه حق.

But if they reject anything that is related as being said by the Prophet ﷺ and do not acknowledge it, then they would be disbelievers, even if they believed in some of what has been related from the Prophet ﷺ. If they reject a part of it, they are disbelievers in the whole of it. It is imperative to believe in all of it, whether it is in line with or goes against our whims and desires, because it is the truth.

أما من كذب ببعض الأحاديث الصحيحة فهو كافر، فلو رد حديثًا في البخاري، والحديث صحيح، وقال: أنا لا أومن بهذا الحديث ولا أصدقه؛ لأنه يخالف العلم الحديث، فسبحان الله! كلام النبي صلىٰ الله عليه وسلم يُتهم، وكلام البشر

لا يتهم؟ أيضاً العلم الحديث قد لا يخالف الأحاديث الصحيحة، والحمد لله، فمثلاً ورد في حديث الذباب الذي ينكره هؤلاء أن في أحد جناحيه داءً وفي الآخر دواءً، والطب يقر بهذا أن السم يعالج بضده، وبما يناقضه، والذباب فيه النقيضان، فإنه إذا وقع في الماء فإنه يرفع الجناح الذي فيه الدواء، ويغمس الجناح الذي فيه السم، فالنبي صلىٰ الله عليه وسلم أمر بغمسه بجناحه الذي فيه الدواء، فيغالب السم، فهذا يقره الطب ولا يرده، ولكنه لما خالف أذواق هؤلاء الجهال صاروا يتكلمون بهذا الكلام، وهذا كفر والعياذ بالله، ولهم مقالات شنيعة نحو السنة، يردونها ويشككون فيها، ويقولون إن النبي صلىٰ الله عليه وسلم قال: «**أنتم أعلم بأمر دنياكم**»، يقولون هذا وهم يدعون أنهم دعاة للإسلام، وهذا موقفهم من سنة النبي صلىٰ الله عليه وسلم، فهؤلاء الجهال يقولون: هذه من أمور الدنيا، والنبي عليه الصلاة والسلام يقول: «**أنتم أعلم بأمر دنياكم**» فمعناه: أنهم يُجهِّلون النبي صلىٰ الله عليه وسلم.

If someone disbelieves in some of the authentic *ḥadīth*s, on the other hand, then he is also a disbeliever. If someone rejects a *ḥadīth* in *al-Bukhārī*, and the *ḥadīth* is authentic, and he says, I do not believe in this *ḥadīth* because it contradicts modern science, then *Subḥḥāna ʾllāh!* Would you have doubts about what the Prophet ﷺ has said and not have doubts about what people say? Moreover, modern science may not be contrary to the authentic *ḥadīth*s, praise be to Allah. It is related, for instance, in the *ḥadīth* about the fly – which these people reject – that in one of its wings is a disease, and in the other is a cure. Medicine confirms the fact that poison is treated with its antidote and with what counteracts it. Flies have both of these counteracting agents, so if a fly lands in water, the wing that has the remedy removes and absorbs the wing that has the poison. So, the Prophet ﷺ commanded us to submerge the wing that has the remedy[55], so that it can overwhelm the poison. This is confirmed by medicine. However, since it is at odds with the tastes of those ignorant people, they say such things, and this is disbelief, and Allah ﷻ is our refuge. They also make some of the most abominable statements against the Sunnah. They reject it and cast doubts on it, saying

55 It is related that Abū Hurayrah ؓ said: The Messenger of Allah ﷺ said: "If a fly lands in the drink of one among you, then let them submerge it and then remove it, for in one of its wings is a disease, and in the other is a cure." Al-Bukhārī, no. 3320, 5782.

that the Prophet ﷺ said, "You know your worldly matters better."[56] They say so whilst at the same time claiming to be preachers of Islām. This is their stance when it comes to the Sunnah of the Prophet ﷺ. These ignorant souls say that these are worldly matters and that the Prophet ﷺ said, "You know your worldly matters better." What this means is that they are calling the Prophet ﷺ ignorant.

وقوله: (معترفين) (مصدقين) لا يكفي الاعتراف والتصديق إلا على مذهب المرجئة، بل لابد مع ذلك من العمل بما جاء به، ولابد من الإخلاص في ذلك.

The author says: '*acknowledge*' and '*believe*', but it does not suffice to acknowledge and believe, except according to the doctrines of the Murji'ah alone. Rather, there has to be action in accordance with what is related, and there also has to be sincerity in that.

المتن

(١٢٦) وَلا نَخُوضُ فِي اللهِ، وَلا نُمارِي فِي دِينِ اللهِ.

(126) And we do not have vain dialogues about Allah and we do not dispute over Allah's religion.

الشرح

لا نخوض في الله، بل نؤمن به وبصفاته وأسمائه، ولا نؤولها ونصرفها عن ظاهرها، ونأتي بمعانٍ ما أرادها الله ولا أرادها النبي صلى الله عليه وسلم، اتباعاً لأهوائنا وعقولنا القاصرة، وهذا كفر بالله عز وجل.

We do not hold any vain dialogues about Allah ﷻ but instead believe in His names and attributes, and we neither interpret them nor shift them from their outward meanings. We do not come up with meanings that neither

---

56 Muslim, no. 2363.

Allah nor His Prophet ﷺ intended so as to follow our whims and desires and our limited minds. That would be to disbelieve in Allah ﷻ.

وكذلك في دين الله لا نماري - أي نجادل- ونقول: هذا نؤمن به وهذا نتوقف في الإيمان به، فما دام ثبت في الكتاب والسنة فليس فيه مجال للخوض، بل نؤمن به ونُسَلّم، وإن كان في عقولنا ما لا يدرك هذا الشيء، فعقولنا قاصرة، ولو كانت كاملة لما احتاجت إلىٰ النبي صلىٰ الله عليه وسلم، ولما احتاجت البشرية إلىٰ الرسل، فدل علىٰ أن العقول قاصرة، وأنه لابد من إرسال الرسل؛ لإحقاق الحق وإبطال الباطل.

We also do not indulge in disputation or argumentation regarding Allah's religion and say, "We believe in this but are undecided on believing in that." As long as something is an established part of the Qurʾān and Sunnah, then there is no room for discussion. Rather, we believe in it and accept it, even if our minds are somewhat unable to comprehend it. Our minds are limited. If they were perfect, we would not require the Prophet ﷺ to be sent to us, and humanity would not require messengers to be sent. This is evidence that the mind is limited and that it is necessary for the messengers to be sent to realize truth and invalidate falsehood.

المتن

(١٢٧) وَلا نُجادِلُ فِي الْقُرْآنِ، وَنَشْهَدُ أَنَّهُ كَلامُ رَبِّ الْعالَمِينَ.

(127) And we do not dispute over the Qurʾān, and we testify that it is the word of the Lord of the Worlds.

الشرح

قوله: (**لا نجادل في القرآن**) يشمل عدم القول بأنه ليس من عند الله، كما يقوله

الكفار، ويقولون: هو من عند محمد صلىٰ الله عليه وسلم.

The author says: **"... we do not dispute over the Qur'ān":** This includes that we do not say that the Qur'ān is not from Allah ﷻ as the disbelievers say. They say that it is from Muḥammad ﷺ.

وكذلك الجدال في تفسير معاني القرآن، فلا نفسر القرآن من عند أنفسنا، فالقرآن لا يفسر إلا بما جاء في كتاب الله أو ما جاء في سنة رسول الله صلىٰ الله عليه وسلم، أو ما قاله الصحابة أو ما قاله التابعون، أو ما اقتضته اللغة العربية التي نزل بها.

The same goes for disputing about explanation of the meanings of the Qur'ān. We are not to interpret the Qur'ān on our own accord. The Qur'ān is only to be interpreted according to what has been related in the Qur'ān or Sunnah of the Messenger of Allah ﷺ or what the Companions or the successors (*tābi'ūn*) have said, or what the Arabic language, in which it was revealed, dictates.

فلا نقول فيه بعقولنا القاصرة، إنما يفسره الله سبحانه الذي نزله، أو النبي عليه الصلاة والسلام الذي وُكل إليه بيانه، أو الصحابة الذين تتلمذوا علىٰ المصطفىٰ عليه الصلاة والسلام، أو التابعون الذين رووا عن تلاميذ النبي صلىٰ الله عليه وسلم، أو باللغة التي نزل بها؛ لأنه نزل بلسان عربي مبين. أما تفسيره بما يقوله الطبيب الفلاني أو المفكر الفلاني أو الفلكي الفلاني، فالنظريات تختلف، فاليوم نظرية وغداً نظرية تبطلها؛ لأنها من عمل البشر، فلا يُفسَّر كلام الله بهذه الأشياء التي تتبدل وتتغير كما يفعله الجهال اليوم ويقولون: هذا من الإعجاز العلمي.

Thus, we do not speak about the Qur'ān with our inadequate minds, but rather its interpretation is only made by Allah ﷻ, who revealed it, or the Prophet ﷺ who was entrusted with expounding it, or the Companions, who learned it from the Prophet ﷺ or the Tābi'ūn who related it as being heard by the students (Companions) of the Prophet ﷺ, or the Arabic language, in which it was revealed, because it was revealed in *a clear Arabic tongue.* As for interpreting the Qur'ān according to what some doctor or intellectual or astronomer says... the theories of today can be invalidated by the theories of tomorrow, because they are the work of man. Therefore, the word of Allah ﷻ is not to be interpreted according to these things that change and are modified. This is what some ignorant people do today and call it a scientific miracle.

قوله: **(ونشهد أنه كلام رب العالمين)** نشهد أن القرآن كلام الله تكلم الله به حقيقة، وسمعه جبريل من الله، وبلغه إلىٰ النبي صلىٰ الله عليه وسلم، وبلغه محمد عليه الصلاة والسلام إلىٰ أمته، وبلغته أمته كل جيل إلىٰ الجيل الذي بعده، نحن نكتبه ونقرؤه ونحفظه، وهو بذلك كلام الله ما هو بكلامنا، ولا كلام النبي صلىٰ الله عليه وسلم، ولا كلام جبريل عليه السلام.

The author says: **"And we testify that it is the word of the Lord of the Worlds."** We testify that the Qurʾān is the word of Allah ﷻ and that Allah ﷻ literally spoke that word. Jibrīl ﵇ heard it from Allah ﷻ and delivered it to the Prophet ﷺ, and Muḥammad ﷺ delivered it to his Ummah, and the Ummah passed it down from generation to generation. We write it down, recite it, and memorize it, yet it is still the speech of Allah ﷻ and not our own speech, nor is it the speech of the Prophet ﷺ or Jibrīl ﵇.

المتن

(١٢٨) نَزَلَ بِهِ الرُّوحُ الْأَمِينُ، فَعَلَّمَهُ سَيِّدَ الْمُرْسَلِينَ مُحَمَّدًا ﷺ.

(128) *Al-Rūh al-Amīn* (The Trusted Spirit) descended with it and taught it to the Chief of the Messengers, Muḥammad ﷺ.

الشرح

الروح الأمين هو جبريل، وسمي بهذا لأنه مؤتمن لا يغير ولا يبدل؛ مؤتمن علىٰ ما حمله الله، لا يتهم بالخيانة كما تقوله اليهود يقولون: جبريل عدونا. أو كما يقوله غلاة الشيعة: إن الرسالة لعلي ولكن جبريل خان وبلغها إلىٰ محمد صلىٰ الله عليه وسلم. فهذا تكذيب لله؛ لأن الله سماه أميناً.

The *Trusted Spirit* is Jibrīl ﷺ. He is named so because he was trusted not to change or alter anything and was entrusted to do what Allah ﷻ commanded him to do. He is not to be suspected as being disloyal, such as what Jews say, "Jibrīl is our enemy!" Or like what extremist Shi'ites say, that the message was meant for 'Alī but Jibrīl betrayed and delivered it to Muḥammad ﷺ. This is disbelief in Allah ﷻ because He called him *trusted*.

فأنزل الله في اليهود: ﴿قُلْ مَن كَانَ عَدُوًّا لِّجِبْرِيلَ فَإِنَّهُۥ نَزَّلَهُۥ عَلَىٰ قَلْبِكَ بِإِذْنِ ٱللَّهِ مُصَدِّقًا لِّمَا بَيْنَ يَدَيْهِ﴾ [البقرة:٩٧]، ثم قال: ﴿مَن كَانَ عَدُوًّا لِّلَّهِ وَمَلَـٰٓئِكَتِهِۦ وَرُسُلِهِۦ وَجِبْرِيلَ وَمِيكَىٰلَ فَإِنَّ ٱللَّهَ عَدُوٌّ لِّلْكَـٰفِرِينَ ۝﴾ [البقرة: ٩٨].

Allah revealed the following verse concerning the Jews: **{Say, 'Whoever is an enemy to Gabriel – it is [none but] he who has brought the Qur'ān down upon your heart, [O Muḥammad], by the permission of Allah, confirming that which was before it.'}** [Qur'ān 2:97] Then, He says: **{Whoever is an enemy to Allah and His angels and His messengers and Gabriel and Michael – then indeed, Allah is an enemy to the disbelievers.}** [Qur'ān 2: 98]

من عادىٰ جبريل، أو ملكًا من الملائكة، فإن الله عدوه وكذا من عادىٰ رسولاً من الرسل، فهو كافر، ومن عادىٰ وليًّا من أولياء الله فإنه مبارز الله بالمحاربة، كما صح في الحديث، فجبريل علَّمه للنبي صلىٰ الله عليه وسلم، قال تعالىٰ: ﴿عَلَّمَهُۥ شَدِيدُ ٱلْقُوَىٰ ۝﴾ [النجم:٥] وضمير المفعول في (علمه) راجع إلىٰ النبي صلىٰ الله عليه وسلم، وشديد القوىٰ: جبريل عليه الصلاة والسلام، فعلَّم النبي صلىٰ الله عليه وسلم بأمر الله.

If anyone takes Jibrīl ﷺ or any angel as an enemy, then Allah ﷻ is an enemy to that person. Likewise, if someone takes one of the Messengers of Allah as an enemy, then he is a disbeliever. And anyone who takes one of Allah's allies (*awliyā'*) as an enemy, has waged war against Allah ﷻ, as authentically related in a *ḥadīth*.[57] This is because Jibrīl ﷺ taught it to the Prophet

---

57 It is related that Abū Hurayrah ؓ said: The Messenger of Allah ﷺ said: "Allah Almighty said: 'He who has shown enmity to one of my allies has declared war against Me. And My servants do not draw nearer to Me by anything more beloved to Me than what I have obligated upon them. And if My servant keeps drawing near to Me by do-

ﷺ. Allah ﷻ says: **{Taught to him by one intense in strength.} [Qurʾān 53:5]** The pronoun of the object ('him') in '*taught to him*' refers to the Prophet ﷺ; and '*one intense in strength*' refers to Jibrīl عليه السلام. He taught him at the command of Allah ﷻ.

المتن

(١٢٩) وَهُوَ كَلامُ اللهِ تَعالَىٰ لا يُساوِيهِ شَيْءٌ مِنْ كَلامِ الْمَخْلُوقِينَ.

(129) It is the speech of Allah, the Most High and there is nothing on its level from the speech of created beings.

الشرح

هو كلام الله، تكلم به سبحانه حقيقة، وسمعه جبريل من الله حقيقة، وبلغه إلىٰ النبي صلىٰ الله عليه وسلم من غير زيادة ولا نقصان ﴿لَّا يَأْتِيهِ ٱلْبَٰطِلُ مِنۢ بَيْنِ يَدَيْهِ وَلَا مِنْ خَلْفِهِۦ﴾ [فصلت:٤٢]، ﴿وَإِن كَادُوا۟ لَيَفْتِنُونَكَ عَنِ ٱلَّذِىٓ أَوْحَيْنَآ إِلَيْكَ لِتَفْتَرِىَ عَلَيْنَا غَيْرَهُۥ ۖ وَإِذًا لَّٱتَّخَذُوكَ خَلِيلًا ﴿٧٣﴾ وَلَوْلَآ أَن ثَبَّتْنَٰكَ لَقَدْ كِدتَّ تَرْكَنُ إِلَيْهِمْ شَيْـًٔا قَلِيلًا ﴿٧٤﴾ إِذًا لَّأَذَقْنَٰكَ ضِعْفَ ٱلْحَيَوٰةِ وَضِعْفَ ٱلْمَمَاتِ ثُمَّ لَا تَجِدُ لَكَ عَلَيْنَا نَصِيرًا ﴿٧٥﴾﴾ [الإسراء:٧٣-٧٥] فالرسول يبلغ القرآن، لا ينقص ولا يزيد ولا يبدل ﴿وَلَوْ تَقَوَّلَ عَلَيْنَا بَعْضَ ٱلْأَقَاوِيلِ ﴿٤٤﴾ لَأَخَذْنَا مِنْهُ بِٱلْيَمِينِ ﴿٤٥﴾ ثُمَّ لَقَطَعْنَا مِنْهُ ٱلْوَتِينَ ﴿٤٦﴾﴾ [الحاقة:٤٤-٤٦].

It is the speech of Allah ﷻ, which He spoke in reality. Jibrīl عليه السلام heard it from Allah ﷻ, in reality, and he delivered it to the Prophet ﷺ without addition or omission. **{Falsehood cannot approach it from before it or from behind it.} [Qurʾān 41:42] {And indeed, they were about to tempt you away from that which We revealed to you in order to [make] you invent about Us something else; and then they would have taken you as a friend. And if We had not strengthened you, you would have almost inclined to them a little. Then [if you had], We would have**

---

ing beyond the obligations, then I will love him....'" Al-Bukhārī, no. 6502.

made you taste double [punishment in] life and double [after] death. Then you would not find for yourself against Us a helper.} [Qur'ān 17:73-75] Thus, the Messenger ﷺ delivered the Qur'ān without addition, omission, or alteration. **{And if Muḥammad had made up about Us some [false] sayings, We would have seized him by the right hand; Then We would have cut from him the aorta.} [Qur'ān 69:44-46]**

وهو كلام الله، سبحانه وتعالىٰ كما نزل، فالله حفظه من الزيادة والنقص: ﴿إِنَّا نَحْنُ نَزَّلْنَا ٱلذِّكْرَ وَإِنَّا لَهُۥ لَحَـٰفِظُونَ ۝٩﴾ [الحجر:٩]

It is the speech of Allah ﷻ, as it was revealed. Allah ﷻ has preserved it from additions and omissions. **{Indeed, it is We who sent down the Qur'ān and indeed, We will be its guardian.} [Qur'ān 15:9]**

المتن

(١٣٠) وَلا نَقُولُ بِخَلْقِهِ، وَلا نُخالِفُ جَماعَةَ الْمُسْلِمِينَ.

(130) We do not say that it was created, and we do not oppose the united community (*jamā'ah*) of the Muslims.

الشرح

لا نقول: القرآن مخلوق، كما تقول الجهمية، فهذا كفر وجحود لكلام الله، ووصف لله بالنقص وأنه لا يتكلم، والذي لا يتكلم يكون ناقصاً ولا يكون إلهاً.

We do not say that the Qur'ān is created, as the Jahmīyyah sect says. This is disbelief and rejection of the speech of Allah ﷻ. It also implies a shortcoming to Allah ﷻ, namely that He does not speak, as anything that does not speak is imperfect and is not a deity.

ولهذا لما قال قوم السامري: هذا إلهكم وإله موسىٰ، يعنون العجل أو التمثال، قال الله جل وعلا: ﴿أَفَلَا يَرَوْنَ أَلَّا يَرْجِعُ إِلَيْهِمْ قَوْلًا وَلَا يَمْلِكُ لَهُمْ ضَرًّا وَلَا نَفْعًا ۝٨٩﴾ [طه:٨٩] فقال: ﴿أَلَّا يَرْجِعُ إِلَيْهِمْ قَوْلًا﴾ أي: لا يتكلم، فدل علىٰ بطلان

عبادتهم له.

To this effect, the people of the Samaritan said: **{This is your god and the god of Moses.} [Qur'ān 20:88]** They were referring to the calf or the statue. Allah ﷻ says: **{Did they not see that it could not return to them any speech and that it did not possess for them any harm or benefit?} [Qur'ān 20:89]** The Almighty says, ***'that it could not return to them any speech'***, meaning that it does not speak. This is evidence for the wrongfulness of their worship of it.

وفي الآية الأخرىٰ: ﴿أَلَمْ يَرَوْا۟ أَنَّهُۥ لَا يُكَلِّمُهُمْ وَلَا يَهْدِيهِمْ سَبِيلًا﴾ [الأعراف:١٤٨] والكلام صفة كمال، وعدم الكلام صفة نقص، فالله سبحانه وتعالىٰ منزه عن صفات النقص، ومتصف بصفات الكمال.

In another verse, Allah ﷻ says: **{Did they not see that it could neither speak to them nor guide them to a way?} [Qur'ān 7:148]** Speech is an attribute of perfection, and the inability to speak is an attribute of imperfection. Allah ﷻ transcends all attributes of imperfection, and He is characterized by attributes of perfection.

(ولا نخالف جماعة المسلمين) فجماعة المسلمين يؤمنون بأنه منزل حقيقة غير مخلوق، منه بدأ وإليه يعود، هذه عقيدة المسلمين في القرآن.

"And we do not oppose the united community *(jamā'ah)* of Muslims": The united community of Muslims believes that it was revealed in reality and is not a created thing. From Him it began and to Him shall it return. This is the doctrine of the Muslims concerning the Qur'ān.

وكذلك لا نخالف جماعة المسلمين في كل ما اجتمعوا عليه من أمور الدين. قال تعالىٰ: ﴿وَمَن يُشَاقِقِ ٱلرَّسُولَ مِنۢ بَعْدِ مَا تَبَيَّنَ لَهُ ٱلْهُدَىٰ وَيَتَّبِعْ غَيْرَ سَبِيلِ ٱلْمُؤْمِنِينَ نُوَلِّهِۦ مَا تَوَلَّىٰ وَنُصْلِهِۦ جَهَنَّمَ ۖ وَسَآءَتْ مَصِيرًا ﴿١١٥﴾﴾.

Likewise, we do not oppose the united community of Muslims in anything that they have agreed on in matters of religion. Allah ﷻ says: **{And whoever opposes the Messenger after guidance has become clear to him, we will give him what he has taken and drive him into Hell, and evil it**

is as a destination.}

(من الله بدأ) وليس كما يقول بعض الضلال: إن جبريل أخذه من اللوح المحفوظ، بل سمعه من الله مباشرة، **(وإليه يعود)** أي: في آخر الزمان، يرفع القرآن إلىٰ الله عز وجل، وهذا من علامات الساعة، فيُنزع القرآن من المصاحف وصدور الرجال، فلا يبقىٰ في الأرض.

'From Allah it began': It is not as some misguided people have said: That Jibrīl took it from *al-Lawḥ al-Maḥfūẓ* (the Preserved Tablet). Rather, he heard it directly from Allah ﷻ. *'To Him it shall return'*: That is to say, in the end of times the Qur'ān will ascend to Allah ﷻ, which is one of the signs of the Hour. The Qur'ān will be removed from the codices and from people's hearts and will not remain on earth.

المتن

(١٣١) وَلا نُكَفِّرُ أَحَدًا مِنْ أَهْلِ الْقِبْلَةِ بِذَنْبٍ، ما لَمْ يَسْتَحِلَّهُ.

(131) We do not declare anyone from *Ahl al-Qiblah* (the people of the *qiblah*) a disbeliever over sin, so long as they do not say it is lawful.

الشرح

(ولا نكفّر أحداً من أهل القبلة بذنب ما لم يستحله) هذا كما سبق أن الذنب إذا لم يكن كفراً أو شركاً مخرجاً من الملة، فإننا لا نُكَفّر به المسلم، بل نعتقد أنه مؤمن ناقص الإيمان، معرض للوعيد وتحت المشيئة. هذه عقيدة المسلم، ما لم يستحله، فإذا استحل ما حرم الله فإنه يكفر، كما لو استحل الربا أو الخمر أو الميتة أولحم الخنزير أو الزنا، إذا استحل ما حرم الله كفر بالله، وكذلك العكس: لو حرم ما أحل الله كفر: ﴿ٱتَّخَذُوٓاْ أَحۡبَارَهُمۡ وَرُهۡبَٰنَهُمۡ أَرۡبَابٗا مِّن دُونِ ٱللَّهِ وَٱلۡمَسِيحَ ٱبۡنَ مَرۡيَمَ﴾ [التوبة:٣١] وجاء تفسير الآية بأنهم أحلوا لهم الحرام وحرموا عليهم

الحلال فأطاعوهم.

As mentioned, as long as the sin is not an act of disbelief or idolatry that removes one from the religion, we do not declare any Muslim an unbeliever on account of it. Rather, we believe that he is a believer with incomplete faith, and who is under threat and under Allah's ﷻ will. This is the belief of a Muslim, as long as he does not declare that sin to be lawful. If anyone says that which Allah ﷻ has forbidden is lawful, like if someone says that *ribā* (usury), *khamr* (wine), or the flesh of an unslaughtered animal (*maytah*), or the flesh of swine, or *zinā* (fornication) is lawful, then they have disbelieved in Allah ﷻ. The opposite is also true: if someone says that what Allah ﷻ has made lawful is unlawful, then they have also disbelieved. **{They have taken their scholars and monks as lords besides Allah, and [also] the Messiah, the son of Mary. And they were not commanded except to worship one God; there is no deity except Him. Exalted is He above whatever they associate with Him.} [Qur'ān 9:31]** It has been related concerning the interpretation of this verse that they declared as lawful what was unlawful to them and declared as unlawful what was lawful to them, and they obeyed them.[58]

أما لو فعل الذنب وهو لم يستحله بل يعترف أنه حرام فهذا لا يكفر ولو كان الذنب كبيرة دون الشرك والكفر لكنه يكون مؤمناً ناقص الإيمان أو فاسقاً بكبيرته مؤمن بإيمانه.

On the other hand, if someone commits a sin but does not claim that it is lawful, rather acknowledges the fact that it is forbidden, then we do not declare such a person an unbeliever, even if it were any major sin below *shirk* and disbelief. Even so, such a person is a believer with a shortcoming in faith, or a *fāsiq* (sinner) because of his great sin and a believer because of his faith.

وقوله: (لا نكفر بذنب) ليس علىٰ إطلاقه، فتارك الصلاة متعمداً يكفر، كما دل

58 It is related that ʿAdī ibn Ḥātim ﷺ said: "I came to the Prophet ﷺ and I had a crucifix of gold around my neck, so he said: 'O ʿAdī, remove this idol from you.' I heard him read from *Sūrat Barāʾah*: ***'They have taken their scholars and monks as lords besides Allah'.*** He said: 'Verily, they did not worship them but if they (their scholars and monks) declared something to be lawful to them, they made it lawful, and if they declared something unlawful to them, they made it unlawful.'" Al-Tirmidhī, no. 3095.

علىٰ ذلك الكتاب والسنة.

The author says: **"We do not declare anyone a disbeliever over sin":** This is with an exception: Someone who deliberately abandons *ṣalāh* (prayer) has committed an act of disbelief[59], as evidenced in the Qur'ān and Sunnah.

المتن

(١٣٢) وَلا نَقُولُ: لا يَضُرُّ مَعَ الْإِيمانِ ذَنْبٌ لِمَنْ عَمِلَهُ.

(132) We do not say that sin does not affect the faith of the one who commits it.

الشرح

كما تقوله المرجئة، يقولون: ما دام مصدقًا بقلبه فهو مؤمن كامل الإيمان، أما الأعمال فأمرها هيّن، فالذي لا يصلي ولا يصوم ولا يحج ولا يزكي ولا يعمل شيئًا من أعمال الطاعة، يقولون: هو مؤمن بمجرد ما في قلبه! وهذا من أعظم الضلال.

As the Murji'ites say, that as long as someone affirms faith in his heart then he is a believer with complete faith. Deeds, on the other hand, are insignificant. Therefore, someone who does not pray, fast, perform *Ḥajj* (pilgrimage), pay *zakāh* (alms), nor does he do any acts of obedience, they say that he is a believer simply because of what lies in his heart! This is one of the most major forms of misguidance.

فالرد عليهم أن الذنوب تضر علىٰ كل حال، منها ما يزيل الإيمان بالكلية، ومنها ما لا يزيله بالكلية بل ينقصه وصاحبها معرض للوعيد المرتب عليها.

The response to them is that sins have a negative effect in all states: Some of

59 It is related that Buraydah ibn al-Ḥuṣayb al-Aslami ﷺ said: "The Messenger of Allah ﷺ said: "The covenant that stands between us and them is the *ṣalāh*, so whoever abandons it has disbelieved." Aḥmad, 5/346, 355; al-Tirmidhī, no. 2621; al-Nasā'ī, 1/231; Ibn Mājah, no. 1079.

them invalidate faith altogether while some of them do not. Rather, they detract from faith and the one who commits them falls under the consequent threat.

المتن

(١٣٣) نَرْجُو لِلْمُحْسِنِينَ مِنَ الْمُؤْمِنِينَ أَنْ يَعْفُوَ عَنْهُمْ، وَيُدْخِلَهُمُ الْجَنَّةَ بِرَحْمَتِهِ، وَلا نَأْمَنُ عَلَيْهِمْ، وَلا نَشْهَدُ لَهُمْ بِالْجَنَّةِ.

(133) We hope that [Allah] will forgive the good believers (*muḥsinīn*) and send them to Jannah via His mercy, but we do not claim that they are totally secure, nor do we testify that they will go to Jannah.

الشرح

هذا بحث للشهادة لمعين أنه من أهل الجنة، أو أنه من أهل النار، نحن لا نشهد لأحد بجنة أو نار إلا بدليل، إلا من شهد له المصطفىٰ عليه الصلاة والسلام أنه من أهل الجنة، شهدنا له بذلك، ومن شهد له النبي صلىٰ الله عليه وسلم بالنار شهدنا له بذلك، هذا بالنسبة إلىٰ المعينين، أما بالنسبة إلىٰ العموم فنعتقد أن الكافرين في النار، وأن المؤمنين في الجنة.

This is a discussion about testifying to whether a specific person is one of the dwellers of Jannah or whether he is one of the dwellers of the Fire. We do not testify that anyone is either in Jannah or in the Fire without evidence. However, if the Prophet ﷺ gave testimony that someone is among the dwellers of Jannah, then we attest to that, and if the Prophet ﷺ gave testimony that someone is in the Fire, we attest to that likewise. This is with respect to specific individuals. However, in a general sense, we believe that the disbelievers are in the Fire and the believers are in Jannah.

أما علىٰ وجه الخصوص فلا نحكم لأحد إلا بالدليل، لكن نرجو للمحسن ونخاف علىٰ المسيء. هذه عقيدة المسلمين.

In a specific sense, though, we do not pass judgment about anyone in specific without evidence. However, we hope well for good believers and fear for those who do wrong. This is the doctrine of the Muslims.

المتن

(١٣٤) وَنَسْتَغْفِرُ لِمُسِيئِهِمْ، وَنَخافُ عَلَيْهِمْ، وَلا نُقَنِّطُهُمْ.

(134) We ask forgiveness for sinful Muslims and fear for them, but do not lose hope for them.

الشرح

نستغفر للمسيء؛ لأنه أخونا، وندعو له بالتوبة والتوفيق؛ وإن كان مذنبًا، وهذا حق الإيمان علينا ﴿وَٱسْتَغْفِرْ لِذَنۢبِكَ وَلِلْمُؤْمِنِينَ وَٱلْمُؤْمِنَٰتِ﴾ [محمد:١٩].

We ask forgiveness for bad Muslims because they are our brothers. We pray for them to repent and be given grace, although they are guilty of sin. It is our duty of faith towards them. **{And ask forgiveness for your sin and for the believing men and believing women.} [Qur'ān 47:19]**

ولا نُقنّطُ المذنب من رحمة الله كما تقوله الخوارج والمعتزلة، لا نقنطه من رحمة الله، بل هو معرض للوعيد وتحت المشيئة، وإن تاب تاب الله عليه عز وجل: ﴿إِنَّهُۥ لَا يَاْيْـَٔسُ مِن رَّوْحِ ٱللَّهِ إِلَّا ٱلْقَوْمُ ٱلْكَٰفِرُونَ ﴿٨٧﴾﴾ [يوسف:٨٧] ﴿قَالَ وَمَن يَقْنَطُ مِن رَّحْمَةِ رَبِّهِۦٓ إِلَّا ٱلضَّآلُّونَ ﴿٥٦﴾﴾ [الحجر:٥٦] ﴿قُلْ يَٰعِبَادِىَ ٱلَّذِينَ أَسْرَفُواْ عَلَىٰٓ أَنفُسِهِمْ لَا تَقْنَطُواْ مِن رَّحْمَةِ ٱللَّهِ﴾ [الزمر: ٥٣].

We do not place any sinner beyond any hope for Allah's ﷻ mercy, as do the Khārijites and Muʿtazilites. We do not say that there is no hope for such people but rather that they are under threat and under Allah's ﷻ will. Allah ﷻ is forgiving of those who turn to Him in repentance. **{Indeed, no one despairs of relief from Allah except the disbelieving people.} [Qur'ān 12:87] {And who despairs of the mercy of his Lord except for those**

astray?} [Qur'ān 15:56] {Say, 'O My servants who have transgressed against themselves [by sinning], do not despair of the mercy of Allah.'} [Qur'ān 39: 53]

والوعيدية الذين هم الخوارج ومن سار في ركابهم، هم الذين يُقنّطون الناس من رحمة الله، ويخرجونهم من الملة بذنوبهم، وإن كانت دون الشرك.

The 'threat sect' (*al-waʿīdīyah*), namely the Khārijites and those who tread their path, are the ones who say there is no hope for people in terms of Allah's ﷻ mercy. They call people disbelievers on account of sins, even those less serious than polytheism.

المتن

(١٣٥) والْأَمْنُ والْإِياسُ يَنْقُلانِ عَنْ مِلَّةِ الْإِسْلامِ.

(135) Loss of fear [of Allah's punishment] and loss of hope [of Allah's mercy] remove one from Islām.

الشرح

من أصول العقيدة الإسلامية: الخوف والرجاء، وهما من أعظم أصول العقيدة، والخوف والرجاء لابد من الجمع بينهما، لا يكفي الاقتصار على واحد منهما فقط، كما قال تعالى في وصف أنبيائه: ﴿إِنَّهُمْ كَانُوا۟ يُسَٰرِعُونَ فِى ٱلْخَيْرَٰتِ وَيَدْعُونَنَا رَغَبًا وَرَهَبًا﴾ [الأنبياء: ٩٠].

Among the fundamental principles of the Islamic faith are *fear* and *hope*. They are two of the *greatest* principles of faith. Fear and hope have to be evoked in combination. It is not sufficient to have only one of them. Allah ﷻ says, describing His Prophets: **{Indeed, they used to hasten to good deeds and supplicate Us in hope (*raghaban*) and fear (*rahaban*).} [Qur'ān 21:90]**

رغباً: هذا هو الرجاء، ورهباً: هذا هو الخوف، وقال سبحانه وتعالى: ﴿أُوْلَٰٓئِكَ

﴿ٱلَّذِينَ يَدْعُونَ يَبْتَغُونَ إِلَىٰ رَبِّهِمُ ٱلْوَسِيلَةَ أَيُّهُمْ أَقْرَبُ وَيَرْجُونَ رَحْمَتَهُۥ وَيَخَافُونَ عَذَابَهُۥٓ ۚ إِنَّ عَذَابَ رَبِّكَ كَانَ مَحْذُورًا ۝٥٧﴾ [الإسراء:٥٧] فهم يجمعون بين الخوف والرجاء.

Raghaban [lit. 'desire'] means *rajā'* (hope), and *rahaban* is *khawf* (fear). Allah ﷻ says: **{Those whom they invoke seek means of access to their Lord, [striving as to] which of them would be nearest, and they hope for His mercy and fear His punishment. Indeed, the punishment of your Lord is ever feared.} [Qur'ān 17:57]** Thus, they combine between fear and hope.

وقال جل وعلا: ﴿أَمَّنْ هُوَ قَٰنِتٌ ءَانَآءَ ٱلَّيْلِ سَاجِدًا وَقَآئِمًا يَحْذَرُ ٱلْءَاخِرَةَ وَيَرْجُوا۟ رَحْمَةَ رَبِّهِۦ ۗ﴾ [الزمر:٩]. ولابد معهما من المحبة لله، فلابد من هذه الأمور الثلاثة: المحبة لله، والخوف منه سبحانه وتعالىٰ، والرجاء لفضله.

Allah ﷻ also says: **{Is one who is devoutly obedient during periods of the night, prostrating and standing [in prayer], fearing the Hereafter and hoping for the mercy of his Lord, [like one who does not]?} [Qur'ān 92:9]** Along with these, there also has to be love for Allah ﷻ. All of these three things are necessary: Love for Allah ﷻ, fear of Him, and hope for His bounty.

فمن اقتصر علىٰ المحبة فقط فهو صوفي، فالصوفية يعبدون الله عز وجل بالمحبة، ولا يخافون ولا يرجون، يقول قائلهم؛ أنا لا أعبده طمعاً في جنته، ولا خوفاً من ناره، وإنما أعبده للمحبة فقط، وهذا ضلال والعياذ بالله.

Anyone who confines himself to love alone is a *Ṣūfī* (mystic). The *Ṣūfīs* worship Allah ﷻ through love but they do not fear or have hope [for anything]. A *Ṣūfī* may say, "I do not worship Allah ﷻ out of desire for Jannah, nor out of fear of the Fire; I worship Him only for the sake of love". Such is sheer misguidance and Allah ﷻ is our refuge.

ومن عبد الله بالخوف فقط فهو من الخوارج؛ لأن الخوارج أخذوا جانب الخوف والوعيد فقط، فكفروا بالمعاصي.

If someone worships Allah ﷻ in fear alone, then he is a Khārijite. That is because the Khārijites hold fast to the aspect of fear and focus on the threat of sins only, so they declare others disbelievers on account of sins.

ومن عبد الله بالرجاء فقط فهو من المرجئة، الذين أخذوا جانب الرجاء فقط، وتركوا جانب الخوف.

If someone worships Allah ﷻ in hope alone, then he is a Murjiʾite. The Murjiʾites are those who hold fast to the aspect of hope alone and disregard the aspect of fear.

أما أهل التوحيد فيعبدون الله بجميع الثلاث: بالحب والخوف والرجاء، ثم إن الخوف لا يكون معه قنوط، فإن كان معه قنوط من رحمة الله صار كفراً ﴿إِنَّهُۥ لَا يَاْيْـَٔسُ مِن رَّوْحِ ٱللَّهِ إِلَّا ٱلْقَوْمُ ٱلْكَٰفِرُونَ ۝٨٧﴾ [يوسف:٨٧] قال الخليل عليه الصلاة والسلام: ﴿قَالَ وَمَن يَقْنَطُ مِن رَّحْمَةِ رَبِّهِۦٓ إِلَّا ٱلضَّآلُّونَ ۝٥٦﴾ [الحجر:٥٦].

The people of *tawḥīd* worship Allah ﷻ with all three: with love, fear, and hope. Furthermore, the fear they have is not accompanied by despair. If it is accompanied by despair from Allah's ﷻ mercy, it then becomes disbelief. **{Indeed, no one despairs of relief from Allah except the disbelieving people.} [Qurʾān 12:87]** Ibrāhīm ﵇ said: **{And who despairs of the mercy of his Lord except for those astray?} [Qurʾān 15:56]**

وكذلك الرجاء لا يكون رجاء مع الأمن من مكر الله وعدم الخوف، وهذا مذهب المرجئة، وهو مذهب ضال ﴿أَفَأَمِنُواْ مَكْرَ ٱللَّهِۚ فَلَا يَأْمَنُ مَكْرَ ٱللَّهِ إِلَّا ٱلْقَوْمُ ٱلْخَٰسِرُونَ ۝٩٩﴾ [الأعراف:٩٩] فالرجاء فقط كفر، والخوف دون الرجاء كفر، ولذلك قال المصنف: ينقلان عن ملة الإسلام.

Likewise, hope is not hope if accompanied by fearlessness (*amn*) of Allah's ﷻ plan (*makr*), which is the doctrine of the Murjiʿites, and which is wayward from the path. **{Then did they feel secure from the plan of Allah? But no one feels secure from the plan of Allah except thc losing people.} [Qurʾān 7:99]** Thus, hope alone is disbelief, so is fear alone without hope. Hence, the author said that they become disbelievers.

لذا يقول بعض السلف: يجب علىٰ العبد أن يكون بين الخوف والرجاء؛ يعني: يسوي بينهما، كجناحي الطائر، وجناحا الطائر معتدلان، لو اختل واحد منهما سقط، فكذلك العبد بين الخوف والرجاء كجناحي الطائر.

This is why some of the predecessors said that the servant of Allah has to be in a state between fear and hope, that is, to have an equal amount of each, like the wings of a bird. The wings of a bird are even, and if one of them were not so, the bird would fall from the sky. Likewise, a servant of Allah should be in a balanced state between fear and hope like the wings of a bird.

❀❀❀

المتن

(١٣٦) وَسَبِيلُ الْحَقِّ بَيْنَهُما لِأَهْلِ الْقِبْلَةِ.

(136) The right path for *Ahl al-Qiblah* is between the two.

الشرح

(**الحق بينهما**) أي: الخوف والرجاء (**لأهل القبلة**) أي: المسلمين، سُمُّوا أهل القبلة؛ لأنهم يصلون إلىٰ الكعبة، أما من لا يصلي إلىٰ الكعبة فليس من المسلمين لأن الله أمر بالتوجه إلىٰ الكعبة، فالواجب اتباع أمره سبحانه حينما نسخ الاستقبال لبيت المقدس، فالمؤمن يدور مع الأوامر؛ لأنه عبد لله ﴿وَمَا جَعَلْنَا ٱلْقِبْلَةَ ٱلَّتِي كُنتَ عَلَيْهَآ إِلَّا لِنَعْلَمَ مَن يَتَّبِعُ ٱلرَّسُولَ مِمَّن يَنقَلِبُ عَلَىٰ عَقِبَيْهِ﴾ [البقرة:١٤٣].

"Is between the two": I.e. between fear and hope. Muslims are called *ahl al-qiblah* (the people of the *qiblah*) because they pray toward the Ka'bah. Anyone who does not pray towards the Ka'bah is not one of the Muslims because Allah ﷺ commanded us to face the Ka'bah in prayer. It is incumbent to follow His command as He abrogated prayer in the direction of Bayt al-Maqdis. The believers revolve around the commands because they are servants of Allah ﷺ. **{And We did not make the *qiblah* which you used to face except that We might make evident who would follow the**

Messenger from who would turn back on his heels.} [Qurʾān 2:143]

المتن

(١٣٧) وَلا يَخْرُجُ الْعَبْدُ مِنَ الْإِيمانِ إِلّا بِجُحُودِ ما أَدْخَلَهُ فِيهِ.

(137) One does not leave the faith unless they reject what enters them into it.

الشرح

هذا الكلام فيه مؤاخذة؛ لأن قصر الكفر علىٰ الجحود مذهب المرجئة، ونواقض الإسلام كثيرة، منها: الجحود، ومنها: الشرك بالله عز وجل، ومنها: الاستهزاء بالدين أو بشيء منه ولو لم يجحد، وهي نواقض كثيرة ذكرها العلماء والفقهاء في أبواب الردة، ومنها: تحليل الحرام وتحريم الحلال.

This statement entails some criticism, because it is the doctrine of the Murjiʾites to restrict disbelief to outright rejection (*juḥūd*). There are many things that render someone's acceptance of Islām invalid, including rejection (*juḥūd*), polytheism (*shirk*), mocking Islām or a part of it, even without rejection. There are many invalidators which the scholars of Islām and experts of Islamic law (*fuqahāʾ*) have listed in the chapters of apostasy (*riddah*). Another example is to declare lawful what is unlawful and to declare unlawful what is lawful.

وذكر شيخ الإسلام محمد بن عبد الوهاب منها عشرة، وهي أهمها، وإلا فالنواقض كثيرة. فقصرُ نواقض الإسلام علىٰ الجحود فقط غلط. وبعض الكتّاب المتعالمين اليوم يحاولون إظهار هذا المذهب من أجل أن يصير الناس في سعة من الدين، ما دام أنه لم يجحد فهو عندهم مسلم، إذا سجد للصنم وقال: أنا ما جحدت، وأنا معترف بالتوحيد، إنما هو ذنب من الذنوب. أو ذبح لغير الله أو سب الله أو سب الرسول أو سب الدين، يقولون: هذا مسلم لأنه؛ لم يجحد،

وهذا غلط كبير، وهذا يضيع الدين تماماً، فلا يبقىٰ دين فالواجب الحذر من هذا الخطر العظيم.

Shaykh al-Islām Muḥammad ibn ʿAbd al-Wahhāb mentioned ten invalidators of Islām; they are the most important of them, however, there are many. So it is wrong to limit the nullifiers of Islām to denial alone. Some writers of today who feign to be learned have tried to champion this doctrine so as to accommodate to people's religious persuasions. For them, as long as someone is not a denier (of the faith), he is a Muslim. If they prostrate themselves before idols and say, 'I have not denied anything, I acknowledge that Allah is one,' then that is only a sin. Or if someone slaughters an animal in sacrifice to anything besides Allah or directs an insult towards the Messenger of Allah or Islām, they say, 'He is a Muslim because he has not denied anything.' This is a great mistake and it is complete divestment of the religion as there would be no religion left by that. So it is obligatory to beware of this great danger.

المتن

(١٣٨) والْإِيمانُ: هُوَ الْإِقْرارُ بِاللِّسانِ، والتَّصْدِيقُ بِالْجَنانِ.

(138) Faith is to attest with the tongue and believe with the heart.

الشرح

هذا تعريف المرجئة، قصروا الإيمان علىٰ الإقرار باللسان والتصديق بالجنان.

This is the definition according to the Murji'ites; they limit faith to attestation with the tongue and belief with the heart.

فالقول الحق: أن الإيمان قول باللسان، واعتقاد بالقلب، وعمل بالجوارح، فالأعمال داخلة في حقيقة الإيمان، وليست بشيء زائد عن الإيمان، فمن اقتصر علىٰ القول باللسان والتصديق بالقلب دون العمل، فليس من أهل الإيمان الصحيح.

The true view is that faith is the word of the tongue, the belief of the heart and the action of the limbs. Thus, action is included in the reality of faith, and it is not something additional to it. Therefore, whoever confines the matter to the word of the tongue and the belief of the heart without action, he would not be from those of correct faith.

فالإيمان - كما قال العلماء - : قول باللسان وتصديق بالجنان وعمل بالجوارح، يزيد بالطاعة وينقص بالعصيان.

So, faith, according to the scholars of Islām, is: the word of the tongue, the belief of the heart and the action of the limbs. It increases with obedience and decreases with disobedience.

قال تعالىٰ: ﴿وَإِذَا تُلِيَتْ عَلَيْهِمْ ءَايَٰتُهُۥ زَادَتْهُمْ إِيمَٰنًا وَعَلَىٰ رَبِّهِمْ يَتَوَكَّلُونَ ۝٢﴾ [الأنفال:٢] وقال: ﴿فَأَمَّا ٱلَّذِينَ ءَامَنُوا۟ فَزَادَتْهُمْ إِيمَٰنًا﴾ [التوبة:١٢٤] وقال: ﴿وَيَزْدَادَ ٱلَّذِينَ ءَامَنُوٓا۟ إِيمَٰنًا﴾ [المدثر: ٣١] هذه الآيات تدل علىٰ زيادة الإيمان والنقص، كما في قوله عليه الصلاة والسلام: «**من رأىٰ منكم منكراً فليغيره بيده، فإن لم يستطع فبلسانه، فإن لم يستطع فبقلبه وذلك أضعف الإيمان**» فدل علىٰ أن الإيمان ينقص. وفي رواية: «**وليس وراء ذلك من الإيمان حبة خردل**» دل علىٰ أن الإيمان ينقص، حتىٰ يكون علىٰ وزن حبة خردل.

Allah ﷻ says: **{And when His verses are recited to them, it increases them in faith.} [Qur'ān 8:2]** Allah ﷻ also says: **{As for those who believed, it has increased them in faith.} [Qur'ān 9:124]** Allah ﷻ also says: **{And those who have believed will increase in faith.} [Qur'ān 74:31]** These verses are evidence that faith increases and decreases, as the Prophet ﷺ attests: "If any one of you sees an evil, then let him change it with their hands, and if they cannot, then with their tongue, and if he cannot, then with their heart, and that is the weakest of faith."[60] This is evidence that faith decreases. In another version: "There is not a mustard seed of faith beyond that."[61] This is evidence that faith decreases until it is the weight of a mustard seed.

60 Muslim, no. 49.
61 Muslim, no. 50.

وكما في الحديث الصحيح: «أخرجوا من النار من كان في قلبه أدنىٰ أدنىٰ مثقال حبة من خردل من إيمان».

In another authentic *ḥadīth*: "Bring out of the Fire anyone who has the smallest, smallest weight of a mustard seed of faith."[62]

فالإيمان قول باللسان واعتقاد بالقلب وعمل بالأركان يزيد بالطاعة وينقص بالعصيان، هذا تعريفه الصحيح المأخوذ من الكتاب والسنة.

Faith is the word of the tongue, the belief of the heart and the action of the body parts (limbs); it increases with obedience and decreases with disobedience. This is the correct definition as taken from the Qur'ān and Sunnah.

فليس كما تقوله الحنفية: قول باللسان واعتقاد بالجنان فقط.

It is not as the Ḥanafī scholars say: The word of the tongue and belief of the heart (*jinān*) alone.

وليس كما تقوله الكرامية: قول باللسان فقط.

It is also not as the Karāmīyyah sect says: The word of the tongue alone.

وليس كما تقوله الأشاعرة: اعتقاد القلب فقط.

It is also not as the Ashāʿirah say: The belief of the heart alone.

وليس كما تقوله الجهمية: هو المعرفة بالقلب فقط.

It is also not as the Jahmiyyah say: The understanding (*maʿrifah*) of the heart alone.

فالمرجئة أربع طوائف، أبعدها الجهمية، وعلىٰ قولهم يكون فرعون مؤمنـًا؛ لأنه عارف، وإبليس يكون مؤمنـًا؛ لأنه عارف بقلبه.

Thus, there are four denominations of the Murji'ites, the farthest from the truth being the Jahmīs. According to their proposition, Pharaoh would be a believer because he *knew,* and Iblīs would also be a believer because he knew in his heart.

62 Al-Bukhārī, no. 7510; Muslim, no. 192.

وعلىٰ قول الأشاعرة: إنه التصديق بالقلب، يكون أبو لهب وأبو طالب وأبو جهل وسائر المشركين يكونون مؤمنين؛ لأنهم موقنون بقلوبهم ومصدقون، يصدقون النبي صلىٰ الله عليه وسلم في قلوبهم، ولكن منعهم الكبر والحسد من اتباعه صلىٰ الله عليه وسلم.

The Ash'arīs say that it is the belief (confirmation) of the heart. Then, Abū Lahab, Abū Ṭālib, and all of the other idolaters would be believers because there was certainty in their hearts and they believed. They believed the Prophet ﷺ in their hearts, however, pride and envy prevented them from following him.

واليهود يعترفون أنه رسول الله صلىٰ الله عليه وسلم في قلوبهم، ولكن الحسد والكبر: ﴿ٱلَّذِينَ ءَاتَيْنَٰهُمُ ٱلْكِتَٰبَ يَعْرِفُونَهُۥ كَمَا يَعْرِفُونَ أَبْنَآءَهُمْ﴾ [البقرة:١٤٦]، وقال في المشركين: ﴿قَدْ نَعْلَمُ إِنَّهُۥ لَيَحْزُنُكَ ٱلَّذِى يَقُولُونَ فَإِنَّهُمْ لَا يُكَذِّبُونَكَ وَلَٰكِنَّ ٱلظَّٰلِمِينَ بِـَٔايَٰتِ ٱللَّهِ يَجْحَدُونَ ﴿٣٣﴾﴾ [الأنعام:٣٣]

The Jews acknowledged that he was the Messenger of Allah ﷺ in their hearts, however, it was a matter of pride and envy. **{Those to whom We gave the Scripture know him as they know their own sons.} [Qur'ān 2:146]** Allah ﷻ says about the idolaters: **{We know that you, [O Muḥammad], are saddened by what they say. And indeed, they do not call you untruthful, but it is the verses of Allah that the wrongdoers reject.} [Qur'ān 6:33]**

فمعنىٰ ﴿لَا يُكَذِّبُونَكَ﴾ أي أنهم يصدقونك.

'They do not call you untruthful' means that they believe you.

وأبو طالب يقول:

ولقد علمت أن دين محمد   من خير أديان البرية دينا

لولا الملامة أو حذار مسبةٍ   لرأيتني سمحاً بذاك مبينا

Abū Ṭālib said: "I know that the religion of Muḥammad is among the best religions of all creations. Were it not for blame and fear of insult, I would have declared faith openly."

المتن

(١٣٩) وَجَمِيعُ ما صَحَّ عَنْ رَسُولِ اللهِ ﷺ مِنَ الشَّرْعِ والْبَيانِ كُلُّهُ حَقٌّ.

(139) All of the legislations and teachings authentically reported from the Messenger of Allah ﷺ are the truth.

الشرح

هذا كلام طيب، كل ما صح عن رسول الله صلىٰ الله عليه وسلم فهو حق، بخلاف من يقولون: إن ما ورد عن رسول الله صلىٰ الله عليه وسلم ينقسم إلىٰ متواتر وآحاد، فلا يأخذون إلا بالمتواتر، ويقولون: أحاديث الآحاد تفيد العلم، ولا تفيد اليقين، ولا يستدل بها في العقيدة، وهذا باطل، فكل ما صح عن النبي صلىٰ الله عليه وسلم - متواتراً أو آحاداً، فإنه يفيد العلم، وتبنىٰ عليه العقيدة؛ لأنه صح عن الرسول صلىٰ الله عليه وسلم، وقال تعالىٰ: ﴿وَمَآ ءَاتَىٰكُمُ ٱلرَّسُولُ فَخُذُوهُ ...﴾ [الحشر:٧].

These are soothing words. Everything that the Messenger of Allah ﷺ was authentically related as having said or done is the truth. In contrast to those who say that the reports of the Messenger of Allah ﷺ can be classified into *mutawātir* (handed down concurrently through many *isnāds*) and *āḥād* ("singular", less than *mutawātir*). They only accept the *mutawātir* accounts and say that the *āḥād ḥadīths* do not provide knowledge (*'ilm*) nor certainty (*yaqīn*), and so they should not be used as evidence in matters of creed. This is false. Anything authentically reported from the Prophet ﷺ (whether *mutawātir* or *āḥād*) is a source of knowledge and matters of creed are to be based on it, due to it being authentically traced back to the Messenger of Allah ﷺ. Allah ﷻ says: **{And whatever the Messenger has given you – take.} [Qur'ān 59:7]**

فإذا صح عن النبي صلىٰ الله عليه وسلم حديث عمل به في كل شيء، بشرط أن يكون قد صح عن النبي صلىٰ الله عليه وسلم، فهناك طوائف الآن يشككون في السنة؛ منهم من يقول: لا يجوز العمل بالسنة مطلقاً، ويكفي العمل بالقرآن فقط، وهناك من يقول: يؤخذ من السنة المتواتر فقط، وكلا الطائفتين ضال.

If a *ḥadīth* is authentically traced to the Prophet ﷺ, it is to be acted upon in all matters, provided that it is correctly attributed to the Prophet ﷺ. There are groups now that are sceptical about the Sunnah, and some of them say that it is not right to act in accordance with the Sunnah unrestrictedly ([t] i.e. regardless of authenticity), and that it suffices to act in accordance with the Qurʾān[63]. There are also some people who say that the only thing that is acceptable from the Sunnah is that which is *mutawātir*. Both groups are astray.

فالواجب علىٰ المسلم أن يعتقد أن كل ما صح عن النبي صلىٰ الله عليه وسلم فهو حق، والرسول صلىٰ الله عليه وسلم عمل بخبر الواحد في وقائع كثيرة؛ رؤية الهلال؛ جاءه ابن عمر وأخبره بأنه رأىٰ الهلال فأمر الناس بالصيام، وجاءه أعرابي وأخبره أنه رأىٰ الهلال فقال له: «**أتشهد أن لا إله إلا الله؟ أتشهد أن محمداً رسول الله؟**» قال: نعم، فأمر النبي صلىٰ الله عليه وسلم الناس بالصيام، وهو خبر واحد.

It is obligatory for a Muslim to believe that all that is authentically attributed to the Prophet ﷺ is the truth. The Messenger of Allah ﷺ acted upon the testimony of a single person in many instances. In the sighting of the new moon, for example: Ibn ʿUmar ؓ came and told him that he had seen the new moon, so he commanded the Muslims to fast. A Bedouin Arab came to him and told him that he saw the new moon, so he asked him: "Do you testify that there is no God but Allah? Do you testify that Muḥammad is

63 It is related that al-Miqdām ibn Maʿdīkarib al-Kindī ؓ said: "The Messenger of Allah ﷺ said: 'Verily, I have been given the Book and its like as well. Verily, I have been given the Qurʾān and its like as well. Verily, there will soon come a man full and reclining on a couch, saying, 'Upon you is the Qurʾān. Whatever lawful thing you find in it, make lawful, and whatever unlawful thing you find in it, make unlawful.'" Aḥmad, 4/130; Abū Dāwūd, no. 3804, 4604. Aḥmad (according to a similar wording), 4/132; al-Tirmidhī, no. 2664; Ibn Mājah, no. 3193; al-Dārimī, no. 592.

the Messenger of Allah?" He said: "Yes". So, the Prophet ﷺ commanded the people to fast[64]. This was a singular narration.

كان الرسول صلىٰ الله عليه وسلم يرسل رسله آحاداً، وما كان يرسل جماعات، والمرسل إليهم يعملون بما بلغهم المندوب عن الرسول صلىٰ الله عليه وسلم.

The Prophet ﷺ used to also send his messengers individually. He did not send groups. Those who received the messages would have had to act upon what they heard from the single delegate of the Messenger of Allah ﷺ.

المتن

(١٣٩) والإِيمانُ واحِدٌ وَأَهْلُهُ فِي أَصْلِهِ سَواءٌ.

(139) Faith is one, and its people in regards to it are equal.

الشرح

هذا غلط؛ لأن الإيمان ليس واحداً، وليس أهله سواء، بل الإيمان يتفاضل، ويزيد وينقص، إلا عند المرجئة.

This is a mistake, because faith is not one, and the people of faith are not equal. Rather, there is disparity in faith and it increases and decreases. Only the Murji'ites believe otherwise.

والتصديق بالقلب ليس الناس فيه سواءً، فليس إيمان أبي بكر الصديق كإيمان الفاسق من المسلمين؛ لأن الفاسق من المسلمين إيمانه ضعيف جداً، وإيمان أبي بكر الصديق يعدل إيمان الأمة كلها، فليس الناس في أصله سواءً. هذا من ناحية أصله.

Affirmation in the heart is also not equal amongst the people. The faith of Abū Bakr al-Ṣiddīq ؓ is not like that of an open sinner among the Muslims,

64 Al-Tirmidhī, no. 691; Abū Dāwūd, no. 2340; Ibn Mājah, no. 1652; Ibn Khuzaymah, no. 1923; Ibn Ḥibbān, no. 870; al-Ḥākim, 1/424.

because the latter has very weak faith, whereas the faith of Abū Bakr al-Ṣiddīq amounts to the faith of the entire *Ummah*[65]. So people are not the same in the essence (*aṣl*) of faith, either. This is in terms of its essence (*aṣl*).

كذلك من ناحية العمل، الناس يتفاضلون في العمل، منهم كما قال الله عز وجل: ﴿ثُمَّ أَوْرَثْنَا ٱلْكِتَٰبَ ٱلَّذِينَ ٱصْطَفَيْنَا مِنْ عِبَادِنَا ۖ فَمِنْهُمْ ظَالِمٌ لِّنَفْسِهِۦ﴾ [فاطر:٣٢] هذا العاصي الذي معصيته دون الشرك، فإنه ظالم لنفسه؛ لأنه معرض نفس للخطر ﴿ومنهم مقتصد﴾ وهو الذي يعمل الواجبات ويتجنب المحرمات.

Likewise, when it comes to action: there is disparity between people in terms of actions, as Allah ﷻ says about some of them: **{Then we caused to inherit the Book those We have chosen of Our servants; and among them is he who wrongs himself.} [Qur'ān 35:32]** This is the sinner whose sin is less than polytheism, he wrongs himself as he is placing himself in danger. **{And among them is he who is moderate}** This is the one who meets his obligations and avoids doing what is forbidden.

﴿مِنْهُمْ سَابِقٌۢ بِٱلْخَيْرَٰتِ بِإِذْنِ ٱللَّهِ﴾ [فاطر:٣٢] وهذا هو الذي يعمل الواجبات والمستحبات، ويترك المحرمات والمكروهات وبعض المباحات من باب الاحتياط. فالأمة ليست سواء، فصارت ثلاث طوائف، فمنها الظالم لنفسه، ومنها المقتصد، ومنها السابق بالخيرات، فدل علىٰ أن الإيمان متفاضل.

{And among them is he who is foremost in good deeds by the permission of Allah.} [Qur'ān 35:32] This is the one who does what is obligatory and what is desirable (*mustaḥabbāt*), and refrains from what is forbidden

---

65 It is related that 'Abdullah ibn 'Umar ﷺ said: "We used to compare people as to who was the best in the time of the Prophet ﷺ. We said Abū Bakr was the best, then 'Umar ibn al-Khaṭṭāb, and then 'Uthmān." Al-Bukhārī, no. 3655. In another version: "In the time of the Prophet ﷺ we did not hold Abū Bakr to be equal to anyone, and then 'Umar, and then 'Uthmān. Then, we would leave the Companions of the Prophet ﷺ as not having any superiority among them." (no. 3698)

It is related that Muḥammad ibn al-Ḥanafīyyah said: "I said to my father (i.e. 'Ali ﷺ): 'Who is the best of all people after the Messenger of Allah ﷺ?' He said: 'Abu Bakr.' I said: 'Then who?' He said: 'Then 'Umar.' And I feared that he would say 'Uthmān. I said: 'Then you?' He said: 'I am but a man from among the Muslims.'" Al-Bukhārī, no. 3671.

and undesirable, as well as some things that are permissible to be on the safe side. The Muslims are not, then, the same. There are three groups: one group wrongs itself, one group is moderate, and the last is foremost in good deeds. This is evidence that there is disparity between people in terms of faith.

✿✿✿

المتن

(١٤١) والتَّفاضُلُ بَيْنَهُمْ بِالْخَشْيَةِ والتُّقَىٰ، وَمُخالَفَةِ الْهَوَىٰ، وَمُلازَمَةِ الْأَوْلَىٰ.

(141) They differ only in their fear of Allah, piety, abstention from inclinations (*hawā*), and pursuance of what is best.

الشرح

هذا لا يكفي لأن معناه إخراج الأعمال عن مسمىٰ الإيمان، وأنه إذا صدق بقلبه ونطق بلسانه فهو مؤمن كامل الإيمان، والناس لا يتفاضلون في ذلك. وهذا خطأ كبير؛ لأن التفاضل يحصل بما ذكره وبالأعمال الصالحة.

This is not enough, because it implies that the actions are not encompassed within the term *faith*. This also means that if someone believes in their heart and utters it on the tongue, then they are Muslims of complete faith, and that there is no disparity between people. This is a major mistake, because there is disparity in what he mentions here as well as in righteous deeds.

✿✿✿

المتن

(١٤٢) والْمُؤْمِنُونَ كُلُّهُمْ أَوْلِياءُ الرَّحْمَنِ، وَأَكْرَمُهُمْ عِنْدَ اللهِ أَطْوَعُهُمْ وَأَتْبَعُهُمْ لِلْقُرْآنِ.

(142) All of the faithful are *awliyā'* (allies) of the Most Merciful. The most honourable of them to Allah are those who obey Him most and

follow the Qur'ān best.

الشرح

هذا حق، فالمؤمنون كلهم أولياء الله، يعني: أحبابه، فالله يحب المؤمنين ويحب المتقين ويحب المحسنين ويحب التوابين ويحب المتطهرين، كما أنه يبغض الكافرين ويبغض الفاسقين، فالله يحب ويبغض على الأعمال.

This is correct. All of the faithful are allies of Allah ﷻ, they are His loved ones. Allah ﷻ loves the faithful, the pious, those who do much good, those who repent and those who purify themselves. Likewise, He hates the unbelievers and open sinners. Allah ﷻ loves and hates according to deeds.

فكل مؤمن يكون ولياً لله، وتتفاضل الولاية، بعضهم أفضل من بعض، قال جل وعلا: ﴿أَلَآ إِنَّ أَوْلِيَآءَ ٱللَّهِ لَا خَوْفٌ عَلَيْهِمْ وَلَا هُمْ يَحْزَنُونَ ۝٦٢ ٱلَّذِينَ ءَامَنُوا۟ وَكَانُوا۟ يَتَّقُونَ ۝٦٣﴾ [يونس:٦٢-٦٣] فمن الناس من ولايته مع الله تامة، ومنهم من ولايته مع الله ناقصة، ومنهم من هو عدو لله بعيد عن الله سبحانه وتعالى.

Everyone who has faith is an ally (*walī*) of Allah ﷻ, and there is also disparity in this alliance. Some are superior to others. Allah ﷻ says: **{Unquestionably, [for] the allies of Allah there will be no fear concerning them, nor will they grieve. Those who believed and were God-fearing.} [Qur'ān 10:62-63]** Some people have complete alliance with Allah ﷻ, some have incomplete alliance, whilst others are enemies of Allah ﷻ and are distant from Him.

فكل من فيه إيمان وتقوى فهو ولي الله، ولكن الولاية تتفاضل بحسب الأعمال، فمنهم من ولايته كاملة، ومنهم من هو ولي من وجه، وهو المؤمن الفاسق، ولي لله بطاعته، عدو لله بمعصيته ومخالفته.

Anyone who has faith and piety is an ally of Allah ﷻ. However, there is disparity in alliance according to deeds. Some of them have complete alliance while some of them, namely openly sinful believers, are allies in one respect. They are allies to Allah ﷻ according to their obedience and enemies to Allah ﷻ according to their disobedience and contravention.

ومنهم من هو عدو خالص كالكافر والمشرك.

Some of them are pure enemies, like the disbelievers and polytheists.

هذا هو الحق، أما من يرىٰ أنه ليس لله ولي إلا من بُنِيَ علىٰ قبره مشهد أو ضريح، والذي ليس عليه ضريح هذا فليس بولي؟ كما عند القبوريين! فهذا باطل.

This is the truth of the matter. It is falsehood to believe that only those whose graves have tombstones or mausoleums built are Allah's ﷻ allies, and that those whose graves do not have mausoleums are not His allies, as is commonly the case with the grave-worshippers. This is falsehood.

المتن

(١٤٣) والْإِيمانُ: هُوَ الْإِيمانُ بِاللهِ، وَمَلائِكَتِهِ، وَكُتُبِهِ، وَرُسُلِهِ، والْيَوْمِ الْآخِرِ، والْقَدَرِ خَيْرِهِ وَشَرِّهِ، وَحُلْوِهِ وَمُرِّهِ مِنَ اللهِ تَعالَىٰ.

(143) Faith is to have faith in Allah, His Angels, His Books, His Messengers, the Last Day, and *qadar* (predestination) – its good and bad, sweet and bitter – it is from Allah, The Most High.

الشرح

تعريف الإيمان هو كما سبق: قول باللسان وتصديق بالقلب وعمل بالجوارح، يزيد بالطاعة وينقص بالعصيان، وأما ما ذكره المصنف هنا فهي أركانه كما بينها النبي صلىٰ الله عليه وسلم لما سأله جبريل «**قال: أخبرني عن الإيمان، قال: الإيمان أن تؤمن بالله وملائكته وكتبه ورسله واليوم الآخر وتؤمن بالقدر خيره وشره**».

Faith has already been defined. It is the statement of the tongue, attestation of the heart, and the actions of the limbs; it increases by obedience, and decreases by disobedience[66]. What the author mentions here are the pillars of

66 Al-Bukhārī reported in The Book of Faith: Chapter: The Increase and Decrease of Faith, He said: "Allah says: ***{And We increased them in guidance}***, ***{and those who***

faith, as stated by the Prophet ﷺ when asked by Jibrīl عليه السلام. He said: "Tell me about faith." He replied: "Faith is to believe in Allah, His angels, His books, His Messengers, the Last Day, and in *qadar*, whether good or bad."[67]

وله خصال كثيرة، كما في قوله صلىٰ الله عليه وسلم: «الإيمان بضع وسبعون شعبة – أو بضع وستون شعبة – أعلاها قول: لا إله إلا الله، وأدناها إماطة الأذىٰ عن الطريق» لكن هذه الستة هي الأركان والدعائم التي يقوم عليها.

It has many characteristics, such as in the statement of the Prophet ﷺ: "Faith has seventy-odd branches – or sixty-odd branches[68] – and the highest one is to say, 'There is no God but Allah', and the lowest is to remove harm from the road."[69] These six, on the other hand, are the pillars and foundations that it stands on.

وتقدم الكلام عن الإيمان بالله، والإيمان بالملائكة، والإيمان بالرسل، والإيمان بالكتب، تقدم كل هذا، ولكنه متفرق في أول هذه العقيدة.

We have already discussed faith in Allah ﷻ, faith in the angels, faith in the Messengers and faith in the books. All of these have been mentioned previously, however, separately during earlier parts of this declaration of creed.

المتن

(١٤٤) وَنَحْنُ مُؤْمِنُونَ بِذَلِكَ كُلِّهِ.

(144) We believe in all of that;

الشرح

---

have believed will increase in faith.} Allah ﷻ says: ***{This day I have perfected for you your religion.}*** He who leaves something from perfection is then imperfect.

67 Al-Bukhārī, no. 50; Muslim, no. 10.

68 In Arabic *biḍʿ* is any number between three to nine, therefore *biḍʿ wa sabʿūn* and *biḍʿ wa sitūn* is anywhere between seventy three to seventy nine and sixty three to sixty nine. [Translator's note]

69 Al-Bukhārī, no. 9; Muslim, no. 35 (this wording is from Muslim).

يجب الإيمان بهذا كله، فإن جحد شيئاً من هذه الأركان فإنه ليس بمؤمن؛ لأنه نقص ركناً من أركان الإيمان.

It is obligatory to have faith in all of those things. If someone denies any of these pillars, then he is not a believer, because he would be missing a pillar of faith.

المتن

(١٤٥) لا نُفَرِّقُ بَيْنَ أَحَدٍ مِنْ رُسُلِهِ، وَنُصَدِّقُهُمْ كُلَّهُمْ عَلَىٰ ما جاءُوا بِهِ.

(145) And we make no distinction between any of His Messengers. We believe in all of them and what they preached.

الشرح

هذا سبق، أنه يجب الإيمان بجميع الرسل من أولهم إلىٰ آخرهم، من سمىٰ الله منهم في القرآن ولم يسمَّ؛ فنؤمن بجميع الرسل الذين أرسلهم الله إلىٰ عباده، فمن آمن ببعضهم وكفر ببعض فهو كافر بالجميع؛ لو جحد نبياً واحداً فإنه يكون كافراً بجميع الأنبياء ﴿إِنَّ ٱلَّذِينَ يَكۡفُرُونَ بِٱللَّهِ وَرُسُلِهِۦ وَيُرِيدُونَ أَن يُفَرِّقُواْ بَيۡنَ ٱللَّهِ وَرُسُلِهِۦ وَيَقُولُونَ نُؤۡمِنُ بِبَعۡضٖ وَنَكۡفُرُ بِبَعۡضٖ وَيُرِيدُونَ أَن يَتَّخِذُواْ بَيۡنَ ذَٰلِكَ سَبِيلًا ١٥٠ أُوْلَٰٓئِكَ هُمُ ٱلۡكَٰفِرُونَ حَقّٗاۚ﴾ [النساء: ١٥٠-١٥١].

This was mentioned previously: it is obligatory to have faith in all of the Messengers, from the first to the last, those whom Allah ﷻ has named in the Qur'ān and those whom He has not named. We believe in all of the Messengers that Allah has sent to His slaves. If an individual believes in some of them and disbelieves in others, then he is a disbeliever in all of them. Likewise if one were to deny only a single prophet, he has disbelieved in all of the prophets. **{Indeed, those who disbelieve in Allah and His messengers and wish to discriminate between Allah and His messengers and say, 'We believe in some and disbelieve in others,' and wish to adopt a way in between – Those are the disbelievers, truly. And We have prepared**

for the disbelievers a humiliating punishment.} [Qurʾān 4:150-151]

فاليهود كفار؛ لأنهم كفروا بنبيين كريمين، كفروا بعيسىٰ عليه الصلاة والسلام، وكفروا بمحمد صلىٰ الله عليه وسلم، والنصارىٰ كفار؛ لأنهم جحدوا رسالة النبي محمد صلىٰ الله عليه وسلم، فالذين يقولون اليوم: اليهود والنصارىٰ مسلمون ومؤمنون، وأنهم أهل أديان، ويجب التقارب بين الأديان والحوار بين الأديان، هذا خلط وضلال والعياذ بالله، خلط بين الحق والباطل، والإيمان والكفر لأنه بعد بعثة محمد صلىٰ الله عليه وسلم ليس هناك دين صحيح إلا الإسلام ﴿وَمَن يَبْتَغِ غَيْرَ ٱلْإِسْلَٰمِ دِينًا فَلَن يُقْبَلَ مِنْهُ وَهُوَ فِى ٱلْءَاخِرَةِ مِنَ ٱلْخَٰسِرِينَ ۝٨٥﴾ [آل عمران:٨٥].

Thus, the Jews are disbelievers because they disbelieve in two honourable prophets: ʿĪsā ﷺ and Muḥammad ﷺ. Christians are also disbelievers because they deny the message of Muḥammad ﷺ. So, the people of today who say that Jews and Christians are Muslims and believers, and that they belong to divine religions, and that there has to be rapprochement between these religions and interfaith dialogue, this is mixing [good with bad] and an error, and Allah is our refuge. This is to mix truth with falsehood and faith with disbelief, because after the dispatch of the Prophet ﷺ no religion is correct besides Islām. **{And whoever desires other than Islām as a religion – never will it be accepted from him, and he, in the Hereafter, will be among the losers.} [Qurʾān 3:85]**

فالإسلام نسخ كل ما قبله، وأمر الإنس والجن واليهود والنصارىٰ والأميين وجميع العرب والعجم، أمروا باتباع المصطفىٰ صلىٰ الله عليه وسلم، فلا إيمان إلا باتباع هذا الرسول صلىٰ الله عليه وسلم.

Islām abrogated everything before it. It commanded man and jinn, Jews, Christians, the illiterate, Arabs and non-Arabs to follow the Chosen One ﷺ. So, there is no faith without following the Messenger ﷺ.

المتن

(١٤٦) وَأَهْلُ الْكَبَائِرِ مِنْ أُمَّةِ مُحَمَّدٍ ﷺ فِي النَّارِ لا يُخَلَّدُونَ، إِذا ماتُوا وَهُمْ مُوَحِّدُونَ،

(146) Those who commit major sins from the Ummah of Muḥammad ﷺ shall not be in Hell forever, if they die worshipping Allah alone;

الشرح

الكبائر هي الذنوب التي دون الشرك وفوق الصغائر، وضابط الكبيرة هو: كل ذنب رُتب عليه حد، أو ختم بغضب أو لعنة أو نار، أو تبرئ الرسول صلىٰ الله عليه وسلم من فاعله، فإن هذا كبيرة، كقوله: «**من غشنا فليس منا**»، «**من حمل علينا السلاح فليس منا**».

The major sins are those that are less serious than polytheism and more serious than minor sins (*ṣaghā'ir*). The guideline for determining the major sins is that they are every sin that results in a prescribed punishment (*ḥadd*), or is concluded with the anger of Allah ﷻ, curse or the Fire. Or a sin that the Messenger of Allah ﷺ has disavowed whoever does it, then this is a major sin, such as in his saying: "Whoever deceives us is not one of us."[70] And: "Whoever draws a weapon on us is not one of us."[71]

كل هذه الاعتبارات تدل علىٰ أن الذنب كبيرة، ولكنها دون الشرك، فصاحبها لا يخرج من الإيمان، وإنما يكون مؤمناً ناقص الإيمان، أو يسمىٰ فاسقاً، هذا مذهب أهل السنة والجماعة، لا يكفرون بالكبائر التي دون الشرك، ولكن لا يمنحون صاحبها اسم الإيمان المطلق، ولكن يمنحونه إيماناً مقيداً؛ فيقال: مؤمن بإيمانه، فاسق بكبيرته.

All of these considerations indicate that if someone commits a major sin (that is less serious than polytheism) then he has not left the faith but is rather a believer of less faith, or is a sinner (*fāsiq*). This is the doctrine of

70 Muslim, no. 101.
71 Al-Bukhārī, no. 6874; Muslim, no. 98, 100, 101.

Ahl al-Sunnah wa ʾl-Jamāʿah: they do not declare anyone a disbeliever on account of any major sin besides polytheism; however, they do not grant a sinner the label of a believer in an absolute manner, rather they grant it in a conditional manner. So it is said that he is a believer due to his faith, and a sinner due to his major sin.

فلا يقال: هو مؤمن كامل الإيمان، كما تقوله المرجئة، ولا يقال: هو خارج من الإسلام، كما تقوله الخوارج والمعتزلة.

It should not be said that a sinner who committed a major sin is a complete believer, as the Murjiʾites say. It should also not be said that they have left Islām, as the Khārijites and Muʿtazilites say.

إذاً: فالناس في صاحب الكبيرة التي هي دون الشرك ثلاث طوائف:

Hence, there are three groups when it comes to a person who commits a major sin that is less than polytheism:

الخوارج والمعتزلة: أخرجوه من الإسلام، لكن الخوارج أدخلوه في الكفر، والمعتزلة لم يدخلوه، وقالوا: هو في منزلة بين المنزلتين، ولكنهم أخرجوه من الإسلام.

The Khārijites and Muʿtazilites, who exclude major sinners from Islām; however, the Khārijites say that the person becomes a disbeliever, whereas the Muʿtazilites instead say that he is ʿin a status between two positions (*manzilah bayn al-manzilatayn*). Nonetheless, they exclude him from Islām.

المرجئة قالوا: هو مؤمن كامل الإيمان، طالما أنه يعتقد في قلبه الإيمان عند جمهورهم وينطق بلسانه عند بعضهم، فإنه مؤمن كامل الإيمان، ولا تنقص هذه المعاصي من إيمانه، وإن كانت كبائر، وهذا ضلال أيضاً.

The Murjiʾites say that he is a believer with complete faith, as long as he believes in his heart (according to the majority of them) and as long as he pronounces it on his tongue (according to some of them). Then he is a believer with complete faith, and sins do not at all detract from his faith, even if they were major ones. This is also misguidance.

أما القول الحق فهو مذهب أهل السنة والجماعة: أن صاحب الكبيرة دون الشرك مؤمن، وليس بكافر، لكنه ناقص الإيمان. فهذا يجب معرفته، ويجب أن ترسخه في عقلك، فأهل الشر زاد شرهم في هذا الوقت، وصاروا يظهرون مذهب الإرجاء ليروجوه على الناس، وليستروا على أنفسهم ما هم فيه من الضلال.

The true way, however, is the doctrine of **Ahl al-Sunnah wa 'l-Jamā'ah**. Someone who commits a major sin below polytheism is a believer, not a disbeliever, but his faith has shortcomings. It is obligatory to know this, and it has to be entrenched in your mind. The evil of the evil people has increased in these times, championing the doctrine of the Murji'ah and promoting it to people in order to conceal the misguidance that they themselves belong to.

فهذا معرفته من أوجب الواجبات على طالب العلم اليوم.

So, it is one of the greatest obligations for students of [Islamic] knowledge today to know this.

المتن

(١٤٧) وَإِنْ لَمْ يَكُونُوا تائِبِينَ، بَعْدَ أَنْ لَقُوا اللهَ عارِفِينَ مُؤْمِنِينَ، وَهُمْ فِي مَشِيئَتِهِ وَحُكْمِهِ إِنْ شاءَ غَفَرَ لَهُمْ، وَعَفا عَنْهُمْ بِفَضْلِهِ، كَما ذَكَرَ عز وجل فِي كِتابِهِ: ﴿ وَيَغْفِرُ ما دُونَ ذَلِكَ لِمَنْ يَشاءُ﴾ [النساء: ٤٨]، وَإِنْ شاءَ عَذَّبَهُمْ فِي النّارِ بِعَدْلِهِ.

(147) Even if they do not repent, as long as they meet Allah as knowing believers. They are under the will and judgment of Allah, if He wills, He may forgive them and He may pardon them by His grace, as Allah has said in His Book: *{...but He forgives what is less than that for whom He wills.}* If He wills, He may punish them in Hell out of justice.

الشرح

نعم، هذا هو المذهب الحق: أن أصحاب الكبائر التي دون الشرك ليسوا كفاراً، وأنهم إذا لقوا الله ولم يتوبوا من هذه الكبائر فإنهم تحت المشيئة، إن شاء عذبهم بقدر ذنوبهم، ثم يخرجهم من النار ويدخلهم الجنة بتوحيدهم وإيمانهم، لا يخلدون في النار، والدليل على ذلك قوله تعالى: ﴿إِنَّ ٱللَّهَ لَا يَغْفِرُ أَن يُشْرَكَ بِهِۦ وَيَغْفِرُ مَا دُونَ ذَٰلِكَ لِمَن يَشَآءُ﴾ [النساء:٤٨]، لكن قوله: (عارفين مؤمنين) فيه إجمال، فلو قال: (موحدين) كما قال أولاً لكان أحسن.

Yes, this is the right doctrine: that those who commit major sins less than polytheism are not disbelievers. If they meet Allah without repenting from these sins, then they are under Allah's will. If He so wills, He will punish them according to the extent of their sins and then bring them out of the Fire and admit them to Jannah on account of them deifying Him alone (i.e. *tawḥīd*) and having faith, and they will not abide in the Fire forever. Evidence for that is the statement of Allah ﷻ: **{Indeed, Allah does not forgive association with Him, but He forgives what is less than that for whom He wills.} [Qur'ān 4:48]** However, there is some ambiguity and brevity in the author's statement: "knowing believers". If he were to say, "those who deify Allah ﷻ alone" (*muwaḥḥidīn*), instead, as he had said earlier, it would have been better.

وإن شاء الله أمضى فيهم الوعيد، ولكنهم لا يخلدون في النار، هذا مذهب أهل السنة والجماعة، وهذا هو المذهب الحق، بخلاف الخوارج الذين يقولون: إنهم في النار على أي حال، وإنهم خالدون فيها، فمن دخل النار عندهم لا يخرج منها. وخلاف المرجئة القائلين: إنهم لا يمرون على النار أبداً، فهذا غلط، بل لا نضمن لهم النجاة، فهم تحت المشيئة.

And if Allah ﷻ wills, He could carry out the threats on them, but they will not abide in the Fire forever. This is the doctrine of Ahl al-Sunnah wa 'l-Jamā'ah and this is the doctrine of truth, as opposed to the Khārijites, who say that they will be in the Fire in any case, and that they will abide in it forever. So, for them, anyone who enters the Fire does not come out. In contrast, the Murji'ites say that they will never even pass through the Fire. This is wrong. Rather, we cannot guarantee that they will be saved as they are under Allah's will.

إن شاء عفا عنهم بفضله، وإن شاء عذبهم بعدله، وما ظلمهم الله سبحانه وتعالى، بل عذبهم بأعمالهم التي أوجبت لهم ذلك، فالله لا يعذب من لم يعصه، ولا يساوي بين العاصي وبين المؤمن المستقيم، ﴿أَفَنَجْعَلُ ٱلْمُسْلِمِينَ كَٱلْمُجْرِمِينَ ۝٣٥ مَا لَكُمْ كَيْفَ تَحْكُمُونَ ۝٣٦﴾ [القلم: ٣٥-٣٦] ﴿أَمْ نَجْعَلُ ٱلَّذِينَ ءَامَنُوا۟ وَعَمِلُوا۟ ٱلصَّٰلِحَٰتِ كَٱلْمُفْسِدِينَ فِى ٱلْأَرْضِ أَمْ نَجْعَلُ ٱلْمُتَّقِينَ كَٱلْفُجَّارِ ۝٢٨﴾ [ص:٢٨].

If He wills, He will forgive them out of His grace, and if He wills, He will punish them out of His justice. But Allah ﷻ does not wrong them; He punishes them for their actions, which are the cause for that. Allah ﷻ does not punish those who do not disobey Him, and He does not equate between a sinner and an upright Muslim. **{Then will We treat the Muslims like the criminals? What is [the matter] with you? How do you judge?} [Qur'ān 68:35-36] {Or should we treat those who believe and do righteous deeds like corrupters in the land? Or should We treat those who fear Allah like the wicked?} [Qur'ān 38:28]**

هذا استنكار من الله عز وجل، ﴿أَمْ حَسِبَ ٱلَّذِينَ ٱجْتَرَحُوا۟ ٱلسَّيِّـَٔاتِ أَن نَّجْعَلَهُمْ كَٱلَّذِينَ ءَامَنُوا۟ وَعَمِلُوا۟ ٱلصَّٰلِحَٰتِ سَوَآءً مَّحْيَاهُمْ وَمَمَاتُهُمْ ۚ سَآءَ مَا يَحْكُمُونَ ۝٢١﴾ [الجاثية: ٢١].

This is a criticism from Allah the Almighty. **{Or do those who commit evils think We will make them like those who have believed and done righteous deeds – [make them] equal in their life and their death? Evil is that which they judge.} [Qur'ān 45: 21]**

المتن

(١٤٨) ثُمَّ يُخْرِجُهُمْ مِنْها بِرَحْمَتِهِ وَشَفاعَةِ الشّافِعِينَ مِنْ أَهْلِ طاعَتِهِ،

(148) Then they will be brought out of Hell because of His mercy and the intercession of the obedient Muslims.

الشرح

كما صحت بذلك الأخبار عن رسول الله صلىٰ الله عليه وسلم: أن عصاة الموحدين يخرجون من النار، إما بفضل الله تعالىٰ، وإما بشفاعة الشافعين بإذن الله تعالىٰ، والشفاعة حق، ولكن لا تكون إلا بإذن الله، وأن يكون المشفوع فيه من أهل التوحيد، لا من الكافرين ولا من المشركين ولا من المنافقين.

As it has been authentically reported from the Messenger of Allah ﷺ. Those who believe in Allah alone but are sinful will be brought out of the Fire[72], either by the grace of Allah ﷻ or via intercession of the intercessors with the permission of Allah ﷻ. Intercession is true, but it is only by the permission of Allah ﷻ. It is permissible on behalf of those who worship Allah ﷻ alone (*al-muwaḥḥidūn*), and not on behalf of the disbelievers, idolaters, and hypocrites (*munāfiqūn*).

❁❁❁

المتن

(١٤٩) ثُمَّ يَبْعَثُهُمْ إِلَىٰ جَنَّتِهِ.

(149) Then, He will send them to Paradise.

الشرح

بعد إخراجهم من النار، ورد أنهم يخرجون من النار كالفحم محترقين، ثم يلقون

---

72 For example, it is related in the *ḥadīth* of the intercession as attributed to Anas ﷺ that the Messenger of Allah ﷺ said: "Bring out of the Fire anyone who said, 'There is no God but Allah', and who had the weight of a grain of barley of good in his heart. Then, bring out of the Fire anyone who said, 'There is no God but Allah', and who had the weight of a grain of wheat of good in his heart. Then, bring out of the Fire anyone who said, 'There is no God but Allah', and had the weight of a speck of good in his heart." Al-Bukhārī, no. 7410; Muslim, no. 193.

في نهر يسمىٰ: نهر الحياة، فتنبت أجسامهم ولحومهم، ثم بعد ذلك إذا هُذبوا ونُقوا أُذن لهم في دخول الجنة، فيدخلون في الجنة.

After being removed from the Fire. It has been related that they will be brought out of the Fire burnt like charcoal. They will later be cast into the River of Life and their bodies and flesh will sprout [like plants.] Afterwards, when they are cleansed and purified, they will be allowed to enter Jannah, and they will enter it.[73]

المتن

(١٥٠) وَذَلِكَ بِأَنَّ اللهَ تَعالَىٰ تَوَلَّىٰ أَهْلَ مَعْرِفَتِهِ، وَلَمْ يَجْعَلْهُمْ فِي الدَّارَيْنِ كَأَهْلِ نُكْرَتِهِ الَّذِينَ خابُوا مِنْ هِدايَتِهِ، وَلَمْ يَنالُوا مِنْ وَلايَتِهِ.

(150) This is because Allah is the ally of those who know Him and He has not made them the same in both abodes as those who have denied Him, those who missed out on His guidance and failed to avail His alliance.

الشرح

قال تعالىٰ: ﴿أَمْ حَسِبَ ٱلَّذِينَ ٱجْتَرَحُواْ ٱلسَّيِّـَٔاتِ أَن نَّجْعَلَهُمْ كَٱلَّذِينَ ءَامَنُواْ وَعَمِلُواْ ٱلصَّٰلِحَٰتِ﴾ [الجاثية:٢١]، وقوله تعالىٰ: ﴿أَمْ نَجْعَلُ ٱلْمُتَّقِينَ كَٱلْفُجَّارِ ﴿٢٨﴾﴾ [ص:٢٨] إلىٰ غير ذلك من الآيات التي تدل علىٰ أن الله لا يسوي بين أهل طاعته وأهل معصيته، ولا بين أهل الإيمان وأهل الكفر، بل يجازي كلاً بعمله.

Allah the Most High says: **{Or do those who commit evils think We will make them like those who have believed and done righteous deeds.}**

73 It is related that Abū Sa'īd al-Khudrī ﷺ said that the Prophet ﷺ said: "When the people of Jannah enter Jannah, and the people of the Fire enter the Fire, Allah will say, 'Bring out of the Fire anyone who has the weight of a mustard seed of faith in his heart.' So they are to be brought out, and by that time, they will have burnt and become like coal. Then, they will be cast into the River of Life and will sprout as a seed sprouts on a flood bank." The Prophet ﷺ said: "Behold! It sprouts yellow and twisted." Al-Bukhārī, no. 5060; Muslim, no. 184, 185.

[Qur'ān 45:21] Allah ﷻ also says: **{Or should We treat those who fear Allah like the wicked?} [Qur'ān 38:28]** These, along with other verses, indicate that Allah ﷻ does not treat the obedient and the disobedient, or the believers and disbelievers equally, but rather repays each according to their actions.

(ولم يجعلهم في الدارين كأهل نكرته الذين خابوا من هدايته ولم ينالوا من ولايته) بل ميز بينهم سبحانه في الدنيا وفي الآخرة، ميز بين أهل الطاعة والمعصية، وبين أهل الكفر والإيمان، في الدنيا وفي الآخرة، ميز بينهم في الدنيا في صفاتهم وعلاماتهم وأفعالهم، فليست أفعال أولياء الله وأهل الطاعة مثل أفعال أعدائه ولا أقوالهم ولا تصرفاتهم، انظر إلىٰ الناس الآن، وانظر إلىٰ تصرفاتهم، انظر إلىٰ تصرفات المتقين والمؤمنين، وانظر إلىٰ تصرفات الفسقة والعاصين، وانظر إلىٰ تصرفات الكفار والملحدين، هذا في الدنيا.

"He has not made them the same in both abodes as those who have denied Him, those who missed out on His guidance and failed to avail His alliance": Rather, Allah ﷻ has made each distinct in this world and in the afterlife. He has made the obedient distinct from the disobedient, and the disbelievers distinct from the believers in this world and in the afterlife. He has made them distinct in their characteristics, distinguishing features, and actions; so, the actions of the allies of Allah ﷻ and the obedient are not like the actions, speech, and behaviour of the enemies of Allah ﷻ. Look at the people of today. Look at how they behave. Look at the behaviour of the pious and the faithful and look at the behaviour of the sinners, the disobedient, the disbelievers and heretics. This is in this world.

وفي الآخرة كذلك يميز الله بينهم، فهؤلاء يكرمهم بجنته، وهؤلاء يعذبهم بناره وعقوبته؛ لأنه سبحانه حكيم يضع الأمور في مواضعها، فلا يضع الرحمة إلا فيمن يستحقها، ولا يضع سبحانه وتعالىٰ العذاب إلا فيمن يستحقه. لكن قوله: **(أهل معرفته)** فيه قصور وإيهام أن الإيمان هو مجرد المعرفة كما يقوله غلاة المرجئة فلو قال: (أهل طاعته) لكان أحسن وأوضح.

In the afterlife, Allah ﷻ will make each type of people distinct as well. Allah

ﷻ gives some the honour of Jannah and punishes others with His Fire and punishment. Allah is Most Wise; He keeps everything in its right place. He gives mercy only to those who deserve it and He gives punishment only to those who deserve it. That said, the author said: "*those who know Him* (*ahl al-ma'rifah*)". This falls short and perpetuates the misconception that faith is knowledge (*ma'rifah*) alone, as believed by extreme Murji'ites. If he were to have said, 'those who are obedient', it would have been better and clearer.

المتن

(١٥١) اللَّهُمَّ يا وَلِيَّ الإِسْلامِ وَأَهْلِهِ ثَبِّتْنا عَلَىٰ الإِسْلامِ حَتَّىٰ نَلْقاكَ بِهِ.

(151) O Allah, O ally of Islām and the Muslims, keep us steadfast upon Islām until we meet You with it.

الشرح

هذا من أجمل كلام المصنف يرحمه الله!

These are some of the most beautiful words of the author رحمه الله.

إنه لما ذكر هذه المسائل العظيمة الخطيرة سأل الله التثبيت، ألا يضله الله مع أصحاب هذه الضلالات وأصحاب هذه المقالات الضالة، فهذا من الفقه والحكمة؛ أن الإنسان لا يغتر بعلمه، ويقول: أنا أعرف التوحيد وأعرف العقيدة، وليس عليّ خطر، هذا غرور بل عليه أن يخاف من سوء الخاتمة والضلال، يخاف أن ينخدع بأهل الضلال، كم من معتدل انحرف، خصوصاً إذا اشتدت الفتن، يصبح الرجل مسلماً ويمسي كافراً، ويمسي مؤمناً ويصبح كافراً، ويبيع دينه بعرض من الدنيا، كما صح الحديث بذلك.

After mentioning these great and serious issues, he asks Allah ﷻ to allow him to remain steadfast, that Allah ﷻ does not lead him astray along with the people who belong to those misguided ways and utterers of those words of misguided heresy. This demonstrates his understanding and wisdom, insofar as one should not be deceived by his own knowledge and say, "I know about *tawḥīd,* I know about *ʿaqīdah,* I'm not in any danger". This is deception. Rather, he must fear having a bad ending and going astray, and being misled by those who have strayed from the path. Many an upright person have deviated from the path, especially when the trials and tribulations are strong, [wherein] a man is a Muslim by day and a disbeliever by night, and a Muslim by night and a disbeliever by day; he trades his religion for the goods of the world, as authentically reported in the *ḥadīth*.[74]

الفتن إذا جاءت يسأل الإنسان الله الثبات، ولا يقول: أنا لست علىٰ خطر، أنا عارف وأنا أصلي، نعم، أنت عارف وتصلي والحمد لله، لكن عليك خطر وعليك أن تخاف، أنت أفضل أم إبراهيم عليه الصلاة والسلام؟ قال: ﴿وَٱجْنُبْنِي وَبَنِيَّ أَن نَّعْبُدَ ٱلْأَصْنَامَ ﴿٣٥﴾﴾ [إبراهيم:٣٥]

When tribulations come, a person has to ask Allah ﷻ for steadfastness[75]. One should not say, "I'm not at risk, I know and I pray". Yes, you know and you pray, *al-ḥamdu lillāh.* But you are at risk, and you have to show concern. Who is better, you or Ibrāhīm ﷺ? He said: **{My Lord, make this city [Makkah] secure and keep me and my sons away from worshipping idols.} [Qurʾān 14:35]**

إبراهيم خاف علىٰ نفسه من عبادة الأصنام، مع أنه هو الذي كسّرها وحطّمها

---

74 It is related that Abū Hurayrah ؓ said that the Messenger of Allah ﷺ said: "Hasten to action before there comes tribulations like the darkness of night: a man will be a believer by day and a disbeliever by night, or a believer by night and an unbeliever by day, trading his religion for some goods of the world." Muslim, no. 118.

75 It is related that Jābir ؓ said: The Messenger of Allah ﷺ used to say: "O You who turns the hearts, make my heart steadfast upon Your religion." We said: "O Messenger of Allah, do you fear for us though we have believed in you and in what you've brought?" He said: "Yes. Verily, the hearts are between two of Allah's fingers, He turns them as He wills." Al-Tirmidhī, no. 2145; Ibn Mājah, no. 3834; al-Ḥākim, 1/525, 526, 4/321. Al-Ḥākim said it is *ṣaḥīḥ* and al-Dhahabī concurred. Al-Tirmidhī said: "This *ḥadīth* is *ḥasan."*

Muslim presented it as being related by ʿAbdullāh ibn ʿAmr ibn al-ʿĀṣ ؓ who said that he heard the Messenger of Allah ﷺ say: "The hearts of the sons of Ādam are all between two fingers of the fingers of the All Merciful, as one heart; He turns it as He wills." Then, the Messenger of Allah ﷺ said: "O Allah, You who turn the hearts, turn our hearts to obey You." Muslim, no. 2654.

بيده، ولقي في ذلك العذاب والإهانة في سبيل الله عز وجل، ومع هذا يقول: ﴿وَٱجْنُبْنِي وَبَنِيَّ أَن نَّعْبُدَ ٱلْأَصْنَامَ ۝٣٥﴾ [إبراهيم:٣٥] ولم يقل: أنا الآن نجوت، بل طلب من الله أن يجنبه وبنيه أن يعبدوا الأصنام، فالإنسان يخاف دائماً من ربه عز وجل، وكم من مهتد ضل، وكم من مستقيم انحرف، وكم من مؤمن كفر وارتد، وكم من ضال هداه الله، وكم من كافر أسلم، فالأمر بيد الله سبحانه وتعالىٰ.

Ibrāhīm ﷺ feared that he would worship idols, even though he broke and shattered them with his hands and subsequently received punishment and insult for the sake of Allah ﷻ. Even so, he said: **{Make this city [Makkah] secure and keep me and my sons away from worshipping idols.} [Qur'ān 14:35]** He did not say, "I'm saved now". Instead, he asked Allah ﷻ to keep him and his sons from worshipping idols. A person should always fear his Lord, the Almighty. Many people who were once on the path have gone stray, and many who were upright have deviated, and many believers have disbelieved and apostatised, and many who were once lost were then guided by Allah ﷻ, and many who were disbelievers submitted [to Allah as Muslims]. The matter is in Allah's hands.

المتن

(١٥٢) وَنَرَىٰ الصَّلاةَ خَلْفَ كُلِّ بَرٍّ وَفاجِرٍ مِنْ أَهْلِ الْقِبْلَةِ، وعَلَىٰ مَنْ ماتَ مِنْهُمْ.

(152) We believe *ṣalāh* is to be prayed behind every righteous or sinful person from *Ahl al-Qiblah* and over everyone that dies from them.

الشرح

هذا فيه مسألتان:

This involves two issues:

الأولىٰ: أن الصلاة عمل وإحسان، فإذا فعلها الناس خصوصاً ولاة الأمور،

فإنهم عملوا معروفاً وإحساناً، وفي ترك الصلاة خلفهم فيه محظور عظيم، من شق العصا، وتفريق الكلمة، وسفك الدماء وهذا خطر عظيم، فيجب أن يُتلافىٰ.

First: That prayer (*ṣalāh*) is an act of worship and a good deed, hence when people – especially those who have authority (leaders) – perform it, they do a good deed. Further to the point, the consequences of deserting prayer behind them are serious and disturbing as it causes things such as, secession from the united community, disunion and bloodshed, which are great dangers and thus have to be avoided.

قال عليه الصلاة والسلام: «**صلوا خلف من قال: لا إله إلا الله، وعلىٰ من قال: لا إله إلا الله**»، هذا من حيث العموم، فكيف بولاة الأمور الذين في منابذتهم ومخالفتهم شق لعصا الطاعة، وتفريق الكلمة، وآثار سيئة علىٰ المسلمين؟

The Prophet ﷺ said: "Pray behind anyone who says, 'There is no God but Allah', and over anyone who says, 'There is no God but Allah.'"[76] This is general to all Muslims, so with even greater reason, it should apply to the rulers, the opposition of whom causes fraying of the community, disunion, and has adverse effects on the Muslims.

هذا مذهب أهل السنة والجماعة، يصلون الجمع والجماعات، ويجاهدون في سبيل الله مع كل أمير، براً كان أو فاجراً، ما لم يخرج عن الإسلام.

This is the doctrine of Ahl al-Sunnah wa 'l-Jamāʿah: They pray [together] in the Friday prayer and the [daily] congregations. They fight in Allah's cause with every *amīr,* whether righteous or sinful, as long as that *amīr* has not left Islām.

هذا أصل من أصول أهل السنة والجماعة، من عهد الصحابة إلىٰ عهد الأئمة، وهو الذي عليه إجماع المسلمين من أهل السنة والجماعة.

This is a fundamental principle of Ahl al-Sunnah wa 'l-Jamāʿah, from the time of the Companions to the time of the *imāms*. It is also that which the Muslims of Ahl al-Sunnah wa 'l-Jamāʿah unanimously agree on.

---

76 Al-Dāraquṭnī, 2/43, no. 1743.

المسألة الثانية: الصلاة علىٰ جنازة المسلم وإن كان فاسقًا، ما لم يخرج من الإسلام، فهو مسلم له ما للمسلمين وعليه ما علىٰ المسلمين، أما إذا خرج عن الإسلام فلا يصلىٰ عليه؛ لأنه ليس بمسلم، وليس كل إنسان يَحكُمُ علىٰ الناس بالردة، إنما يحكم بذلك أهل العلم والبصيرة بالرجوع إلىٰ قواعد أهل السنة والجماعة، أما كل أحد فلا يحكم بذلك، وإن كانت نيته طيبة ومقصده حسنًا، إنما الحكم لأهل البصيرة والراسخين في العلم.

The second issue is that *ṣalāh* is to be prayed over all dead Muslims, even if they were sinners, as long as they did not apostatise. They are treated as Muslims and have the same rights and duties as all Muslims. On the other hand, if they apostatise, then funeral prayers should not be offered over them because they are not Muslims. However, it is not the right of every person to judge whether someone has apostatised. Instead, it is only the right of people of knowledge and insight by referring to the principles of Ahl al-Sunnah wa 'l-Jamāʿah. Therefore it is not right for every person to make such a judgment, even if he has good intentions. Such judgments are only to be made by those who have insight and firmly grounded knowledge.

المتن

(١٥٣) وَلَا نُنَزِّلُ أَحَدًا مِنْهُمْ جَنَّةً وَلَا نَارًا.

(153) We do not place any of them in Paradise or Hell.

الشرح

نحن لا نشهد لأحد، مهما بلغ من الصلاح والتقىٰ، لا نشهد له بالجنة؛ لأننا لا نعلم الغيب، ولا نحكم لأحد من المسلمين بالنار مهما عمل من المعاصي، لا نحكم عليه بالنار؛ لأننا لا ندري بما خُتم له وما مات عليه، وهذا في المعيّن.

We do not testify that anyone, regardless of their level of righteousness and piety, will be in Paradise, because we do not know the unseen. We also do not judge that any Muslim will be in the Fire; regardless of what sins he does, because we do not know how his life will be sealed and what he will die upon[77]. This is regarding specific individuals.

فنحن ما لنا إلا الظاهر فقط، وكذلك لا يحكم لأحد بالنار، إلا من شهد له بذلك الرسول صلىٰ الله عليه وسلم، سواء بجنة أو نار، مثل العشرة المبشرين بالجنة، وهم الخلفاء الراشدون الأربعة، وسعد بن أبي وقاص، وسعيد بن زيد بن عمرو بن نفيل، وعبد الرحمن بن عوف، والزبير بن العوام، وأبو عبيدة عامر بن الجراح، وطلحة بن عبيد الله، رضي الله عنهم.

We do not have the right to judge except by what is apparent. Similarly, we are not to judge that someone will be in the Fire unless the Messenger of Allah ﷺ testified to that. That goes for both Jannah and the Fire. Examples are the ten promised Jannah, namely, the four Rightly-Guided Caliphs, Saʿd ibn Abī Waqqāṣ, Saʿīd ibn Zayd ibn ʿAmr ibn Nufayl, ʿAbd al-Raḥmān ibn ʿAwf, al-Zubayr ibn al-ʿAwwām, Abū ʿUbaydah ibn al-Jarrāḥ, and Ṭalḥah ibn ʿUbayd Allāh ﷺ.[78]

وكذلك شهد رسول الله صلىٰ الله عليه وسلم لثابت بن قيس بن شماس الأنصاري، شهد له بالجنة، وكذلك رجل من الأنصار قال: «**يدخل عليكم رجل من أهل الجنة**» فدخل رجل تنطف لحيته من وضوئه، وبيده اليسرىٰ نعلاه، ثم جلس في الحلقة، وفي اليوم الثاني والثالث قال عليه الصلاة والسلام نفس المقالة، ودخل نفس الرجل، وهذا من باب التأكيد، وإلا فشهادة واحدة تكفي، وقد تابعه عبد الله بن عمرو - رضي الله عنهما - حتىٰ يعلم عمله الذي بسببه بشر بالجنة، فلم يجد عنده كثير عبادة، وجده محافظًا علىٰ الفرائض،

77 It is related that Sahl ibn Saʿd al-Sāʿidī ﷺ said that the Messenger of Allah ﷺ said: "Actions are judged according to the last of them." Al-Bukhārī, no. 6493.

78 It is related that Saʿīd ibn Zayd ﷺ said among some men that the Messenger of Allah ﷺ said: "Ten are in Jannah: Abū Bakr is in Jannah, ʿUmar is in Jannah, and so are ʿUthmān, ʿAlī, al-Zubayr, Ṭalḥah, ʿAbd al-Raḥmān, Abū ʿUbaydah, and Saʿd ibn Abī Waqqāṣ." He said: He counted those nine and kept silent about the tenth, so people said: "We implore you by Allah, who is the tenth?" He said: "You have implored me in Allah's name. Abu ʿl-Aʿwar is in Jannah." Al-Tirmidhī, no. 3757. Abu ʿĪsā said: "Abu ʿl-Aʿwar is Saʿīd ibn Zayd ibn ʿAmr ibn Nawfal. I heard Muḥammad [i.e. al-Bukhārī] say: 'It is more authentic than the prior *ḥadīth*.'"

ويقوم من الليل، وكان إذا استيقظ من الليل ذكر الله وسبح وهلل، فلما أراد عبد الله أن يغادر قال للرجل: إني سمعت رسول الله عليه الصلاة والسلام يقول كذا وكذا، فأردت أن أسبر عملك، فقال الرجل: ما هو إلا ما رأيت. فلما ولّىٰ دعاه وقال: إلا أنني لا أجد في قلبي غلاً علىٰ مسلم، قال: هذا الذي لا نطيقه.

The Messenger of Allah ﷺ also attested to Thābit ibn Qays ibn Shammās al-Anṣārī ؓ being in Jannah, as well as a man of the Anṣār. He said: "A man from the people of Jannah will enter your place." So a man with water trickling from his beard from his ablution entered with his sandals in his left hand. Then, he sat in the circle. On the second and third day, the Prophet ﷺ said the same thing and the same man entered. This was for the sake of emphasis; otherwise, one testimony is enough. ʿAbdullāh ibn ʿAmr ؓ followed the man to learn what act was the reason for him to be promised Jannah. He did not, however, find that he performed much worship. He did find that he was mindful of the obligations, stood for prayer at night, and when he woke at night, he would remember and glorify Allah's ﷻ name and declare Him as one. When ʿAbdullāh was about to leave, he said to the man: "I heard the Messenger of Allah ﷺ say such-and-such, so I wanted to carefully observe what you do." The man said: "It is only as you have seen." But when he went off, he called him and said: "However, I find no malice in my heart toward any Muslim." He said: "It is this, and this is what is beyond ourabilities."[79]

الحاصل: أن النبي صلىٰ الله عليه وسلم إذا شهد لأحد بالجنة، فإننا نشهد له بالجنة، ونقطع له بالجنة، وأما غيره فلا نقطع له، ولكن نرجو له الخير. وكذلك الكافر المعين لا نحكم عليه بالنار؛ لأنه قد يتوب ويموت علىٰ التوبة، يختم له بخير، لكننا نخاف عليه، هذا من حيث التعيين.

To summarise: If the Prophet ﷺ testifies to someone being in Jannah, we also testify to them being in Jannah, and we are certain that they will be in Jannah. On the other hand, we cannot be certain about anyone else, but we wish them the best. We also do not determine that specific disbelievers will be in the Fire. That is because they may repent and die having repented

79 Aḥmad, *Musnad,* 3:166; ʿAbd al-Razzāq, *Muṣannaf,* no. 20,559; al-Baghwaī, *Sharḥ al-Sunnah*, no. 3535; al-Nasāʾī, *ʿAmal al-Yawm wa ʾl-Laylah,* no. 863; al-Bayhaqī, *Shuʿab al-Īmān,* no. 6605.

from their sins and ended their lives in a good way. Nonetheless, we fear they will be in the Fire. This is in terms of specific individuals.

أما من حيث العموم: فنقطع أن المسلمين في الجنة، ونقطع أن الكفار من أهل النار.

In general terms, on the other hand, we can definitively determine that Muslims will be in Jannah, and disbelievers will be in the Fire.

المتن

(١٥٤) وَلا نَشْهَدُ عَلَيْهِمْ بِكُفْرٍ وَلا بِشِرْكٍ وَلا بِنِفاقٍ، ما لَمْ يَظْهَرْ مِنْهُمْ شَيْءٌ مِنْ ذَلِكَ.

(154) We do not testify for any of them disbelief, polytheism, or hypocrisy as long as they do not outwardly demonstrate any of that;

الشرح

الأصل في المسلم: العدالة، وهذه قاعدة عظيمة فلا نسيء الظن فيه ولا نتجسس عليه، ولا نتتبعه، لكن إن ظهر لنا شيء حكمنا به عليه، وإن لم يظهر شيء فلا نسيء الظن بالمسلمين، فنعامله بما يظهر منه، ونحن لسنا مكلفين بالبحث عن الناس والتحري عنهم والحكم عليهم، لم يكلفنا الله بذلك.

The default rule is that every Muslim is upright. This is a great maxim which one should not forget. Therefore, we are not to harbour suspicions regarding any Muslim, or spy or snoop on them; however, if something is outward, we pass judgment according to that. On the other hand, if there is nothing outward, then we do not have suspicions about Muslims, and we treat them in a way that corresponds to what outwardly appears of them. It is not our duty to search or investigate people's affairs or pass judgment upon them, and Allah ﷻ has not made it our duty to do so.[80]

80 It is related that Ibn ʿUmar ﵁ said: The Messenger of Allah ﷺ climbed the pulpit

المتن

(١٥٥) وَنَذَرُ سَرائِرَهُمْ إِلَىٰ اللهِ تَعالَىٰ.

(155) And we leave their private affairs to Allah the Most High.

الشرح

نحسن الظن بهم، وسرائرهم إلىٰ الله تعالىٰ، ولم نكلف أن نبحث عن الناس وعن أحوالهم، والواجب ستر المسلم وإحسان الظن به، والتآخي بين المسلمين ﴿ إِنَّمَا ٱلْمُؤْمِنُونَ إِخْوَةٌ﴾ [الحجرات:١٠].

We have a good opinion about them, and their private affairs are left to Allah the Most High. It is not our duty to investigate people and their affairs. What is obligatory is to hide the faults of Muslims, to have a good opinion about them and to maintain brotherhood among the Muslims. **{The believers are but brothers.} [Qur'ān 49:10]**[81]

المتن

---

and yelled out: "O you who have submitted (*aslama*) on the tongue but whose faith has not reached the heart, do not cause trouble to the Muslims, do not insult them, and do not track their secret faults. Whoever tracks the secret faults of their Muslim brother, Allah will track theirs, and if Allah tracks someone's secret faults, He exposes them, even if they were in the middle of their home."

One day, Ibn 'Umar looked at the Ka'bah and said: "How great you are, and how great is your sanctity! And the sanctity of a believer is greater to Allah than you." Al-Tirmidhī, no. 2032. Al-Tirmidhī said: This *ḥadīth* is *ḥasan gharīb*.

81 It is related that Ibn 'Umar ﷺ said that the Messenger of Allah ﷺ said: "A Muslim is the brother of a Muslim. He does not wrong him and he does not forsake him. He who fulfils the needs of his brother, Allah fulfils his needs; and he who alleviates the plight of a Muslim, Allah will alleviate a plight from the plights of the Day of Judgment; and he who shields a Muslim, Allah will shield him on the Day of Judgment." Al-Bukhārī, no. 2442; Muslim, no. 2580.

(١٥٦) وَلا نَرَىٰ السَّيْفَ عَلَىٰ أَحَدٍ مِنْ أُمَّةِ مُحَمَّدٍ ﷺ إِلَّا مَنْ وَجَبَ عَلَيْهِ السَّيْفُ.

(156) We do not believe in fighting anyone from the Ummah of Muḥammad ﷺ except those whom it is obligatory to fight.

الشرح

لا يجوز قتل المسلم، واستباحة دمه؛ لأن الله عصمه بالإسلام، قال عليه الصلاة والسلام: «**أُمرت أن أُقاتل الناس حتىٰ يقولوا: لا إله إلا الله، فإذا قالوها فقد عصموا مني دماءهم وأموالهم إلا بحقها، وحسابهم علىٰ الله**».

It is not permissible to kill a Muslim or to declare his blood as lawful, because Allah has made the Muslim sanctified via his Islām. The Prophet ﷺ said: "I have been commanded to fight people until they say, 'There is no God but Allah'. If they do so, they sanctify their blood and property from me, except for what is due, and Allah is their judge."[82]

فمن أظهر الإسلام ونطق بالشهادتين، ولم يظهر منه ناقض من نواقض الإسلام، فإن دمه حرام، فلا يجوز الاعتداء عليه وسفك دمه، قال عليه الصلاة والسلام: «**إن دماءكم وأموالكم وأعراضكم عليكم حرام، كحرمة يومكم هذا في شهركم هذا في بلدكم هذا**» قال هذا في خطبته بمنىٰ يوم النحر.

So, if someone seems outwardly a Muslim, utters the testimonies of faith and is not seen to invalidate his faith in any way, his blood is sacred. It is wrong to commit any offense against him or to shed his blood. The Prophet ﷺ said: "Your blood, property, and honour are sacred to you as this day, this month, and this land are sacred." He said this in his sermon at Minā on the Day of Sacrifice.[83]

هل هناك أشد من هذا؟ فحرمة المؤمن عند الله أعظم من حرمة الكعبة؛ لأن النبي صلىٰ الله عليه وسلم لما نظر إلىٰ الكعبة قال: «**ما أشد حرمتك! وحرمة المسلم أعظم عند الله من حرمتك**» أو كما قال عليه الصلاة والسلام.

---

82 Al-Bukhārī, no. 25, 392 and 2946; Muslim, no. 21 and 22.

83 Al-Bukhārī, no. 67; Muslim, no. 1679.

Is there anything more serious than this? The sanctity of a believer is greater than the sanctity of the Ka'bah, because the Prophet ﷺ said, while looking at the Ka'bah: "How sacred is your sanctity! And the sanctity of a Muslim is greater to Allah than your sanctity," or as he ﷺ stated.[84]

وجاء عنه عليه الصلاة والسلام: «**لا يحل دم امرئ مسلم إلا بإحدىٰ ثلاث: الثيب الزاني، والنفس بالنفس، والتارك لدينه المفارق للجماعة**».

It has also been related that the Prophet ﷺ said: "It is not lawful to violate the blood of a Muslim except for three: a previously married/deflowered fornicator, a life for a life and one who leaves his religion and splits away from the community."[85]

الأول: الثيب الزاني، هو المحصن الذي سبق أن وطأ زوجته في نكاح صحيح وهما عاقلان بالغان حران، فإذا زنىٰ رُجم حتىٰ الموت.

First: The non-virgin fornicator (*al-thayyib al-zānī*), which is the *muḥṣan* (previously married) who is confirmed to have had intercourse with his wife in a valid marriage while both parties were of sound mind and were free adults (not slaves). If such a person commits fornication (*zinā*), he is to be stoned to death.

الثاني: المسلم إذا تعدّىٰ علىٰ المسلم فقتله ظلماً وعدواناً، وطالب أولياء المقتول بالقصاص فيُقتل ﴿يَـٰٓأَيُّهَا ٱلَّذِينَ ءَامَنُوا۟ كُتِبَ عَلَيْكُمُ ٱلْقِصَاصُ فِى ٱلْقَتْلَى﴾ [البقرة:١٧٨] أي : فرض عليكم، وقال تعالىٰ: ﴿وَكَتَبْنَا عَلَيْهِمْ فِيهَآ أَنَّ ٱلنَّفْسَ بِٱلنَّفْسِ﴾ [المائدة:٤٥].

Second: If a Muslim commits an act of assault against another Muslim and kills him unjustly and wrongfully, and the relatives of the person who was killed demand retribution (*qiṣāṣ*), then he is to be killed. **{O you who have believed, prescribed for you is legal retribution for those murdered.} [Qur'ān 2:178]** I.e. [*kutiba 'alaykum* means:] it has been prescribed for you. Allah ﷻ also says: **{And We ordained for them therein a life for a**

84 This dictum is verified to have been correctly attributed to Ibn 'Umar, as presented by al-Tirmidhī, no. 2037. Al-Tirmidhī said: "This *ḥadīth* is *ḥasan gharīb*."
85 Al-Bukhārī, no. 6878; Muslim, no. 1676.

life.} [Qurʾān 5:45]

والثالث: هو المرتد، فيقتل حد الردة.

Third: An apostate. Such a person is to be killed according to the prescribed penalty of apostasy.

وما عدا الثلاثة فدم المسلم محرَّم حرمةً عظيمة.

Other than these three types, the blood of a Muslim is highly sacred.

كذلك البغي، إن بغىٰ علىٰ المسلمين ولو كان مسلماً فالبغاة يقاتلون؛ لأنهم يريدون أن يفرقوا كلمة المسلمين، ويخرجوا علىٰ إمامهم، فيجب قتالهم ﴿وَإِن طَآئِفَتَانِ مِنَ ٱلْمُؤْمِنِينَ ٱقْتَتَلُوا۟ فَأَصْلِحُوا۟ بَيْنَهُمَا ۖ فَإِنۢ بَغَتْ إِحْدَىٰهُمَا عَلَى ٱلْأُخْرَىٰ فَقَٰتِلُوا۟ ٱلَّتِى تَبْغِى حَتَّىٰ تَفِىٓءَ إِلَىٰٓ أَمْرِ ٱللَّهِ ۚ﴾ [الحجرات:٩] وتُستحل دماؤهم من أجل كفهم عن البغي، ولصيانة جماعة المسلمين وكلمتهم وحفظ الأمن.

The same applies to rebels/assailants. If anyone, even a Muslim, rebels against a Muslim, then they are to be fought. This is because they seek to disunite the Muslims and because they would be revolting against their leader, so it is incumbent to fight them. **{And if two factions among the believers should fight, then make settlement between the two. But if one of them oppresses the other, then fight against the one that oppresses until it returns to the ordinance of Allah.} [Qurʾān 49:9]** Their blood is shed in order to stop them from transgressing, to maintain the united community of Muslims and to maintain security.

وكذلك تستباح دماء قطاع الطريق ﴿إِنَّمَا جَزَٰٓؤُا۟ ٱلَّذِينَ يُحَارِبُونَ ٱللَّهَ وَرَسُولَهُۥ وَيَسْعَوْنَ فِى ٱلْأَرْضِ فَسَادًا أَن يُقَتَّلُوٓا۟ أَوْ يُصَلَّبُوٓا۟ أَوْ تُقَطَّعَ أَيْدِيهِمْ وَأَرْجُلُهُم مِّنْ خِلَٰفٍ أَوْ يُنفَوْا۟ مِنَ ٱلْأَرْضِ ۚ﴾ [المائدة:٣٣] فجزاؤهم علىٰ حسب جرائمهم.

It is also lawful to shed the blood of highway robbers (*quṭṭāʿ al-ṭarīq*). **{Indeed, the penalty for those who wage war against Allah and His Messenger and strive upon earth [to cause] corruption is none but that they be killed or crucified or that their hands and feet be cut off from opposite sides or that they be exiled from the land.} [Qurʾān 5:33]**

Their penalty is according to their crime.

فهؤلاء أحل الله قتلهم؛ لدفع شرهم وعدوانهم .

Allah ﷻ has made it lawful to kill those types of people as defence against their evil and aggression.

❁❁❁

المتن

(١٥٧) وَلا نَرَىٰ الْخُرُوجَ عَلَىٰ أَئِمَّتِنا وَوُلاةِ أُمُورِنا.

(157) We do not believe in revolting against our leaders and governors;

الشرح

هذه مسألة عظيمة، فمن أصول أهل السنة والجماعة: أنهم لا يرون الخروج على ولاة أمر المسلمين ﴿يَـٰٓأَيُّهَا ٱلَّذِينَ ءَامَنُوٓاْ أَطِيعُواْ ٱللَّهَ وَأَطِيعُواْ ٱلرَّسُولَ وَأُوْلِي ٱلْأَمْرِ مِنكُمْۖ﴾ [النساء:٥٩] وقال عليه الصلاة والسلام: «**من يطع الأمير فقد أطاعني، ومن يعصِ الأمير فقد عصاني**» فلا يجوز الخروج عليهم؛ ولو كانوا فساقًا لأنهم انعقدت بيعتهم، وثبتت ولايتهم، وفي الخروج عليهم ولو كانوا فساقًا مفاسد عظيمة، من شق العصا، واختلاف الكلمة، واختلال الأمن، وتسلط الكفار على المسلمين.

This issue is of great importance. One of the principles of Ahl al-Sunnah wa 'l-Jamā'ah is that they do not believe that it is correct to revolt against those who govern the Muslims. **{O you who have believed, obey Allah and obey the Messenger and those in authority among you.} [Qur'ān 4:59]** The Messenger of Allah ﷺ said: "He who obeys the emir has obeyed me, and he who disobeys the emir has disobeyed me". Therefore, it is impermissible to revolt against them, even if they are sinners, because they have been given the pledge of allegiance and stand established as leaders. Revolting against them, even if they were sinners, results in a number of evils, such as sedition, disunion, disruption of security, and allowing the disbelievers to gain authority over the Muslims.[86]

قال شيخ الإسلام رحمه الله تعالىٰ: (ما خرج قوم علىٰ إمامهم إلا كانت حالتهم بعد الخروج أسوأ من حالتهم قبل الخروج) أو كما ذكر.

Shaykh al-Islām [Ibn Taymiyah] ﷺ said: "A people have not revolted against their leader except that the situation after the revolt became worse than the situation before it," or as he mentioned.

وهذا حتىٰ عند الكفار، إذا قاموا علىٰ ولي أمرهم وخرجوا عليه، فإنه يختل أمنهم ويصبحون في قتل وقتيل، ولا يقر لهم قرار، كما هو مشاهد في الثورات التي حدثت في التاريخ، فكيف بالخروج علىٰ إمام المسلمين؟ فلا يجوز الخروج علىٰ الأئمة وإن كانوا فساقاً، ما لم يخرجوا عن الدين، قال عليه الصلاة والسلام: «**اسمعوا وأطيعوا إلا أن تروا كفراً بواحاً عندكم من الله فيه برهان**» فالفسق والمعاصي لا توجب الخروج عليهم، خلافاً للخوارج والمعتزلة الذين يرون الخروج عليهم إن كان عندهم معاصٍ وحصل منهم فسق، فيقولون: هذا هو الأمر بالمعروف والنهي عن المنكر، ويقصدون به الخروج علىٰ ولاة أمور المسلمين.

This is also true for a disbelieving leader. When people revolt against their leaders, it disturbs their own security, they end up killing each other, and there is much instability, as observed in the revolutions that have occurred throughout history. So what about revolting against a Muslim leader? It is not permissible to revolt against Muslim leaders even if they were sinners, as long as they do not apostatise. The Prophet ﷺ said: "Hear and obey unless you see disbelief that is so outright that you have proof from Allah in it." Thus, sin and disobedience (to Allah ﷻ) are not causes for revolution. Even so, the Khārijites and Muʿtazilites hold the view that it is an obligation to revolt against anyone who has committed sins. They say that it falls under enjoining right and forbidding wrong. By that, they mean to revolt against

86 Al-Bukhārī, no. 2957; Muslim, no. 1835.

those governing the Muslims.[87]

فأصول المعتزلة خمسة:

Muʿtazilites have five basic principles:

الأول: التوحيد، ومعناه: نفي الصفات، ويرون من يثبت الصفات فهو مشرك.

One. *Tawḥīd* (oneness of Allah ﷻ). It means the rejection of all of His attributes, and they hold that anyone who affirms the attributes is an idolater.

الثاني: العدل، ومعناه: نفي القدر، فيقولون: إن إثبات القدر جور وظلم، ويجب العدل علىٰ الله.

Two. Justice (*ʿadl*). It means the rejection of predestination (*qadar*). They say it is oppression and injustice to affirm the predestination of Allah ﷻ, and that it is incumbent upon Allah ﷻ to be just.

الثالث: الأمر بالمعروف والنهي عن المنكر، ويريدون به الخروج علىٰ أئمة المسلمين إن كان عندهم معاصٍ دون الكفر. وهذا هو المنكر بنفسه، وليس من المعروف في شيء.

Three. Enjoining good and forbidding wrong. But by this, they mean revolution against Muslim leaders who commit sins that are less serious than disbelief. This itself is wrong (*munkar*) and it is far from anything right (*maʿrūf*).

الرابع: المنزلة بين المنزلتين، وهو الحكم علىٰ أصحاب الكبائر بالخروج من الإسلام، وعدم الدخول في الكفر، وأما الخوارج فيحكمون عليه بالكفر.

Four. The intermediary status (*al-manzilah bayn al-manzilatayn*). This means that those who commit major sins are judged as having left Islām but haven't entered into disbelief (*kufr*), [rendering them neither Muslims nor non-Muslims.] The Khārijites, on the other hand, hold that such people are disbelievers.

87 Al-Bukhārī, no. 7056; Muslim, no. 1709.

الخامس : إنفاذ الوعيد، ومعناه، أن من مات على معصية وهي كبيرة من الكبائر دون الشرك، فهو خالد مخلد في النار، فهم يوافقون الخوارج في مصيره في الآخرة، ويخالفون الخوارج في أنه في منزلة بين المنزلتين، وألّف فيها القاضي عبد الجبار – من أئمتهم– كتاباً سماه: شرح الأصول الخمسة.

Five. The enforcement of threats (*infādh al-waʿīd*). It means that anyone who dies having committed a major sin less serious than idolatry will abide in the Fire forever. Thus, they are in agreement with the Khārijites as far as one's fate in the afterlife, but they disagree with the Khārijites as far as their intermediary status between Islām and disbelief. One of their leaders, al-Qāḍī ʿAbd al-Jabbār, authored a book about this entitled, *Sharḥ al-Uṣūl al-Khamsah.*

المتن

(١٥٨) وَإِنْ جارُوا.

(158) Even if they commit injustice.

الشرح

الجور معناه: الظلم، وإن تعدوا وظلموا الناس بأخذ أموالهم، وضرب ظهورهم، أو يقتلون المسلم، فلا يرون الخروج عليهم؛ لقوله عليه الصلاة والسلام: «**اسمع وأطع وإن أخذ مالك وجلد ظهرك**».

The word *al-jawr* (injustice) is a synonym of *al-ẓulm.* If they transgress and commit wrongs against people by taking their property and striking their backs, or killing Muslims, then [we] hold that there is to be no revolt against them. The Prophet ﷺ said: "Hear and obey, even if he takes your property and flogs your back."[88]

فالصبر عليهم أولى من الخروج؛ لما في الخروج من المفاسد العظيمة، فهذا

88 Muslim, no. 1847, presented as being related by Hudhayfah ibn Yamān.

من باب ارتكاب أخف الضررين لدفع أعلاهما، وهي قاعدة عند أهل السنة والجماعة، والنبي صلىٰ الله عليه وسلم أمر بالصبر علىٰ جور الولاة وإن ظلموا وجاروا وإن فسقوا.

Patience with them is better than revolt, because revolt entails great evil, so it is a matter of committing the lesser of two harms to avoid the greater one. This is a principle held by Ahl al-Sunnah wa 'l-Jamā'ah. And the Prophet ﷺ commanded patience with the injustices of the authorities even if they do wrong, commit injustice or sin.

المتن

(١٥٩) وَلا نَدْعُو عَلَيْهِمْ.

(159) Nor do we supplicate against them.

الشرح

لا يجوز الدعاء عليهم: لأن هذا خروج معنوي، مثل الخروج عليهم بالسلاح، وكونه دعا عليهم؛ لأنه لا يرىٰ ولايتهم، فالواجب الدعاء لهم بالهدىٰ والصلاح، لا الدعاء عليهم، فهذا أصل من أصول أهل السنة والجماعة، فإذا رأيت أحداً يدعو علىٰ ولاة الأمور، فاعلم أنه ضال في عقيدته، وليس علىٰ منهج السلف، وبعض الناس قد يتخذ هذا من باب الغيرة والغضب لله عز وجل، لكنها غيرة وغضب في غير محلهما؛ لأنهم إذا زالوا حصلت المفاسد.

It is impermissible to pray against them because this is a symbolic form of revolt, and it is like revolting with weapons, as it means not holding their authority to be legitimate. What is obligatory is to pray for them to have guidance and righteousness, not to pray against them. This is one of the foundational principles of Ahl al-Sunnah wa 'l-Jamā'ah. So, if you see someone praying against the authorities, you should know that they have strayed from the right creed and do not follow the methodology of the early Muslims. Some people see this as a matter of zeal or discontentment over the infringement of Allah's ﷻ laws. However, it is zeal and discontentment in the wrong manner, because if they were to be removed, evils would occur.

قال الإمام الفضيل بن عياض – رحمه الله – ويروي ذلك عن الإمام أحمد يقول: (لو أني أعلم أن لي دعوة مستجابة لصرفتها للسلطان).

Al-Imām al-Fuḍayl b. ʿIyāḍ ﵀ said and cited al-Imām Aḥmad as saying: "If I knew that one of my supplications would be answered, I would supplicate for the leader."

والإمام أحمد صبر في المحنة، ولم يثبت عنه أنه دعا عليهم أو تكلم فيهم، بل صبر وكانت العاقبة له، هذا مذهب أهل السنة والجماعة.

Al-Imām Aḥmad showed patience during the Great Trial[89], and it is not established from him that he supplicated against them (the authorities) or spoke ill of them. Instead, he was patient and the final outcome was in his favour. This is the methodology of Ahl al-Sunnah wa ʾl-Jamāʿah.

فالذين يدعون علىٰ ولاة أمور المسلمين ليسوا علىٰ مذهب أهل السنة والجماعة، وكذلك الذين لا يدعون لهم، وهذا علامة أن عندهم انحرافًا عن عقيدة أهل السنة والجماعة.

Those who supplicate against the Muslim authorities are not upon the way of Ahl al-Sunnah wa ʾl-Jamāʿah. Moreover, those not supplicating for them show a sign that they have some deviation from the creed of Ahl al-Sunnah wa ʾl-Jamāʿah.

وبعضهم ينكر علىٰ الذين يدعون في خطبة الجمعة لولاة الأمور، ويقولون: هذه مداهنة، هذا نفاق، هذا تزلف. سبحان الله! هذا مذهب أهل السنة والجماعة، بل من السنة الدعاء لولاة الأمور؛ لأنهم إذا صلحوا صلح الناس، فأنت تدعو

89 The Great Trial refers to a controversy that arose during the time of al-Imām Aḥmad about whether the Qurʾān was created. The ruler asked him to say that it was created (therefore, implying that it will eventually perish) yet he completely refused and endured much torture due to this. Fortunately, though, his opinion prevailed and Allah brought him safely out of his trial. [Translator's note]

لهم بالصلاح والهداية والخير، وإن كان عندهم شر، فهم ما داموا علىٰ الإسلام فعندهم خير، فما داموا يُحَكِّمون الشرع، ويقيمون الحدود، ويصونون الأمن، ويمنعون العدوان عن المسلمين، ويكفون الكفار عنهم، فهذا خير عظيم، فيدعىٰ لهم من أجل ذلك. وما عندهم من المعاصي والفسق، فهذا إثمه عليهم، ولكن عندهم خير أعظم، ويُدعىٰ لهم بالاستقامة والصلاح فهذا مذهب أهل السنة والجماعة، أما مذهب أهل الضلال وأهل الجهل، فيرون هذا من المداهنة والتزلف، ولا يدعون لهم، بل يدعون عليهم.

Some people even criticize those who supplicate for the authorities during Friday sermons. They say that it is flattery, hypocrisy, and adulation. *Subḥāna 'llāh!* The way of Ahl al-Sunnah wa 'l-Jamā'ah, rather of the Sunnah, is to supplicate for the authorities, because if they are righteous, their people will also be righteous. So, you should supplicate for them to be righteous and rightly guided and for good [things for them,] even if they have done some evils. As long as they are Muslims, there is some good in them. As long as they seek judgment from the Islamic law, uphold the statutes, maintain security, defend against aggression towards the Muslims and protect them from the disbelievers, then there is much good and supplication should be made for them on that basis. On the other hand, whatever sins they have committed, then it is they who are to bear the blame, but the good that they do is greater. Supplications should also be made for them to be upright and righteous. This is the way of Ahl al-Sunnah wa 'l-Jamā'ah. On the other hand, the way of those who have gone astray and the ignorant is the belief that such is flattery and bootlicking. They do not supplicate for them, rather they do so against them.

والغيرة ليست في الدعاء عليهم، فإن كنت تريد الخير؛ فادعُ لهم بالصلاح والخير، فالله قادر علىٰ هدايتهم وردهم إلىٰ الحق، فأنت هل يئست من هدايتهم؟ هذا قنوط من رحمة الله، وأيضـًا الدعاء لهم من النصيحة، كما قال عليه الصلاة والسلام: «**الدين النصيحة، الدين النصيحة، الذين النصيحة**» قلنا: لمن يا رسول الله ؟ قال: «**لله ولكتابه ولرسوله ولأئمة المسلمين وعامتهم**».

It is not 'protective jealousy [for the religion]' to pray against them. If you wish to do good, pray for good and righteousness for them. Allah is able to guide them to the path and bring them back to what is right. Have you, nonetheless, given up hope for them to be rightly guided? This is a form of despair of Allah's mercy (*qunūṭ min raḥmati llāh*). Furthermore, supplicating for them means having sincerity (*naṣīḥah*) towards them, as the Prophet ﷺ said: "Faith is good will, faith is good will, faith is good will." "Towards whom, O Messenger of Allah?" He said: "Towards Allah, His Book, His Messenger, and the *imāms* and common folk among the Muslims."

فهذا أصل عظيم يجب التنبه له، وبخاصة في هذه الأزمنة.

This is a great fundamental principle that has to be given notice, especially in these times.[90]

المتن

(١٦٠) وَلا نَنْزِعُ يَدًا مِنْ طاعَتِهِمْ.

(160) Or disobey them.

الشرح

(ولا ننزع يداً من طاعتهم) هذا تأكيد لما سبق، حتىٰ ولو حصل منهم ظلم وجور ومعاصٍ وكبائر دون الشرك، فإننا لا ننزع يداً من طاعتهم، ولا نخرج عليهم ولا نعصيهم ﴿يَٰٓأَيُّهَا ٱلَّذِينَ ءَامَنُوٓاْ أَطِيعُواْ ٱللَّهَ وَأَطِيعُواْ ٱلرَّسُولَ وَأُوْلِي ٱلۡأَمۡرِ مِنكُمۡۖ﴾ [النساء:٥٩] بل نجاهد معهم، ونشهد الجمع والجماعات والأعياد معهم؛ من أجل اجتماع كلمة المسلمين.

This is to emphasize the aforementioned, even if they were to commit wrongs, injustices, acts of disobedience, and major sins below polytheism, we do not disobey them, nor do we revolt against or disobey them. **{O you**

---

90 Muslim, no. 55; al-Bukhārī presented it with a discontinuous route of transmission in *kitāb al-īmān, bāb qawl al-nabī ṣallāʾllāhu ʿalayhi wa sallam, al-dīn al-naṣīḥah lillāhi wa li-rasūlihī wa li-aimmat al-muslimīn wa li-ʿāmmatihim*.

who have believed, obey Allah and obey the Messenger and those in authority among you.} [Qur'ān 4:59] Rather, we fight in *jihād* with them, and we observe all congregations of the daily, Friday, and Eid prayers with them, for the sake of unity among Muslims.

المتن

(١٦١) وَنَرَىٰ طاعَتَهُمْ مِنْ طاعَةِ اللهِ عز وجل فَرِيضَةً، ما لَمْ يَأْمُرُوا بِمَعْصِيَةٍ.

(161) We believe that obedience to them is obedience to Allah the Almighty, a statute, as long as they do not command to sin.

الشرح

قال تعالىٰ: ﴿يَٰٓأَيُّهَا ٱلَّذِينَ ءَامَنُوٓاْ أَطِيعُواْ ٱللَّهَ وَأَطِيعُواْ ٱلرَّسُولَ وَأُوْلِي ٱلْأَمْرِ مِنكُمْۖ﴾ [النساء:٥٩] فالله أمر بطاعة ولاة الأمر من المسلمين، أما الكافر فلا طاعة له علىٰ المسلمين ﴿وَلَن يَجْعَلَ ٱللَّهُ لِلْكَٰفِرِينَ عَلَى ٱلْمُؤْمِنِينَ سَبِيلًا ١٤١﴾ [النساء:١٤١] لأنه قال: ﴿وَأُوْلِي ٱلْأَمْرِ مِنكُمْ﴾ يعني المسلمين. فتجب طاعتهم إلا إذا أمروا بمعصية، فإنه لا طاعة لمخلوق في معصية الله، فلا تطعه في تلك المعصية، لكن ليس المعنىٰ أن تخرج عليه وتنزع الطاعة مطلقًا، بل لا تطعه في تلك المعصية، وأطعه فيما عداها، مما ليس بمعصية وقال عليه الصلاة والسلام: «**إنما الطاعة في المعروف**».

Allah ﷻ says: **{O you who have believed, obey Allah and obey the Messenger and those in authority among you.} [Qur'ān 4:59]** So, Allah commands obedience to the authorities from the Muslims. On the other hand, it is not the Muslims' duty to obey a disbeliever. **{And never will Allah give the disbelievers over the believers a way [to overcome them].} [Qur'ān 4:141]** Because Allah said: *"those in authority among you"*, that is, among the Muslims. It is obligatory to obey them unless they command us to disobey Allah, as there is no obedience to the creation if it means disobeying Allah ﷻ. We are not to obey them in any such disobedience. However, that does not mean that we are to revolt against them and renounce our obedience altogether. It only means that we are not to obey them in that sin, but we obey them in everything besides that, i.e. in that which is not sinful. The Prophet ﷺ said: "Obedience is in what is good."[91]

المتن

(١٦٢) وَنَدْعُو لَهُمْ بِالصَّلاحِ والْمُعافاةِ.

(162) We supplicate for them to be righteous and well.

الشرح

ندعو الله أن يرجعهم إلىٰ الحق، ويصحح ما عندهم من الخطأ، ندعو لهم بالصلاح؛ لأن صلاحهم صلاح للمسلمين، وهدايتهم هداية للمسلمين، ونفعهم يتعدّىٰ لغيرهم، فأنت إن دعوت لهم دعوت للمسلمين.

We supplicate that Allah ﷻ brings them back to what is right (i.e. The Truth) and corrects their wrongs. We pray that they be set aright, because their righteousness means the righteousness of the Muslims, and them being rightly guided means that the Muslims will be rightly guided. The effects of the good things that they do are felt by others as well. So, if you supplicate for them, you are supplicating for all of the Muslims.

المتن

(١٦٣) وَنَتَّبِعُ السُّنَّةَ والْجَماعَةَ، وَنَجْتَنِبُ الشُّذُوذَ والْخِلافَ والْفُرْقَةَ.

(163) We follow the Sunnah and the *jamā'ah* (united community), and we avoid anomalies, discord, and division.

91 Al-Bukhārī, no. 4340 and 7145; Muslim, no. 1840.

الشرح

هذا أصل عظيم من أصول أهل السنة والجماعة، وهو اتباع سنة النبي صلىٰ الله عليه وسلم، قال عليه الصلاة والسلام: «**فإنه من يعش منكم فسيرىٰ اختلافاً كثيراً، فعليكم بسنتي وسنة الخلفاء الراشدين المهديين من بعدي، تمسكوا بها وعضوا عليها بالنواجذ، وإياكم ومحدثات الأمور، فإن كل محدثة بدعة، وكل بدعة ضلالة، وكل ضلالة في النار**» فلما أمر بالسنة، نهىٰ عن البدعة.

This is one of the important fundamental principles of Ahl al-Sunnah wa 'l-Jamā'ah, namely the following of the Sunnah of the Prophet ﷺ. The Prophet ﷺ said: "Anyone who lives among you (after me) will see much disagreement, so hold on to my Sunnah and the Sunnah of the rightly guided caliphs to come after me. Hold on to it and bite on it with your molars. And beware of newly introduced matters, as every newly introduced matter is an innovation, and every innovation is misguidance, and all misguidance is in the Hell Fire." So, when he commanded holding on to the Sunnah, he forbade innovation (*bid'ah*).[92]

والبدعة: ما أُحدث في الدين مما ليس منه؛ لقوله عليه الصلاة والسلام: «**من عمل عملاً ليس عليه أمرنا فهو رد**»، وكل عبادة وكل عمل يتقرب به العبد لله، وليس عليه دليل من الكتاب ولا السنة، فهو بدعة، وإن كان قصد فاعله التقرب إلىٰ الله فهو إنما يبعده عن الله، ولا يثاب عليه؛ بل يعاقب، فالسنة ما كان عليه دليل من الكتاب أو السنة.

Innovation is anything that is newly introduced into the religion which was not originally part of it. The Prophet ﷺ said: "He who does an act that is not in accordance with our affair, then it is rejected." Every form of worship and every act through which a person seeks to draw nearer to Allah ﷻ, which is not supported by any evidence in the Qur'ān and Sunnah, is an innovation, regardless of whether the intent of the one who does it is to draw nearer to Allah ﷻ. It only takes one away from Allah ﷻ, and one is not rewarded for it, but in fact is to be punished. Thus, the Sunnah is what is in

92 Abū Dāwūd, no. 4607; al-Tirmidhī, no. 2681; Ibn Mājah, no. 42.

accord with evidence from the Qurʾān and Sunnah.[93]

والبدع كثيرة جداً، فالناس يُحدثُون بدعاً كثيرة، فالبدع لا تُقرّ ولا يُعمل بها مهما كانت وممن صدرت، ومن البدع ما يعمل من الاحتفالات بالمولد النبوي، فهو بدعة، ليس عليه دليل من الكتاب ولا السنة ولا هدي الخلفاء الراشدين، ولا من هدي القرون المفضلة التي شهد لها رسول الله صلىٰ الله عليه وسلم بالخيرية، إنما أُحدث بعد هذه القرون لما فشا الجهل، وأول من أحدث المولد: الشيعة الفاطميون، ثم أخذه الأغرار المتسبون لأهل السنة عن حسن نية وقصد، ويزعمون أنه من محبة الرسول، وليس ذلك من محبته، إنما المحبة بالاتباع لا الابتداع:

There are many kinds of innovations as the people have introduced many different forms of them. Innovations are neither to be adopted nor acted upon, regardless of what they are or who they have originated from. One innovation is the celebration of the Prophet's ﷺ birthday (*al-mawlid*). It is an innovation for which there is no evidence from the Qurʾān, or the Sunnah, or the guidance of the Rightly-Guided Caliphs (*al-khulafāʾ al-rāshidīn*), or from the generations of virtue[94], whose virtue has been attested to by the Prophet ﷺ. The birthday (*mawlid*) was introduced after these generations, when ignorance spread. The first people to have introduced the *mawlid* were the Shiʾite Fāṭimids. The first people attributing to Ahl al-Sunnah to fall for this accepted it out of good intentions, claiming that it was out of love for the Prophet ﷺ. However, it is not out of love for him, as love for him is only by following him, not by innovating.

One poet said:

تعصي الإله وأنت تزعم حبه   هذا لعمري في القياس شنيع

93 Muslim, no. 1718; al-Bukhārī, presented it according to the following wording: "Whoever introduces a matter into our affair which is not from it, then it is rejected." (no. 2697).

94 This is a reference to the "best three generations", namely the generation of the Prophet ﷺ then that which followed and then that which followed them. We are to follow in the footsteps of those three generations and try our best to emulate them. [Translator's note]

لو كان حبك صادقاً لأطعته إن المحب لمن يحب مطيع

You disobey Allah in your claim of love for Him?
This is a gravely mistaken analogy.

If your love were sincere, you would have instead obeyed Him,
As the lover is indeed obedient to his beloved.

فعلامة المحبة الصادقة: الاتباع، أما الابتداع فهي علامة علىٰ الكراهة؛ لأن النبي صلىٰ الله عليه وسلم حذر من البدعة، وأنت تحييها وتحدثها، فمعنىٰ ذلك أنك تكره السنة، وإذا كنت تكره السنة فأنت تكره الرسول فإن كنت تريد الخير فتب إلىٰ الله وارجع، أما العناد والمكابرة فهذا اختيار سيئ لنفسك.

The sign of sincere love is following [the Sunnah]. Innovation, on the other hand, is a sign of detest, because the Prophet ﷺ warned against innovation. Then you, [O innovator,] revive and introduce them! This means that you hate the Sunnah, and if you hate the Sunnah, then you hate the Messenger of Allah ﷺ. If you would like to do something good, then turn to Allah in repentance and cease. Obstinacy and pride, on the other hand, are foul choices to make for yourself in that situation.

وكذلك نلزم الجماعة ونترك الشذوذ؛ فلا نأتي بعمل ولا بقول شاذ ليس عليه عمل المسلمين وقولهم؛ لأن هذا يُفرّق الكلمة ويحدث العداوة، فما دام المسلمون يمشون علىٰ منهج الكتاب والسنة، فلا نترك ما هم عليه لقول شاذ، فالشذوذ والمخالفات لا تجوز، والحمد لله، المسلمون يبحثون عن الحق، وإجماعهم «**إن الله تعالىٰ لا يجمع أمتي علىٰ ضلالة**»، حتىٰ الحديث إن ورد عن طريق وسند صحيح، لكن فيه مخالفة لما هو أصح منه؛ فيسمىٰ حديثاً شاذاً عند المحدثين.

In addition [to the Sunnah], we stick to the united community of Muslims (*jamāʿah*) and leave deviations or oddities (*shudhūdh*). We do not act in accordance with any irregular practices or opinions that are not in accord with the practices and opinions of the Muslims because this causes disunion and creates enmity. So, as long as the Muslims tread upon the path of the Qur'ān and Sunnah, we don't forsake what they follow for the irregular opinions. Irregularity and transgression are not permissible. Thanks to Allah, Muslims seek the truth, and their agreement is the fact that "Allah ﷻ does not unite my Ummah in error." Although this *ḥadīth* has been presented with an authentic chain of transmission, it is somewhat inconsistent with what is more established as authentic, so it is called a *shādh* (irregular) *ḥadīth* according to the *ḥadīth* scholars.[95]

فيجب التثبت في هذه الأمور، ولا ننبش في أقوال وأفعال مهجورة ونؤلف فيها ونشوش علىٰ الناس أمور دينهم، والشذوذ: مخالفة ما عليه جماعة المسلمين، والخلاف ضد الاتفاق، والفرقة ضد الاجتماع، والشذوذ ضد الائتلاف، أما أن نبحث عن الشاذ، فهذا تضليل للأئمة وتجهيل لهم، وهل أنت أوتيت علماً أكثر من علمهم، وخصصت بعلم لم يصلوا إليه؟ وما آل إليه بعض الناس من هذه الأمور في العصور المتأخرة التي يفشو فيها الجهل، وأغلب ما يصدر ذلك عن واحد متعالم وليس بعالم، ولم يدرس العقيدة الصحيحة والفقه، إنما تفقه علىٰ نفسه وصار يضيف إلىٰ دين الله ما ليس منه، وهذه مصيبة، فالعلم ليس بفوضىٰ، إنه يحتاج إلىٰ ضوابط وفقه ودراية.

Such matters have to be verified, and we do not try to exhume opinions and practices that have been abandoned, and then write about them and confuse people about their religion. Deviation, or irregularity (*shudhūdh*), means to be inconsistent or disagree with what the Muslim community follows. Disagreement is the opposite of agreement; division (*furqah*) is the opposite of unity (*ijtimāʿ*), and irregularity is the opposite of accord (*iʾtilāf*). Seeking after irregular opinions means claiming that the Muslim *imāms* were misguided and ignorant. Have you been given more knowledge than them? Or have you been given special knowledge that they were unable to attain? It has gotten to the point that, in recent times where ignorance is widespread, some people follow such matters. The majority of that originates from one pretending to be knowledgeable but who is not, in fact, knowledgeable, who has not studied the correct doctrine or jurisprudence but instead learned the law at his own hands and thus ended up making additions to Allah's ﷻ reli-

95 Al-Tirmidhī, no. 2172.

gion that are not from it. This is a misfortune, as knowledge is not chaotic; it requires guidelines, understanding, and comprehension.

المتن

(١٦٤) وَنُحِبُّ أَهْلَ الْعَدْلِ والْأَمانَةِ، وَنُبْغِضُ أَهْلَ الْجَوْرِ والْخِيانَةِ.

(164) We love those who are just and fulfil their trusts and hate those who are unjust and disloyal.

الشرح

المحبة عمل قلبي ، والمحبة على قسمين:

Love is an act of the heart. There are two kinds of love:

أولاً: محبة طبيعية، كمحبة الإنسان لأهله وزوجته وأولاده، ومحبته لأصدقائه، ومحبته للأكل والشرب، فهذه المحبة لا تدخل في أمر العبادة.

One. Natural love, such as the love a person has for his family, wife, and children, and the love he has for his friends, and the love he has for his food and drink. This kind of love is not included in matters of worship.

ثانياً: محبة دينية، وهذه على نوعين:

Two. Love as associated with religion.

وهذه على نوعين:

There are two kinds of the second type:

النوع الأول: محبة الله سبحانه وتعالى، وهي أعظم أنواع العبادة، يقول ابن القيم:

The first kind is love for Allah the Almighty, which is the greatest kind of worship. Ibn al-Qayyim said:

وعبادة الرحمن غاية حبه   مع ذل عابده هما قطبان

وعليهما فلك العبادة دائر   ما دار حتىٰ قامت القطبان

To serve the All Merciful is *to have the greatest love* for Him with the *inferiority of His slaves*, these are two poles,

And the orbit of worship revolves around them until the two poles stand.

عبادة الرحمن غاية حبه، أي: منتهىٰ حبه، وتدور عليها أمور العبادات كلها، فهي نوع عظيم من أنواع العبادة، لا يجوز أن يُحب أحد مع الله ﴿وَمِنَ ٱلنَّاسِ مَن يَتَّخِذُ مِن دُونِ ٱللَّهِ أَندَادًا يُحِبُّونَهُمْ كَحُبِّ ٱللَّهِ﴾ [البقرة:١٦٥] هذا شرك في المحبة، التي هي أعظم أنواع العبادة، ولذلك قال: ﴿وَٱلَّذِينَ ءَامَنُوٓاْ أَشَدُّ حُبًّا لِّلَّهِ﴾ [البقرة:١٦٥]

To worship the All Merciful is to have the greatest love for Him: that is, ultimate love, which all matters of worship revolve around. It is a great kind of worship, and it is not permissible to love anyone alongside Allah ﷻ. **{And [yet], among the people are those who take other than Allah as equals [to Him]. They love them as they [should] love Allah.} [Qurʾān 2:165]** This is polytheism in love, which (i.e. love) is the greatest kind of worship, and that is why He ﷻ says: **{But those who believe are stronger in love for Allah.} [Qurʾān 2:165]**

فالمؤمنون لا يحبون إلا الله، ومحبتهم أشد من محبة أهل الأصنام لأصنامهم؛ لأن محبة الله لا تنقطع في الدنيا ولا في الآخرة، أما محبة غيره من المعبودين فتنقطع في الآخرة، وتحصل العداوة بين من عبد من دون الله ومن عبده ﴿وَإِذَا حُشِرَ ٱلنَّاسُ كَانُواْ لَهُمْ أَعْدَآءً وَكَانُواْ بِعِبَادَتِهِمْ كَٰفِرِينَ ۝٦﴾ [الأحقاف:٦]، ﴿وَقَالَ إِنَّمَا ٱتَّخَذْتُم مِّن دُونِ ٱللَّهِ أَوْثَٰنًا مَّوَدَّةَ بَيْنِكُمْ فِى ٱلْحَيَوٰةِ ٱلدُّنْيَا ثُمَّ يَوْمَ ٱلْقِيَٰمَةِ يَكْفُرُ بَعْضُكُم بِبَعْضٍ وَيَلْعَنُ بَعْضُكُم بَعْضًا وَمَأْوَىٰكُمُ ٱلنَّارُ﴾ [العنكبوت:٢٥].

The believers love nothing more than Allah ﷻ, and their love for Allah ﷻ is greater than the love idolaters have for their idols, because love of Allah ﷻ neither discontinues in the world nor in the hereafter. On the other hand, the love of things besides Him that are worshipped discontinues in the hereafter, and there will be enmity between the things that are worshipped besides Allah ﷻ and those who worship them. **{And when the people are gathered [that Day], they [who were invoked] will be enemies to them, and they will be deniers of their worship.} [Qur'ān 46:6] {You have only taken, other than Allah, idols as [a bond of] affection among you in the worldly life. Then on the Day of Resurrection you will deny one another and curse one another, and your refuge will be the Fire...} [Qur'ān 29:25]**

النوع الثاني: المحبة في الله ولأجل الله، وذلك بأن تحب ما يحبه الله من الأعمال والأشخاص، وتحب أهل الإيمان والتقوى، ﴿إِنَّ ٱللَّهَ يُحِبُّ ٱلتَّوَّٰبِينَ وَيُحِبُّ ٱلْمُتَطَهِّرِينَ ﴿٢٢٢﴾﴾ [البقرة:٢٢٢]، ﴿إِنَّ ٱللَّهَ يُحِبُّ ٱلْمُحْسِنِينَ ﴿١٩٥﴾﴾ [البقر:١٩٥]، فأنت تحبهم؛ لأن الله يحبهم، وفي مقدمة هؤلاء: الملائكة، والأنبياء والرسل، والأولياء والصالحون، وجميع المؤمنين.

The second kind is love for Allah ﷻ and for the sake of Allah ﷻ. That is via loving whatever acts and people that Allah loves. You love the faithful and the pious. **{Indeed, Allah loves those who are constantly repentant and loves those who purify themselves.} [Qur'ān 2:222] {Indeed, Allah loves the doers of good.} [Qur'ān 2:195]** So you love them because Allah ﷻ loves them. At the forefront of those individuals are the angels, the Prophets, the Messengers, the allies of Allah (*awliyā'*), the righteous and all of the faithful.

وهذه تسمى المحبة في الله، وهي أوثق عرى الإيمان، كما جاء في الحديث: «**أوثق عرى الإيمان: الحب في الله والبغض في الله**»، وقال عليه الصلاة والسلام: «**ثلاث من كن فيه وجد حلاوة الإيمان**» ذكر منها: «**أن يحب المرء لا يحبه إلا لله**».

This is called *love for the sake of Allah* and is the firmest thing upon which one lays hold of faith, as it is related in a *ḥadīth*: "The firmest thing upon which one lays hold of faith is love for Allah's sake and hate for Allah's sake."[96] The Prophet ﷺ said: "There are three things that if one has them,

96 Al-Ṭabarānī, *al-Muʿjam al-Kabīr,* 11/215, no. 11537.

they have found the sweetness of faith,"[97] – and one of those things is: "that they love someone for nothing more than Allah's sake."

فتحب أولياء الله لأن الله يحبهم، وتبغض أعداء الله لأن الله يبغضهم، فيكون الحب والبغض من أجل الله، وليس طمعاً في الدنيا، فلا يجد العبد حلاوة الإيمان حتىٰ يحب في الله ويبغض في الله، ويوالي ويعادي الله.

So, you should love the allies of Allah because Allah loves them and hate the enemies of Allah because Allah hates them. So your love and hate are for the sake of Allah, not for the desire of this world. A person does not taste the sweetness of faith unless he loves for the sake of Allah and hates for the sake of Allah, and also takes allies and enemies for the sake of Allah.

قال ابن عباس رضي الله عنهما: «**صارت عامة مؤاخاة الناس علىٰ أمر الدنيا، وذلك لا يجدي علىٰ أهله شيئاً**».

Ibn 'Abbās ﷺ said: "It has become that the majority of fraternity amongst people is for matters of the world, and that is of no use to those people."

وهذه المحبة تبقىٰ في الدنيا والآخرة، وأما محبة الدنيا فتنقطع، وتكون عداوة في الآخرة ﴿ٱلْأَخِلَّآءُ يَوْمَئِذٍۭ بَعْضُهُمْ لِبَعْضٍ عَدُوٌّ إِلَّا ٱلْمُتَّقِينَ ۝٦٧﴾ [الزخرف:٦٧].

This kind of love remains in this world and in the hereafter, but the love of the world discontinues and becomes hatred in the hereafter. **{Close friends, that Day, will be enemies to each other, except for the righteous.} [Qur'ān 43:67]**

وتبغض الشخص من أجل الله، وليس من أجل أنه أساء إليك؛ بل تبغضه؛ لأنه عدو لله، وهذه ملة إبراهيم عليه الصلاة والسلام: الحب والبغض في الله، ﴿قَدْ كَانَتْ لَكُمْ أُسْوَةٌ حَسَنَةٌ فِىٓ إِبْرَٰهِيمَ وَٱلَّذِينَ مَعَهُۥٓ إِذْ قَالُوا۟ لِقَوْمِهِمْ إِنَّا بُرَءَٰٓؤُا۟ مِنكُمْ وَمِمَّا تَعْبُدُونَ مِن دُونِ ٱللَّهِ كَفَرْنَا بِكُمْ وَبَدَا بَيْنَنَا وَبَيْنَكُمُ ٱلْعَدَٰوَةُ وَٱلْبَغْضَآءُ أَبَدًا حَتَّىٰ تُؤْمِنُوا۟ بِٱللَّهِ وَحْدَهُۥٓ﴾ [الممتحنة:٤].

97 Al-Bukhārī, no. 16; Muslim, no. 43.

And you hate someone for the sake of Allah, not because of any offense that they did to you, but rather you hate them because they are an enemy to Allah. This is the religion of Ibrāhīm ﷺ: To love and hate for Allah's sake. **{There has already been for you an excellent pattern in Abraham and those with him, when they said to their people, 'Indeed, we are disassociated from you and from whatever you worship other than Allah. We have denied you, and there has appeared between us and you animosity and hatred forever until you believe in Allah alone.'} [Qur'ān 60:4]**

ومن السبعة الذين يظلهم الله في ظله يوم لا ظل إلا ظله «**رجلان تحابا في الله، اجتمعا عليه وتفرقا عليه**» فالحب في الله والبغض في الله أمره عظيم؛ لأنه فرقان بين الحق والباطل ﴿يَـٰٓأَيُّهَا ٱلَّذِينَ ءَامَنُوٓاْ إِن تَتَّقُواْ ٱللَّهَ يَجۡعَل لَّكُمۡ فُرۡقَانًا﴾ [الأنفال:٢٩]، فالمؤمن يكون عنده فرقان، يفرق بين هذا وهذا.

Amongst the seven people whom Allah will shade on the Day when there is no shade but His are "two men who loved for the sake of Allah and came together and departed for that purpose." Loving and hating for Allah's sake is a matter of great importance, as it is a criterion between truth and falsehood. **{O you who have believed, if you fear Allah, He will grant you a criterion.} [Qur'ān 8:29]** A believer should have a criterion by which to make a distinction between this and that.[98]

وقد ذكر العلماء أن الناس في المحبة علىٰ ثلاثة أقسام:

The scholars of Islām have noted that people are of three types when it comes to love:

القسم الأول: منهم من يحب محبة خالصة ليس معها بغضاء، وهم الملائكة والرسل عليه الصلاة والسلام، وخُلّص المؤمنين كالصحابة ﴿رَبَّنَا ٱغۡفِرۡ لَنَا وَلِإِخۡوَٰنِنَا ٱلَّذِينَ سَبَقُونَا بِٱلۡإِيمَٰنِ وَلَا تَجۡعَلۡ فِي قُلُوبِنَا غِلّٗا لِّلَّذِينَ ءَامَنُواْ﴾[الحشر:١٠] وكذلك السلف الصالح وأهل السنة والجماعة؛ لصفاء ما هم عليه من العقيدة وما هم عليه من الحق؛ لطاعتهم لله ورسوله.

98 Al-Bukhārī, no. 660; Muslim, no. 1031.

The first type of people includes those who have a right to sincere and pure love not accompanied by hate. These are the angels and Messengers as well as the pure believers, such as the Companions, **{'Our Lord, forgive us and our brothers who preceded us in faith and put not in our hearts [any] resentment toward those who have believed.'} [Qur'ān 59:10]** And the righteous early Muslims and Ahl al-Sunnah wa 'l-Jamāʿah. This is because they adhere to a pure creed and because of the truth they are upon, as they obeyed Allah and the Messenger of Allah.

القسم الثاني: من يبغض بغضاً خالصاً ليس معه محبة، وهم الكفار، أعداء الله ﴿يَٰٓأَيُّهَا ٱلَّذِينَ ءَامَنُواْ لَا تَتَّخِذُواْ عَدُوِّى وَعَدُوَّكُمْ أَوْلِيَآءَ﴾ [الممتحنة:١] أي: أحباء تحبونهم وتوالونهم وتناصرونهم، وتدافعون عنهم، بل الواجب التبرؤ منهم؛ لأنهم أعداء الله ﴿لَّا تَجِدُ قَوْمًا يُؤْمِنُونَ بِٱللَّهِ وَٱلْيَوْمِ ٱلْءَاخِرِ يُوَآدُّونَ مَنْ حَآدَّ ٱللَّهَ وَرَسُولَهُۥ وَلَوْ كَانُوٓاْ ءَابَآءَهُمْ أَوْ أَبْنَآءَهُمْ أَوْ إِخْوَٰنَهُمْ أَوْ عَشِيرَتَهُمْ أُوْلَٰٓئِكَ كَتَبَ فِى قُلُوبِهِمُ ٱلْإِيمَٰنَ وَأَيَّدَهُم بِرُوحٍ مِّنْهُ وَيُدْخِلُهُمْ جَنَّٰتٍ تَجْرِى مِن تَحْتِهَا ٱلْأَنْهَٰرُ﴾ [المجادلة: ٢٢] والمقصود بالروح هنا: قوة الإيمان .

The second type of people are those who have a right to pure and sincere hate, not accompanied by love. These are the disbelievers, the enemies of Allah. **{O you who have believed, do not take My enemies and your enemies as allies.} [Qur'ān 60:1]** That is to say, do not take them as loved ones, thus neither love them, give them your alliance and aid nor defend them. Instead, it is a duty to disavow them because they are the enemies of Allah. **{You will not find a people who believe in Allah and the Last Day having affection for those who oppose Allah and His Messenger, even if they were their fathers or their sons or their brothers or their kindred. Those – He has decreed within their hearts faith and supported them with spirit from Him. And We will admit them to gardens beneath which rivers flow.} [Qur'ān 58:22]** What *spirit* means here is 'strength of faith'.

القسم الثالث: من يجتمع فيه محبة وبغض، وهو المؤمن العاصي، يحب من وجه، ويبغض من وجه، تحبه لما فيه من الخير والطاعة، وتبغضه لما فيه من

المعاصي والمخالفة، هكذا ينبغي علىٰ المسلم أن يميز.

The third type of people are those who combine both love and hate. These are the sinful believers; they are loved in one respect and hated in another. You love them for their goodness and obedience and you hate them for their sin and wrongdoing. A Muslim ought to make distinctions between people according to this.

والمحبة بابها باب عظيم ينبغي التنبه له ومعرفته؛ لأن عليه مداراً عظيماً في العقيدة وأمور الدين، فالإنسان لا يمشي إمعة، لا يدري من يحب ومن يبغض، بل يجعل المحبة والبغضاء ميزاناً يفرق بين أولياء الله وأولياء الشيطان، ولا يجعله ميزاناً دنيوياً وهوىٰ، فمن وافقه علىٰ دنياه وهواه وأعطاه شيئاً من الدنيا أحبه، ولو كان من أكفر الناس وأفسقهم، وإن لم يعطه شيئاً أبغضه، ولو كان من أصلح الصالحين، فهذا لا يجوز.

Love is a matter of great importance, and it deserves attention and knowledge, because creed and matters of religion largely revolve around it. A person should not be a yes-man, not knowing who to love and hate; rather, he should place love and hate on a scale [based on the] criterion between the allies of Allah ﷻ and the allies of Shayṭān, and one should not make it a scale based on worldly matters and desires, thus loving anyone who is in conformity with his interests and inclinations or who gives him some mundane things of the world, even if that person were the most faithless or sinful of all people, and hating one who does not give him anything [worldly,] even if he were the most righteous of all people. This is not permissible.

المتن

(١٦٥) وَنَقُولُ: اللهُ أَعْلَمُ فِيما اشْتَبَهَ عَلَيْنا عِلْمُهُ.

(165) And when something is unclear to us, we say "Allah knows best."

الشرح

هذه مسألة عظيمة، وهي مسألة العلم فالإنسان لا يقول ما لا يعلم، إن علم شيئاً قال به، وإن جهل شيئاً فلا يقول به، ولا يقول في أمور الدين والعبادات ولا يدخل فيها بغير علم، بل يتوقف، ويقول: الله أعلم.

This is an issue of great importance: It is the issue of knowledge. We do not speak about something of which we do not have knowledge. If a person has knowledge of something, he should say it; if not, then he should not say anything. Also a person should not speak about religious matters, such as worship, without knowledge. Rather he should stop and say, "Allah knows best."

والإمام مالك إمام دار الهجرة، جاءه رجل فسأله عن أربعين مسألة، فأجاب عن أربع منها، وقال في الباقي: لا أدري، فقال الرجل: أنا جئتك من كذا وكذا علىٰ راحلتي وتقول: لا أدري؟ قال له الإمام: اركب راحلتك، وارجع إلىٰ البلد الذي جئت منه، وقل: سألت مالكاً فقال: لا أدري!!

Al-Imām Mālik was the Imām of Dār al-Hijrah. A man came and asked him about forty issues. He answered four of them and said in respect to the rest: "I do not know." So, the man said: "I have come to you from such and such place on my camel, and you say, 'I do not know'?" Al-Imām Mālik told him: "Ride your camel, and go back to the land you came from and say, 'I asked Mālik and he said, "I do not know"'!"

والنبي صلىٰ الله عليه وسلم إذا سئل عن شيء لم ينزل عليه فيه وحي فإنه ينتظر حتىٰ ينزل عليه وحي، كذلك الصحابة إذا سألهم رسول الله صلىٰ الله عليه وسلم عن شيء لا يعلمونه قالوا: «الله ورسوله أعلم»، لا يتخرصون. فهذا الباب عظيم وخطير، والله عز وجل جعل القول عليه بغير علم مرتبة فوق الشرك به سبحانه وتعالىٰ: ﴿قُلْ إِنَّمَا حَرَّمَ رَبِّيَ ٱلْفَوَٰحِشَ مَا ظَهَرَ مِنْهَا وَمَا بَطَنَ وَٱلْإِثْمَ وَٱلْبَغْيَ بِغَيْرِ ٱلْحَقِّ وَأَن تُشْرِكُوا۟ بِٱللَّهِ مَا لَمْ يُنَزِّلْ بِهِۦ سُلْطَٰنًا وَأَن تَقُولُوا۟ عَلَى ٱللَّهِ مَا لَا تَعْلَمُونَ ﴿٣٣﴾﴾ [الأعراف:٣٣]، وقال سبحانه: ﴿وَلَا تَقْفُ مَا لَيْسَ لَكَ بِهِۦ عِلْمٌ ۚ إِنَّ ٱلسَّمْعَ وَٱلْبَصَرَ وَٱلْفُؤَادَ كُلُّ أُو۟لَٰٓئِكَ كَانَ عَنْهُ مَسْـُٔولًا ﴿٣٦﴾﴾ [الإسراء:٣٦].

Whenever the Prophet ﷺ was asked about something concerning which no revelation came to him, he would wait until he received the divine revelation. Also, whenever the Companions were asked by the Messenger ﷺ about something that they did not know, they would say, "Allah and His Messenger know best," and they did not make fabrications. This is a great and serious matter. Allah has made speaking about Him without knowledge one grade above polytheism. The Most High says: **{Say, 'My Lord has only forbidden immoralities – what is apparent of them and what is concealed – and sin, and oppression without right, and that you associate with Allah that for which He has not sent down authority, and that you say about Allah that which you do not know.'} [Qur'ān 7:33]** Allah ﷻ says: **{And do not pursue that of which you have no knowledge. Indeed, the hearing, the sight and the heart – about all those [one] will be questioned.} [Qur'ān 17:36]**

يا أخي، يسعك أن تقول: لا أدري، ومن قال: لا أدري، فقد أجاب، ولا تتخرص وتخوض في أحكام الشرع بغير بصيرة، وقول: لا أدري، فيما لا تعلم، ليس نقصاً فيك، بل العكس، هو كمال؛ لأنه ورع وتقوىٰ، والناس يحمدونك علىٰ هذا.

My dear brothers, it is enough to say, "I do not know". If you say that, then you have given an answer. And do not guess or involve yourself in the laws of the Religion without discernment. To say "I do not know" about something you do not know is not a fault but rather an ideal, because it is a sign of piety and care, and others will praise you for it.

كثير من المنتسبين إلىٰ العلم - وبخاصة في هذه الأزمنة المتأخرة التي قل فيها الفقهاء وكثر القراء - يفتون ويحكمون ويتخبطون في الأحكام الشرعية في وسائل الإعلام وغيرها بغير بصيرة، ومن فضل الله أنهم انكشفوا أمام الناس بجهلهم، وفضحهم الله عز وجل، ولو أنهم ستروا أنفسهم وتوقفوا عما ليس لهم به علم وتورّعوا؛ لكان ذلك أكمل وأجل لهم عند الله وعند الناس، فلنعتبر بهذا.

Many people who associate themselves with knowledge – especially in these later times when scholars are few and reciters are many – issue legal opinions and rulings and they recklessly enter into discourse about the laws of the Religion without knowledge, on the media and elsewhere. By the grace of Allah ﷻ, their ignorance has been exposed to the masses, and Allah the

Almighty has shamed them. Were they to shield themselves and abstain from matters that they do not have knowledge about and show some piety, it would have been more ideal, and Allah ﷻ would have honoured them in the eyes of people. Let us take warning from that.

المتن

(١٦٦) وَنَرَىٰ الْمَسْحَ عَلَىٰ الْخُفَّيْنِ فِي السَّفَرِ والْحَضَرِ، كَما جاءَ فِي الْأَثَرِ.

(166) We believe in wiping the *khuffs* while traveling or as a resident, as related in the reports.

الشرح

لماذا جاء بهذه المسألة - وهي مسألة فقهية - في العقيدة؟ لأن هذه المسألة أنكرها المبتدعة، وأثبتها أهل السنة، والمسح على الخفين تواترت به الأحاديث عن النبي صلىٰ الله عليه وسلم.

This is an issue of jurisprudence, so why is it presented in a creedal treatise? Because innovators have rejected this issue and Ahl al-Sunnah have affirmed it. Wiping over the *khuffs* has been related concurrently (*mutawātir*) in reports from the Prophet ﷺ.

وممن اشتهر عنهم إنكار المسح علىٰ الخفين: الرافضة، ويخالفون أهل السنة والجماعة في ذلك، ويخالفون الأحاديث الثابتة، فالمسح ثابت، يوم وليلة للمقيم، وثلاثة أيام بلياليهن للمسافر، وهذه رخصة وتسهيل من الله علىٰ عباده.

Some of those who are known for their rejection of wiping the *khuffs* are the Rāfiḍites. They are at variance with Ahl al-Sunnah wa 'l-Jamā'ah regarding that and at variance with the *ḥadīth* reports that have been established as authentic. Wiping the *khuffs* is something established. It is valid for one day and one night for someone who is settled as a resident, and three days and three nights for someone who is travelling. This is a concession and facilitation from Allah ﷻ to His servants.

فالرافضة ينكرون المسح علىٰ الخفين، ويقولون بالمسح علىٰ الرجلين، وهذا من أكبر المغالطة، فلا أحد يقول بالمسح علىٰ الرجلين، وهكذا من ترك الحق ابتلاه الله بالباطل.

The Rāfiḍites reject the wiping of the *khuffs* and say instead that the wiping [in the Qur'ān] is of the feet, which is one of the greatest fallacies, as none [of the scholars] were of that opinion. Thus Allah ﷻ does afflict those who abandon the truth with falsities.

استدل الرافضة علىٰ المسح علىٰ الرجلين: بقوله تعالىٰ: ﴿وَٱمۡسَحُواْ بِرُءُوسِكُمۡ وَأَرۡجُلِكُمۡ﴾ [المائدة:٦] بقراءة الجر، حيث عطف الأرجل علىٰ الرؤوس في هذه القراءة، والرؤوس ممسوحة، وعندهم الكعبان معقد الشراك، مجمع القدم مع العقب ويسمىٰ عرش الرِّجْل.

The Rāfiḍites cite as evidence for wiping the feet the saying of the Most High: **{And wipe over your heads and your feet} [Qur'ān 5:6]** according to the variant reading of the Qur'ān with the genitive case (*jarr*). '*Feet*' is syntactically conjoined with '*heads*' in this reading and the heads are wiped over [thus it means, *wipe over your heads and your feet*]. Also, in their view, the word *al-ka'bān* (ankles) means the place where the straps or laces are tied, the place where the foot and the heel meet, which is also called the '*arsh* (throne) of the foot.

وعند أهل السنة والجماعة أن المراد بالكعبين: العظمان الناتئان في أسفل الساق، مجمع الساق مع الرجل، فالمسح للرجلين باطل؛ لأن المشهور من قراءة الآية: الفتح، عطف علىٰ المغسولات، علىٰ ﴿وُجُوهَكُمۡ وَأَيۡدِيَكُمۡ﴾ [المائدة:٦] وأدخل الممسوح بين المغسولات من أجل الترتيب، ولو أخر لفهم أن مسح الرأس يكون بعد غسل الرجلين.

In the view of Ahl al-Sunnah wa 'l-Jamā'ah, *ka'bayn* means the ankles. So the wiping of the feet is incorrect, as the common reading of the verse is with a *fatḥah*, [in the accusative case,] conjoined with the parts of the body that are washed: ***{wash your faces and your arms.}*** The part of the body to be wiped is inserted between the parts of the body to be washed for the sake of sequence. If it was placed after them, it would imply that the wiping of the head is to be done after the washing of the feet.

أما قراءة (وأرجلكم) بالجر فهي صحيحة، ولكن عنها أربعة أجوبة الجواب الأول أن وجه الجر هنا علىٰ المجاورة، وهذه لغة عند العرب، مثل أن تقول: هذا جحر ضب خربٍ، خربٍ ليست صفة لضب، إنما هي صفة لجحر، وجحر مرفوع.

The reading of *feet* in the genitive case is, however, correct, but nonetheless, there are four responses. The first response is that the genitive case is based on adjacency, and this is according to one dialect of Arabic. One may say, for instance, *hadhā juḥr ḍabbin kharibin* (this is a destroyed lizard's hole). Here, *destroyed* is not an adjective of *lizard* [as the matching case would suggest], but rather of *hole,* and *hole* is in the nominative case (*marfūʿ*), so it would be expected that the matching adjective would also be *marfūʿ* (nominative).

ولكن من أجل المجاورة، ومن أجل سهولة النطق جُرّت للمجاورة.

However, because of adjacency, and for the sake of ease of pronunciation, it is in the genitive case because it is adjacent [to a word in the genitive case].

والثاني: أن المراد بالمسح: الغسل، فالغسل يسمىٰ مسحًا، تقول: تمسحت بالماء، يعني اغتسلت به، فالمراد بمسح الرجلين غسلهما، بدليل قراءة النصب.

Second: That *wipe* (*masḥ*) means *wash* (*ghusl*). *Ghusl* is sometimes termed as *masḥ*. One may say, *tamassaḥtu bi ʾl-māʾ* [lit. *I wiped with water*], that is, *ightasaltu bihi* (*I washed with it*). Thus, *wiping the feet* means *washing them,* as evidenced by the reading with the accusative case.

الجواب الثالث: أن المشهور من القراءتين: قراءة النصب وهنا لا إشكال.

The third response is that the more known of the two readings is the reading where *feet* is in the accusative, and so there is no contradiction.

الجواب الرابع: أن غسل الرجلين هو صفة وضوء رسول الله صلىٰ الله عليه

وسلم التي نقلها عنه أصحابه، لم يرد في حديث واحد - ولو ضعيف - أن رسول الله عليه الصلاة والسلام مسح رجليه، وكذلك ما ثبت ذلك عن أصحابه، بل لما رأىٰ صلىٰ الله عليه وسلم رجلاً في رجله لمعة لم يصبها الماء، أمره بإعادة الوضوء، وقال عليه الصلاة والسلام: «**ويل للأعقاب من النار**»؛ لأن صاحبها يغفل عنها، وقد لا يصيبها الماء وذلك بسبب التساهل والغفلة، والأمر في هذا واضح.

The fourth response is that washing the feet is the manner of ablution of the Messenger of Allah ﷺ which the Companions have transmitted to us. Moreover, it has not been presented in a single *ḥadīth* (not even a weak one) that the Messenger of Allah ﷺ wiped his feet, and it has not been verified that his companions did so either. In fact, when the Prophet ﷺ once saw that water had not touched a spot of the foot of one man, he commanded him to repeat his ablution. And the Prophet ﷺ said: "The woe of the Fire betides the heels"[99] because people are negligent in washing the heels and water may not reach them because of leniency and negligence. This matter is clear.

المتن

(١٦٧) والْحَجُّ والْجِهادُ ماضِيانِ مَعَ أُولِي الْأَمْرِ مِنَ الْمُسْلِمِينَ، بَرِّهِمْ وَفاجِرِهِمْ إِلَىٰ قِيامِ السّاعَةِ، لا يُبْطِلُهُما شَيْءٌ وَلا يَنْقُضُهُما.

(167) Ḥajj and *jihād* shall continue until the coming of the Hour, under the Muslim rulers, whether pious or impious. Nothing shall abrogate or undo them.

الشرح

تقدمت مسألة الصلاة خلف الأئمة، سواء كانوا أبراراً أو فجّاراً، فنصلي خلفهم امتثالاً لأمر النبي صلىٰ الله عليه وسلم؛ لأنه أمرنا بطاعتهم، ونهانا عن مخالفتهم،

99 Al-Bukhārī, no. 60, 96 and 163; Muslim, no. 241.

والصحابة – رضوان الله عليهم – امتثلوا أمره، فكانوا يصلون خلف الأمراء، وإن كانوا يفعلون بعض الكبائر، مثل الحجاج وغيره.

The issue of being led by every *imām*, be they righteous or unrighteous, in prayer, was mentioned previously. We pray behind them in compliance with the command of the Prophet ﷺ as he commanded us to obey them and forbade us from disobeying them. The Companions complied with this command: They used to pray behind rulers, such as al-Ḥajjāj and others, even if they were guilty of major sins.

وهذا الفعل من أجل جمع الكلمة، هذا مذهب أهل السنة والجماعة، خلاف الخوارج والمعتزلة.

This action is for the sake of unity and is the doctrine of Ahl al-Sunnah wa 'l-Jamā'ah, as opposed to the Khārijites and Mu'tazilites.

وقوله: (**نرىٰ الحج والجهاد**): يجب علىٰ المسلمين كل سنة أن يقيموا الحج، أما الأفراد: فإذا حج أحدهم مرة واحدة فإنه تكفيه، ومن زاد فتطوع.

"[We believe] that Ḥajj and *jihād*": It is the duty of the Muslims to hold the Ḥajj (pilgrimage) every year. On the other hand, it is enough for individuals to perform the Ḥajj rites only once, and anything more is voluntary.

والذي يقيم الحج؟ هو إمام المسلمين هو الذي يقود الحجيج، ويعلن يوم عرفة، ويقف بهم بعرفة، ويفيض إلىٰ مزدلفة، وهكذا يتبعونه في المشاعر، وسواء الإمام أو من ينوب عنه، ولا يكون الأمر فوضىٰ.

The one who hosts the Ḥajj rituals is the *imām* of the Muslims. He leads the pilgrims, announces the Day of 'Arafah, stays with them at 'Arafah [for *wuqūf*] and goes forth with them to Muzdalifah. Muslims thus follow him in the Ḥajj rites, regardless whether it is with the *imām* or someone representing him, as the matter should not be done chaotically.

وأهل السنة والجماعة يحجون مع إمامهم، قال عليه الصلاة والسلام: «**الصوم يوم يصوم الناس، والأضحىٰ يوم يضحي الناس**».

Ahl al-Sunnah wa 'l-Jamā'ah perform Ḥajj with their *imām*. The Prophet ﷺ said: "The fast is the day when the Muslims fast, and the sacrifice is the day when the Muslims sacrifice."[100]

هذه أمة الإسلام، يصومون جمعيًا إذا اتفقت المطالع، ويحجون جميعًا، ويصلون العيد جميعًا، فالجماعة من سمة أهل السنة، والافتراق من سمة أهل البدع والضلال. والجهاد: المراد به: قتال الكفار والبغاة من المسلمين وقتال الخوارج، نقاتل مع إمام المسلمين؛ فنقاتل البغاة لبغيهم وليس لكفرهم ﴿وَإِن طَآئِفَتَانِ مِنَ ٱلْمُؤْمِنِينَ ٱقْتَتَلُوا۟ فَأَصْلِحُوا۟ بَيْنَهُمَا ۖ فَإِنۢ بَغَتْ إِحْدَىٰهُمَا عَلَى ٱلْأُخْرَىٰ فَقَـٰتِلُوا۟ ٱلَّتِى تَبْغِى حَتَّىٰ تَفِىٓءَ إِلَىٰٓ أَمْرِ ٱللَّهِ ۚ﴾ [الحجرات:٩].

The community of Islām fast together if they share a common area of sighting (*maṭāli'*). They perform the rites of Ḥajj and pray *ṣalāt al-'īd* (Eid prayer) together. Unity is a feature of Ahl al-Sunnah while division is a feature of the people of innovation and misguidance. What is meant by *jihād* is to fight the disbelievers and transgressors/rebels among the Muslims, and also to fight the Khārijites. We fight alongside the *imām* of the Muslims. We fight transgressors because of their transgression and not because of their disbelief. **{And if two factions among the believers should fight, then make settlement between the two. But if one of them oppresses the other, then fight against the one that oppresses until it returns to the ordinance of Allah.} [Qur'ān 49:9]**

وقتال الكفار من أجل نشر التوحيد، وقمع الشرك.

Fighting the disbelievers is done in order to spread monotheism and suppress polytheism.

وقتال الكفار على نوعين:

There are two kinds of fighting against the disbelievers:

النوع الأول: قتال دفاع، وهذه الحالة تكون في حالة ضعف المسلمين، فإنه إذا

100 Al-Tirmidhī, no. 696; Abū Dāwūd, according to a similar wording (*lafẓ*), no. 232; Ibn Mājah, no. 1660. Al-Tirmidhī said: "This *ḥadīth* is *ḥasan gharīb*."

داهم العدو بلادهم وجب عليهم قتالهم، فيجب على جميع من يحمل السلاح قتالهم؛ من أجل دفع العدو عن أرضهم.

One. To fight in defence *(qitāl al-difāʿ)*, which is in a state of the weakness of the Muslims. If an enemy attacks their land, then it is incumbent upon them to fight them. It is the duty of anyone who is able to 'bear arms' to fight them, in order to defend their land against the enemy.

النوع الثاني: قتال طلب، وذلك إن كان المسلمون أقوياء، فإنهم يغزون العدو في بلادهم، ويدعونهم إلى الله، فإن أجابوا وإلا قاتلوهم من أجل إعلاء كلمة الله ﴿ وَقَٰتِلُوهُمْ حَتَّىٰ لَا تَكُونَ فِتْنَةٌ وَيَكُونَ ٱلدِّينُ كُلُّهُۥ لِلَّهِ﴾ [الأنفال:٣٩].

Two. Fighting in pursuit of the enemy (*qitāl al-ṭalab*). That is to say that if the Muslims have strength, they invade the enemies within their lands and call on them to worship Allah alone. They either accept or the Muslims fight them in order to raise the word of Allah ﷻ. **{And fight them until there is no *fitnah* and [until] the religion, all of it, is for Allah.} [Qurʾān 8:39]**

ذكر ابن القيم رحمه الله أن الجهاد مر بمراحل:

Ibn al-Qayyim ﷺ said that *jihād* went through stages:

المرحلة الأولى: كان منهياً عنه فيها، وهذا يوم كان النبي صلى الله عليه وسلم والمسلمون بمكة، فكانوا مأمورين بكف الأيدي وإقام الصلاة وإيتاء الزكاة ﴿ أَلَمْ تَرَ إِلَى ٱلَّذِينَ قِيلَ لَهُمْ كُفُّوٓاْ أَيْدِيَكُمْ وَأَقِيمُواْ ٱلصَّلَوٰةَ وَءَاتُواْ ٱلزَّكَوٰةَ﴾ [النساء:٧٧]

The first stage: Being prohibited, which was when the Prophet ﷺ and the Muslims were in Makkah. They were commanded to refrain from fighting, pray the *ṣalāh* and give alms (*zakāh*). **{Have you not seen those who were told, 'Restrain your hands [from fighting] and establish prayer and give *zakāh*?'} [Qurʾān 4:77]**

فالمنع لأن المسلمين لا يستطيعون وليس لهم دولة ولا قوة، وكان الله يأمر نبيه بالصبر والصفح والانتظار، إلى أن يأتي الفرج، ومن قاتل في هذه المرحلة فإنه

يكون قد عصىٰ الله ورسوله؛ لأنه يترتب علىٰ القتال في هذه المرحلة الإضرار بالمسلمين وبالدعوة، وتسلط الكفار علىٰ المسلمين.

The prohibition was on account of the Muslims neither being able nor having an established state or strength. Allah commanded His Prophet to have patience, forgiveness, and to wait until relief was to come. Anyone who fought during this stage would have been disobedient to Allah ﷻ and the Messenger of Allah, because fighting in this stage would have resulted in harm to the Muslims, and to the propagation of Islām, and in the disbelievers gaining full authority over the Muslims.

المرحلة الثانية: لما هاجر النبي صلىٰ الله عليه وسلم إلىٰ المدينة وقامت دولة الإسلام، أُذن له بالقتال ولم يؤمر ﴿أُذِنَ لِلَّذِينَ يُقَٰتَلُونَ بِأَنَّهُمْ ظُلِمُواْ وَإِنَّ ٱللَّهَ عَلَىٰ نَصْرِهِمْ لَقَدِيرٌ ۝٣٩ ٱلَّذِينَ أُخْرِجُواْ مِن دِيَٰرِهِم بِغَيْرِ حَقٍّ إِلَّآ أَن يَقُولُواْ رَبُّنَا ٱللَّهُ وَلَوْلَا دَفْعُ ٱللَّهِ ٱلنَّاسَ بَعْضَهُم بِبَعْضٍ لَّهُدِّمَتْ صَوَٰمِعُ وَبِيَعٌ وَصَلَوَٰتٌ وَمَسَٰجِدُ يُذْكَرُ فِيهَا ٱسْمُ ٱللَّهِ كَثِيرًا﴾ [الحج:٣٩-٤٠] فأذن لهم بدون أمر، فكانت هذه تهيئة لهم، فالأمور الشاقة يشرعها الله شيئًا فشيئًا؛ من أجل التسهيل علىٰ النفوس.

The second stage: When the Prophet ﷺ migrated to Madīnah and the Islamic state was established. It was then that it was made permissible to fight, but it was not a command. **{Permission [to fight] has been given to those who are being fought, because they were wronged. And indeed, Allah is competent to give them victory. [They are] those who have been evicted from their homes without right – only because they say, 'Our Lord is Allah.' And were it not that Allah checks the people, some by means of others, there would have been demolished monasteries, churches, synagogues, and mosques in which the name of Allah is much mentioned.} [Qur'ān 22:39-40]** It was permitted but not commanded. This was a preliminary step, as Allah ﷻ prescribes difficult things in a gradual manner in order to make matters easy on the souls.

المرحلة الثالثة: أُمر بقتال من قاتل، والكف عمن لم يقاتل ﴿وَقَٰتِلُواْ فِي سَبِيلِ ٱللَّهِ ٱلَّذِينَ يُقَٰتِلُونَكُمْ وَلَا تَعْتَدُوٓاْ إِنَّ ٱللَّهَ لَا يُحِبُّ ٱلْمُعْتَدِينَ ۝١٩٠﴾ [البقرة:١٩٠] وهذا يسمىٰ قتال الدفع.

The third stage: The command to fight those who fight and to refrain from fighting those who do not fight. **{Fight in the way of Allah those who fight you but do not transgress. Indeed. Allah does not like transgressors.} [Qur'ān 2:190]** This is termed as defensive fighting (*qitāl al-dafʿ*).

المرحلة الرابعة: لما قوي المسلمون، وكانت لهم شوكة، وللإسلام دولة، أُمروا بالقتال مطلقاً ﴿فَإِذَا ٱنسَلَخَ ٱلۡأَشۡهُرُ ٱلۡحُرُمُ فَٱقۡتُلُواْ ٱلۡمُشۡرِكِينَ حَيۡثُ وَجَدتُّمُوهُمۡ وَخُذُوهُمۡ وَٱحۡصُرُوهُمۡ وَٱقۡعُدُواْ لَهُمۡ كُلَّ مَرۡصَدٖۚ﴾ [التوبة:٥]، ﴿وَقَٰتِلُوهُمۡ حَتَّىٰ لَا تَكُونَ فِتۡنَةٞ وَيَكُونَ ٱلدِّينُ كُلُّهُۥ لِلَّهِۚ﴾ [الأنفال:٣٩].

The fourth stage: When the Muslims became strong, had prowess [in warfare] and Islām had a state, they were commanded to fight in an absolute sense. **{And when the sacred months have passed, then kill the polytheists wherever you find them and capture them and besiege them and sit in wait for them at every place of ambush.} [Qur'ān 9:5] {And fight them until there is no *fitnah* and [until] the religion, all of it, is for Allah.} [Qur'ān 8:39]**

فأمر الله بالقتال مطلقاً، فلما صاروا متهيئين ولهم قوة وعندهم استعداد، فشرع رسول الله صلىٰ الله عليه وسلم في الغزو، غزوة بدر وأحد والخندق وهكذا، حتىٰ جاء الفتح، ودخل الناس في دين الله أفواجاً، ثم توفي رسول الله صلىٰ الله عليه وسلم، ثم حصلت الردة فقاتلهم أبو بكر، فلما فرغ منهم شرع في الجهاد للكفار، فجيّش الجيوش لقتال فارس والروم، وتوفي، ثم جاء عمر رضي الله عنه فواصل الفتوح حتىٰ أسقط دولة كسرىٰ وقيصر، ونشر الدين وصارت سيطرتهم علىٰ جميع الأرض مشارقها ومغاربها، هذا هو القتال في الإسلام.

Thus, Allah ﷻ commanded them to fight in an absolute sense. Thus, when they became prepared, had strength and were equipped, the Messenger of Allah ﷺ commanded them to engage in battle: The battles of Badr, Uḥud, Khandaq (the Trench), and so on, all until the Conquest of Makkah and when people accepted Allah's ﷻ religion in crowds. Then, the Messenger of Allah ﷺ passed away and the great apostasy (*riddah*) occurred, so Abū Bakr ؓ fought the apostates. When he was finished with them, he began to engage in *jihād* against the disbelievers, built an army to fight the Persians and Romans and then died. Then, 'Umar ﷺ came and continued the conquests until the states of Khosrau and Caesar crumbled, thus spreading the religion of Islām and gaining sway in the entire world, the east and the west. This is fighting in Islām.

ومن ينظم القتال ويقوده؟ هو الإمام، فنحن نتبع الإمام، فإن أُمرنا بالغزو نغزو، ولا نغزو بغير إذن الإمام؛ فهذا لا يجوز؛ لأنه من صلاحيات الإمام ﴿يَٰٓأَيُّهَا ٱلَّذِينَ ءَامَنُواْ مَا لَكُمْ إِذَا قِيلَ لَكُمُ ٱنفِرُواْ فِى سَبِيلِ ٱللَّهِ ٱثَّاقَلْتُمْ إِلَى ٱلْأَرْضِ﴾ [التوبة:٣٨].

So who regulates and acts as the leader in the fighting? It is the *imām* and we are to follow him. If we are commanded to engage in battle, then we engage in battle and do not carry out an invasion without the authorisation of the *imām*. It is impermissible to do so because it is one of the executive powers of the *imām*. **{O you who have believed, what is [the matter] with you that, when you are told to go forth in the cause of Allah, you adhere heavily to the earth?} [Qur'ān 9:38]**

فالقتال من صلاحيات الإمام، فإذا استنفر الإمام الناس للقتال وجب على كل من أطاق حمل السلاح، ولا يشترط في الإمام الذي يقيم الحج والجهاد أن يكون غير عاصٍ، فقد يكون عنده بعض المعاصي والمخالفات، لكن ما دام أنه لم يخرج من الإسلام فيجب الجهاد والحج معه، وصلاحه وقوته للمسلمين وفساده على نفسه، أما الجهاد والحج ففي صالح المسلمين، كذلك الصلاة، فإن أصاب كنا معه، وإن أخطأ فنتجنب إساءته، لكن لا نخرج ونشق عصا الطاعة، هذا مذهب أهل السنة والجماعة، وعليه تقوم مصالح المسلمين.

Fighting is one of the executive powers of the *imām*, so when the *imām* summons the people to battle, it is incumbent upon every person able to bear arms. It is not a condition that the *imām*, who upholds the Ḥajj and *jihād*, is not a sinner: he may have committed some sins and transgressions, but as long as he does not forsake the religion of Islām, it is incumbent to participate in Ḥajj and *jihād* with him. His righteousness and strength are to the advantage of the Muslims yet his unrighteousness is only against himself. *Jihād* and Ḥajj, in light of this, are to the advantage of the Muslims, and so is the prayer. Therefore, if he is correct, then we are with him, and if he is mistaken, then we do not take part in his misdeed, but we also do not revolt against him or renounce our obedience. This is the way of Ahl al-Sunnah wa ʾl-Jamāʿah and what is to the best interest of the Muslims is founded upon this.

أما أهل البدع والضلال فيرون الخروج على ولاة الأمور، وهذا مذهب الخوارج، ونحن نبرأ إلى الله من هذا المذهب.

The people of innovation and misguidance, on the other hand, believe in revolting against the authorities. This is the doctrine of the Khārijites and we dissociate ourselves in front of Allah ﷻ from that doctrine.

المتن

(١٦٨) وَنُؤْمِنُ بِالْكِرامِ الْكاتِبِينَ، فَإِنَّ اللهَ قَدْ جَعَلَهُمْ عَلَيْنا حافِظِينَ.

(168) We believe in the angels that write down our deeds. Allah has made them protectors over us.

الشرح

الإيمان بالملائكة عليهم السلام هو أحد أركان الإيمان. وهذه الأصول موجودة في القرآن ﴿وَلَٰكِنَّ ٱلْبِرَّ مَنْ ءَامَنَ بِٱللَّهِ وَٱلْيَوْمِ ٱلْءَاخِرِ وَٱلْمَلَٰٓئِكَةِ وَٱلْكِتَٰبِ وَٱلنَّبِيِّۦنَ ...﴾ [البقرة:١٧٧]، ﴿ءَامَنَ ٱلرَّسُولُ بِمَآ أُنزِلَ إِلَيْهِ مِن رَّبِّهِۦ وَٱلْمُؤْمِنُونَ ۚ كُلٌّ ءَامَنَ بِٱللَّهِ وَمَلَٰٓئِكَتِهِۦ وَكُتُبِهِۦ وَرُسُلِهِۦ﴾ [البقرة:٢٨٥] فنؤمن بالملائكة وأنهم خلق من خلق الله، وأنهم من عالم الغيب، لا نراهم، خلقهم الله من نور، ووكل إليهم أموراً، يقومون بتنفيذها والقيام بها، كل له عمل موكل به، ومع ذلك فهم يعبدون الله عز وجل لا يفترون ﴿يُسَبِّحُونَ ٱلَّيْلَ وَٱلنَّهَارَ لَا يَفْتُرُونَ ﴿٢٠﴾﴾ [الأنبياء:٢٠]، ﴿عِبَادٌ مُّكْرَمُونَ ﴿٢٦﴾ لَا يَسْبِقُونَهُۥ بِٱلْقَوْلِ وَهُم بِأَمْرِهِۦ يَعْمَلُونَ ﴿٢٧﴾﴾ [الأنبياء:٢٦-٢٧] وهم أقسام، ومن أقسامهم:

Belief in the angels is one of the pillars of faith. These fundamental principles are presented in the Qur'ān. **{But [true] righteousness is [in] one who believes in Allah, the Last Day, the angels, the Book, and the prophets.} [Qur'ān 2:177]** So, we believe in the angels, that they are one kind of Allah's ﷻ creatures and that they are part of the world of the unseen (*'ālam al-ghayb*). We do not see them; Allah ﷻ created them from light.[101] And He entrusted them to carry out different tasks, they persevere in accomplishing and fulfilling them. Each is assigned with a task, and at the same time they worship their Lord without slackening. **{They exalt [Him] night and day [and] do not slacken.} [Qur'ān 21:20] {They are [but] honoured servants. They cannot precede Him in word, and they act by His command.} [Qur'ān 21:26-27]** They are of different types. Amongst those types are:

الحفظة: وهم الذين وكل الله إليهم حفظ بني آدم، وحفظ أعمالهم، فكل عبد من بني آدم معه أربعة يحفظونه بالليل والنهار، اثنان حفظة، واحد عن اليمين وواحد عن اليسار، الذي عن اليمين يكتب الحسنات، والذي عن اليسار يكتب السيئات ﴿مَّا يَلْفِظُ مِن قَوْلٍ إِلَّا لَدَيْهِ رَقِيبٌ عَتِيدٌ ۝١٨﴾ [ق:١٨].

The *ḥafaẓah,* or *guardian angels.* They are those whom Allah ﷻ has entrusted to guard the children of Ādam ﷺ and record their deeds. Every person among the descendants of Ādam ﷺ has four of them who watch over him at night and day: two are recorders, one on the right and one on the left. The one on the right writes down all good deeds and the one on the left writes down all bad deeds. **{Man does not utter any word except that with him is an observer prepared [to record].} [Qur'ān 50:18]**

وملكان آخران؛ واحد أمامه وواحد خلفه، يحفظونه من الاعتداء عليه، ما دام الله قد كتب له البقاء ﴿لَهُۥ مُعَقِّبَٰتٌ مِّنۢ بَيْنِ يَدَيْهِ وَمِنْ خَلْفِهِۦ يَحْفَظُونَهُۥ مِنْ أَمْرِ ٱللَّهِ﴾ [الرعد:١١] فالملائكة يدفعون عنه الأخطار، فإذا تم الأجل تخلوا عنه، فأصابه ما كتب الله له، فنحن نؤمن بهذا، وإذا آمنا بذلك فإننا نستحيي من الملائكة

101 It is related that 'Ā'ishah said: The Messenger of Allah ﷺ said: 'The angels were created from light, the jinns were created from a smokeless flame of fire, and Ādam was created from what has been described to you.' Muslim, no. 2996.

الكرام، فلا نعمل أعمالاً سيئة، ولا نتكلم بألفاظ باطلة؛ لأنها تسجل علينا.

There are two other angels, one at the front and one at the back and they guard the person from harm for as long as Allah ﷻ has written for him to stay alive. **{For each one are successive [angels] before and behind him who protect him by the decree of Allah.} [Qur'ān 13:11]** The angels defend him against danger, and when his term is up, they abandon him and what Allah ﷻ has written for him takes place. We believe in this. Thus, if we believe in this, then we would be ashamed to do bad deeds or enter into false speech in the presence of the honoured angels because they record them against us.

المتن

(١٦٩) وَنُؤْمِنُ بِمَلَكِ الْمَوْتِ، الْمُوَكَّلِ بِقَبْضِ أَرْواحِ الْعالَمِينَ.

(169) We believe in the Angel of Death, who is appointed to take the souls of people;

الشرح

قال سبحانه: ﴿وَهُوَ ٱلْقَاهِرُ فَوْقَ عِبَادِهِۦ وَيُرْسِلُ عَلَيْكُمْ حَفَظَةً حَتَّىٰٓ إِذَا جَآءَ أَحَدَكُمُ ٱلْمَوْتُ تَوَفَّتْهُ رُسُلُنَا﴾ [الأنعام:٦١] يعني من الملائكة، فالرسل قد يكونون من الملائكة، وقد يكونون من البشر ﴿ٱللَّهُ يَصْطَفِى مِنَ ٱلْمَلَٰٓئِكَةِ رُسُلًا وَمِنَ ٱلنَّاسِ﴾ [الحج:٧٥]، ﴿تَوَفَّتْهُ رُسُلُنَا وَهُمْ لَا يُفَرِّطُونَ ﴿٦١﴾﴾ [الأنعام:٦١]، ﴿وَلَوْ تَرَىٰٓ إِذْ يَتَوَفَّى ٱلَّذِينَ كَفَرُوا۟ ٱلْمَلَٰٓئِكَةُ يَضْرِبُونَ وُجُوهَهُمْ وَأَدْبَٰرَهُمْ﴾ [الأنفال:٥٠]، وقال في آية أخرى: ﴿يَتَوَفَّىٰكُم مَّلَكُ ٱلْمَوْتِ﴾ [السجدة:١١].

Allah ﷻ says: **{And He is the subjugator over His servants, and He sends over you guardian-angels until, when death comes to one of you, Our messengers.} [Qur'ān 6:61]** That is, messengers from amongst the angels, as the messengers may be from the angels or from mankind. **{Allah chooses from the angels messengers and from the people.} [Qur'ān 22:75] {Our messengers take him, and they do not fail [in their du-**

ties].} [Qur'ān 6:61] {And if you could but see when the angels take the souls of those who disbelieved... They are striking their faces and their backs.} [Qur'ān 8:50] Allah ﷻ says in another verse: {The angel of death will take you.} [Qur'ān 32:11]

ففي بعض الآيات أسند الموت إلىٰ الملائكة، وفي بعض الآيات أسند الموت إلىٰ ملك واحد، فدل هذا علىٰ أن الملائكة لهم رئيس هو ملك الموت.

In some verses, death is attributed to more than one angel whilst in other verses it is attributed to one angel. This indicates that the angels have a head angel, who is the Angel of Death.

ومسألة الموت لا أحد ينازع فيها، أما ملك الموت وأعوانه فينكرهم بعض بني آدم، ولكن الإيمان بالملائكة أصل من أصول الإسلام والإيمان الثابتة بالكتاب والسنة، فمن أنكر وجود الملائكة عمومًا أو ملكًا من الملائكة فهو كافر؛ لأنه جحد ركنًا من أركان الإيمان.

There is no one who contests the issue of death, but the Angel of Death and his helpers are denied by some of the children of Ādam. Nonetheless, faith in the angels is a fundamental principle of Islām and of faith as established in the Qur'ān and Sunnah; so if one were to deny the existence of angels in general or of any angel in particular, they would be a disbeliever for denying one of the pillars of faith.

۞۞۞

المتن

(١٧٠) وَبِعَذَابِ الْقَبْرِ لِمَنْ كَانَ لَهُ أَهْلًا، وَسُؤَالِ مُنْكَرٍ وَنَكِيرٍ فِي قَبْرِهِ عَنْ رَبِّهِ وَدِينِهِ وَنَبِيِّهِ، عَلَىٰ مَا جَاءَتْ بِهِ الأَخْبَارُ عَنْ رَسُولِ اللهِ صَلَّىٰ اللهُ عَلَيْهِ وَآلِهِ وَسَلَّمَ، وَعَنِ الصَّحَابَةِ رِضْوَانُ اللهِ عَلَيْهِمْ.

(170) And in the punishment of the grave for those who deserve it; and in the questions posed by Munkar and Nakīr in the grave about their Lord, their religion and their prophet, according to the ac-

counts related from the Messenger of Allah ﷺ and the Companions ﷺ.

الشرح

ذكر شيخ الإسلام في العقيدة الواسطية أن الإيمان باليوم الآخر يدخل فيه كل ما بعد الموت من عذاب القبر ونعيمه ومن البعث ومن العرض والحساب والميزان وتطاير الصحف والجنة والنار، ومن أنكر شيئاً منها فإنه لا يكون مؤمناً باليوم الآخر.

Shaykh al-Islam mentioned in *al-ʿAqīdat al-Wāsiṭīyah* that faith in the Last Day includes everything that happens after death. Examples of these are: The punishment and pleasure of the grave, the resurrection, the presentation (*al-ʿarḍ*), the balance, the dispersing (*taṭāyur*) of the records, Paradise and the Fire. Anyone who denies any of that is not a believer in the Last Day.

واليوم الآخر وما فيه من أمور الغيب التي لا ندخل فيها بعقولنا وأفكارنا، إنما نعتمد علىٰ ما جاء في الكتاب والسنة، ولا نتدخل في هذه الأمور، ولا نقول فيها إلا بالدليل.

The Last Day and the matters of the unseen that constitute it are not based on our minds and thoughts, rather we rely instead on what is presented in the Qurʾān and Sunnah. We do not interfere in such matters and we do not say anything about them without evidence.

والقبر برزخ بين الدنيا والآخرة والبرزخ معناه الفاصل بين شيئين ﴿وَمِن وَرَآئِهِم بَرْزَخٌ إِلَىٰ يَوْمِ يُبْعَثُونَ ﴿١٠٠﴾﴾ [المؤمنون: ١٠٠].

The grave is a *barzakh* (partition) between the world and the hereafter. *Barzakh* is *anything that separates two things.* **{And behind them is a barrier (*barzakh*) until the Day they are resurrected.} [Qurʾān 23:100]**

القبر محطة انتظار، وينتقل الناس بعده إلىٰ البعث والحساب، وذكر ابن القيم رحمه الله أن الدور ثلاث:

The grave is a waiting stop which people move from to the resurrection and judgment. Ibn al-Qayyim ﷺ said that there are three abodes:

الأولىٰ: دار الدنيا: وهي محل العمل والكسب من خير أو شرف.

One. The abode of the world, which is a place of work and acquisition of good and honour.

الثانية: دار البرزخ، وهي دار مؤقتة، ولهذا يخطئ من يقول مثواه الأخير.

Two. The abode of the *barzakh*, which is a temporary abode, and so it is a mistake to say '*final resting place*[102]'.

الثالثة: دار القرار، وهي الجنة أو النار: ﴿وَإِنَّ ٱلْآخِرَةَ هِيَ دَارُ ٱلْقَرَارِ ۝٣٩﴾ [غافر:٣٩].

Three. The abode of settlement (*qarār*), which is Paradise or the Fire. **{And indeed, the Hereafter – that is the home of [permanent] settlement.} [Qur'ān 40:39]**

فإذا وضع الميت في قبره ودفن وانصرف الناس عنه، وإنه ليسمع قرع نعالهم، كما في الحديث، فإنه تُعاد روحه في جسده، وهذه حياة برزخية لا يعلمها إلا الله، والله علىٰ كل شيء قدير، وبعد أن تُعاد روحه في جسده ويُحيىٰ حياة أخرىٰ فيأتيه ملكان فيسألانه ثلاثة أسئلة: من ربك؟ وما دينك؟ وما نبيك؟

When the dead are placed in the graves and buried and all the people leave them, they hear the sounds of their footsteps, as related in a *ḥadīth.* This is because their souls are brought back to their bodies and this is the life of the *barzakh.* None has full knowledge of it but Allah ﷻ and He is able to do all things. After the soul is brought back to the body and another life is given, two angels come and ask three questions: "Who is your Lord? What is your religion? Who is your prophet?"[103]

فإن أجاب بجواب صحيح فاز وربح، وصارت حفرته روضة من رياض الجنة،

102 Some Arabs use this phrase to refer to the grave.

103 Aḥmad, 4/287, 295; Abū Dāwūd, no. 4753; al-Ḥākim, 1/37-40. Al-Ḥākim said that it is *ṣaḥīḥ.*

ثم يوم القيامة يصير من أهل الجنة. وإن أخفق في الجواب، ولم يجب، فإن قبره يصير حفرة من حفر النار، ويُضيّقُ عليه قبره حتىٰ تختلف عليه أضلاعه، والأول يوسع له في قبره مد بصره، ويفتح له باب من الجنة يأتيه من روحها وريحانها، وهذا يضيق عليه في قبره حتىٰ تختلف عليه أضلاعه، ثم يفتح له باب من النار فيأتيه من حرها وسمومها، والعياذ بالله.

Those who answer correctly have succeeded and triumphed. Their grave becomes a garden from the gardens of Jannah and then on the Day of Judgment, they will be from amongst the people of Jannah. If anyone fails to answer, their grave will become a pit from the pits of the Fire. Their grave will close in on them so that their ribs are crushed together. The grave of the former will expand as far as the sight can see, and a door of Jannah will be opened unto them, and its comfort and sweet scent will come to them. The grave of the latter closes in on them so that their ribs are crushed together, and then a door of the Fire is opened unto them and its heat and flames come to them (Allah's refuge is sought).

فالإجابة الصحيحة والتي يُثبت الله قائلها: أن يقول: ربي الله، وديني الإسلام، ونبيّ محمد صلىٰ الله عليه وسلم ﴿يُثَبِّتُ ٱللَّهُ ٱلَّذِينَ ءَامَنُواْ بِٱلْقَوْلِ ٱلثَّابِتِ فِى ٱلْحَيَوٰةِ ٱلدُّنْيَا وَفِى ٱلْءَاخِرَةِ﴾ [إبراهيم:٢٧].

The correct answer, the answer by which Allah ﷻ gives steadiness to the one who says it, is that one says, 'my Lord is Allah, my religion is Islām, and my prophet is Muḥammad ﷺ.' **{Allah keeps firm those who believe, with the firm word, in the worldly life and in the Hereafter.} [Qur'ān 14:27]**

وهذا بسبب الإيمان بالله ورسوله، وليس بسبب التعلم أو الثقافة، فمن ليس عنده إيمان فإنه يتلكأ في الإجابة، وهو المنافق الذي يُظهر الإيمان في الدنيا ويُبطن الكفر، فإنه لا يستطيع الإجابة ويقول: هاه، هاه، لا أدري، سمعت الناس يقولون شيئًا فقلته، فيضرب بمرزبة من حديد يسمعها كل شيء إلا الإنسان، ولو سمعها الإنسان لصعق ﴿وَيُضِلُّ ٱللَّهُ ٱلظَّٰلِمِينَ ۚ وَيَفْعَلُ ٱللَّهُ مَا يَشَآءُ ٢٧﴾ [إبراهيم:٢٧].

Steadiness to answer these questions comes from faith in Allah ﷻ and His

Messenger ﷺ, not because of being learned or cultured. Those who do not have faith dawdle before they answer; they are the hypocrites, who appear to have faith in the world but conceal their disbelief. Such people will not be able to answer, they will stutter and say, '*I don't know, I heard people say something, so I said it*'. They will be struck with a large hammer of iron and everything will hear it except for mankind; if a man were to hear it he would fall unconscious. **{And Allah sends astray the wrongdoers. And Allah does what He wills.} [Qur'ān 14:27]**

المتن

(١٧١) والْقَبْرُ رَوْضَةٌ مِنْ رِياضِ الْجَنَّةِ، أَوْ حُفْرَةٌ مِنْ حُفَرِ النِّيرانِ.

(171) The grave is either one of the gardens of Paradise or one of the pits of Hell.

الشرح

قد يقول قائل: الميت يصير تراباً، فكيف يعذب وهو تراب؟ نقول: الله قادر علىٰ أن يعذبه وهو تراب، وقادر علىٰ أن يحمي عليه التراب.

One may say that the dead become dust, so how can one be punished when one is dust? We say, Allah ﷻ is able to punish them as dust and He is able to heat the dust over him.

وقد يقول قائل: ما كل الناس يدفنون، بعضهم يُلقىٰ في البحر، وبعضهم تأكله السباع، فكيف يأتيه العذاب؟ نقول: نعم يأتيه العذاب، في أي مكان كان، وكذلك يأتيه الملكان، والإيمان بهذا هو من الإيمان بالغيب، ومن الإيمان بخبر الله ورسوله، أما الذي لا يؤمن بذلك ويعتمد علىٰ عقله وفكره، فهذا هو الضلال المبين.

Someone may say: Not everyone is buried. Some are cast into the sea and some are eaten by wild animals, so how can they receive punishment? We say, yes, the punishment is received, wherever the person may be, and the two angels will come. To have faith in this constitutes having faith in the unseen and in what Allah ﷻ and His Messenger ﷺ have told. Not believing in this, and instead depending on reason and thought, is the plainest error.

وعذاب القبر ونعيمه دلت عليه أدلة من الكتاب والسنة، بل قال العلماء: إن الأحاديث متواترة عن رسول الله صلىٰ الله عليه وسلم، ومن كذب بالأمر المتواتر يكون كافراً.

The punishment and pleasure of the grave are supported by evidence from the Qurʾān and Sunnah. In fact, scholars of Islām say that the *ḥadīth* reports that go back to the Messenger of Allah ﷺ are *mutawātir,* or related so consistently that there could be no collusions. Anyone who denies a command that is *mutawātir* is a disbeliever.

فالمعتزلة لا يؤمنون بما يحدث في القبر؛ لأنهم عقلانيون، وهم الذين يبنون الأمور علىٰ عقولهم، ويسمون أدلة الشرع ظنية، فأما أدلة العقل عندهم فهي يقينية، فهكذا يقولون، وهؤلاء هم العقلانيون، وهم المعتزلة ومن سار علىٰ نهجهم من العقلانيين في هذه العصور.

The Muʿtazilites do not believe in the events of the grave because they are rationalists (*ʿaqlānīyūn*) and base all matters on logic. They call the evidence as laid out in the Revelation as presumptive (*ẓannī*) and in their view; logical evidence constitutes absolute truths (*yaqīnī*). This is what they say. They are the rationalists, i.e. the Muʿtazilites and the rationalists who tread the same path in these times.

ومن أدلة عذاب القبر: قول الله عز وجل في قوم فرعون: ﴿ٱلنَّارُ يُعۡرَضُونَ عَلَيۡهَا غُدُوّٗا وَعَشِيّٗاۚ وَيَوۡمَ تَقُومُ ٱلسَّاعَةُ أَدۡخِلُوٓاْ ءَالَ فِرۡعَوۡنَ أَشَدَّ ٱلۡعَذَابِ ۝٤٦﴾ [غافر:٤٦]
فقوله: النار يعرضون عليها غدواً وعشياً، هذا في القبر.

Among the evidence of the punishment of the grave is the saying of Allah ﷻ concerning the people of Pharaoh: **{The Fire, they are exposed to it morning and evening. And the Day the Hour appears [it will be said], 'Make the people of Pharaoh enter the severest punishment.'}**

[Qur'ān 40:46] As He says, ***'the Fire, they are exposed to it morning and evening'***: this is in the grave.

﴿وَإِنَّ لِلَّذِينَ ظَلَمُوا۟ عَذَابًا دُونَ ذَٰلِكَ وَلَٰكِنَّ أَكْثَرَهُمْ لَا يَعْلَمُونَ ﴿٤٧﴾﴾ [الطور:٤٧]

فقوله: ﴿عَذَابًا دُونَ ذَٰلِكَ﴾ قالوا: إنه عذاب القبر.

{And indeed, for those who have wronged is a punishment before that, but most of them do not know.} [Qur'ān 52:47] As He says, ***'a punishment before that'***, it is said that it is the punishment of the grave.

وقيل هو: العذاب في الدنيا: ما يصيبهم من القتل والسبي وضرب الجزية وغير ذلك، والآية تشمل المعنيين، وقوله تعالىٰ: ﴿وَلَنُذِيقَنَّهُم مِّنَ ٱلْعَذَابِ ٱلْأَدْنَىٰ دُونَ ٱلْعَذَابِ ٱلْأَكْبَرِ لَعَلَّهُمْ يَرْجِعُونَ ﴿٢١﴾﴾ [السجدة:٢١] العذاب الأدنىٰ هو عذاب القبر، والأكبر هو عذاب يوم القيامة.

It is also said that it is the punishment of this world, such as death, captivity, imposition of the *jizyah* (tribute) and other things that they suffer. The verse is inclusive of both things. Allah ﷻ also says: **{And we will surely let them taste the lesser/nearer punishment short of the greater punishment that perhaps they will repent.} [Qur'ān 32:21]** The *nearer* or *lesser punishment* is the punishment of the grave, and the *greater* one is that of the Day of Judgment.

أما السنة فتواترت الأحاديث بإثبات عذاب القبر، منها: في الصحيح أنه عليه الصلاة والسلام مر علىٰ قبرين فقال: **«إنهما ليعذبان، ولا يعذبان في كبير، أما أنه كبير - أو: بلىٰ إنه لكبير - أما أحدهما فكان يمشي بالنميمة، وأما الآخر فإنه لا يستبرئ من بوله»**.

As for the Sunnah, the *ḥadīth*s that confirm the punishment of the grave have been related concurrently. In the *Ṣaḥīḥ*, it is related that the Prophet ﷺ passed by two graves and said, "They are being punished, but they are not being punished for something great, indeed it is something great [or: but indeed it is something great][104]. One of them used to go around

104 That is, it is a sin that people underestimate however in the eyes of Allah ﷻ it is great.

tale-bearing and the other used to not protect himself from his urine."[105]

وكذلك الحديث الصحيح الذي أمر فيه النبي صلىٰ الله عليه وسلم بالاستعاذة من أربع **«أعوذ بالله من عذاب جهنم، ومن عذاب القبر، ومن فتنة المحيا والممات، ومن فتنة المسيح الدجال»**.

Additionally, in an authentic *ḥadīth,* the Prophet ﷺ commanded us to seek refuge in Allah ﷻ from four things: "I seek refuge in Allah from the punishment of the Fire, and from the punishment of the grave, and from the trials of life and death, and from the trial of the Dajjāl."[106]

وغير ذلك من الأدلة، وقد يشاهد بعض الناس ما يحصل من عذاب القبر من أجل العظة والعبرة.

There is also more evidence. Some people have witnessed elements of the grave's punishment so that it would serve as a warning and a caution.

ذكر الحافظ ابن رجب في كتابه «أهوال القبور وأحوالها أهلها إلىٰ يوم النشور» ذكر عجائب، وذكر ابن القيم في كتابه «الروح» عجائب.

Al-Ḥāfiẓ Ibn Rajab mentioned some astonishing things [related to this] in his book *Ahwāl al-Qubūr wa Aḥwāluhā Ahlihā ilā Yawm al-Nushūr,* and so did Ibn al-Qayyim in his book, *al-Rūḥ.*

وقوله: **(علىٰ ما جاءت به الأخبار عن رسول الله صلىٰ الله عليه وسلم)**؛ لأن ما في القبر من النعيم والعذاب من أمور الغيب، فلا نثبت إلا ما جاء به الدليل، ولا ننكر ما جاء به، هذا مذهب أهل السنة والجماعة.

"According to the accounts related from the Messenger of Allah ﷺ": It means that the punishment and pleasure of the grave are matters of the unseen and, thus, we cannot affirm anything unless it is based on evidence that has been related. We also cannot deny what has been related. This is the doctrine of Ahl al-Sunnah wa ʾl-Jamāʿah.

105 Al-Bukhārī, no. 218; Muslim, no. 292.

106 Al-Tirmidhī, no. 3613. Al-Tirmidhī said: This *ḥadīth* is *ḥasan ṣaḥīḥ.*

المتن

(١٧٢) وَنُؤْمِنُ بِالْبَعْثِ وَجَزاءِ الأَعْمالِ يَوْمَ الْقِيامَةِ، والْعَرْضِ والْحِساب، وَقِراءَةِ الْكِتابِ، والثَّوابِ والْعِقابِ، والصِّراطِ والْمِيزانِ.

(172) We believe in the Resurrection and Judgment on the Judgment Day. We believe in the *'Ardh* [when men are presented before their Lord], the *Ḥisāb* [when their deeds are tallied], and the Book being read. We believe in reward and punishment, the *Ṣirāṭ* (Path) and the *Mīzān* (Balance).

الشرح

بعد البرزخ يبعث الناس من قبورهم، فهذه القبور تضم الأجساد وتحفظها، فإذا جاء البعث فإن الله ينشئ هذه الأجسام كما خلقها أول مرة، لا ينقص منها شيء ﴿كَمَا بَدَأْنَآ أَوَّلَ خَلْقٍ نُّعِيدُهُۥ وَعْدًا عَلَيْنَآ إِنَّا كُنَّا فَٰعِلِينَ ١٠٤﴾ [الأنبياء:١٠٤].

After the *barzakh,* people will be resurrected from their graves, and graves contain and preserve the bodies. When the resurrection comes, Allah ﷻ will create these bodies once again as He created them the first time and they will be in no way incomplete. **{As We began the first creation, We will repeat it. [That is] a promise binding upon Us. Indeed, We will do it.} [Qur'ān 21:104]**

فتعاد كما كانت، بحيث لو مر شخص علىٰ رجل يعرفه لقال: هذا فلان، ثم يأمر الله إسرافيل فينفخ في الصور النفخة الثانية، فتطير الأرواح إلىٰ أجسادها.

They will return to how thcy were insofar as if someone were to walk past someone they knew, they would say, 'this is such and such person'. Then, Allah will command Isrāfīl to blow in the *ṣūr,* or horn, for the second time and the souls will fly to their bodies.

والمحشر: مجمع الأمم، يجمع الله الأولين والآخرين بعد البعث، فالله علىٰ كل شيء قدير، والإيمان بالعبث أحد أركان الإيمان الستة، كما في الحديث.

The *maḥshar*, or *place of gathering*, is the place where the communities will be gathered. Allah gathers the first and last after the resurrection. Allah is able to do all things, and faith in the resurrection is one of the six pillars of faith, as related in a *ḥadīth*.

وأنكر البعث المشركون والملاحدة بناء على عقولهم، فقالوا: ﴿أَءِذَا مِتْنَا وَكُنَّا تُرَابًا وَعِظَـٰمًا أَءِنَّا لَمَبْعُوثُونَ ۝ أَوَءَابَآؤُنَا ٱلْأَوَّلُونَ ۝﴾ [الواقعة:٤٧-٤٨] وذكر الله إنكارهم هذا في عدة مواضع، مثل: ﴿قَالَ مَن يُحْىِ ٱلْعِظَـٰمَ وَهِىَ رَمِيمٌ ۝﴾ [يس:٧٨].

The *mushrikūn* (the idolaters of Makkah) and the atheists (*al-malāḥidah*) deny the resurrection on the basis of rationality. They say: {**'When we die and become dust and bones, are we indeed to be resurrected? And our forefathers [as well]?'**} [Qurʾān 56:47-48] Allah mentions this denial in a number of instances, such as: {**'Who will give life to bones while they are disintegrated?'**} [Qurʾān 36:78]

والله عز وجل ذكر أدلة عقلية على البعث ﴿وَهُوَ ٱلَّذِى يَبْدَؤُاْ ٱلْخَلْقَ ثُمَّ يُعِيدُهُ وَهُوَ أَهْوَنُ عَلَيْهِ﴾ [الروم:٢٧]. وهذا من باب ضرب المثل، فالذي خلقهم من ماء مهين، ألا يقدر أن يخلقهم من تراب ويعيدهم كما كانوا؟ ﴿أَيَحْسَبُ ٱلْإِنسَـٰنُ أَن يُتْرَكَ سُدًى ۝ أَلَمْ يَكُ نُطْفَةً مِّن مَّنِىٍّ يُمْنَىٰ ۝ ثُمَّ كَانَ عَلَقَةً فَخَلَقَ فَسَوَّىٰ ۝ فَجَعَلَ مِنْهُ ٱلزَّوْجَيْنِ ٱلذَّكَرَ وَٱلْأُنثَىٰ ۝ أَلَيْسَ ذَٰلِكَ بِقَـٰدِرٍ عَلَىٰ أَن يُحْـِۧىَ ٱلْمَوْتَىٰ ۝﴾ [القيامة:٣٦:٤٠].

Allah ﷻ also provides rational evidence for the resurrection. {**And it is He who begins creation; then He repeats it, and that is [even] easier for Him.**} [Qurʾān 30:27] This is for the purpose of offering an example: He who created them from a vile form of water is (with more reason) able to create them from dust and bring them back to how they were. {**Does man think that he will be left neglected? Had he not been a sperm from semen emitted? Then he was a clinging clot, and [Allah] created [his form] and proportioned [him] and made of him two mates, the male and the female. Is not that [Creator] Able to give life to the dead?**} [Qurʾān 75:36-40]

ومن الأدلة: إحياء أرض يابسة قاحلة بيضاء ما فيها شيء، ثم ينزل الله عليها المطر، ففي أيام قليلة تهتز بالنبات.

Further evidence is the revival of the barren and arid earth, which is white and has nothing on it. Allah ﷻ sends down the rain upon it and in a few days, the land shakes with the sprouting of vegetation.

أليس الذي يحيي الأرض بعد موتها بقادر على أن يعيد خلق الإنسان؟ فهذا شيء معقول وشيء محسوس ﴿وَءَايَةٌ لَّهُمُ ٱلْأَرْضُ ٱلْمَيْتَةُ أَحْيَيْنَـٰهَا﴾ [يس:٣٣] بعد أن كانت ميتة فأحياها بالنبات ﴿وَتَرَى ٱلْأَرْضَ هَامِدَةً فَإِذَآ أَنزَلْنَا عَلَيْهَا ٱلْمَآءَ ٱهْتَزَّتْ وَرَبَتْ﴾ [الحج:٥].

Isn't He who gives life to the earth after its death able to re-create man? This is something rational and something tangible. **{And a sign for them is the dead earth. We have brought it to life;} [Qur'ān 36:33]** - after it is dead and He gives it life by sprouting vegetation. **{And you see the earth barren, but when We send down upon it rain, it quivers and swells.} [Qur'ān 22:56]**

ومن الأدلة على البعث أيضـًا: أن الله عز وجل لو لم يبعث الناس ويجازيهم لكان خلقه عبثـًا، والله سبحانه وتعالى منزه عن العبث ﴿أَفَحَسِبْتُمْ أَنَّمَا خَلَقْنَـٰكُمْ عَبَثًا وَأَنَّكُمْ إِلَيْنَا لَا تُرْجَعُونَ ﴿١١٥﴾ فَتَعَـٰلَى ٱللَّهُ ٱلْمَلِكُ ٱلْحَقُّ﴾ [المؤمنون:١١٥-١١٦].

Also evidence for the resurrection is the fact that were Allah ﷻ not to resurrect people and repay them for their deeds, His creation of them would have been in vain. However, Allah ﷻ is far exalted above doing anything in vain. **{Then did you think that We created you uselessly and that to Us you would not be returned?" So exalted is Allah, the Sovereign, the Truth.} [Qur'ān 23:115-116]**

فالإنسان الذي يفني نفسه بالعبادة والطاعة في الدنيا فيموت ولا يبعث!؟ كذلك الكافر يعيث في الأرض فساداً ويفعل الفواحش ويموت ولا يبعث!؟ هذا لا يكون من حكمة الله ﴿أَمْ حَسِبَ ٱلَّذِينَ ٱجْتَرَحُوا۟ ٱلسَّيِّـَٔاتِ أَن نَّجْعَلَهُمْ كَٱلَّذِينَ ءَامَنُوا۟ وَعَمِلُوا۟ ٱلصَّـٰلِحَـٰتِ سَوَآءً مَّحْيَاهُم وَمَمَاتُهُمْ ۚ سَآءَ مَا يَحْكُمُونَ ﴿٢١﴾﴾ [الجاثية:٢١]،

وقال سبحانه: ﴿أَفَنَجۡعَلُ ٱلۡمُسۡلِمِينَ كَٱلۡمُجۡرِمِينَ ۝٣٥ مَا لَكُمۡ كَيۡفَ تَحۡكُمُونَ﴾ [القلم:٣٥-٣٦]، ﴿وَمَا خَلَقۡنَا ٱلسَّمَآءَ وَٱلۡأَرۡضَ وَمَا بَيۡنَهُمَا بَٰطِلٗاۚ ذَٰلِكَ ظَنُّ ٱلَّذِينَ كَفَرُواْۚ فَوَيۡلٞ لِّلَّذِينَ كَفَرُواْ مِنَ ٱلنَّارِ ۝٢٧ أَمۡ نَجۡعَلُ ٱلَّذِينَ ءَامَنُواْ وَعَمِلُواْ ٱلصَّٰلِحَٰتِ كَٱلۡمُفۡسِدِينَ فِي ٱلۡأَرۡضِ أَمۡ نَجۡعَلُ ٱلۡمُتَّقِينَ كَٱلۡفُجَّارِ ۝٢٨﴾ [ص:٢٧-٢٨].

So, could it be so that someone spends their entire life serving and obeying Allah in the world, and then he dies and is not resurrected?! Similarly, a disbeliever wreaks havoc on earth and commits all kinds of immoralities and then he dies and is not resurrected?! This is not from the wisdom of Allah. **{Or do those who commit evils think We will make them like those who have believed and done righteous deeds – [make them] equal in their life and their death? Evil is that which they judge.} [Qurʾān 45:21]** Allah ﷻ also says: **{Then will We treat the Muslims like the criminals? What is [the matter] with you? How do you judge?} [Qurʾān 68:35-36] {And We did not create the heaven and the earth and that between them aimlessly. That is the assumption of those who disbelieve, so woe to those who disbelieve from the Fire. Or should we treat those who believe and do righteous deeds like corrupters in the land? Or should We treat those who fear Allah like the wicked?} [Qurʾān 38:27-28]**

فالمؤمن قد لا ينعم في الدنيا، ويكون في ضيق وشدة، فلا ينال جزاء عمله!؟ والكافر ينعم ويبطش ويفسد في الأرض ولا ينال جزاءه!؟ هذا لا يليق بحكمة الله عز وجل.

A believer may not have any pleasure in this life, and live in poverty and hardships; so would it be reasonable to say that he would not be rewarded for his deeds? A disbeliever may have pleasure and live ruthlessly and cause mischief on earth; so would it be reasonable to say that he will not be penalized? This does not befit Allah's ﷻ wisdom.

والبعث معناه القيام من القبور ﴿يَوۡمَ يَقُومُ ٱلنَّاسُ لِرَبِّ ٱلۡعَٰلَمِينَ ۝٦﴾ [المطففين:٦] (وجزاء الأعمال) كما سبق: أن المحسنين والمسيئين لا ينالون جزاءهم في الدنيا، إنما ذلك في دار الآخرة.

The resurrection (*al-ba'th*) means to rise from the graves. **{The Day when mankind will stand before the Lord of the worlds?} [Qur'ān 83:6]** The *judgment* (*jazā' al-a'māl*), or *repayment of deeds,* means, as mentioned previously, that those who do good and those who do bad do not receive repayment in this world but rather they receive it in the abode of the hereafter.

(والعرض) يعني: علىٰ الله ﴿يَوْمَئِذٍ تُعْرَضُونَ لَا تَخْفَىٰ مِنكُمْ خَافِيَةٌ ﴿١٨﴾﴾ [الحاقة:١٨]، ﴿وَعُرِضُوا عَلَىٰ رَبِّكَ صَفًّا لَّقَدْ جِئْتُمُونَا كَمَا خَلَقْنَاكُمْ أَوَّلَ مَرَّةٍ﴾ [الكهف:٤٨] يعرضون علىٰ الله عز وجل حفاة عراة، غرلاً، أي: غير مختونين.

The *'arḍ* means *to be presented* before Allah. **{That Day, you will be presented [for judgment]; not hidden among you is anything concealed.} [Qur'ān 69:18] {And they will be presented before your Lord in rows, [and He will say], 'You have certainly come to Us just as We created you the first time.'} [Qur'ān 18:48]** They will be presented before Allah the Almighty barefoot, naked and with foreskin (uncircumcised).

(والحساب) علىٰ الأعمال: تقرير الحسنات وتقرير السيئات، هذا بالنسبة للمؤمنين، أما الكافر فإنه لا يحاسب حساب موازنة بين حسناته وسيئاته، وإنما يقرر بذنوبه وكفره؛ لأنه ليس له حسنات.

The *tallying* (*ḥisāb*) of the deeds is the report of good deeds and the report of bad deeds. This is in relation to the believer. The disbeliever, on the other hand, is not to be called to account for the scales of good deeds and bad deeds but rather only made to acknowledge his sins and disbelief, because he has no good deeds.

والمؤمنون منهم من يدخل الجنة بغير حساب، ومنهم من يحاسب حساباً يسيراً وينقلب إلىٰ أهل مسروراً، وهو العرض، ومنهم من يُناقش الحساب، وفي الحديث: «**من نوقش الحساب عُذِّب**». وهذه درجات المؤمنين.

Some of the believers will enter Paradise without being called to account and some will have an easy account and will then turn happily back to their families. This is the *presentation*. Some of them will be called to a more thorough account. According to one *ḥadīth,* "Whoever is called to account will be punished."[107] These are the degrees of the believers.

(والكتب): صحائف الأعمال التي عملوها في الدنيا، كل يعطىٰ يوم القيامة كتابه وصحيفة أعماله التي عملها في الدنيا، مكتوب فيها كل شيء ﴿وَوُضِعَ ٱلْكِتَـٰبُ فَتَرَى ٱلْمُجْرِمِينَ مُشْفِقِينَ مِمَّا فِيهِ وَيَقُولُونَ يَـٰوَيْلَتَنَا مَالِ هَـٰذَا ٱلْكِتَـٰبِ لَا يُغَادِرُ صَغِيرَةً وَلَا كَبِيرَةً إِلَّآ أَحْصَىٰهَا﴾ [الكهف:٤٩].

The *records* (*kutub*) are the scrolls (*ṣaḥāʾif*) of deeds that were done in the world. Each will be given a record and a scroll of the deeds that they did in the world and everything will be written in it. **{And the record [of deeds] will be placed [open], and you will see the criminals fearful of that within it, and they will say, 'Oh, woe to us! What is this book that leaves nothing small or great except that it has enumerated it?'} [Qur'ān 18:49]**

وقال سبحانه: ﴿وَكُلَّ إِنسَـٰنٍ أَلْزَمْنَـٰهُ طَـٰٓئِرَهُۥ فِى عُنُقِهِۦ ۖ وَنُخْرِجُ لَهُۥ يَوْمَ ٱلْقِيَـٰمَةِ كِتَـٰبًا يَلْقَىٰهُ مَنشُورًا ﴿١٣﴾ ٱقْرَأْ كِتَـٰبَكَ كَفَىٰ بِنَفْسِكَ ٱلْيَوْمَ عَلَيْكَ حَسِيبًا ﴿١٤﴾﴾ [الإسراء:١٣-١٤].

Allah ﷻ also says: **{And [for] every person We have imposed his fate upon his neck, and We will produce for him on the Day of Resurrection a record which he will encounter spread open. [It will be said], "Read your record. Sufficient is yourself against you this Day as accountant."} [Qur'ān 17:13-14]**

وقال سبحانه: ﴿فَأَمَّا مَنْ أُوتِىَ كِتَـٰبَهُۥ بِيَمِينِهِۦ فَيَقُولُ هَآؤُمُ ٱقْرَءُوا۟ كِتَـٰبِيَهْ ﴿١٩﴾ إِنِّى ظَنَنتُ أَنِّى مُلَـٰقٍ حِسَابِيَهْ ﴿٢٠﴾ فَهُوَ فِى عِيشَةٍ رَّاضِيَةٍ ﴿٢١﴾ فِى جَنَّةٍ عَالِيَةٍ ﴿٢٢﴾﴾ [الحاقة: ١٩-٢٢] فهذا الصنف من الناس يفرح ويسره أن يطلع الناس علىٰ كتابه.

Allah ﷻ also says: **{So as for he who is given his record in his right hand, he will say, 'Here, read my record! Indeed, I was certain that I would be meeting my account.' So he will be in a pleasant life – In an elevated garden.} [Qur'ān 69:19-20]** This class of people will rejoice and be glad that people see their records.

107 Al-Bukhārī, no. 6536; Muslim, no. 2876.

﴿وأما من أوتى كتابه بشماله فيقول ياليتنى لم أوت كتابيه ۝٢٥ ولم أدر ما حسابيه ۝٢٦ ياليتها كانت القاضية ۝٢٧﴾ [الحاقة:٢٥-٢٧] يعني : يا ليتني لم أبعث، وكان الموت هو القاضي عليّ ولم أبعث ﴿مَآ أَغْنَىٰ عَنِّي مَالِيَهْۜ ۝٢٨ هَلَكَ عَنِّي سُلْطَٰنِيَهْ ۝٢٩﴾ [الحاقة: ٢٨-٢٩].

{But as for he who is given his record in his left hand, he will say, 'Oh, I wish I had not been given my record and had not known what is my account. I wish my death had been the decisive one.'} [Qur'ān 69:25-27] That is to say: I wish I had not been resurrected and death was the end of my life without resurrection. **{My wealth has not availed me. Gone from me is my authority.} [Qur'ān 69: 28-29]**

وهذا تطاير الصحف، إما باليمين أو بالشمال.

This is the dispersing of the records and it is either in the right or the left hand.

(والثواب والعقاب) الثواب علىٰ الحسنات، والعقاب علىٰ السيئات.

The *reward* and *punishment* are the reward for good deeds and the punishment for bad deeds.

(والصراط) وهو: الجسر المنصوب علىٰ متن جهنم، أحدُّ من السيف، وأدقُّ من الشعر، وأحرُّ من الجمر، يمر الناس عليه علىٰ قدر أعمالهم، فمنهم من يمر كالبرق الخاطف، ومنهم من يمر كالريح، ومنهم من يمر كأجاويد الخيل، ومنهم من يمر كركاب الإبل، ومنهم من يمر عدواً ومنهم من يمر مشياً، ومنهم من يمر حبواً، ومنهم من تلقطه كلاليب علىٰ حافتي الجسر وتقذفه في النار، وهذه أمور غيب، فلا يُدخلُ الإنسان عقله فيها، وكل الناس يمرون علىٰ الصراط ﴿وَإِن مِّنكُمْ إِلَّا وَارِدُهَاۚ كَانَ عَلَىٰ رَبِّكَ حَتْمًا مَّقْضِيًّا ۝٧١ ثُمَّ نُنَجِّي ٱلَّذِينَ ٱتَّقَواْ وَّنَذَرُ ٱلظَّٰلِمِينَ فِيهَا جِثِيًّا ۝٧٢﴾ [مريم:٧١-٧٢].

The *ṣirāṭ* is the bridge that is raised above Hell. It is sharper than a sword, finer than a hair and hotter than burning coal. People will cross it according to their deeds: Some will cross it like a flash of lightning, some like the passing of the wind, some like racehorses and some like riding camels. Some will cross it running, some walking and some crawling; some of them will be snatched by hooks (*kalālīb*) on both sides of the bridge, which will cast them into the Fire. These are matters of the unseen, so a person cannot intervene in them with his mind. All people will come to cross the *ṣirāṭ*. **{And there is none of you except he will come to it. This is upon your Lord an inevitability decreed. Then We will save those who feared Allah and leave the wrongdoers within it, on their knees.} [Qur'ān 19:71-72]**

وتوزن الحسنات، فإن رجحت حسناته فاز، وإن رجحت سيئاته علىٰ حسناته خاب وخسر ﴿وَٱلْوَزْنُ يَوْمَئِذٍ ٱلْحَقُّ ۚ فَمَن ثَقُلَتْ مَوَٰزِينُهُۥ فَأُو۟لَٰٓئِكَ هُمُ ٱلْمُفْلِحُونَ ۝٨ وَمَنْ خَفَّتْ مَوَٰزِينُهُۥ فَأُو۟لَٰٓئِكَ ٱلَّذِينَ خَسِرُوٓا۟ أَنفُسَهُم بِمَا كَانُوا۟ بِـَٔايَٰتِنَا يَظْلِمُونَ ۝٩﴾ [الأعراف :٨-٩].

The good deeds will be weighed, and if one's good deeds have the greater weight, then one will have succeeded. Yet if one's bad deeds outweigh their good ones, then one is forsaken and is in loss. **{And the weighing [of deeds] that Day will be the truth. So those whose scales are heavy – it is they who will be the successful. And those whose scales are light – they are the ones who will lose themselves for what injustice they were doing toward Our verses.} [Qur'ān 7:8-9]**

وتكرر ذكر الوزن والميزان في آيات كثيرة، وهذا من عدل الله عز وجل، وأنه لا يظلم أحداً. والميزان حقيقي، له كفتان: توضع الحسنات في كفّه، وتوضع السيئات في كفة، فأيهم رجحت حسناته فاز، وأيهم رجحت سيئاته فخسر ﴿وَنَضَعُ ٱلْمَوَٰزِينَ ٱلْقِسْطَ لِيَوْمِ ٱلْقِيَٰمَةِ فَلَا تُظْلَمُ نَفْسٌ شَيْـًٔا ۖ وَإِن كَانَ مِثْقَالَ حَبَّةٍ مِّنْ خَرْدَلٍ أَتَيْنَا بِهَا ۗ وَكَفَىٰ بِنَا حَٰسِبِينَ ۝٤٧﴾ [الأنبياء:٤٧].

The *weighing* and the *balance* are repeatedly mentioned throughout several verses. It is out of Allah's justice that He does not wrong anyone. The balance is real and it has two scales. Good deeds will be placed on one scale and bad deeds will be placed on another. Those whose good deeds are the weightiest are the successful and those whose bad deeds are the weightiest are the losers. **{And We place the scales of justice for the Day of Resurrection, so no soul will be treated unjustly at all. And if there is [even] the weight of a mustard seed, We will bring it forth. And sufficient are We as accountant.} [Qur'ān 21:47]**

المتن

(١٧٣) والْجَنَّةُ والنّارُ مَخْلُوقَتانِ، لا تَفْنَيانِ أَبَدًا وَلا تَبِيدانِ.

(173) Paradise and Hell are both creations that shall never perish nor die out.

الشرح

ومما يكون في يوم القيامة: الجنة دار المتقين، والنار دار المجرمين، قال الله تعالىٰ في الجنة: ﴿أُعِدَّتْ لِلْمُتَّقِينَ ﴿١٣٣﴾﴾ [آل عمران:١٣٣]، وقال في النار: ﴿أُعِدَّتْ لِلْكَٰفِرِينَ ﴿٢٤﴾﴾ [البقرة:٢٤] فهما داران باقيتان، وهما المستقر والنهاية.

Among the things that will be in existence on the Day of Judgment are Paradise, the abode of the righteous and the Fire, the abode of the criminals. Allah ﷻ says concerning Paradise: **{Prepared for the righteous.} [Qur'ān 3:133]** And He says concerning the Fire: **{Prepared for the disbelievers.} [Qur'ān 2:24]** They are two everlasting abodes, places of settlement and of the end.

(**وإن الله تعالىٰ خلق الجنة والنار قبل الخلق وخلق لهما أهلاً**). والجنة والنار مخلوقتان الآن، هذا مذهب أهل السنة والجماعة، قال تعالىٰ: ﴿أُعِدَّتْ لِلْمُتَّقِينَ﴾، وقال: ﴿أُعِدَّتْ لِلْكَٰفِرِينَ﴾ وأعدت: فعل ماضٍ، والنبي صلىٰ الله عليه وسلم كان عنده أصحابه، فسمعوا وجبة، يعني: شيء سقط، فقال: «**أتدرون ما هذا؟**» قالوا: الله ورسوله أعلم، قال: «**هذا حجر رمي به في جنهم منذ سبعين خريفًا، والآن وصل إلىٰ قعرها**» فدل علىٰ أن النار قد خلقت.

"And [we believe] that Allah created Paradise and Hell before creating mankind, and He created people for them."[108] Paradise and the Fire have already been created; they are now in existence. This is the doctrine of Ahl al-Sunnah wa 'l-Jamāʿah. Allah ﷻ says: ***{Prepared for the righteous}*** and He says: ***{prepared for the disbelievers.}*** *Prepared* is a past tense verb. Once, the Prophet ﷺ was with his Companions and they heard something fall. He said: "Do you know what this is?" They said, "Allah and His Messenger know best." He said: "This is a stone that was thrown into *Jahannam* (the Fire) seventy autumns ago and now it has reached its bottom."[109] This indicates that the Fire has already been created.

وقال عليه الصلاة والسلام في الحر والبرد: **«إنهما نفسان لجنهم: نفس في الشتاء وهو أشد ما تجدون من البرد، ونفس في الصيف وهو أشد ما تجدون من شدة الحر»**، وقال عليه الصلاة والسلام: **«إذا اشتد الحر فأبردوا بالصلاة، فإن شدة الحر من فيح جنهم»**.

The Prophet ﷺ also said that heat and cold are two breaths of *Jahannam*: "One breath in the winter, which is the most intense cold you feel; and one breath in the summer, which is the most intense heat you feel."[110] The Prophet ﷺ also said: "When it is very hot, pray when it is cooler, for the intensity of the summer's heat is from the vehemence of the raging heat of Jahannam."[111]

وكذلك الميت في قبره يفتح له باب إلىٰ الجنة، والكافر باب إلىٰ النار، فهذا يدل علىٰ وجود الجنة والنار، وأنكر هذا أهل الضلال، ويقولون: تخلقان يوم القيامة.

Moreover, a gate of Jannah is opened unto the dead [believer] in their graves and a gate of the Fire is opened unto a disbeliever. This is evidence of the existence of Paradise and the Fire. The people of misguidance have denied this and said that they are to be created on the Day of Judgment.

108 [T] The commentator has mentioned the next point in the source text here.
109 Al-Bukhārī, no. 538; Muslim, no. 616.
110 Al-Bukhārī, no. 537; Muslim, no. 617.
111 Al-Bukhārī, no. 538; Muslim, no. 616.

المتن

(١٧٤) وَإِنَّ اللهَ تَعالَىٰ خَلَقَ الْجَنَّةَ والنّارَ قَبْلَ الْخَلْقِ، وَخَلَقَ لَهُما أَهْلًا.

(174) And [we believe] that Allah created Paradise and Hell before creating mankind, and He created people for them.

الشرح

الله قدر للجنة أهلاً، وكذلك للنار أهلاً، فعلىٰ حسب عملهم يجازون.

Allah ﷻ has predetermined that some people belong to Paradise and that others belong to the Fire. They are repaid according to their deeds.

المتن

(١٧٥) فَمَنْ شاءَ مِنْهُمْ إِلَىٰ الْجَنَّةِ فَضْلًا مِنْهُ، وَمَنْ شاءَ مِنْهُمْ إِلَىٰ النّارِ عَدْلًا مِنْهُ.

(175) Whoever He wills goes to Paradise out of His grace and whoever He wills goes to Hell out of His justice.

الشرح

الجنة لا تُنال بالعمل، إنما هو سبب، وإنما الجنة تنال بفضل الله، فمهما عمل ابن آدم من الأعمال الصالحة وإن كثرت فإنها لا تقابل الجنة، إنما تنال بفضل الله عز وجل، والعمل الصالح سبب ﴿ٱدْخُلُوا۟ ٱلْجَنَّةَ بِمَا كُنتُمْ تَعْمَلُونَ ۝٣٢﴾ [النحل: ٣٢] أي: بسبب ما كنتم تعملون.

Paradise is not attained through deeds, but deeds are only a cause; Paradise is only attained by the grace of Allah. Whatever good deeds the son of Ādam does (even if they are great), they do not correspond to Paradise. Rather, Paradise is only attained by the grace of Allah the Almighty. Good deeds are but a cause: **{Enter Paradise for what you used to do,} [Qur'ān 16:32]**

- meaning, *because* of what you used to do.

ودخول النار بسبب الكفر، عدلاً من الله، أدخله النار، لا بظلم، إنما أدخله بسبب عمله.

The entering of the Fire is because of disbelief and it is out of Allah's ﷻ justice that He makes people enter the Fire. He does not wrong them but rather causes them to enter it because of their deeds.

المتن

(١٧٦) وَكُلٌّ يَعْمَلُ لِما قَدْ فَرِغَ لَهُ، وَصائِرٌ إِلَىٰ ما خُلِقَ لَهُ.

(176) Each person acts for whatever has been decided for him and will go to the place for which he was created.

الشرح

إن كان من أهل السعادة فإنه يعمل بعمل أهل السعادة، ومن كان من أهل الشقاوة فسيعمل بعمل أهل الشقاوة، قال عليه الصلاة والسلام: «**اعملوا فكل ميسر لما خلق له**».

If someone is one of the fortunate, they do the deeds of the fortunate; and if someone is one of the wretched, they do the deeds of the wretched. The Prophet ﷺ said: "Work, for each has had made easy that for which he was created."[112]

وقال تعالىٰ: ﴿إِنَّ سَعْيَكُمْ لَشَتَّىٰ ۝٤ فَأَمَّا مَنْ أَعْطَىٰ وَٱتَّقَىٰ ۝٥ وَصَدَّقَ بِٱلْحُسْنَىٰ ۝٦ فَسَنُيَسِّرُهُۥ لِلْيُسْرَىٰ ۝٧ وَأَمَّا مَنۢ بَخِلَ وَٱسْتَغْنَىٰ ۝٨ وَكَذَّبَ بِٱلْحُسْنَىٰ ۝٩ فَسَنُيَسِّرُهُۥ لِلْعُسْرَىٰ ۝١٠﴾ [الليل: ٤-١٠].

Allah ﷻ also says: **{Indeed, your efforts are diverse. As for he who gives and fears Allah and believes in the best [reward], We will ease him**

112 Al-Bukhārī, no. 1362; Muslim, no. 2647.

toward ease. But as for he who withholds and considers himself free of need and denies the best [reward], We will ease him toward difficulty.} [Qur'ān 92:4-10]

فالأعمال هي التي تحكمك، إن كانت صالحة فأنت ميسر لليسرىٰ، وإن كانت سيئة فأنت ميسر للعسرىٰ.

So, it is the actions that you are to be judged by: if they are good, the path of ease (*al-yusrā*) is made easy for you; and if they are bad, the path of difficulty (*al-ʿusrā*) is made easy for you.

المتن

(١٧٧) والْخَيْرُ والشَّرُّ مُقَدَّرانِ عَلَىٰ الْعِبادِ.

(177) Good and bad have been decreed for all.

الشرح

سبق بحث هذا في القدر، والإيمان بالقدر - كما سبق - هو أحد أركان الإيمان الستة، كما قال عليه الصلاة والسلام: «**الإيمان أن تؤمن بالله وملائكته وكتبه ورسله واليوم الآخر، وتؤمن بالقدر خيره وشره**».

This has already been discussed in the section on *qadar* (predestination), which is one of the six pillars of faith, as the Prophet ﷺ said: "Faith is to believe in Allah, His angels, His books, His Messengers, the Last Day and in *qadar*, whether good or bad."[113]

والمؤلف أخذ هذا المعنىٰ من نص الحديث.

The author derived this description from the explicit text of the *ḥadīth*.

فالخير والشر بتقدير الله عز وجل؛ لأنه لا يقع شيء في هذا الكون إلا بقضاء الله

113 Al-Bukhārī, no. 50; Muslim, no. 10.

وقدره، لابد من الإيمان بذلك.

Good and bad are both predestined by Allah ﷻ because nothing in the universe happens outside of Allah's ﷻ decree and predestination. It is necessary to believe in that.

فالله عز وجل خلق الخير والشر لحكمة ﴿وَنَبْلُوكُم بِٱلشَّرِّ وَٱلْخَيْرِ فِتْنَةً ۖ وَإِلَيْنَا تُرْجَعُونَ ﴿٣٥﴾﴾ [الأنبياء:٣٥] يتميز بذلك أهل الإيمان والتوحيد والانقياد لله، وأهل الكفر والشرك والإلحاد، ولو لم يكن هناك خير لما حصل التمييز.

Allah ﷻ created the good and the bad out of wisdom. **{And We test you with evil and with good as trial; and to Us you will be returned.} [Qur'ān 21:35]** Thereby, the people of faith, *tawḥīd,* and obedience to Allah ﷻ are distinguished from the people of disbelief, polytheism, and heresy. If there were no good, this distinction would not be realised.

فالخير يحبه الله ويخلقه ويقدره، والشر يبغضه الله ويسخطه، ولكن يخلقه ويقدره لحكمة، للابتلاء والامتحان، لو لم يوجد الشر ما ظهر الكفر وعداوة الأنبياء والرسل، ولو لم يوجد الخير لما ظهر الجهاد والأمر بالمعروف والنهي عن المنكر والموالاة والمعاداة، ولا تميز الناس.

Allah ﷻ loves, destines and decrees good. He hates and is displeased with the bad, but He creates and destines it for an underlying reason and with wisdom: To try and test people. If there was no evil, there would be no disbelief or enmity towards prophets and messengers. If there was no good, there would be no *jihād,* commanding the right, forbidding the wrong and alliance and enmity [for the sake of Allah] and people would not be distinguished from each other.

قد يعترض معترض ويقول: الله يبغض الشرك والكفر، فكيف يقدر ذلك؟ ونقول: قدر ذلك لحكمة؛ ليتميز الناس ﴿مَّا كَانَ ٱللَّهُ لِيَذَرَ ٱلْمُؤْمِنِينَ عَلَىٰ مَآ أَنتُمْ عَلَيْهِ حَتَّىٰ يَمِيزَ ٱلْخَبِيثَ مِنَ ٱلطَّيِّبِ ۗ وَمَا كَانَ ٱللَّهُ لِيُطْلِعَكُمْ عَلَى ٱلْغَيْبِ﴾ [آل عمران:١٧٩] فنحن لا نعلم المطيع من العاصي إلا بالأعمال، فهي تميز الشقي من السعيد.

Someone could try to challenge this and say, "Allah hates polytheism and unbelief, so how could He have predetermined them?" We say: Allah ﷺ predetermined that with wisdom, to distinguish people from each other. {Allah would not leave the believers in that [state] you are in [presently] until He separates the evil from the good.} [Qur'ān 3:179] The only way for us to know whether someone is obedient or disobedient is through actions, as they distinguish the wretched from the fortunate.

فالأمور لا تصلح إلا إذا وجدت المتضادات.

Matters are not set right unless opposites exist.

❁❁❁

المتن

(١٧٨) والاِسْتِطَاعَةُ الَّتِي يَجِبُ بِهَا الْفِعْلُ مِنْ نَحْوِ التَّوْفِيقِ الَّذِي لا يَجُوزُ أَنْ يُوصَفَ الْمَخْلُوقُ بِهِ، فَهِيَ مَعَ الْفِعْلِ، وَأَمَّا الِاسْتِطَاعَةُ مِنْ جِهَةِ الصِّحَّةِ والْوُسْعِ والتَّمَكُّنِ وَسَلامَةِ الآلاتِ فَهِيَ قَبْلَ الْفِعْلِ، وَبِهَا يَتَعَلَّقُ الْخِطَابُ، وَهُوَ كَمَا قَالَ تَعَالَىٰ ﴿لا يُكَلِّفُ اللهُ نَفْسًا إِلّا وُسْعَها﴾ [البقرة: ٢٨٦].

(178) Enablement, by which an action is obligatory, is an example of the divinely given ability that creation cannot be described as having [intrinsically], for it occurs concurrent with the action. As for ability inasmuch as one has health, capacity, faculties, and sound appendages: they occur prior to the act. The instruction pertains to [the latter], and that is as Allah says: {Allah does not charge a soul except [with that within] its capacity.} [Qur'ān 2:286]

الشرح

الاستطاعة هي القدرة من الإنسان، وهي علىٰ قسمين:

Ability (*istiṭā'ah*) is the ability of man. There are two types:

الأول: استطاعة يتعلق بها التكليف والأمر والنهي.

One. The capacity associated with *taklīf* (an order or prohibition people will be held accountable for), commands, and prohibitions.

الثاني: استطاعة يستطيع بها الإنسان الفعل والتنفيذ.

Two. The capacity by which a person is able to act and put into effect.

القسم الأول: الاستطاعة التي يتعلق بها التكليف، معناها: الوسع، أن يكون عند الإنسان وسع، أن يفعل أو لا يفعل، عنده إمكانية وتمكن، فالتكليف يتعلق بهذه الاستطاعة، فالإنسان الذي ليس عنده تمكن واستطاعة لا يكلف، كالمجنون والصغير، فلا يكلف فلا يُؤمر ولا يُنهىٰ، ولكن الصغير إن بلغ سبع سنوات فإن عنده استطاعة فيُؤمر بالصلاة من باب الاستحباب والتربية، والتدريب علىٰ فعل العبادة، فلا تجب عليه إلا إذا بلغ فيكلف، وهذا النوع يكون قبل الفعل.

The first type, ability which is connected to *taklīf* (legal responsibility), means that a person possesses the capacity to either do or not do something i.e. they have the possibility and capabilities. *Taklīf* is related to this type of ability. Someone who does not have the means or the ability is not held accountable for obligations, as with an insane person or minor. They are not accountable and are thus neither subject to commands nor prohibitions. However, when a minor reaches seven years of age, they have some ability, so they are commanded to pray. [Commanding them to pray] is a matter of desirability, education and training children to do acts of worship. It is not an obligation until the child reaches maturity and becomes accountable. This kind of ability exists before action.

القسم الثاني: الاستطاعة التي يكون فيها التنفيذ، وإيجاد الشيء، فهذه تكون مع الفعل فالحج مثلاً فيه الاستطاعتان، قال تعالىٰ: ﴿وَلِلَّهِ عَلَى ٱلنَّاسِ حِجُّ ٱلْبَيْتِ مَنِ ٱسْتَطَاعَ ...﴾ [آل عمران:٩٧] فهذه استطاعة تمكن، فيجب الحج علىٰ من يستطيع، والسبيل هو الزاد والراحلة، فيجب عليه الحج إذا وجدهما؛ لأن عنده تمكناً، هذه استطاعة قبل الفعل، أما الاستطاعة مع الفعل - وهو مباشرة الحج - فقد لا يكون عنده قدرة مثل المريض المزمن أو الكبير الهرم، فهذا لا يستطيع

استطاعة تنفيذ وفعل، ويستطيع استطاعة تكليف، فهذا يجب عليه الحج في ذمته.

The second type is the ability that involves the implementation and realisation of things. This kind runs concurrently with the action. For example, Ḥajj involves both kinds of ability. Allah ﷻ says: **{And [due] to Allah from the people is a pilgrimage to the House – for whoever is able...} [Qur'ān 22:97]** This refers to the ability by which someone attains all the necessary means to be able. If so, Ḥajj is a duty on those who are able to do it. The *sabīl,* or *way* [mentioned in the verse], is the supplies and means of transportation to complete the journey. It is a duty to perform Ḥajj if those things are available, because one thereby has the ability. This kind of ability occurs before the action. The kind of ability occurring with the action, on the other hand, which is the actual carrying out of the Ḥajj, may not be within someone's ability, as is the case with a chronically ill person or someone who is old and decrepit. Such a person is not able to put the action into effect, but he or she has the ability as far as *taklīf* is concerned; and so such a person is liable in relation to the obligation of Ḥajj.

ومثل دخول وقت الصلاة يوجب الصلاة علىٰ المكلف، ويكون التنفيذ بحسب استطاعته، فالمريض يصلي قائماً، فإن لم يستطع فقاعداً، فإن لم يستطع فعلىٰ جنب، فالصلاة تجب عليه علىٰ كل حال؛ لأنه في استطاعته ذلك، وهذه الاستطاعة قبل الفعل، أما التي مع الفعل قد تكون معدومة نهائياً، وقد تكون موجودة، ولكن ليست تامة، فيجب عليه علىٰ قدر استطاعته.

Another example is that the beginning of the time of prayer renders the prayer obligatory to those who are accountable, but the carrying out of the prayer occurs according to the ability: An ill person prays standing, if unable, then sitting, and if unable, then upon their side. Thus, prayer is obligatory under all circumstances, as a person is able to do it. This is the ability before the action. The ability with the action may be completely absent, or it may be present but incomplete, and it would thus be one's duty to do what is within one's ability.

﴿فَٱتَّقُواْ ٱللَّهَ مَا ٱسۡتَطَعۡتُمۡ﴾ [التغابن:١٦]، ﴿لَا يُكَلِّفُ ٱللَّهُ نَفۡسًا إِلَّا وُسۡعَهَاۚ﴾ [البقرة:٢٨٦].

{So fear Allah as much as you are able.} [Qur'ān 64:16] {Allah does not charge a soul except [with that within] its capacity.} [Qur'ān 2:286]

وفيه فرق بين الاستطاعتين:

Here, the two kinds of ability are differentiated:

فالأولىٰ يتعلق الخطاب بها، كما قال تعالىٰ: ﴿لَا يُكَلِّفُ ٱللَّهُ نَفْسًا إِلَّا وُسْعَهَا﴾ [البقرة:٢٨٦]، والثانية يتعلق بها التنفيذ.

The first is associated with the commands, as Allah ﷻ says: **{Allah does not charge a soul except [with that within] its capacity} [Qur'ān 2:286]** and the second is associated with the performance.

المتن

(١٧٩) وَأَفْعالُ الْعِبادِ خَلْقُ اللهِ، وَكَسْبٌ مِنَ الْعِبادِ.

(179) Man's actions are the creations of Allah and the works of man.

الشرح

هذه المسألة حصل فيها نزاع ومزلة أقدام ومضلة أفهام، هل الأفعال مخلوقة لله أو هي من خلق العباد؟

This issue involved some controversy, causing feet to slip and understandings to err: Are actions the creations of Allah or are they the creations of Allah's slaves?

القول الأول: قول الجبرية والجهمية: إن العبد مجبور، ليس له دخل في الأفعال، فهي محض خلق الله عز وجل، فصلاته التي يؤديها ليس باختياره، إنما هو مجبور وهؤلاء غلوا في إثبات قدرة الله.

The former pronouncement is that of the Jabrī and Jahmī sects, that men are under divine 'compulsion' and do not have the power to intervene in their own actions, they are purely the creations of Allah the Almighty. Thus, the prayer that one prays is not by choice but rather by compulsion. This sect is extreme in its affirmation of Allah's ﷻ omnipotence.

وقولهم هذا ضلال مبين، ومعناه أن الله يظلمهم ويعذبهم علىٰ شيء ليس لهم فيه اختيار، وليس لهم فيه استطاعة، وإنما الله يعذب العبد علىٰ فعل غيره، ويثيبه علىٰ شيء لم يفعله، وهذا المذهب أخبث المذاهب.

This view of theirs is a manifest error. It means that Allah wrongs them and punishes them for something that is not within their choice, and not within their ability. It also means that Allah punishes His slaves for the actions of someone else and rewards them for something that they did not do. This is one of the most vile doctrines.

القول الثاني: وهو مضاد للقول الأول تمامًا، وهو قول المعتزلة، يقولون: الأفعال من إنتاج العبد وإرادته المطلقة ومشيئته، وليس لله تدخل فيها، وإنما العبد هو الذي يخلق فعل نفسه، فهؤلاء غالوا في إثبات قدرة العبد.

The latter pronouncement, which is the complete opposite of the former and is the view of the Muʿtazilites, is that actions are the product of people. People have an absolute free will; Allah ﷻ does not intervene but instead the person creates his own actions. This sect is extreme in its affirmation of the ability of the created beings.

ويلزم من قولهم أن الله عاجز، وأن الله يشاركه غيره في الخلق والإيجاد، وهذا قول المجوس، ولذلك المعتزلة سُمُّوا: مجوس هذه الأمة، فالمجوس يقولون: إن للكون خالقين، خالق للخير وخالق للشر، والمعتزلة زادوا عليهم وقالوا: كل يخلق فعل نفسه، فأثبتوا خالقين.

A necessary consequence of this view of theirs is that Allah is unable to do something and that others share with Allah in creating and originating. This is the belief of the Zoroastrians and therefore, the Muʿtazilites have been named the Zoroastrians of this Ummah (*majūs al-ummah*).[114] The

114 It is related that Ibn 'Umar ﷺ said: The Prophet ﷺ said: "The *Qadarīs* are the

Zoroastrians [or: *majūs*] believe that there are two creators in the universe: a creator of good and a creator of evil. The Muʿtazilites add to that, saying that each individual creates his own actions and thus they assert the existence of [many] creators.

والمذهب التوسط مذهب أهل السنة والجماعة، علىٰ ضوء الكتاب والسنة، قالوا: أفعال العباد هي فعلهم بإرادتهم ومشيئتهم، وهي خلق الله عز وجل ﴿وَٱللَّهُ خَلَقَكُمۡ وَمَا تَعۡمَلُونَ ۝٩٦﴾ [الصافات:٩٦] ﴿ٱللَّهُ خَٰلِقُ كُلِّ شَيۡءٖۖ وَهُوَ عَلَىٰ كُلِّ شَيۡءٖ وَكِيلٞ ۝٦٢﴾ [الزمر:٦٢] ﴿هَلۡ مِنۡ خَٰلِقٍ غَيۡرُ ٱللَّهِ يَرۡزُقُكُم مِّنَ ٱلسَّمَآءِ وَٱلۡأَرۡضِۚ﴾ [فاطر:٣]

The moderate doctrine, in light of the Qur'ān and Sunnah, is that of Ahl al-Sunnah wa 'l-Jamāʿah. They believe that the actions of people are their actions in terms of their own will and volition and that they are creations of Allah ﷻ. **{While Allah created you and that which you do?} [Qur'ān 37:96] {Allah is the Creator of all things, and He is, over all things, Disposer of affairs.} [Qur'ān 39:62] {Is there any creator other than Allah who provides for you from the heaven and earth?} [Qur'ān 35:3]**

فالله منفرد بالخلق والتقدير، والعبد له مشيئته وإرادته، وله فعل، فهو باختياره يذهب إلىٰ المسجد، وباختياره يذهب إلىٰ المسارح؛ لأن عنده قدرة، والإنسان الذي لم يعطه الله قدرة ولا استطاعة فهذا قد عذره الله، مثل المجنون والمكره، فليس عنده إرادة، وليس عنده قصد، أما من عنده إرادة وقصد، فهذا الذي يختار الفعل لنفسه، والعقاب والثواب يقع علىٰ فعله، وليس علىٰ فعل الله عز وجل.

Thus, Allah ﷻ is Alone in His creation and predestination, and people have wills and volitions. So they go to the mosque by choice, and they go to the theatre by choice, because they have the ability. A person that Allah has not given the power and ability is excused by Allah, such as an insane person or someone under compulsion. Such a person does not have a will or intent. But if someone does have a will and intent, then they choose the action on

---

Majūs (Zoroastrians) of this *ummah*. If they are ill, do not visit them; and if they die, do not attend their funerals." Abū Dāwūd, no. 4691.

their own accord and intent, and the punishment and reward are based on their action and not the action of Allah the Almighty.

قال الله تعالىٰ: ﴿إِنَّ ٱلَّذِينَ ءَامَنُواْ﴾ [البقرة:٦٢] [النساء:٥٩]، ﴿إِنَّ ٱلَّذِينَ كَفَرُواْ﴾ [آل عمران:١١٦] أسند الإيمان إليهم، وكذلك أسند الكفر ﴿أَطِيعُواْ ٱللَّهَ وَأَطِيعُواْ ٱلرَّسُولَ﴾ [النساء:٥٩] ﴿وَمَن يُطِعِ ٱللَّهَ وَرَسُولَهُۥ﴾ [النور:٥٢] أسند الأفعال إلىٰ العباد.

Allah the Most High says: **{Indeed, those who believed.} [Qur'ān 2:62; 4:59] {Indeed, those who disbelieve.} [Qur'ān 3:116]** Here, both faith and disbelief are attributed to people. **{Obey Allah and obey the Messenger.} [Qur'ān 4:59] {And whoever obeys Allah and His Messenger.} [Qur'ān 24:52]** Here, actions are attributed to people.

والدليل علىٰ أن العبد له إرادة وقصد: قوله تعالىٰ: ﴿وَمَا تَشَآءُونَ إِلَّآ أَن يَشَآءَ ٱللَّهُۚ إِنَّ ٱللَّهَ كَانَ عَلِيمًا حَكِيمًا ٣٠﴾ [الإنسان:٣٠]، فأثبت الله سبحانه له مشيئة وللعبد مشيئة، وجعل مشيئة العبد تحت مشيئته سبحانه ﴿لِمَن شَآءَ مِنكُمۡ أَن يَسۡتَقِيمَ ٢٨﴾ [التكوير: ٢٨] شاء، أي: باختياره، وفي هذا رد علىٰ الجبرية. ﴿إِلَّآ أَن يَشَآءَ ٱللَّهُۚ﴾ [الإنسان:٣٠] في هذا رد علىٰ القدرية.

Evidence that people have a will and intent is the fact that Allah ﷻ says: **{And you do not will except that Allah wills. Indeed, Allah is ever Knowing and Wise.} [Qur'ān 76:30]** Here, Allah ﷻ establishes that both He and His slaves have a will. He said that the will of the slave is under His will: **{For whoever wills among you to take a right course.} [Qur'ān 81:28]** Whoever wills, that is, by one's own choice, and this is a response to the Jabriyyah sect. **{Except that Allah wills.} [Qur'ān 76:30]** This is a response to the Qadariyyah sect.

المتن

(١٨٠) وَلَمْ يُكَلِّفْهُمُ اللهُ تَعالَىٰ إِلَّا ما يُطِيقُونَ.

(180) Allah does not obligate them to do except that which they are able;

الشرح

قال تعالى: ﴿لَا يُكَلِّفُ ٱللَّهُ نَفْسًا إِلَّا وُسْعَهَا﴾ [البقرة:٢٨٦]، ﴿رَبَّنَا وَلَا تُحَمِّلْنَا مَا لَا طَاقَةَ لَنَا بِهِۦ﴾ [البقرة:٢٨٦]، ﴿يُرِيدُ ٱللَّهُ بِكُمُ ٱلْيُسْرَ وَلَا يُرِيدُ بِكُمُ ٱلْعُسْرَ﴾ [البقرة:١٨٥]، فالله لا يكلف العباد ما لا يطيقون، إلا من باب العقوبة، كما حمّل بني إسرائيل بسبب تعنتهم ﴿فَبِظُلْمٍ مِّنَ ٱلَّذِينَ هَادُوا۟ حَرَّمْنَا عَلَيْهِمْ طَيِّبَٰتٍ أُحِلَّتْ لَهُمْ وَبِصَدِّهِمْ عَن سَبِيلِ ٱللَّهِ كَثِيرًا ﴿١٦٠﴾ وَأَخْذِهِمُ ٱلرِّبَوٰا۟﴾ [النساء:١٦٠-١٦١].

Allah ﷻ says: **{Allah does not charge a soul except [with that within] its capacity.} [Qur'ān 2:286] {Our Lord, and burden us not with that which we have no ability to bear.} [Qur'ān 2:286] {Allah intends for you ease and does not intend for you hardship.} [Qur'ān 2:185]** So, Allah ﷻ does not hold anyone to account for something that is beyond one's capacity, unless it is a form of punishment, as He laid a great burden upon the Children of Israel because of their stubbornness. **{For wrongdoing on the part of the Jews, We made unlawful for them [certain] good foods which had been lawful to them, and for their averting from the way of Allah many [people], and [for] their taking of usury.} [Qur'ān 4:160-161]**

فالله عاقبهم فكلفهم بما لا يطيقون، ولذلك جاء في الدعاء ﴿رَبَّنَا وَلَا تَحْمِلْ عَلَيْنَآ إِصْرًا كَمَا حَمَلْتَهُۥ عَلَى ٱلَّذِينَ مِن قَبْلِنَا﴾ [البقرة:٢٨٦] فالله - فضلاً منه وإحساناً - لا يكلف العباد إلا ما يطيقون، رحمة منه، فهو رحيم ﴿إِنَّ ٱللَّهَ بِٱلنَّاسِ لَرَءُوفٌ رَّحِيمٌ ﴿١٤٣﴾﴾ [البقرة:١٤٣].

Allah ﷻ punished them and laid upon them a burden that they were unable to bear; and therefore, it is presented in the supplication: **{Our Lord, and lay not upon us a burden like that which You laid upon those before us.} [Qur'ān 2:286]** Thus, out of His grace and kindness, He does not hold His servants accountable for anything that is beyond their powers. This is out of His mercy, as He is the Most Merciful. **{Indeed Allah is, to the people, Kind and Merciful.} [Qur'ān 2:143]**

المتن

(١٨١) وَلا يُطِيقُونَ إِلّا ما كَلَّفَهُمْ.

(181) And they are only able to do what He obligated them to do.

الشرح

هذا فيه نظر؛ بل يطيقون أكثر مما كلفهم، ولكن الله يريد بهم اليسر ولا يريد بهم العسر، فالله وضع عنهم المشقة، وشرع لهم الدين اليسر، ونهاهم عن الزيادة علىٰ الاعتدال، فلا يجوز للإنسان أن يصلي كل الليل، وكذلك لا يجوز له ترك الزواج، قال عليه الصلاة والسلام: «**أما أنا فأصلي وأنام وأتزوج النساء وأصوم وأفطر، فمن رغب عن سنتي فليس مني**»، فالله لا يكلف ما يشق عليهم، والله لو كلفهم لأطاقوا، ولكن لا يرضىٰ لهم المشقة والعسر.

This is questionable. Rather, they are able to do more than what He has obligated them to. However, Allah ﷻ wants to make matters easy on them rather than difficult. Thus, Allah ﷻ has rid them of their burdens and has prescribed for them a religion of ease and has forbidden doing more than what is moderate. So it is not permissible for someone to pray for the entire night or to abandon marriage. The Prophet ﷺ said: "But I pray and I sleep, and I marry women, and I fast and I break my fast; so whoever forsakes my *sunnah* is not of me."[115] Allah does not obligate anyone to do what causes distress, and were Allah to obligate people, they would have had the faculties to do so; however, He is not pleased with them having hardship and distress.

المتن

(١٨٢) وَهُوَ تَفْسِيرُ: «لا حَوْلَ وَلا قُوَّةَ إِلّا بِاللهِ». نَقُولُ: لا حِيلَةَ لِأَحَدٍ، وَلا حَرَكَةَ

115 Al-Bukhārī, no. 5063; Muslim, no. 1401.

لِأَحَدٍ، وَلَا تَحَوُّلَ لِأَحَدٍ عَنْ مَعْصِيَةِ اللهِ إِلَّا بِمَعُونَةِ اللهِ، وَلَا قُوَّةَ لِأَحَدٍ عَلَىٰ إِقَامَةِ
طَاعَةِ اللهِ وَالثَّبَاتِ عَلَيْهَا إِلَّا بِتَوْفِيقِ اللهِ.

(182) This is what it means to say, *"Lā ḥawla wa lā quwwata illā bi 'llāh"* (There is neither change nor strength but from Allah). We say: There is no ploy or movement for anyone, and no one can turn from Allah's disobedience, without Allah's help; and there is no strength for anyone to obey Allah and be steadfast upon doing so without Allah's grace.

الشرح

(لا حول) أي: لا تحول من حال إلىٰ حال (إلا بالله) عز وجل وإعانته. وكذلك:
ليس لك قوة إلا من قوة الله عز وجل، ففي هذا تسليم وبراءة من الحول والقوة،
فالإنسان لا يُعجب بحوله ولا بقوته، وإنما يرجع إلىٰ الله عز وجل، فتستعين
بالله، فيعينك علىٰ الطاعة، ومن التحول من المعصية إلىٰ الطاعة، ومن الكفر
إلىٰ الإسلام، فكل شيء بحول الله وقوته، ولو وكلك إلىٰ حولك لم تستطع،
وكذلك الكد والكسب لطلب المال، هذا الكد والتعب منك، ولكن التوفيق
ووضع البركة من الله عز وجل.

Lā ḥawla, that is, there is *no turning* from one state to another *except by Allah* (*illā bi 'llāh*), the Almighty, and by His help. Likewise, it means *"you have no strength unless it is by the strength of Allah"*. This entails submission and the disavowal of one's own ability to *change* (*ḥawl*) and one's own strength (*quwwah*). One should not be impressed by one's own power and strength but should instead return to Allah the Almighty and ask for help in being obedient and in making the shift from sin to obedience, and from disbelief to Islām. All things are through Allah's intervention and strength; and if He were to entrust you to yourself, you would not be able to do anything. Nonetheless, the toil and work you do to seek money emanates from you, however, success and blessing are from Allah the Almighty.

❀❀❀

المتن

(١٨٣) وَكُلُّ شَيْءٍ يَجْرِي بِمَشِيئَةِ اللهِ تَعالَىٰ وَعِلْمِهِ وَقَضائِهِ وَقَدَرِهِ.

(183) Everything happens according to Allah's will, knowledge, decree, and predestination.

الشرح

لا يقع في ملكه شيء إلا بعلمه وتقديره ﴿وَمَا تَشَآءُونَ إِلَّآ أَن يَشَآءَ ٱللَّهُ رَبُّ ٱلْعَٰلَمِينَ ۝٢٩﴾ [التكوير:٢٩].

Nothing occurs in His kingdom without His knowledge and pre-decree. **{And you do not will except that Allah wills – Lord of the worlds.} [Qur'ān 81:29]**

فهو ما قضاه وقدره، وكتبه في اللوح المحفوظ، فكل ما يجري في الكون فهو بقضاء الله وقدره.

It is what He has decreed and predetermined and what is written in the Preserved Tablet. Everything that happens in the universe is by the decree and determination of Allah.

المتن

(١٨٤) غَلَبَتْ مَشِيئَتُهُ الْمَشِيئاتِ كُلَّها.

(184) His will prevails over the will of all others.

الشرح

قال تعالىٰ: ﴿وَمَا تَشَآءُونَ إِلَّآ أَن يَشَآءَ ٱللَّهُ﴾ [التكوير:٢٩] اثبت للعبد مشيئته، ولكنها داخلة تحت مشيئة الله، وأن العبد لا يستطيع المشيئة إلا بمشيئة الله.

Allah ﷻ says: **{And you do not will except that Allah wills – Lord of**

the worlds.} [Qurʾān 81:29] Here, it is affirmed that people have a will; but it is included under Allah's will, i.e. one cannot have a will except by Allah's ﷻ will.

المتن

(١٨٥) وَغَلَبَ قضاؤُهُ الْحِيَلَ كُلَّها.

(185) And His decree prevails over the ploys of all others.

الشرح

مهما عملت من الأسباب ومن الأمور، إذا لم يقدر الله المسبب فلا تنفعك الأسباب، وجميع الأعمال لا تنفع إذا لم يُقدِّر الله عز وجل لك النفع بها، فأنت عليك فعل السبب، والتوفيق على الله، فأنت مأمور بفعل الأسباب.

Whatever means you take, they will not be to your advantage if Allah has not predestined the result. All actions are of no benefit if Allah ﷻ has not predestined that they will benefit you. Your duty is to take the means and success is from Allah. You are commanded to do what is a cause of the result.

المتن

(١٨٦) يَفْعَلُ ما يَشاءُ وَهُوَ غَيْرُ ظالِمٍ أَبَدًا، تَقَدَّسَ عَنْ كُلِّ سُوءٍ وَحَيْنٍ، وَتَنَزَّهَ عَنْ كُلِّ عَيْبٍ وَشَيْنٍ.

(186) He does what He wishes, but He is never unjust. He is pure from every evil and end, and He is free from every flaw.

الشرح

فالله يفعل ما يشاء من الخير والشر، والنعمة والنقمة، وهو غير ظالم لعباده؛

لأنه يضع الأشياء في مواضعها، فيضع النعمة والتوفيق لمن يتأهل لذلك، ويحرم من التوفيق ومن الطاعة من لا يستحق ذلك، وهو غير ظالم، فلا يعذب المطيع الصالح، ولا يثيب العاصي على معصيته.

Allah does whatever He so wills of good or bad, blessing or affliction. He is not unjust to His servants, as He puts matters in their right places. He favours and gives success to those who are suitable for it; and He deprives those who do not deserve to be under His grace and obedience. Yet He is not unjust. He does not punish someone who obeys him and is righteous as He does not reward someone who disobeys Him for his disobedience.

فالله سبحانه الكامل في ذاته، والكامل في أسمائه وصفاته، والكامل في أفعاله وخلقه سبحانه وتعالى.

Thus, Allah the Almighty is perfect in His essence (*dhāt*), perfect in His names and attributes and perfect in His actions and creation.

المتن

(١٨٧) ﴿لا يُسْأَلُ عَمَّا يَفْعَلُ وَهُمْ يُسْأَلُونَ﴾ [الأنبياء: ٢٣].

(187) ***{He is not questioned about what He does, but they will be questioned.}*** **[Qur'ān 21:23]**

الشرح

وكذلك لا يُسأل سبحانه عما يفعل؛ لأن كل شيء يفعله لحكمة، وواقع موقعه، فأما العباد فيسألون؛ لأنهم يخطئون، ويضعون الأمور في غير مواضعها، ففيه فرق بين الخالق والمخلوق، فالله لا يقع في أفعاله خلل، أما العبد فعنده ظلم وحسد وكبر، وعنده أمور تقتضي أنه يخطئ في أموره وتصرفاته.

Allah ﷻ is not to be questioned about what He does, because everything He does is with wisdom and is done in the proper way. People, on the other hand, are questioned, because they are prone to make mistakes and to put things out of place. There is a difference between the Creator and created things. There is nothing that Allah ﷻ does that is flawed. People, on the other hand, are full of injustice, envy and pride, and they have traits that dictate them making mistakes in their affairs and actions.

المتن

(١٨٨) وَفِي دُعاءِ الأَحْياءِ وَصَدَقاتِهِمْ مَنْفَعَةٌ لِلأَمْواتِ.

(188) As for the dead, they will benefit from the supplications and *ṣadaqah* (charity) of the living.

الشرح

هذه مسألة فقهية، ولها تعلق بالعقيدة:

This is a matter of jurisprudence (*fiqh*), but it is associated with creed (*ʿaqīdah*):

قال عليه الصلاة والسلام: **«إذا مات ابن آدم انقطع عمله إلا من ثلاث: صدقة جارية، أو علم ينتفع به، أو ولد صالح يدعو له»**.

The Prophet ﷺ said: "When the son of Ādam dies, all of his deeds come to an end except for three: ongoing charity, beneficial knowledge or a righteous child who prays for him."[116]

فالعبد ينقطع عمله بموته، إلا ما تسبب في بقائه بعد موته، مثل الصدقة الجارية، كوقف مسجد أو مدرسة يدرس فيها، فما دام نفعها فأجرها يجري ما دام هذا الوقف ينتفع به.

One's deeds come to an end after death, except for that which is a cause for remaining after death, such as an ongoing charity, like founding a mosque or a school. As long as there is benefit, the reward is ongoing as long as this charitable trust (*waqf*) is a source of benefit.

116 Muslim, no. 1631.

(أو علم) بأن يكون قد درّس الفقه أو العقيدة، وصار له تلاميذ، فيجري عليه أجر تعليمه، أو ألّف كتباً تنفع الناس، فيجري أجره، وهذا من العلم الذي علّمه.

The second deed mentioned was beneficial knowledge, e.g. that one has taught jurisprudence or creed and has students, the reward for one's teaching is then ongoing, or if one authored books that are of benefit to people, one's reward is ongoing. This is from knowledge that one teaches.

(أو ولد صالح يدعو له) فهو تزوج من أجل إعفاف نفسه، وطلباً للذرية الصالحة، فجاءه ولد صالح، وهذا مما تسبب فيه، قال عليه الصلاة والسلام: **«إن أطيب ما أكلتم من كسبكم، وإن أولادكم من كسبكم»**.

"Or a righteous child who prays for him": One marries to be chaste and to have righteous offspring, so when such a person is given a righteous child, it is something that he is a cause in. The Prophet ﷺ said: "The best of what you consume is what you have worked for, and your children are something you have worked for."[117]

فإن كان صالحاً يدعو له بعد موته، فإن دعاءه يصل إليه، وهذا من عمله الذي تسبب فيه فينفعه عمل غيره.

If children are righteous, they supplicate for their parents after death and their supplications reach them. It counts as a person's deeds since one plays a role in it, so the deeds of someone else are of benefit to that person.

وغير هذه المسألة محل الخلاف، قال سبحانه: ﴿وَأَن لَّيْسَ لِلْإِنسَٰنِ إِلَّا مَا سَعَىٰ ۝٣٩﴾ [النجم:٣٩] منطوق الآية: أن عمل الإنسان لا ينفع غيره، إلا ما تسبب فيه، فأخذ طائفة من العلماء بهذه الآية، وقال: لا ينفعه إلا عمله مطلقاً، لكن النبي صلىٰ الله عليه وسلم أخبر بأشياء تنفع الميت من عمل غيره، مثل الدعاء والاستغفار ﴿رَبَّنَا ٱغْفِرْ لَنَا وَلِإِخْوَٰنِنَا ٱلَّذِينَ سَبَقُونَا بِٱلْإِيمَٰنِ﴾ [الحشر:١٠]، ﴿وَٱسْتَغْفِرْ لِذَنۢبِكَ وَلِلْمُؤْمِنِينَ وَٱلْمُؤْمِنَٰتِ﴾ [محمد:١٩]، هذا يشمل الأموات أيضاً.

117 Abū Dāwūd, no. 3528; al-Tirmidhī, no. 1362. Al-Tirmidhī said: This *ḥadīth* is *ḥasan ṣaḥīḥ*.

Other issues are points of disagreement, for example, Allah ﷻ says: **{And that there is not for man except that [good] for which he strives.} [Qurʾān 53:39]** Explicitly, the verse pronounces that the works of man are of no benefit to others, except those things in which someone is a cause. Some of the scholars held fast to this verse and said that one does not benefit from anyone's work besides their own, without exception. However, the Prophet ﷺ told us of some things that benefit the dead that are from the deeds of someone else, such as supplications and asking forgiveness. **{Our Lord, forgive us and our brothers who preceded us in faith.} [Qurʾān 59:10] {And ask forgiveness for your sin and for the believing men and believing women.} [Qurʾān 47:19]** This also includes the dead.

والنبي صلىٰ الله عليه وسلم أمر المسلمين إذا دفنوا أخاهم أن يقفوا علىٰ قبره، وأن يستغفروا له ويسألوا له التثبيت، كذلك الصدقة تنفع الميت، جاء رجل إلىٰ النبي صلىٰ الله عليه وسلم وأخبره بأن أمه ماتت، ولو تكلمت لتصدقت، أفأتصدّق عنها؟ قال: «**نعم**».

The Prophet ﷺ also commanded the believers to ask for forgiveness and strength for their brothers when they bury them and stand at their grave sites.[118] Moreover, charity benefits the dead. A man came to the Prophet ﷺ and told him that his mother died and he said that if she were able to will, she would give in charity. He asked, "Should I give charity on her behalf?" He replied: "Yes."[119]

كذلك الحج ينفع غيره، كما جاءت به الأدلة، كما في حديث شبرمة، قال عليه الصلاة والسلام: «**حج عن نفسك، ثم حج عن شبرمة**» فهذا عمل للغير ينفع الميت، كذلك لما جاءت امرأة تسأل النبي صلىٰ الله عليه وسلم عن الحج عن أمها: أنها أدركتها فريضة الحج ولم تحج، أفأحج عنها؟ قال: «**نعم، حجي عن أمك**». فتكون هذه الأشياء: الدعاء والاستغفار والصدقة والحج والعمرة، تكون

118 It is related that ʿUthmān ﷺ said that the Messenger of Allah ﷺ said: "Ask forgiveness and strength for your brother, for he is being asked now." Abū Dāwūd, no. 3221; al-Ḥākim, no. 1/370. Al-Ḥākim said: "This *ḥadīth* is authentic (*ṣaḥīḥ*) and [al-Bukhārī and Muslim] did not cite it."

119 Al-Bukhārī, no. 2760; Muslim, no. 1004.

نافعة للميت من عمل غيره، فتكون مخصصة للآية ﴿وَأَن لَّيۡسَ لِلۡإِنسَٰنِ إِلَّا مَا سَعَىٰ ﴿٣٩﴾﴾ [النجم:٣٩].

The Ḥajj rites can also be to the advantage of someone else, as presented in the evidence, like in 'the *ḥadīth* of Shubrumah'. The Prophet ﷺ said: "Perform Ḥajj on your own behalf and then perform Ḥajj on behalf of Shubrumah."[120] This is the deed of someone else and it is to the advantage of the dead. Also, a woman came to the Prophet ﷺ and asked about Ḥajj on behalf of her mother: "The Ḥajj was obligated upon her in her lifetime, yet she did not perform it. Shall I perform it on her behalf?" He replied: "Yes, perform Ḥajj on your mother's behalf."[121] So, these things: prayer, asking for forgiveness, charity, Ḥajj, and 'Umrah are others' actions that benefit the dead. Therefore, they specify the verse: **{And that there is not for man except that [good] for which he strives.} [Qur'ān 53:39]**

وغلت طائفة في هذا وقالت: ينفع الميت كل شيء من عمل غيره، فيستأجرون المقرئين يقرءون للميت، فمثل هذا العمل لا ينفع الميت ولا الحي؛ لأن القارئ أخذ علىٰ قراءته أجرة، فليس له ثواب، ومن ناحية ثانية: أن هذا الأمر مبتدع، ليس عليه دليل، وسبحان الله! لو جعل الأجرة التي يعطيها المقرئ صدقة عن الميت صار تابعـًا للسنة وينفع الميت، أما علىٰ وجه البدعة فلا ينفع الميت ولا الحي، وهذا نتيجة ترك السنة.

One group went to extremes and said that all of the deeds of others are of benefit to the dead. Hence people even hire Qur'ān reciters to recite Qur'ān for the dead. Deeds such as these are not to the benefit of the dead or the living, because the reciter takes a fee for reciting, so he does not get a divine reward. And from another aspect, doing so is an innovation as there is no evidence to support it. *Subḥāna 'llāh!* If the fee paid to the reciter were given as charity on behalf of the deceased, it would have been in accord with the Sunnah and to the benefit of the deceased. But in an innovated manner, it is neither to the advantage of the dead nor the living. This is the result of abandonment of the Sunnah.

---

120 Abū Dāwūd, no. 1811; Ibn Mājah, no. 2903; Ibn Khuzaymah, no. 3039.
121 Al-Bukhārī, no. 1852.

المتن

(١٨٩) واللهُ تَعالَىٰ يَسْتَجِيبُ الدَّعَواتِ وَيَقْضِي الْحاجاتِ.

(189) Allah the Most High answers supplications and fulfils the needs.

الشرح

هذه من صفات الله عز وجل أنه يجيب من دعاه، قال سبحانه ﴿وَإِذَا سَأَلَكَ عِبَادِى عَنِّى فَإِنِّى قَرِيبٌۖ أُجِيبُ دَعْوَةَ ٱلدَّاعِ إِذَا دَعَانِۖ﴾ [البقرة:١٨٦].

These are some of the attributes of Allah ﷻ, namely that He answers those who supplicate to Him. Allah ﷻ says: **{And when My servants ask you, [O Muḥammad], concerning Me – indeed I am near. I respond to the invocation of the supplicant when he calls upon Me.} [Qur'ān 2:186]**

وأمر الله عز وجل بدعائه فقال: ﴿ٱدْعُونِىٓ أَسْتَجِبْ لَكُمْۚ إِنَّ ٱلَّذِينَ يَسْتَكْبِرُونَ عَنْ عِبَادَتِى سَيَدْخُلُونَ جَهَنَّمَ دَاخِرِينَ ۝٦٠﴾ [غافر:٦٠]، وقال سبحانه: ﴿أَمَّن يُجِيبُ ٱلْمُضْطَرَّ إِذَا دَعَاهُ وَيَكْشِفُ ٱلسُّوٓءَ وَيَجْعَلُكُمْ خُلَفَآءَ ٱلْأَرْضِۗ﴾ [النمل:٦٢]

Allah the Almighty commands us to call upon Him, saying: **{And your Lord says, 'Call upon Me; I will respond to you.' Indeed, those who disdain My worship will enter Hell [rendered] contemptible.} [Qur'ān 40:60]** Allah also says: **{Is He [not best] who responds to the desperate one when he calls upon Him and removes evil and makes you inheritors of the earth?} [Qur'ān 27:62]**

إلىٰ غير ذلك من الآيات التي فيها الأمر بالدعاء وإجابة الدعاء، وهذا من كرمه وجوده وإحسانه، يأمر عباده بدعائه ليستجيب لهم، مع أنه غني عنهم، ولكن لعلمه سبحانه وتعالىٰ بحاجتهم أمرهم بدعائه، وفي الحديث: **«من لا يسأل الله يغضب عليه»**.

There are also other verses that include the command to supplicate and that

Allah answers it. It is out of Allah's generosity and kindness that He commands His servants to supplicate to Him in order that He answers them, although He is free of need of them. However, because He knows their need, He commands them to supplicate to Him. It has been related in a *ḥadīth:* "Allah is angry with those who do not ask of Him."[122]

والدعاء أعظم أنواع العبادة؛ لقوله عليه الصلاة والسلام: «الدعاء هو العبادة».

Supplicating to Allah ﷻ is the greatest kind of worship, as the Prophet ﷺ said: "Supplication is worship."[123]

وكما أنه أمر بدعائه، نهى عن دعاء غيره والإشراك به في الدعاء، فقال: ﴿وَأَنَّ ٱلْمَسَٰجِدَ لِلَّهِ فَلَا تَدْعُواْ مَعَ ٱللَّهِ أَحَدًا ﴿١٨﴾﴾ [الجن:١٨]، ﴿قُلْ إِنَّمَآ أَدْعُواْ رَبِّي وَلَآ أُشْرِكُ بِهِۦٓ أَحَدًا ﴿٢٠﴾﴾ [الجن:٢٠]، ﴿وَمَن يَدْعُ مَعَ ٱللَّهِ إِلَٰهًا ءَاخَرَ لَا بُرْهَٰنَ لَهُۥ بِهِۦ فَإِنَّمَا حِسَابُهُۥ عِندَ رَبِّهِۦٓۚ إِنَّهُۥ لَا يُفْلِحُ ٱلْكَٰفِرُونَ ﴿١١٧﴾﴾ [المؤمنون:١١٧].

As He commanded us to make *du'ā'* to Him, so has He forbidden us from making it to anyone besides Him and from associating anything with Him in prayer or *du'ā'*. Allah says: **{And [He revealed] that the *masjids* are for Allah, so do not invoke with Allah anyone.} [Qur'ān 72:18] {Say, [O Muḥammad], 'I only invoke my Lord and do not associate with Him anyone.'} [Qur'ān 72:20] {And whoever invokes besides Allah another deity for which he has no proof – then his account is only with his Lord. Indeed, the disbelievers will not succeed.} [Qur'ān 23:117]**

فلا يجوز دعاء غير الله، ومن دعا غير الله فهو مشرك، سواء كان المدعو ملكـًا أو نبيـًا أو وليـًا، فقد أشرك الشرك الأكبر ﴿وَمَنْ أَضَلُّ مِمَّن يَدْعُواْ مِن دُونِ ٱللَّهِ مَن لَّا يَسْتَجِيبُ لَهُۥٓ إِلَىٰ يَوْمِ ٱلْقِيَٰمَةِ وَهُمْ عَن دُعَآئِهِمْ غَٰفِلُونَ ﴿٥﴾﴾ [الأحقاف:٥]، ﴿إِن تَدْعُوهُمْ لَا يَسْمَعُواْ دُعَآءَكُمْ وَلَوْ سَمِعُواْ مَا ٱسْتَجَابُواْ لَكُمْۖ وَيَوْمَ ٱلْقِيَٰمَةِ يَكْفُرُونَ

122 Aḥmad, 2/477; al-Tirmidhī, no. 3370; Ibn Mājah, no. 3827; al-Ḥākim, 1/491. Al-Ḥākim said that it is authentic and al-Dhahabī concurred.

123 Abū Dāwūd, no. 1479; al-Tirmidhī, no. 3369; Ibn Mājah, no. 3828. Al-Tirmidhī said: *ḥasan ṣaḥīḥ*.

بِشِرْكِكُمْ﴾ [فاطر:١٤] فسماه شركًا، وقال سبحانه ﴿قُلِ ٱدْعُوا۟ ٱلَّذِينَ زَعَمْتُم مِّن دُونِ ٱللَّهِ لَا يَمْلِكُونَ مِثْقَالَ ذَرَّةٍ فِى ٱلسَّمَٰوَٰتِ وَلَا فِى ٱلْأَرْضِ وَمَا لَهُمْ فِيهِمَا مِن شِرْكٍ وَمَا لَهُۥ مِنْهُم مِّن ظَهِيرٍ ۝٢٢ وَلَا تَنفَعُ ٱلشَّفَٰعَةُ عِندَهُۥٓ إِلَّا لِمَنْ أَذِنَ لَهُۥ﴾ [سبأ:٢٢-٢٣].

So it is impermissible to invoke anything other than Allah ﷻ. Anyone who does this is a polytheist, regardless whether what is prayed to is an angel, a prophet, or a saint (*walī*), and such a person has committed major polytheism (*shirk akbar*). **{And who is more astray than he who invokes besides Allah those who will not respond to him until the Day of Resurrection, and they, of their invocation, are unaware.} [Qurʾān 46:5] {If you invoke them, they do not hear your supplication; and if they heard, they would not respond to you. And on the Day of Resurrection they will deny your association.} [Qurʾān 35:14]** Here, it is called *association* (*shirk*). Allah also says: **{Say, [O Muḥammad], 'Invoke those you claim [as deities] besides Allah.' They do not possess an atom's weight [of ability] in the heavens or on the earth, and they do not have therein any partnership [with Him], nor is there for Him from among them any assistant. And intercession does not benefit with Him except for one whom He permits.} [Qurʾān 34:22-23]**

فالدعاء لا يكون إلا لله، فلا يدعىٰ أحد من دونه من الأحياء أو الأموات، أيًّا كان هذا المدعو.

Thus, *duʿāʾ* is to be made only to Allah; no one from the living or dead is to be supplicated to besides Allah, whatever that thing may be.

والدعاء علىٰ قسمين:

There are two types of supplication:

الأول: دعاء عبادة، وهو الثناء علىٰ الله عز وجل في أسمائه وصفاته وأفعاله، فالذي يسبحه ويكبره ويحمده ويثني عليه قد دعاه دعاء عبادة.

One. Supplication of worship (*duʿāʾ ʿibādah*), which is to praise Allah ﷻ for His names, attributes and actions. If someone glorifies, magnifies and praises Allah ﷻ, then one has supplicated to Him in the form of worship.

الثاني: دعاء مسألة، وهو طلب الحوائج من الله عز وجل، وكلاهما تضمنته سورة الفاتحة، فأولها إلىٰ نصفها دعاء عبادة، إلىٰ قوله ﴿إِيَّاكَ نَعْبُدُ﴾ وآخر السورة مسألة.

Two. Supplication of asking (*du'ā' mas'alah*), which is to request one's needs from Allah ﷻ. Both of these types are included in *Sūrat al-Fātiḥah.* Its start until the middle is 'supplication of worship', up to where Allah ﷻ says: ***{It is You we worship},*** and the last part of the *sūrah* is a 'supplication of asking'.

والعلماء يقولون: دعاء العبادة مستلزم لدعاء المسألة، ودعاء المسألة متضمن لدعاء العبادة.

The scholars say that the supplication of worship dictates the supplication of asking and the supplication of asking is inclusive of the supplication of worship.

والله عز وجل وعد من دعاه أن يستجيب له، وقد يقول قائل: أنا دعوت ولم يستجب لي.

Allah the Almighty has promised to answer anyone who invokes Him. One might say, I made *du'ā'* but it has not been answered.

والجواب أن يُقال: المانع من عندك أنت، الدعاء سبب من الأسباب، والنتيجة لا تحصل إلا إذا انتفت الموانع، فقد يكون مانع من الموانع منع استجابة دعوتك، إما أن تكون دعوت بقلب غافل لاهٍ فأنىٰ يُستجاب لقلب غافل لاهٍ؟ كما في الحديث، أو أنك تأكل الحرام وتشرب الحرام وتلبس الحرام، قال عليه الصلاة والسلام في الذي: «**يطيل السفر، أشعث أغبر، يمد يديه إلىٰ السماء: يا رب، يارب، يارب، ومطعمه حرام وملبسه حرام، وغذي بالحرام، فأنىٰ يُستجاب له**»؟

It is said in response: The impediment is from your side. *Duʿā'* is a cause, and the result is only achieved if all of the impediments are absent. It might be that there is some impediment that impedes the answering of your *duʿā'*. It is either you supplicated with a heedless and negligent heart (and how can a *duʿā'* from a heedless and negligent heart be answered? As related in a *ḥadīth*), or because you eat, drink, and wear what is unlawful. The Prophet ﷺ said regarding one who "has travelled at length, is dishevelled and dusty, and raises his hands to the sky, saying, 'O Lord, O Lord, O Lord'; and yet his food is unlawful, his clothes are unlawful, and he is nourished from what is unlawful. How will his prayers be answered?"[124]

أو يدعو بإثم أو قطيعة رحم، فلا يُستجاب له، هذا من ناحية.

It could also be that someone prays for a sin or to sever family ties, so the invocation is not answered. This is one aspect.

ومن ناحية ثانية: أن الله عز وجل أعلم بمصالحك، قد يعجل لك الإجابة وقد يؤخرها، وقد يصرف عنك من السوء مثلها، وأنت لا تدري، كما في الحديث: **«ما من رجل يدعو الله بدعوة ليس فيها إثم ولا قطيعة رحم إلا أعطاه بها إحدىٰ ثلاث: إما أن يعجل دعوته، وإما أن يؤخرها له، وإما أن يصرف عنه من السوء مثلها»**.

From another aspect, Allah the Almighty knows better what is in your best interests than you do. Allah ﷻ may answer your prayer promptly or delay it, or He may take some harm equal to it away from you, yet you do not know. It has been related in a *ḥadīth:* "Whenever one prays to Allah for something that does not involve sin or the severing of family ties, He gives him one of three things: He either immediately answers it, delays it or keeps an equal amount of evil away from him."[125]

أهل الضلال يقولون: لا حاجة للدعاء؛ لأن الأمر إذا كان قدر فلا يحتاج إلىٰ دعاء؛ لأنه إذا كان الأمر قدر لك فإنه سيأتيك، ولو لم تدع، وإن كان لم يقض لك ويقدر فإنك لو دعوت لم يحصل لك ولا يقدر، وهذا ضلال، والعياذ بالله،

124 Muslim, no. 1015.
125 Al-Tirmidhī, no. 3390.

ومخالف لكلام الله عز وجل.

People of misguidance say, "There is no need to supplicate because matters are predetermined. There is no need for invocation because if something has been written for you, then it will happen, even if you don't supplicate; and if it were not decreed and predetermined for you, then even if you made *du'ā'*, it would not occur or be decreed". This is misguidance and Allah ﷻ is our refuge; it contradicts the speech of Allah ﷻ.

والجواب: أنه لا تعارض بين الدعاء والقضاء والقدر، الذي قضىٰ وقدر هو الذي أمر بالدعاء، والدعاء سبب من الأسباب، والمسبب هو الله عز وجل، وهناك بعض الأشياء قدرت علىٰ أسباب، إذا وجدت أسبابها وجدت مسبباتها، والدعاء سبب.

The response is that there is no contradiction between *du'ā'* and the divine decree and predestination. He who has decreed and predestined has also commanded that we supplicate to Him. *Du'ā'* is a cause and it is Allah ﷻ who is the ultimate causer. Some things are predestined according to the causes and when the causes [i.e. when *du'ā' is made*] come into existence, the results also come into existence, and *du'ā'* is a cause.

المتن

(١٩٠) وَيَمْلِكُ كُلَّ شَيْءٍ وَلا يَمْلِكُهُ شَيْءٌ.

(190) All things are under His dominion, and He is under the dominion of none.

الشرح

من صفات الله عز وجل: أنه يملك كل شيء، فكل ما في الكون فهو ملك له ﴿ تَبَٰرَكَ ٱلَّذِى بِيَدِهِ ٱلْمُلْكُ وَهُوَ عَلَىٰ كُلِّ شَىْءٍ قَدِيرٌ ۝١﴾ [الملك:١]، وقال تعالىٰ: ﴿ لَهُۥ مُلْكُ ٱلسَّمَٰوَٰتِ وَٱلْأَرْضِ ﴾ [الحديد:٢].

Among the attributes of Allah the Almighty is that He possesses everything. All things in the universe are possessions of His. **{Blessed is He in whose hand is dominion, and He is over all things competent.} [Qurʾān 67:1]** Allah ﷻ also says: **{His is the dominion of the heavens and earth.} [Qurʾān 57:2]**

فلا يخرج شيء عن ملكه، والناس وما يملكون فهم ملكه سبحانه وتعالىٰ: ﴿قُلِ ٱللَّهُمَّ مَٰلِكَ ٱلۡمُلۡكِ تُؤۡتِي ٱلۡمُلۡكَ مَن تَشَآءُ وَتَنزِعُ ٱلۡمُلۡكَ مِمَّن تَشَآءُ وَتُعِزُّ مَن تَشَآءُ وَتُذِلُّ مَن تَشَآءُۖ بِيَدِكَ ٱلۡخَيۡرُۖ إِنَّكَ عَلَىٰ كُلِّ شَيۡءٖ قَدِيرٞ ﴿٢٦﴾﴾ [آل عمران:٢٦].

There is nothing outside of His kingdom: all people and all that they possess are part of His kingdom. **{Say, 'O Allah, Owner of Sovereignty, You give sovereignty to whom You will and You take sovereignty away from whom You will. You honour whom You will and You humble whom You will. In Your hand is [all] good. Indeed, You are over all things competent.'} [Qurʾān 3:26]**

فلا أحد يفرض ويلزم ويملي علىٰ الله شيئًا؛ لأن الناس عباد لله فقراء إليه، كما قال سبحانه: ﴿وَرَبُّكَ يَخۡلُقُ مَا يَشَآءُ وَيَخۡتَارُۗ﴾ [القصص:٦٨]، وقال سبحانه: ﴿إِنَّ ٱللَّهَ يَفۡعَلُ مَا يَشَآءُ﴾ [الحج:١٨].

Thus, there is no one who imposes anything upon Allah nor compels Him to do anything nor dictates anything to Him. That is because people are servants of Allah ﷻ who are in need of Him, as Allah ﷻ says: **{And your Lord creates what He wills and chooses; not for them was the choice. Exalted is Allah and high above what they associate with Him.} [Qurʾān 28:68]** Allah ﷻ also says: **{Indeed, Allah does what He wills."} [Qurʾān 22:18]**

وإنما هو سبحانه يدبر الأمر بمفرده، ويجريه علىٰ حكمته سبحانه وتعالىٰ.

It is no one but Allah ﷻ who is in charge of all of the affairs and He is alone. He arranges everything according to His wisdom.

المتن

(١٩١) وَلا غِنَىٰ عَنِ اللهِ تَعالَىٰ طَرْفَةَ عَيْنٍ.

(191) Nothing is independent of Allah, even for the blink of an eye.

الشرح

الله جل وعلا هو الغني الحميد، والخلق كلهم فقراء إلىٰ الله، وما أحد منهم يمكن أن يستغني عن الله.

Allah the Almighty is free of need and He is worthy of praise. All created beings are in need of Allah ﷻ; there is no one that can dispense with Allah .

قال تعالىٰ: ﴿يَـٰٓأَيُّهَا ٱلنَّاسُ أَنتُمُ ٱلْفُقَرَآءُ إِلَى ٱللَّهِ ۖ وَٱللَّهُ هُوَ ٱلْغَنِىُّ ٱلْحَمِيدُ ﴿١٥﴾﴾ [فاطر:١٥]. فلا أحد يمكن أن يستغني عن الله، ولو كان عنده ملك الدنيا، فالملوك فقراء إلىٰ الله، وكذلك الأغنياء، فلا أحد يستغني عن الله، لا الملائكة المقربون ولا من دونهم من الخلق.

Allah ﷻ says: **{O mankind, you are those in need of Allah, while Allah is the Free of need, the Praiseworthy.} [Qur'ān 35:15]** No one can dispense with Allah, even if one had the world as a kingdom. All kings are in need of Allah and likewise all of the rich. There is no one who can dispense with Allah, neither the angels who are drawn near, nor any other creation lower than them.

المتن

(١٩٢) وَمَنِ اسْتَغْنَىٰ عَنِ اللهِ طَرْفَةَ عَيْنٍ فَقَدْ كَفَرَ، وَصارَ مِنْ أَهْلِ الْحَيْنِ.

(192) He who thinks himself independent of Allah for the blink of an eye has disbelieved and has become one of those who will be destroyed.

الشرح

من زعم أنه في غنىً عن الله، وأنه مستغن عن الله، فقد كفر وخرج من الملة، فالواجب على العبد أن يظهر لله ضعفه، ولا يعجبه ما هو فيه من القوة والصحة والغنى؛ لأن الأمور بيد الله عز وجل، فلا يمكن الاستغناء عن الله عز وجل.

If a person claims that he is free of the need of Allah ﷻ and that he can dispense with Allah, then he has disbelieved and abandoned the religion. It is incumbent on each person to demonstrate their weakness to Allah and not to be impressed by their strength, health, and wealth. These matters are in Allah's hands and therefore, it is not possible to dispense with Allah the Almighty.

المتن

(١٩٣) والله يَغْضَبُ وَيَرْضَىٰ، لا كَأَحَدٍ مِنَ الْوَرَىٰ.

(193) Allah becomes angered and pleased, but not like anyone of the creation.

الشرح

من صفات الله عز وجل الفعلية: أنه يغضب ويرضى، قال سبحانه: ﴿وَٱلسَّٰبِقُونَ ٱلْأَوَّلُونَ مِنَ ٱلْمُهَٰجِرِينَ وَٱلْأَنصَارِ وَٱلَّذِينَ ٱتَّبَعُوهُم بِإِحْسَٰنٍ رَّضِيَ ٱللَّهُ عَنْهُمْ وَرَضُواْ عَنْهُ﴾ [التوبة:١٠٠] فالله يرضى عن عباده، قال تعالى: ﴿وَرِضْوَٰنٌ مِّنَ ٱللَّهِ أَكْبَرُ﴾ [التوبة:٧٢]، وقال تعالى: ﴿لَّقَدْ رَضِيَ ٱللَّهُ عَنِ ٱلْمُؤْمِنِينَ إِذْ يُبَايِعُونَكَ تَحْتَ ٱلشَّجَرَةِ﴾ [الفتح:١٨]

Among the active attributes (*al-ṣifat al-fiʿlıyah*) of Allah ﷻ is that He becomes angry and becomes pleased. Allah ﷻ says: **{And the first forerunners [in the faith] among the Muhājirīn and the Anṣār and those who followed them with good conduct – Allah is pleased with them and they are pleased with Him.} [Qur'ān 9:100]** Thus, Allah becomes pleased with His servants. Allah says: **{But approval *(riḍwān)* from Allah is greater.} [Qur'ān 9:72]** Allah ﷻ also says: **{Certainly was Allah pleased with the believers when they pledged allegiance to you, [O Muḥammad], under the tree.} [Qur'ān 48:18]**

وهو كذلك يغضب سبحانه وتعالىٰ: ﴿قُلْ هَلْ أُنَبِّئُكُم بِشَرٍّ مِّن ذَٰلِكَ مَثُوبَةً عِندَ ٱللَّهِ ۚ مَن لَّعَنَهُ ٱللَّهُ وَغَضِبَ عَلَيْهِ﴾ [المائدة: ٦٠] فالله يغضب علىٰ من عصاه ويمقته، والمقت هو أشد البغض، قال تعالىٰ: ﴿وَمَن يَقْتُلْ مُؤْمِنًا مُّتَعَمِّدًا فَجَزَآؤُهُۥ جَهَنَّمُ خَٰلِدًا فِيهَا وَغَضِبَ ٱللَّهُ عَلَيْهِ وَلَعَنَهُۥ وَأَعَدَّ لَهُۥ عَذَابًا عَظِيمًا ﴿٩٣﴾﴾ [النساء: ٩٣].

Allah ﷻ also becomes angry. He says: **{Say, 'Shall I inform you of [what is] worse than that as penalty from Allah? [It is that of] those whom Allah has cursed and with whom He became angry.'} [Qur'ān 5:60]** Allah gets angry and detests those who disobey Him. *Maqt* (detestation) is the most intense form of hatred. Allah ﷻ says: **{But whoever kills a believer intentionally – his recompense is Hell, wherein he will abide eternally, and Allah has become angry with him and has cursed him and has prepared for him a great punishment.} [Qur'ān 4:93]**

والمخلوق يغضب ويرضىٰ، ولا مشابهة بين غضب ورضا المخلوق وغضب ورضا الخالق، رضا الله وغضبه يليقان به سبحانه، ورضا وغضب المخلوق يليقان به كسائر الصفات ﴿لَيْسَ كَمِثْلِهِۦ شَىْءٌ ۖ وَهُوَ ٱلسَّمِيعُ ٱلْبَصِيرُ ﴿١١﴾﴾ [الشورىٰ: ١١]، ليس له مثل في ذاته ولا في أسمائه ولا في صفاته، وإن كانت له أسماء وصفات، وللمخلوق أسماء وصفات، فلا تشابه.

Created beings become angry and become pleased, but there is no resemblance between the anger and contentment of created beings and the anger and contentment of the Creator. Allah's ﷻ anger and contentment befit Him as with all of His other attributes. **{There is nothing like unto Him, and He is the Hearing, the Seeing.} [Qur'ān 42:11]** There is nothing like Him in His essence (*dhāt*) nor in His names and attributes. Although He has names and attributes, and created beings have names and attributes, there is no similarity between them.

وهذا مذهب أهل السنة ولجماعة، يثبتون الرضا والغضب لله عز وجل وغير ذلك من الصفات، وإن كان جنس هذه الصفات موجوداً في المخلوقين، لكن مع الفارق ﴿لَيْسَ كَمِثْلِهِۦ شَىْءٌ ۖ وَهُوَ ٱلسَّمِيعُ ٱلْبَصِيرُ ﴾ [الشورى:١١] كذلك المخلوق سميع بصير، وقال الله عن نفسه: ﴿وَهُوَ ٱلسَّمِيعُ ٱلْبَصِيرُ﴾ وقال في أول الآية: ﴿لَيْسَ كَمِثْلِهِۦ شَىْءٌ﴾ فدل على أن هناك فرقاً بين صفات الخالق وصفات المخلوق وهذا شيء معلوم من كتاب الله وسنة رسول الله صلى الله عليه وسلم واعتقاد أهل السنة والجماعة، أما أهل التأويل والضلال فينفون الأسماء والصفات عن الله؛ لأن جنسها موجود في المخلوقين، ولو أثبتها اقتضى هذا المشابهة - بزعمه - وفي الحقيقة هذا لا يقتضي المشابهة.

This is the doctrine of Ahl al-Sunnah wa ʿl-Jamāʿah. They affirm the contentment (*riḍā*) and anger (*ghaḍab*) of Allah the Almighty, as well as other attributes. Although these attributes exist in kind within created beings, there is a difference. **{There is nothing like unto Him, and He is the Hearing, the Seeing.} [Qurʾān 42:11]** Created beings also have hearing and sight. Allah ﷻ says about Himself that He is the *All Hearing and the All Seeing*. He says earlier on in the verse that there is nothing like Him. This indicates that there is a difference between the qualities of the Creator and the qualities of created things, and this is something known from the Book of Allah, the Sunnah of the Messenger of Allah ﷺ and the creed of Ahl al-Sunnah wa ʿl-Jamāʿah. The people of interpretation (*ahl al-tàwīl*) and misguidance, on the other hand, deny the names and attributes of Allah. This is because the genus of [the names and attributes] exist within created beings. According to them, affirming them has the necessary consequence of attributing likenesses to Allah, but in reality it does not have that necessary consequence.

ولكن هذا الفهم عقيم، ويأولون الغضب بالانتقام، والرضا بالإنعام، فالواجب التسليم لله ولرسوله وما ثبت عنهما، وأن يترك هذه الترهات والتأويلات.

This understanding is futile. They interpret the *anger* of Allah ﷻ as meaning His *vengeance* (*intiqām*) and His *contentment* as His *giving of favours* (*inʿām*). What is obligatory is to submit to Allah and His Messenger and that which has been established from them, and to leave such nonsense and interpretations.

ولذلك لما سئل مالك عن كيفية استواء الله علىٰ عرشه؟ أطرق مالك رأسه خوفاً وحياء من الله، ثم رفع رأسه وقال: (الاستواء معلوم، والكيف مجهول، والإيمان به واجب، والسؤال عنه بدعة).

Hence, when Mālik was asked about *how* Allah rose above the Throne *(istawā 'ala 'l-'arsh)*, Mālik lowered his head out of fear and shyness before Allah, then he raised it and said: "The *istawā* is known, its manner is unknown, to believe in it is incumbent, and to ask about it is an innovation."

المتن

(١٩٤) وَنُحِبُّ أَصْحابَ رسُولِ ﷺ.

(194) We love the Companions of the Messenger of Allah ﷺ.

الشرح

أصحاب: جمع صاحب، والصحابي هو: الذي لقي الرسول وهو مؤمن به ومات علىٰ ذلك، فإن آمن به ولم يلقه فليس بصحابي، ولو كان معاصراً للنبي صلىٰ الله عليه وسلم، كالنجاشي، وكذلك يشترط الإيمان به والموت علىٰ ذلك، فبمجرد الردة والموت عليها تبطل الصحبة وسائر الأعمال، وصحابة رسول الله صلىٰ الله عليه وسلم هم أفضل القرون والأمم بعد الأنبياء والرسل، وذلك لأنهم أدركوا المصطفىٰ عليه الصلاة والسلام وآمنوا به وجاهدوا معه وتلقوا عنه العلم، وأحبهم النبي صلىٰ الله عليه وسلم واختارهم الله لنبيه أصحاباً.

Companions (*aṣḥāb*) is the plural of *ṣāḥib*. A *ṣaḥābī* (companion) is someone who met the Messenger of Allah ﷺ whilst believing in him and who died as such. If someone believed in him but did not meet him, then they are not a Companion, even if that person were a contemporary of the Messenger of Allah ﷺ, such as *al-Najāshī* (Negus). It is also a condition that one believed in him and died as a believer. Apostasy and death as an apostate renders one's status as a Companion, as well as all other deeds, invalid. The Companions of the Messenger of Allah ﷺ were the best of all generations and communities of believers after the Prophets and Messengers of Allah, that is because they made it to see the Messenger of Allah ﷺ and believed in him, joined him in *jihād* and acquired knowledge from him. The Prophet ﷺ also loved them and Allah chose them to be the Companions of His Prophet.

والله يقول: ﴿لَّقَدْ رَضِيَ ٱللَّهُ عَنِ ٱلْمُؤْمِنِينَ إِذْ يُبَايِعُونَكَ تَحْتَ ٱلشَّجَرَةِ فَعَلِمَ مَا فِي قُلُوبِهِمْ فَأَنزَلَ ٱلسَّكِينَةَ عَلَيْهِمْ وَأَثَٰبَهُمْ فَتْحًا قَرِيبًا ﴿١٨﴾﴾ [الفتح:١٨]، وقال سبحانه: ﴿مُّحَمَّدٌ رَّسُولُ ٱللَّهِ ۚ وَٱلَّذِينَ مَعَهُۥٓ أَشِدَّآءُ عَلَى ٱلْكُفَّارِ رُحَمَآءُ بَيْنَهُمْ ۖ تَرَىٰهُمْ رُكَّعًا سُجَّدًا يَبْتَغُونَ فَضْلًا مِّنَ ٱللَّهِ وَرِضْوَٰنًا ۖ سِيمَاهُمْ فِي وُجُوهِهِم مِّنْ أَثَرِ ٱلسُّجُودِ ۚ ذَٰلِكَ مَثَلُهُمْ فِي ٱلتَّوْرَىٰةِ ۚ وَمَثَلُهُمْ فِي ٱلْإِنجِيلِ كَزَرْعٍ أَخْرَجَ شَطْـَٔهُۥ فَـَٔازَرَهُۥ فَٱسْتَغْلَظَ فَٱسْتَوَىٰ عَلَىٰ سُوقِهِۦ يُعْجِبُ ٱلزُّرَّاعَ لِيَغِيظَ بِهِمُ ٱلْكُفَّارَ ۗ وَعَدَ ٱللَّهُ ٱلَّذِينَ ءَامَنُوا۟ وَعَمِلُوا۟ ٱلصَّٰلِحَٰتِ مِنْهُم مَّغْفِرَةً وَأَجْرًا عَظِيمًۢا ﴿٢٩﴾﴾ [الفتح:٢٩]

Allah says: **{Certainly was Allah pleased with the believers when they pledged allegiance to you, [O Muḥammad], under the tree, and He knew what was in their hearts, so He sent down tranquillity upon them and rewarded them with an imminent conquest.} [Qurʾān 48:18]** Allah also says: **{Muḥammad is the Messenger of Allah; and those with him are forceful against the disbelievers, merciful among themselves. You see them bowing and prostrating [in prayer], seeking bounty from Allah and [His] pleasure. Their mark is on their faces from the trace of prostration. That is their description in the Torah. And their description in the Gospel is as a plant which produces its offshoots and strengthens them so they grow firm and stand upon their stalks, delighting the sowers – so that Allah may enrage by them the disbelievers. Allah has promised those who believe and do righteous deeds among them forgiveness and a great reward.} [Qurʾān 48:29]**

والصحابة أفضل القرون؛ لقوله عليه الصلاة والسلام: «خير القرون قرني ثم

الذين يلونهم ثم الذين يلونهم» فهم خير القرون بفضل صحبتهم للنبي عليه الصلاة والسلام، فحبهم إيمان وبغضهم نفاق، قال تعالىٰ: ﴿لِيَغِيظَ بِهِمُ ٱلْكُفَّارَ﴾ [الفتح:٢٩].

The Companions are the best of all generations as the Prophet ﷺ said: "The best of all generations is my generation, then those who follow them and then those who follow."[126] So, they are the best of all generations by virtue of them being the Companions of the Prophet ﷺ. Therefore, loving them is faith and hating them is hypocrisy (*nifāq*). Allah ﷻ says: **{...so that Allah may enrage by them the disbelievers.} [Qur'ān 48:29]**

فالواجب علىٰ المسلمين عموماً حب الصحابة جميعاً، بنص الآية؛ لمحبة الله عز وجل لهم، ولمحبة النبي صلىٰ الله عليه وسلم، ولأنهم جاهدوا في سبيل الله، ونشروا الإسلام في مشارق الأرض ومغاربها، وآزروا الرسول وآمنوا به واتبعوا النور الذي أُنزل معه، هذه عقيدة أهل السنة والجماعة.

It is incumbent upon all Muslims in general to love all of the Companions because Allah ﷻ loved them, and because the Prophet ﷺ loved them. We also love them because they engaged in *jihād* for Allah's sake, spread Islām in the east and the west of the earth and aided and believed in the Messenger of Allah ﷺ. And they followed the light that was sent down to him. This is the creed of Ahl al-Sunnah wa 'l-Jamā'ah.

فالله لما ذكر المهاجرين والأنصار في سورة الحشر، قال سبحانه: ﴿لِلْفُقَرَآءِ ٱلْمُهَٰجِرِينَ ٱلَّذِينَ أُخْرِجُوا۟ مِن دِيَٰرِهِمْ وَأَمْوَٰلِهِمْ يَبْتَغُونَ فَضْلًا مِّنَ ٱللَّهِ وَرِضْوَٰنًا وَيَنصُرُونَ ٱللَّهَ وَرَسُولَهُۥٓ ۚ أُو۟لَٰٓئِكَ هُمُ ٱلصَّٰدِقُونَ ۝٨ وَٱلَّذِينَ تَبَوَّءُو ٱلدَّارَ وَٱلْإِيمَٰنَ مِن قَبْلِهِمْ يُحِبُّونَ مَنْ هَاجَرَ إِلَيْهِمْ وَلَا يَجِدُونَ فِى صُدُورِهِمْ حَاجَةً مِّمَّآ أُوتُوا۟ وَيُؤْثِرُونَ عَلَىٰٓ أَنفُسِهِمْ وَلَوْ كَانَ بِهِمْ خَصَاصَةٌ ۚ وَمَن يُوقَ شُحَّ نَفْسِهِۦ فَأُو۟لَٰٓئِكَ هُمُ ٱلْمُفْلِحُونَ ۝٩ وَٱلَّذِينَ جَآءُو مِنۢ بَعْدِهِمْ يَقُولُونَ رَبَّنَا ٱغْفِرْ لَنَا وَلِإِخْوَٰنِنَا ٱلَّذِينَ سَبَقُونَا بِٱلْإِيمَٰنِ وَلَا تَجْعَلْ فِى قُلُوبِنَا غِلًّا لِّلَّذِينَ ءَامَنُوا۟﴾ [الحشر:٨-١٠]

When mentioning the Muhājirūn (Emigrants) and Anṣār (Helpers) in

126 Reported by al-Bukhārī (2652) and Muslim (2533).

Sūrat al-Ḥashr, Allah ﷻ says: **{For the poor emigrants who were expelled from their homes and their properties, seeking bounty from Allah and [His] approval and supporting Allah and His Messenger, [there is also a share]. Those are the truthful. And [also for] those who were settled in al-Madīnah and [adopted] the faith before them. They love those who emigrated to them and find not any want in their breasts of what the emigrants were given but give [them] preference over themselves, even though they are in privation. And whoever is protected from the stinginess of his soul – it is those who will be the successful. And [there is a share for] those who came after them, saying, 'Our Lord, forgive us and our brothers who preceded us in faith and put not in our hearts [any] resentment toward those who have believed.'} [Qur'ān 59:8-10]**

فهذا موقف المسلمين من صحابة رسول الله عليه الصلاة والسلام، يستغفرون لهم، ويسألون الله أن لا يجعل في قلوبهم بغضـًا للصحابة، وكذلك آل بيت الرسول فلهم حق القرابة وحق الإيمان، ومذهب أهل السنة والجماعة: موالاة أهل بيت النبي عليه الصلاة والسلام.

This is the believers' attitude toward the Companions of the Messenger of Allah ﷺ. They ask forgiveness for them and ask Allah ﷻ not to put any hatred for the Companions in their hearts. The same goes for the family of the Prophet ﷺ, as they enjoy certain rights for their kinship and certain rights for their being believers. The doctrine of Ahl al-Sunnah wa 'l-Jamāʿah involves keeping *walāʾ* (to love and defend) for the family of the Prophet ﷺ.

وأما النواصب: فيوالون الصحابة، ويبغضون بيت النبي عليه الصلاة والسلام، ولذلك سموا بالنواصب؛ لنصبهم العداوة لأهل بيت النبي عليه الصلاة والسلام.

The Nawāṣib sect align themselves with the Companions and hate the family of the Prophet ﷺ, which is why they are called *nawāṣib* [from *n – ṣ – b*]: for their manifesting (*naṣbihim*) hostilities toward the family of the Prophet ﷺ.

والروافض: على العكس، والوا أهل البيت بزعمهم، وأبغضوا الصحابة،

ويلعنونهم ويكفرونهم ويذمونهم.

The Rāfiḍah Shīʿites are the opposite, aligning themselves with the family of the Prophet (*ahl al-bayt*), as they claim, and they hate the Companions. Moreover, they curse them, declare them to be disbelievers and vilify them.

والصحابة يتفاضلون، فأفضلهم الخلفاء الراشدون الأربعة: أبو بكر وعمر وعثمان وعلي، رضي الله عن الجميع، الذين قال فيهم النبي عليه الصلاة والسلام: «**عليكم بسنتي وسنة الخلفاء الراشدين المهديين من بعدي عضوا عليها بالنواجذ**».

The Companions vary in respect of their excellence. The most superior of them are the four Rightly-Guided Caliphs, Abū Bakr, ʿUmar, ʿUthmān, and ʿAlī ﷺ, those concerning whom the Prophet ﷺ said: "Adhere to my *sunnah* and to the *sunnah* of the four rightly guided caliphs to come after me; bite down on them with your molar teeth."[127]

ثم باقي العشرة المبشرين بالجنة وهم: أبو عبيدة عامر بن الجراح، وسعد بن أبي وقاص، وسعيد بن زيد، والزبير بن العوام، وطلحة بن عبيد الله، وعبد الرحمن بن عوف، رضي الله عنهم.

Next in succession are the remaining *ten who were promised Jannah*, namely, Abū ʿUbaydah ʿĀmir ibn al-Jarrāḥ, Saʿd ibn Abī Waqqāṣ, Saʿīd ibn Zayd, al-Zubayr ibn al-ʿAwwām, Ṭalḥah ibn ʿUbayd-Allāh and ʿAbdurraḥmān ibn ʿAwf ﷺ.

ثم أهل بدر ثم أهل بيعة الرضوان، قال تعالىٰ: ﴿لَّقَدْ رَضِيَ ٱللَّهُ عَنِ ٱلْمُؤْمِنِينَ إِذْ يُبَايِعُونَكَ تَحْتَ ٱلشَّجَرَةِ فَعَلِمَ مَا فِى قُلُوبِهِمْ فَأَنزَلَ ٱلسَّكِينَةَ عَلَيْهِمْ وَأَثَٰبَهُمْ فَتْحًا قَرِيبًا ﴿١٨﴾﴾ [الفتح:١٨].

Then come those who fought in the Battle of Badr and then come those who pledged themselves in 'the *pledge of good pleasure*' (*bayʿat al-riḍwān*) about which Allah ﷻ says: **{Certainly was Allah pleased with the believers when they pledged allegiance to you, [O Muḥammad], under**

127 Abū Dāwūd, no. 4607; al-Tirmidhī, no. 2678; Ibn Mājah, no. 42. Al-Tirmidhī said: This *ḥadīth* is *ḥasan ṣaḥīḥ*.

the tree, and He knew what was in their hearts, so He sent down tranquillity upon them and rewarded them with an imminent conquest.} [Qur'ān 48:18]

ثم الذين آمنوا وجاهدوا قبل الفتح، فهم أفضل من الصحابة الذين آمنوا وجاهدوا بعد الفتح، قال تعالىٰ: ﴿لَا يَسْتَوِي مِنكُم مَّنْ أَنفَقَ مِن قَبْلِ ٱلْفَتْحِ وَقَٰتَلَ ۚ أُو۟لَٰٓئِكَ أَعْظَمُ دَرَجَةً مِّنَ ٱلَّذِينَ أَنفَقُوا۟ مِنۢ بَعْدُ وَقَٰتَلُوا۟ ۚ وَكُلًّا وَعَدَ ٱللَّهُ ٱلْحُسْنَىٰ ۚ﴾ [الحديد: ١٠]
والمراد بالفتح: صلح الحديبية.

Then come those who believed and fought in *jihād* before the Conquest of Makkah. They are superior to the Companions who believed and fought in *jihād* after the Conquest of Makkah. Allah ﷻ says: **{Not equal among you are those who spent before the conquest and fought [and those who did so after it]. Those are greater in degree than they who spent afterwards and fought. But to all Allah has promised the best [reward].} [Qur'ān 57:10]** Here, the *conquest* means, the treaty at al-Ḥudaybīyah.

ثم المهاجرون عمومـًا، ثم الأنصار؛ لأن الله قدّم المهاجرين علىٰ الأنصار في القرآن، قال سبحانه: ﴿وَٱلسَّٰبِقُونَ ٱلْأَوَّلُونَ مِنَ ٱلْمُهَٰجِرِينَ وَٱلْأَنصَارِ﴾ [التوبة: ١٠٠]، وقال سبحانه: ﴿لِلْفُقَرَآءِ ٱلْمُهَٰجِرِينَ ٱلَّذِينَ أُخْرِجُوا۟ مِن دِيَٰرِهِمْ وَأَمْوَٰلِهِمْ يَبْتَغُونَ فَضْلًا مِّنَ ٱللَّهِ وَرِضْوَٰنًا وَيَنصُرُونَ ٱللَّهَ وَرَسُولَهُۥٓ ۚ أُو۟لَٰٓئِكَ هُمُ ٱلصَّٰدِقُونَ ۝٨﴾ [الحشر: ٨]
وهؤلاء هم المهاجرون.

Then come the Muhājirūn (Emigrants) in a general sense and then the Anṣār (Helpers), as Allah ﷻ gives precedence to the Muhājirūn over the Anṣār in the Qur'ān. Allah ﷻ says: **{And the first forerunners [in the faith] among the Muhajirīn and the Anṣār...} [Qur'ān 9:100]** Allah ﷻ also says: **{For the poor emigrants who were expelled from their homes and their properties, seeking bounty from Allah and [His] approval and supporting Allah and His Messenger, [there is also a share]. Those are the truthful.} [Qur'ān 59:8]** This is a reference to the Muhājirūn.

ثم قال سبحانه في الأنصار: ﴿وَٱلَّذِينَ تَبَوَّءُو ٱلدَّارَ وَٱلْإِيمَٰنَ مِن قَبْلِهِمْ يُحِبُّونَ مَنْ هَاجَرَ إِلَيْهِمْ وَلَا يَجِدُونَ فِى صُدُورِهِمْ حَاجَةً مِّمَّآ أُوتُواْ وَيُؤْثِرُونَ عَلَىٰٓ أَنفُسِهِمْ وَلَوْ كَانَ بِهِمْ خَصَاصَةٌ وَمَن يُوقَ شُحَّ نَفْسِهِۦ فَأُوْلَٰٓئِكَ هُمُ ٱلْمُفْلِحُونَ ۝٩﴾ [الحشر: ٩].

Allah ﷻ then says in reference to the Anṣār: **{And [also for] those who were settled in al-Madīnah and [adopted] the faith before them. They love those who emigrated to them and find not any want in their breasts of what the emigrants were given but give [them] preference over themselves, even though they are in privation. And whoever is protected from the stinginess of his soul – it is those who will be the successful.} [Qur'ān 59:9]**

فقدّم المهاجرين وأعمالهم علىٰ الأنصار وأعمالهم، مما دل علىٰ أن المهاجرين أفضل؛ لأنهم تركوا أوطانهم وأموالهم وهاجروا في سبيل الله، فدل علىٰ صدق إيمانهم، فجميع الصحابة يجب حبهم وموالاتهم، ولا نتدخل فيما حصل بينهم من حروب، فما حصل بينهم من الحروب فبتأويل منهم، فهم مجتهدون، فمن أصاب منهم فله أجران، ومن أخطأ فله أجر واحد، وكذلك عندهم من الحسنات والفضائل العظيمة التي تُكفِّر ما يقع من الخطأ من بعضهم.

Here, the Muhājirūn and their deeds are given precedence over the Anṣār and their deeds, which is from [the evidence] suggesting that the Muhājirūn are superior, as they left their homeland and property for Allah's ﷻ sake. This is evidence of the sincerity of their faith. It is obligatory to love and align oneself with all of the Companions. We do not involve ourselves in the wars that occurred between them. Whatever wars happened between them was because of an interpretation on their part as they were qualified to exert personal discretions *(mujtahids)*. And so if any one of them were correct, they would have two divine rewards and if they were mistaken, they would have one divine reward. Moreover, they had such good deeds and great virtues that would have expiated any mistakes that some of them might have fallen into.

فالواجب علىٰ المسلمين الترضّي عنهم، وطلب العذر لهم، والدفاع عنهم، فمذهب أهل السنة والجماعة: أنهم لا يتدخلون فيما شجر بين الصحابة رضي

الله عنهم؛ لما لهم من الفضل والسابقة؛ ولقوله عليه الصلاة والسلام: «**لا تسبوا أصحابي، فوالذي نفسي بيده لو أنفق أحدكم مثل أحد ذهبًا ما بلغ مد أحدهم ولا نصيفه**» لفضلهم.

It is the duty of all Muslims to be pleased with them, to seek excuses on their behalf and to defend them. The doctrine of Ahl al-Sunnah wa ʿl-Jamāʿah. is: They do not involve themselves in the disputes that occurred between the Companions because of their virtues and precedence, and because the Prophet ﷺ said: "Do not insult my companions, for, by Him in whose hand lies my soul, if one of you were to give out the like of Mount Uḥud in gold, it would not amount to one *mudd*, and not half a *mudd*, of one of them."[128] This is because of their virtue.

فمن تدخل فيما حصل بين الصحابة وصار في قلبه شيء، فهذا زنديق، فأما من قال: نتدخل فيما حصل بين الصحابة من باب البحث، فهذا خطر عظيم ولا يجوز، ولذلك لما سُئل عمر بن عبد العزيز عما حصل بين الصحابة قال: «أولئك قوم طهّر الله أيدينا من دمائهم، فيجب أن نطهر ألسنتنا من أعراضهم».

So, if someone was to involve himself in what occurred between the Companions and then acquire some doubts in his heart, then that person is a heretic. Also if someone was to say, we discuss what happened between the Companions for the sake of research, then this is very dangerous and it is not permissible. Hence, when ʿUmar ibn ʿAbdul ʿAzīz was asked about what happened between the Companions, he said: "Those are people whom Allah ﷻ has cleansed our hands of their blood, so it is our duty to cleanse our tongues of their honour."

وقال عليه الصلاة والسلام: «**هل أنتم تاركو لي أصحابي؟**» فلا نتدخل فيما حصل بين الصحابة؛ لأنه من مقتضىٰ الإيمان ومن مقتضىٰ النصيحة لله ولرسوله ولكتابه ولعامة المسلمين وخاصتهم.

And the Prophet ﷺ said: "Should you not leave my companions to me?"[129] So we do not involve ourselves in what happened between the Companions

128 Al-Bukhārī, no. 3673; Muslim, no. 2541.

129 Al-Bukhārī presented it according to a similar wording (no. 3661).

as it is a requisite of faith and a requisite of good will towards Allah, His Messenger, His Book, and to the general and elite Muslims not to do so.

المتن

(١٩٥) وَلاَ نُفْرِطُ فِي حُبِّ أَحَدٍ مِنْهُم.

(195) But we do not exceed the limits in our love for any one of them.

الشرح

الإفراط: الغلو، أي: لا نغلوا في حب أحد منهم، كما غلت الرافضة في حب علي رضي الله عنه على زعمهم، وإلا الظاهر أنهم لا يحبونه ولا يحبون المسلمين عموماً، فغلوا فيه حتىٰ قال بعضهم: إن علياً هو الله، وذلك في زمن علي رضي الله عنه، فخدَّ لهم الأخاديد وأحرقهم بالنار غيرةً لله عز وجل. فالغلو ممنوع سواء في الصحابة أو غيرهم، قال سبحانه: ﴿قُلْ يَٰٓأَهْلَ ٱلْكِتَٰبِ لَا تَغْلُوا۟ فِى دِينِكُمْ غَيْرَ ٱلْحَقِّ﴾ [المائدة:٧٧]، والنبي صلىٰ الله عليه وسلم يقول: «**إياكم والغلو، فإنما أهلك من كان قبلكم الغلو**» فنحن نحب أصحاب رسول الله عليه الصلاة والسلام، ولكن لا نغلو فيهم حتىٰ نجعلهم شركاء لله وندعوهم من دون الله، كما تفعل الرافضة والقبوريون، فليس هذا حباً للصحابة، فحبهم باتباعهم والاقتداء بهم والترضي عليهم.

We should not be excessive in our love for any one of them, in the way that the Rāfiḍites have been excessive and immoderate in their love of ʿAlī ﷺ, as they claim. Even so, it is evident that they neither love him nor love the Muslims in general. They are extreme in such a way that some of them say that ʿAlī is Allah, as happened in the era of ʿAlī ﷺ. In light of this, he dug out ditches for them and burned them out of love (lit. protective jealousy) for Allah the Almighty. Excess is prohibited, whether it is for the Companions or for anyone else. Allah ﷻ says: **{Say, 'O People of the Scripture, do not exceed limits in your religion beyond the truth...'} [Qur'ān 5:77]**

And the Prophet ﷺ said: "Beware of excess, for it is not but excess that destroyed those who were before you."[130] Therefore we love the Companions of the Messenger of Allah ﷺ but we are not so excessive that we associate them as partners with Allah ﷻ or supplicate to them besides Allah ﷻ as the Rāfiḍites and grave worshippers do. This is not love for the Companions. Rather, love for them is to follow them, emulate them and pray that Allah be pleased with them.

المتن

(١٩٦) وَلَا نَتَبَرَّأُ مِنْ أَحَدٍ مِنْهُم.

(196) Nor do we dissociate ourselves from any of them.

الشرح

في هذا إشارة إلى الرافضة الذين يتبرؤون من الصحابة، وخاصة أبا بكر، وعمر، وعثمان، بل يكفرون كثيراً من الصحابة، هذا من التفريط، فلا نُفرّط في حبهم؛ لأن التفريط هو ترك محبتهم.

This is a reference to the Rāfiḍites, who disavow the Companions, especially Abū Bakr, ʿUmar, and ʿUthmān, and in fact, they declare many of the Companions to be disbelievers. This is an example of negligence. So we should not be negligent in our love for them, as negligence is to leave off loving them.

المتن

(١٩٧) وَنُبْغِضُ مَنْ يُبْغِضُهُم.

(197) And we hate whoever hates them.

130 Aḥmad, *Musnad,* 1/215, 347; Ibn Mājah, no. 3029.

الشرح

من يبغض الصحابة فإنه يبغض الدين؛ لأنهم هم حملة الإسلام وأتباع المصطفىٰ عليه الصلاة والسلام، فمن أبغضهم فقد أبغض الإسلام؛ فهذا دليل علىٰ أنه ليس في قلوب هؤلاء إيمان، وفيه دليل علىٰ أنهم لا يحبون الإسلام.

Anyone who hates the Companions also hates the religion of Islām, because the Companions are the ones who have transmitted Islām and are the followers of al-Muṣṭafā ﷺ. So whoever hates them, hates Islām. This suggests that those people do not have faith in their hearts, and it also suggests that they do not love Islām.

المتن

(١٩٨) وَبِغَيْرِ الخَيْرِ يَذْكُرُهُم، ولا نَذْكُرُهُم إلاَّ بِخَيْرٍ.

(198) Or says anything other than good about them. We only speak well of them.

الشرح

علىٰ ما سبق فلا يجوز الخوض فيما حصل بينهم؛ بل يجب الإمساك عن ذلك وأن لا يُذكروا إلا بخير.

As mentioned, it is not permissible to delve into what happened between them. In fact, one should refrain from doing so and should say nothing about them besides that which is good.

المتن

(١٩٩) وَحُبُّهُم دِينٌ وإيمانٌ وإحْسانٌ، وَبُغْضُهُم كُفْرٌ ونِفاقٌ وطُغْيانٌ.

(199) Loving them is religious conviction, faith, and kindness, and hating them is disbelief, hypocrisy, and transgression.

الشرح

هذا أصل عظيم يجب علىٰ المسلمين معرفته، وهو محبة الصحابة وتقديرهم؛ لأن ذلك من الإيمان، بغضهم أو بغض أحد منهم من الكفر والنفاق، ولأن حبهم من حب النبي صلىٰ الله عليه وسلم، وبغضهم من بغض النبي صلىٰ الله عليه وسلم.

This is a great foundational principle that all Muslims should know, namely, loving the Companions and valuing them, as this emanates from faith. And hating them, or hating someone from amongst them, emanates from disbelief and hypocrisy. Moreover, love for them emanates from love of the Prophet ﷺ, and hating them comes from hate of the Prophet ﷺ.

المتن

(٢٠٠) وَنُثْبِتُ الْخِلَافَةَ بَعْدَ رَسُولِ اللهِ ﷺ أَوَّلًا لِأَبِي بَكْرٍ الصِّدِّيقِ رضي الله عنه تَفْضِيلًا لَهُ وَتَقْدِيمًا عَلَىٰ جَمِيعِ الْأُمَّةِ، ثُمَّ لِعُمَرَ بْنِ الْخَطَّابِ رضي الله عنه، ثُمَّ لِعُثْمَانَ رضي الله عنه، ثُمَّ لِعَلِيِّ بْنِ أَبِي طَالِبٍ رضي الله عنه، وَهُمُ الْخُلَفَاءُ الرَّاشِدُونَ والْأَئِمَّةُ الْمَهْدِيُّونَ.

(200) We affirm the Caliphate after the Messenger of Allah ﷺ, the first of which was of Abū Bakr ؓ, due to his virtue and precedence over the entire *Ummah;* then, of ʿUmar ibn al-Khaṭṭāb ؓ; then, of ʿUthmān ؓ; then, of ʿAlī ibn Abī Ṭālib ؓ. These are *al-Khulafāʾ al-Rāshidūn* (the Rightly-Guided Caliphs) and the rightly-guided *imāms.*

الشرح

لما فرغ مما يجب للصحابة من المحبة والولاء، وترك بغضهم وبغض من يبغضهم، وعدم التدخل فيما جرىٰ بينهم، شرع في ذكر الخلافة بعد النبي صلىٰ الله عليه وسلم، وهي علىٰ النحو الذي ذكره؛ لأن النبي صلىٰ الله عليه وسلم قدم أبا بكر للصلاة في آخر حياته، وفي هذا إشارة إلىٰ خلافته، ولذلك قال الصحابة لما بايعوه: (رضيك رسول الله صلىٰ الله عليه وسلم لديننا، ألا نرضاك لدنيانا؟) فبايعوه، ولما لأبي بكر من السوابق العظيمة قبل الهجرة وبعدها، وهو أولىٰ الناس بعد النبي صلىٰ الله عليه وسلم، ثم بعده عمر بن الخطاب بعهد من أبي بكر، ثم عثمان بإجماع الصحابة باختيار من أصحاب الشورىٰ الذين عينهم عمر قبل وفاته من العشرة المبشرين بالجنة، وهم خيار الصحابة. وبعد مقتل عثمان وليها علي رضي الله عنه، هذا هو ترتيب الخلافة، فمن زعم أن الخلافة بعد النبي صلىٰ الله عليه وسلم لعلي رضي الله عنه، فهو ضال ومخالف للنبي صلىٰ الله عليه وسلم ولإجماع المسلمين.

After concluding the discussion on what is obligatory in terms of love and loyalty to the Companions, and in terms of not hating them and hating those who hate them, and not entering into discourse about what happened between them, the author begins mentioning the caliphate that followed the Prophet ﷺ, which is according to what the author has mentioned here. The reason is that the Prophet ﷺ put Abū Bakr ﷜ forward to lead the prayer towards the end of his life, which signifies his right of the caliphate. Hence, the companions pledged allegiance to him, and said, 'The Messenger of Allah ﷺ was content with you being in charge of our religion. Should we not then be content with you being in charge of our worldly affairs?' So they pledged allegiance to him as the Caliph. Also, Abū Bakr ﷜ had a great background both before and after the Hijrah. He was the most rightful of all people after the Prophet ﷺ and 'Umar ibn al-Khaṭṭāb ﷜ came after him – via the edict of Abū Bakr, and then came 'Uthmān ﷜ according to the unanimous agreement of the Companions. He was chosen by members of a consultation (*shūrā*) from the ten promised Paradise, the best of all of the Companions, which 'Umar appointed before his death. After 'Uthmān's ﷜ death, 'Alī ﷜ assumed the office of Caliph, and this is the order of the Caliphate. So anyone who claims that the caliphate after the Prophet ﷺ

belonged to 'Alī ﷺ has strayed from the path, and has opposed the Prophet ﷺ as well as the unanimous agreement of the Muslims.

فالشيعة: يزعمون أنها لعلي، ويسمونه الوصي على الأمة، وإنما قصدهم التهويش وإشعال الفتن بين الناس، فهم ليسوا بأحسن نظراً من الصحابة رضي الله عنهم. فالشيعة يقولون: الصحابة ظلمة، وكل وصف ذميم في القرآن المعني به الصحابة عندهم فيصفونهم بأنهم ظالمون وكافرون وضالون، وهذا مما جعل العلماء ينصون على ذكر الخلافة في كتب العقائد؛ لئلا يتأثر أحد بهؤلاء الأرجاس. فترتيب الخلفاء الأربعة على هذا الترتيب هو مذهب أهل السنة والجماعة؛ لأن الصحابة رتبوا هذا الترتيب وأجمعوا عليه، قال شيخ الإسلام ابن تيمية: (من خالف في أمر الخلافة فهو أضل من حمار أهله) .

The Shī'ites, for instance, claim that the succession belonged to 'Alī ﷺ, and they call him the custodian (*waṣī*) of the *Ummah.* But their intent is only to ignite sedition and disorder among people, as their opinion is not greater than that of the Companions ﷺ. The Shī'ites say that the Companions were wrongdoers, and that every vilifying description in the Qur'ān is associated with the Companions, in their view. Thus, they describe them as being wrongdoers, disbelievers and misguided. This is among the reasons why scholars of Islām have explicitly cited the Caliphate after the Prophet (*al-khilāfah*) in the creedal literature – so that no one is affected by such filth. The order of Caliphate of the four rightly-guided caliphs according to this is the doctrine of Ahl al-Sunnah wa 'l-Jamā'ah, because it is the Companions who have given and agreed upon this order. Shaykh al-Islām Ibn Taymiyyah said: "Whoever opposes in the matter of the Caliphate is more astray than his household donkey."

المتن

(٢٠١) وَأَنَّ الْعَشَرَةَ الَّذِينَ سَمّاهُمْ رَسُولُ اللهِ ﷺ وَبَشَّرَهُمْ بِالْجَنَّةِ، نَشْهَدُ لَهُمْ بِالْجَنَّةِ عَلَىٰ ما شَهِدَ لَهُمْ رَسُولُ اللهِ ﷺ، وَقَوْلُهُ الْحَقُّ، وَهُمْ: أَبُو بَكْرٍ، وَعُمَرُ،

وَعُثْمانُ، وَعَلِيٌّ، وَطَلْحَةُ، والزُّبَيْرُ، وَسَعْدٌ، وَسَعِيدٌ، وَعَبْدُ الرَّحْمَنِ بْنُ عَوْفٍ، وَأَبُو عُبَيْدَةَ بْنُ الْجَرّاحِ وَهُوَ أَمِينُ هَذِهِ الْأُمَّةِ رضي الله عنهم أَجْمَعِينَ.

(201) And [we believe] that the ten who the Messenger of Allah ﷺ named and promised Paradise will be in Paradise, according to the testimony of the Messenger of Allah ﷺ who speaks the truth. They are: Abū Bakr, 'Umar, 'Uthmān, 'Alī, Ṭalḥah, al-Zubayr, Sa'd, Sa'īd, 'Abd al-Raḥmān ibn 'Awf and Abū 'Ubaydah ibn al-Jarrāḥ, the trusty of this Ummah. May Allah be pleased with them all.

الشرح

فهؤلاء هم العشرة المشهود لهم بالجنة، وأبو عبيدة رضي الله عنه وصف بأنه أمين هذه الأمة؛ لأنه لما عقد النبي صلىٰ الله عليه وسلم العهد مع أهل نجران، وفرض عليهم الجزية، طلبوا منه أن يبعث إليهم أمينـًا، فاختار أبا عبيدة وقال صلىٰ الله عليه وسلم: «**لأبعثن عليكم أمينـًا، حق أمين**» فاستشرف الصحابة لذلك فبعث أبا عبيدة.

These are the ten people who it has been testified that they will be in Paradise. Abū 'Ubaydah ﷺ is described as being the 'Trusty' of this *Ummah* because when the Prophet ﷺ made a covenant with the people of Najrān and imposed the *jizyah* tribute on them, they requested that he send a trustworthy individual to them, so he chose Abū 'Ubaydah. The Prophet ﷺ said: "I will send someone to you who is truly trustworthy." Upon knowing this, the Companions looked forward to having this honour, and he sent Abū 'Ubaydah.[131]

المتن

(٢٠٢) وَمَنْ أَحْسَنَ الْقَوْلَ فِي أَصْحابِ رَسُولِ اللهِ ﷺ وَأَزْواجِهِ الطّاهِراتِ مِنْ كُلِّ دَنَسٍ، وَذُرِّيّاتِهِ الْمُقَدَّسِينَ مِنْ كُلِّ رِجْسٍ؛ فَقَدْ بَرِئَ مِنَ النِّفاقِ.

131 Al-Bukhārī, no. 3745; Muslim, no. 2420.

(202) Whoever speaks well of the Prophet's ﷺ Companions and his pure and pious wives, [avoiding] every smear against them, and his sacred progeny, [avoiding] every cruelty against them, he is free from hypocrisy.

الشرح

بعد أن ذكر ما يجب للصحابة انتقل إلىٰ ذكر أهل بيت النبي صلىٰ الله عليه وسلم، وأول أهل البيت هم أزواج النبي صلىٰ الله عليه وسلم؛ قال تعالىٰ: ﴿إِنَّمَا يُرِيدُ ٱللَّهُ لِيُذْهِبَ عَنكُمُ ٱلرِّجْسَ أَهْلَ ٱلْبَيْتِ وَيُطَهِّرَكُمْ تَطْهِيرًا ﴿٣٣﴾﴾ [الأحزاب:٣٣]، هذا خطاب لهن.

After mentioning the rights of the Companions, the author shifts to a discussion about the family of the Prophet (*ahl bayt al-nabī*) ﷺ. First and foremost, the family of the Prophet includes the wives of the Prophet ﷺ. Allah ﷻ says: **{Allah intends only to remove from you the impurity [of sin], O people of the [Prophet's] household, and to purify you with [extensive] purification.} [Qurʾān 33:33]** This is addressed to them.

فأول من يدخل في أهل البيت: زوجاته، ثم قرابته عليه الصلاة والسلام، وهم آل العباس وآل أبي طالب، وآل الحارث بن عبد المطلب.

Thus, the family of the Prophet primarily includes his wives. Then come his ﷺ relatives, namely, the family of al-ʿAbbās, Abū Ṭālib, and the family of al-Ḥārith ibn ʿAbd al-Muṭṭalib.

فالرافضة: يقدحون في عائشة ويصفونها بما برأها الله منه، وهذا تكذيب لله عز وجل ووصف لله بأنه اختار لرسوله امرأة لا تصلح له، وهذا كفر بالله، قال تعالىٰ: ﴿ٱلْخَبِيثَٰتُ لِلْخَبِيثِينَ وَٱلْخَبِيثُونَ لِلْخَبِيثَٰتِ ۖ وَٱلطَّيِّبَٰتُ لِلطَّيِّبِينَ وَٱلطَّيِّبُونَ لِلطَّيِّبَٰتِ ۚ﴾ [النور:٢٦] فالنبي صلىٰ الله عليه وسلم طيب فلا يختار الله له إلا الطيبة.

The Rāfiḍī Shīʿites defame ʿĀʾishah ﵂ and attribute offenses to her that Allah ﷻ has cleared her of. This is denial of what Allah the Almighty has said and it means attributing to Allah that He chose an inappropriate woman to be the wife of His Messenger. This is disbelief in Allah ﷻ. Allah ﷻ says: **{Vile women are for vile men, and vile men are for vile women; and good women are for good men, and good men are for good women.} [Qur'ān 24:26]** The Prophet ﷺ was goodly, so Allah would only choose a good wife for him.

وذرياته المقصود بهم أولاده عليه الصلاة والسلام، وأولاد ابنته فاطمة، وهم الحسن والحسين وأولادهما، هؤلاء ذريته صلى الله عليه وسلم.

What is meant by his *progeny* (*dhurrīyah*) are his ﷺ children and the children of his daughter Fāṭimah i.e. al-Ḥasan al-Ḥusayn, and their offspring. These are the descendants of the Prophet ﷺ.

المتن

(٢٠٣) وَعُلَماءُ السَّلَفِ مِنَ السّابِقِينَ، وَمَنْ بَعْدَهُمْ مِنَ التّابِعِينَ - أَهْلُ الْخَيْرِ والأَثَرِ، وَأَهْلُ الْفِقْهِ والنَّظَرِ - لا يُذْكَرُونَ إلّا بِالْجَمِيلِ، وَمَنْ ذَكَرَهُمْ بِسُوءٍ فَهُوَ عَلَىٰ غَيْرِ السَّبِيلِ.

(203) The *'ulamā'* from the preceding *Salaf* (pious predecessors) and the Tābi'ūn (their successors), the people of goodness and ḥadīth traditions, and the people of *fiqh* and sound reason are only to be spoken of in the best terms. Whoever speaks ill of them is not on the right path.

الشرح

لما فرع - رحمه الله - من حقوق الصحابة وأهل البيت، وما يجب لهم من المحبة والموالاة، وعدم التنقُّص لأحد منهم انتقل إلى الذين يلونهم في الفضيلة وهم العلماء.

Having concluded the discourse on the Companions, the Family of the

Prophet ﷺ and their right to love and loyalty and not detracting from any of them their [high] reputations, the author ﷺ shifted the discourse to those who directly follow them in virtue: the *ʿulamāʾ* (knowledgeable people and scholars).

فعلماء هذه الأمة لهم منزلة وفضل بعد الصحابة؛ لأنهم ورثة الأنبياء؛ لقوله عليه الصلاة والسلام: «**العلماء ورثة الأنبياء**».

The *ʿulamāʾ* of the Ummah enjoy a special status and merit that comes after the Companions, because they are the heirs of the Prophets, as the Prophet ﷺ said: "The *ʿulamāʾ* are the heirs of the Prophets."[132]

والمراد بهم: علماء أهل السنة والجماعة، أهل العلم والنظر والفقه، وأهل الأثر، وهم أهل الحديث.

What is meant by 'the *ʿulamāʾ*' are the learned ones (scholars) of Ahl al-Sunnah wa 'l-Jamāʿah, those who possess knowledge, foresight and understanding, as well as those who are experts of the traditions (*ahl al-athar*), namely, the *ḥadīth* scholars.

فالعلماء على قسمين:

There are two types of *ʿulamāʾ*:

القسم الأول: علماء الأثر، وهم المحدثون الذين اعتنوا بسنة النبي صلى الله عليه وسلم وحفظوها وذبُّوا عنها، وقدموها للأمة صافية نقية، كما نطق بها رسول الله صلى الله عليه وسلم، وأبعدوا عنها كل دخيل وكل كذب، فنحوا الأحاديث الموضوعة وبينوها وحاصروها، فهؤلاء يسمون: علماء الرواية.

One. The experts of transmissions (*ʿulamāʾ al-athar*). They are the ḥadīth masters who have been concerned with the Prophetic Sunnah and with preserving and defending it, who presented it to the *Ummah* in its purest form, as spoken by the Messenger of Allah ﷺ. They remove from it every con-

132 Al-Bukhārī, presented it without a chain of transmission (*muʿallaq*) in *kitāb al-ʿilm: bāb al-ʿilm qabl al-qawl wa ʾl-ʿamal* (The book of knowledge before speech and action); Abū Dāwūd, no. 463; Ibn Mājah, no. 223; al-Tirmidhī, no. 2687.

tamination and lie, put all of the fabricated ḥadīth reports to the side and demonstrate and demarcate them [as being fabrications]. Such people are called scholars of transmission (*'ulamā' al-riwāyah*).

القسم الثاني: وهم الفقهاء، وهم الذين استنبطوا الأحكام، من هذه الأدلة، وبينوا فقهها، وشرحوها وبينوها للناس، فهؤلاء يسمون: علماء الدراية.

Two. The *fuqahā'* (jurists): They are the ones who derive the laws from these evidences, who demonstrate and explain their jurisprudence for the people. They are termed scholars of discernment *('ulamā' al-dirāyah*).

ومنهم من جمع بين العلمين، ويسمون: فقهاء المحدثين، كالإمام أحمد، ومالك، والشافعي، والبخاري.

There are scholars who mastered both kinds of knowledge, and they are termed as the jurists of the ḥadīth masters. Examples are: al-Imām Aḥmad, Mālik, al-Shāfi'ī and al-Bukhārī.

وكل هؤلاء العلماء لهم فضل، والنبي صلىٰ الله عليه وسلم قال: «**نضّر الله أمرأً سمع مقالتي فوعاها فأدّاها كما سمعها**» فالنبي صلىٰ الله عليه وسلم دعا لهم ومدحهم.

All of these learned people are people of virtue. The Prophet ﷺ said: "May Allah give good pleasure to someone who hears what I say, keeps it in mind and then conveys it as he has heard it."[133] Here, the Prophet ﷺ devoted a supplication for such people and praised them.

فالعلماء قاموا بما أوجب الله عليهم من حماية الدين والعقيدة، فبينوا الأحكام، والمواريث، والحلال والحرام، وبينوا أيضـًا فقه الكتاب والسنة، فجعلوا للأمة ثروة عظيمة يستفاد منها ويقاس عليها ما يجد من مشاكل.

The *'ulamā'* have carried out their duty from Allah ﷻ to protect the religion and creed and explain the laws; the laws of inheritance and what is lawful and unlawful. They have also clarified the jurisprudence of the Qur'ān and

133 Ibn Mājah, no. 230, 231, 232 & 3056.

the Sunnah and thus, left a great wealth for the *Ummah* to benefit from and use to measure upon contemporary problems.

والفقه علىٰ قسمين:

Fiqh has two types as well:

القسم الأول: الفقه الأكبر، وهو فقه العقيدة.

One. The greater knowledge (*al-fiqh al-akbar*), which is the knowledge of creed.

القسم الثاني: وهو فقه عملي، لا يقل عن الفقه الأكبر من حيث الأهمية، وهو فقه الأحكام العملية.

Two. Practical knowledge (jurisprudence), or knowledge of the Islamic law which is no less important than 'the greater knowledge'. It is the knowledge of the practical laws.

وفي فضل العلماء جاء في الحديث عن النبي صلىٰ الله عليه وسلم: «**فضل العالم علىٰ العابد كفضل القمر علىٰ سائر الكواكب**» وذلك لأن نفعهم يتعدّىٰ، وفي رواية: «**فضل العالم علىٰ العابد كفضلي علىٰ أدناكم**» فالعلماء لهم احترام ومنزلة.

In reference to the virtue of the *ʿulamāʾ*, it has been reported from the Prophet ﷺ: "The superiority of the learned over the worshipper is like the superiority of the moon over all of the stars."[134] This is because their benefit extends [beyond themselves]. According to another version: "The superiority of the learned to the worshipper is like my superiority to the least of you."[135] Thus, the learned have high esteem and status.

فلا يجوز الطعن فيهم وتنقصهم حتىٰ لو حصل من بعضهم خطأ في الاجتهاد، فهذا لا يقتضي تنقصهم؛ لأنهم قد يخطئون، ومع ذلك هم طالبون للحق، قال

134 Al-Tirmidhī, no. 2687.

135 Al-Tirmidhī, no. 2690.

النبي صلىٰ الله عليه وسلم: «**إذا اجتهد الحاكم فأصاب فله أجران، وإذا اجتهد فأخطأ فله أجر واحد**» وهذا في حق العلماء وليس المتعالمين؛ لأنه لا يحق لهم أن يدخلوا فيما لا يحسنون.

It is not permissible to attack them or to detract from their reputations. Even if some of them were to be mistaken in their discretionary judgments, it does not require detracting from their reputations because it is possible that they might be mistaken, but nonetheless they seek the truth. The Prophet ﷺ said: "If a judge exerts his judgment to the best of his ability and is correct, he will have two rewards. If he exerts his judgment to the best of his ability and is mistaken, then he will have one reward."[136] This is with regard to the *'ulamā'*, who have knowledge, and not to those who feign knowledge, as they do not have the right to involve themselves in something that they are not proficient in.

المتن

(٢٠٤) وَلا نُفَضِّلُ أَحَدًا مِنَ الْأَوْلِياءِ عَلَىٰ أَحَدٍ مِنَ الْأَنْبِياءِ عَلَيْهِمُ السَّلام، وَنَقُولُ: نَبِيٌّ واحِدٌ أَفْضَلُ مِنْ جَمِيعِ الْأَوْلِياءِ.

(204) We do not give superiority to any of the *awliyā'* (Allah's allies) over any of the Prophets. Rather, we say that a single prophet is better than all of the *awliyā'*.

الشرح

انتقل المصنف – رحمه الله – من العلماء إلىٰ الأولياء. والأولياء: جمع ولي، والولاية هي القرب والمحبة، فهم أهل القرب والمحبة من الله عز وجل، وسُمُّوا بالأولياء لقربهم من الله، ولأن الله يحبهم، قال تعالىٰ: ﴿إِنَّ ٱللَّهَ يُحِبُّ ٱلتَّوَّٰبِينَ وَيُحِبُّ ٱلْمُتَطَهِّرِينَ ﴿٢٢٢﴾﴾ [البقرة:٢٢٢] وقال تعالىٰ: ﴿إِنَّ ٱللَّهَ يُحِبُّ ٱلْمُحْسِنِينَ ﴿١٩٥﴾﴾ [البقرة:١٩٥].

136 Al-Bukhārī, no. 7352; Muslim, no. 1716.

The author ﷺ switched the discussion from that of the *ʿulamāʾ* to that of the *awliyāʾ* or allies of Allah ﷻ. *Awliyāʾ* is the plural of *walī*, and *wilāyah* means *closeness* and *love*. Thus, the *awliyāʾ* are those who possess closeness and love from Allah the Almighty. They are called *awliyāʾ* due to their closeness (*qurb*) to Allah, and because Allah ﷻ loves them. Allah ﷻ says: **{Indeed, Allah loves those who are constantly repentant and loves those who purify themselves.} [Qurʾān 2:222]** Allah ﷻ also says: **{Indeed, Allah loves the doers of good.} [Qurʾān 2:195]**

وقد بينهم الله في قوله: ﴿أَلَآ إِنَّ أَوۡلِيَآءَ ٱللَّهِ لَا خَوۡفٌ عَلَيۡهِمۡ وَلَا هُمۡ يَحۡزَنُونَ ۝٦٢ ٱلَّذِينَ ءَامَنُواْ وَكَانُواْ يَتَّقُونَ ۝٦٣﴾ [يونس:٦٢-٦٣]، فالولي لابد أن يجتمع فيه صفتان: الأولىٰ: الإيمان. والثانية: التقوىٰ.

Allah explains who they are in His statement: **{Unquestionably, [for] the allies of Allah there will be no fear concerning them, nor will they grieve, those who believed and were fearful of Allah.} [Qurʾān 10:62-63]** Thus, a *walī* has to have both of these two qualities: faith and piety (*taqwā*).

والناس في الولاية والبغض علىٰ أقسام ثلاثة:

In terms of being loved [i.e. having *wilāyah*] and hated [by Allah], there are three groups of people:

القسم الأول: أولياء الله الخُلَّص من الملائكة والنبيين والصدّيقين والشهداء وصالح المؤمنين.

The first are the pure allies of Allah ﷻ, such as the angels, Prophets, the true in faith (*al-ṣiddīqūn*), martyrs and the righteous believers.

القسم الثاني: أعداء لله عداوة خالصة، كالمشرك والكافر والمنافق النفاق الأكبر، فهؤلاء أعداء الله ورسوله ﴿يَـٰٓأَيُّهَا ٱلَّذِينَ ءَامَنُواْ لَا تَتَّخِذُواْ عَدُوِّي وَعَدُوَّكُمۡ أَوۡلِيَآءَ تُلۡقُونَ إِلَيۡهِم بِٱلۡمَوَدَّةِ وَقَدۡ كَفَرُواْ بِمَا جَآءَكُم مِّنَ ٱلۡحَقِّ﴾ [الممتحنة:١]، وقال تعالىٰ: ﴿لَّا تَجِدُ قَوۡمًا يُؤۡمِنُونَ بِٱللَّهِ وَٱلۡيَوۡمِ ٱلۡأٓخِرِ يُوَآدُّونَ مَنۡ حَآدَّ ٱللَّهَ وَرَسُولَهُۥ وَلَوۡ

كَانُوٓاْ ءَابَآءَهُمۡ أَوۡ أَبۡنَآءَهُمۡ أَوۡ إِخۡوَٰنَهُمۡ أَوۡ عَشِيرَتَهُمۡۚ﴾ [المجادلة:٢٢]، وقال تعالىٰ: ﴿يَٰٓأَيُّهَا ٱلَّذِينَ ءَامَنُواْ لَا تَتَّخِذُواْ ٱلۡيَهُودَ وَٱلنَّصَٰرَىٰٓ أَوۡلِيَآءَۘ بَعۡضُهُمۡ أَوۡلِيَآءُ بَعۡضٖۚ وَمَن يَتَوَلَّهُم مِّنكُمۡ فَإِنَّهُۥ مِنۡهُمۡۗ إِنَّ ٱللَّهَ لَا يَهۡدِي ٱلۡقَوۡمَ ٱلظَّٰلِمِينَ ٥١﴾ [المائدة:٥١].

The second are the pure enemies of Allah ﷻ, like polytheists, disbelievers and those who commit the major form of hypocrisy (*al-nifāq al-akbar*). These are the enemies of Allah ﷻ and His Messenger. **{O you who have believed, do not take My enemies and your enemies as allies, extending to them affection while they have disbelieved in what came to you of the truth.} [Qur'ān 60:1]** Allah ﷻ also says: **{You will not find a people who believe in Allah and the Last Day having affection for those who oppose Allah and His Messenger, even if they were their fathers or their sons or their brothers or their kin.} [Qur'ān 58:22]** Allah ﷻ also says: **{O you who have believed, do not take the Jews and the Christians as allies. They are [in fact] allies of one another. And whoever is an ally to them among you – then indeed, he is [one] of them. Indeed, Allah guides not the wrongdoing people.} [Qur'ān 5:51]**

القسم الثالث: من فيهم ولاية من وجه، وعداوة من وجه، وهو المسلم العاصي، ففيه ولاية بقدر ما معه من طاعة، وفيه عداوة بقدر ما معه من معصية، فكل مسلم ولي لله ولكن علىٰ حسب ما معه من إيمان.

The third are those who are allies in one regard and enemies in another, namely, those of the Muslims who are sinful. They have *wilāyah* in accordance to their obedience and enmity in accordance to their sin. Every Muslim is an ally of Allah ﷻ but only according to how much faith he has.

فمن ادّعىٰ الولاية أو ادعيت له الولاية وليس معه إيمان، وليس فيه تقوىٰ، فإنما هو دجال وكذاب.

If someone claims to be a *walī* or is proclaimed to be one but has neither faith nor piety, then that person is a deceiver (*dajjāl*) and a liar.

وقد يدعون الولاية وهم سحرة وكهنة ومشعوذون وعرافون، وقد كتب شيخ الإسلام كتاباً سمّاه (الفرقان بين أولياء الرحمن وأولياء الشيطان) وبيّن فيه

من يدّعي الولاية، ويُروج علىٰ الناس أشياءً يظن أنها كرامات، وهي خوارق شيطانية، وسيأتي بيانه.

Some may go as far as to claim to be *walīs* but [in reality] they are magicians, soothsayers, charlatans, and diviners. Shaykh al-Islām Ibn Taymiyyah authored a book entitled *al-Furqān bayna awliyā' al-Raḥmān wa awliyā' al-shayṭān* and in it, he exposes those who claim to be *walīs* and who present some things that people believe to be miracles (*karāmāt*), but which are in fact paranormal activities of the *shayṭāns*. This is to be explained later on.

فتجب محبة أولياء الله، والاقتداء بهم، وولايتهم، والقرب منهم.

It is incumbent to love the allies of Allah ﷻ, to follow their example, to be their allies and to be near them.

وقوله : (ولا نفضل أحداً من الأولياء علىٰ أحد من الأنبياء عليهم السلام): رد علىٰ الصوفية، فعندهم غلو في الأولياء. وأنهم عندهم أفضل من الأنبياء وأهل السنة والجماعة لا يغلون في الأولياء وينزلونهم منازلهم، أما الصوفية الضلال فيفضلونهم علىٰ الأنبياء، يقول قائلهم:

مقـام النبوة في منـزل فويـق الرسـول ودون الولـي

The author's statement: **"We do not give superiority to any of the *awliyā'* (Allah's allies) over any of the Prophets"** is a refutation of the Ṣūfīs, as they are excessive with respect to *awliyā'*. To them, they are superior to the Prophets. Ahl al-Sunnah wa 'l-Jamā'ah are not excessive with respect to the *awliyā'*, but place them in their proper place. The misguided Ṣūfīs, on the other hand, consider them superior to the Prophets and say: *The status of a prophet is just above a messenger but under a walī.*

وهذا كفر؛ لأن الأفضل الرسل ثم الأنبياء ثم الأولياء، وسبب تقديم الولي علىٰ النبي عند الصوفية – علىٰ زعمهم – أن الولي يأخذ عن الله مباشرة، والنبي يأخذ بواسطة.

This is disbelief, as the superior ones are the Messengers, then the Prophets and then the *awliyā'*. The reason why *awliyā'* are given precedence to the

Prophets in the view of the Ṣūfīs, as they so claim, is that a *walī* receives divine messages directly from Allah ﷻ and a prophet receives them through an intermediary.

وقوله: **(ونقول: نبي واحد أفضل من جميع الأولياء)**: وهذا لا شك فيه، فجميع الأولياء من أول الخلق إلىٰ آخرهم لا يعادلون نبيًا واحداً، وهذه عقيدة أهل السنة والجماعة.

"Rather, we say that a single prophet is better than all of the *awliyā'*": There is no doubt about this. All of the *awliyā'*, from the first to the last of all creatures, are never equal to a single prophet. And this is the creed of Ahl al-Sunnah wa 'l-Jamā'ah.

المتن

(٢٠٥) وَنُؤْمِنُ بِما جاءَ مِنْ كَراماتِهِمْ، وَصَحَّ عَنِ الثِّقاتِ مِنْ رِواياتِهِمْ.

(205) We believe in the *karāmāt* (miracles) that have occurred from them, and what is authentically reported from them by reliable narrators.

الشرح

هذا بحث عظيم، وهو بحث الكرامات، فالكرامة هي الخارق للعادة، فإن كانت علىٰ يد نبي فهي معجزة، مثل معجزة القرآن، فالإنس والجن عجزوا عن أن يأتوا بمثله، وهي أعظم المعجزات، ومثل معجزة عصا موسىٰ، والتسع الآيات، ومثل إحياء الموتىٰ لعيسىٰ ابن مريم؛ وإن جرت الخارقة علىٰ يد رجل صالح فهو كرامة من الله أجراها علىٰ يده، وليس من عنده، مثل ما حصل لأصحاب الكهف وما حصل لمريم ﴿كُلَّمَا دَخَلَ عَلَيْهَا زَكَرِيَّا ٱلْمِحْرَابَ وَجَدَ عِندَهَا رِزْقًا﴾ [آل عمران:٣٧] فكان يأتيها رزقها وهي تتعبّد الله ولم تخرج من المحراب، وكذلك ما حصل من كرامات لهذه الأمة، وقد ذكر شيخ الإسلام طرفًا منها في

كتابه: الفرقان.

This is a great subject, namely that of *karāmāt* (miracles). A *karāmah* is a paranormal event. If it takes place at the hands of a prophet, then it is a *muʿjizah* (an inimitable miracle presented as a challenge) such as the inimitable challenge of the Qurʾān. Man and jinn lack the ability to produce anything like it and it is the greatest miracle. There are other great miracles like the miracle of Mūsā's ﷺ stick and the nine signs given to him; and like the bringing of the dead to life by ʿĪsā ﷺ, the son of Maryam. If it happens at the hands of a righteous person, then it is a *karāmah* (honour) from Allah, who causes it to occur at one's hand but it does not actually originate from that person. Examples of this are what occurred with the companions of the cave (*aṣḥāb al-kahf*) and what occurred with Maryam. **{Every time Zechariah entered upon her in the prayer chamber, he found with her provision.} [Qurʾān 3:37]** She used to receive sustenance while she devoted herself in worship to Allah, and did not part from her chamber. Similarly, *karāmāt* have occurred to members of this *Ummah*. Shaykh al-Islām mentions several instances of them in his book, *al-Furqān*.

أما إذا جرىٰ الخارق علىٰ يد كاهن أو ساحر فهذا خارق شيطاني، يجري علىٰ يده من أجل الابتلاء والامتحان، فقد يطير في الهواء ويمشي علىٰ الماء ويعمل أعمالاً خارقة للعادة وهي من أعمال الشياطين.

If a paranormal event happens at the hands of a diviner or sorcerer, on the other hand, then it is a satanic paranormal event and it happens at such a person's hands as a trial and test. For instance, one may fly in the air, walk on water or do other paranormal acts, but they are acts of devils.

والضابط: أننا ننظر إلىٰ عمله، فإن كان موافقاً للإسلام، فما يجري علىٰ يده كرامة، وإلا فهو من خدمة الشياطين له.

The guiding principle is that we look at a person's actions. If they are in agreement with Islām then the things that happen at his hands are *karāmāt*. Otherwise, they are a service to him from the devils.

قال تعالىٰ: ﴿وَيَوْمَ يَحْشُرُهُمْ جَمِيعًا يَٰمَعْشَرَ ٱلْجِنِّ قَدِ ٱسْتَكْثَرْتُم مِّنَ ٱلْإِنسِ ۖ وَقَالَ

أَوْلِيَآؤُهُم مِّنَ ٱلْإِنسِ رَبَّنَا ٱسْتَمْتَعَ بَعْضُنَا بِبَعْضٍ﴾ [الأنعام:١٢٨]، فالجني استمتع بالإنسي بالخضوع له وطاعته، والإنسي استمتع بالجني لأنه يخدمه ويحضر له ما يريد.

Allah the Most High says: **{'O company of jinn, you have [misled] many of mankind.' And their allies among mankind will say, 'Our Lord, some of us made use of others.'} [Qur'ān 6:128]** Here, we see that jinns take pleasure in man's subjection and obedience to them, and that man takes pleasure in the jinns because they serve him and bring him what he wants.

قال تعالىٰ: ﴿قَالَ ٱلنَّارُ مَثْوَىٰكُمْ خَٰلِدِينَ فِيهَآ إِلَّا مَا شَآءَ ٱللَّهُ إِنَّ رَبَّكَ حَكِيمٌ عَلِيمٌ ﴿١٢٨﴾ وَكَذَٰلِكَ نُوَلِّي بَعْضَ ٱلظَّٰلِمِينَ بَعْضًا بِمَا كَانُواْ يَكْسِبُونَ ﴿١٢٩﴾﴾ [الأنعام:١٢٨-١٢٩]، فهذه خوارق شيطانية، فالفارق بينها وبين الكرامة: الإيمان والعمل الصالح؛ وهذا هو مذهب أهل السنة والجماعة، أما من عاداهم فقد حصل عنده بسبب فهم الخوارق خلط كثير، فالمعتزلة ومن نحا نحوهم من العقلانيين إلىٰ يومنا هذا ينكرون الكرامات، حتىٰ إن غلاتهم ينكرون بعض المعجزات، ويقولون: هذه لا يثبتها العقل؛ لأنهم يقدمون عقولهم.

Allah ﷻ says: **{He will say, 'The Fire is your residence, wherein you will abide eternally, except for what Allah wills. Indeed, your Lord is Wise and Knowing.' And thus will We make some of the wrongdoers allies of others for what they used to earn.} [Qur'ān 6:128-129]** This is satanic paranormal activity. The difference between it and *karāmāt* is faith and good deeds. This is the doctrine of Ahl al-Sunnah wa 'l-Jamā'ah. Those who oppose Ahl al-Sunnah wa 'l-Jamā'ah have fallen into great confusion on account of the concept of paranormal occurrences. Mu'tazilites and those who have the same tendencies such as the rationalists (*al-'aqlāniyūn*) to this day, deny the existence of *karāmāt*. In fact, extremists among them deny some *mu'jizāt*. They say that such things have not been proven through logic as they give precedence to logic.

الصنف الثاني: وهم القبوريون والصوفيون، غلوا في إثبات الكرامات حتىٰ أثبتوها لأولياء الشيطان، فيثبتونها لمن لا يصلي ولا يصوم إذا جرىٰ علىٰ يده

خارق للعادة، وهي خوارق شيطانية، ومنهم من يغلو في الولي الصالح ويتخذه إلهـًا مع الله كما حدث للقبوريين، فلو قرأت كتاب الشعراني المسمىٰ «طبقات الأولياء» لرأيت العجب العجاب والحكايات الباطلة، فالولي عندهم خرج عن التكاليف ولا يحتاج إلىٰ العبادة.

The grave-worshippers and Ṣūfīs go to excess in their affirmation of *karāmāt* and thus, attribute *karāmāt* to allies of *shayṭān.* They attribute them to people who neither perform the prayer nor fast if something paranormal occurs at the hands of such a person. Yet such instances are satanic paranormal occurrences. There are those from them who go to excess with regard to some righteous *walīs* and associate them as gods and partners with Allah, as is the case with grave-worshippers. If you read a book by al-Shaʿrānī called *Tabaqāt al-Awliyā'*, you would find some of the most astonishing and false accounts. In their view, they are excluded from having any *taklīf* (orders and prohibitions) and are in no need of worshipping or serving Allah.

فالإنسان مهما بلغ من الصلاح والعبادة فإنه لا يخرج عن العبودية، لا الملائكة، ولا الأولياء، ولا الأنبياء، حتىٰ نبينا صلىٰ الله عليه وسلم يقول: «**والله إني لأرجو أن أكون أعلمكم بالله وأتقاكم**»، وهو سيد البشر وخير من مشىٰ علىٰ الأرض، ويقول الله له: ﴿وَٱعْبُدْ رَبَّكَ حَتَّىٰ يَأْتِيَكَ ٱلْيَقِينُ ۝٩٩﴾ [الحجر:٩٩] فما أحد بلغ ما بلغه النبي صلىٰ الله عليه وسلم وما خرج عن عبادة الله.

Regardless of the extent of a person's worship and righteousness, one is never beyond being a servant (of Allah ﷻ). This goes for the angels, *awliyā'* and Prophets. In fact, our Prophet ﷺ said: "By Allah, I have the eager desire to be the most knowledgeable about Allah and God-fearing among you."[137] This is coming from the foremost of all humanity and the best to have walked the earth. Allah ﷻ says to him: **{And worship your Lord until there comes to you the certainty (death).} [Qur'ān 15:99]** There is no one who has ever reached the same heights as the Prophet ﷺ and yet he was not exempted from worshipping Allah.

حتىٰ المسيح صلىٰ الله عليه وسلم يقول الله عز وجل فيه: ﴿لَّن يَسْتَنكِفَ ٱلْمَسِيحُ

137 Al-Bukhārī, no. 5063; Muslim, no. 1110, and both have similar wording.

أَن يَكُونَ عَبْدًا لِّلَّهِ وَلَا ٱلْمَلَٰٓئِكَةُ ٱلْمُقَرَّبُونَ ۚ وَمَن يَسْتَنكِفْ عَنْ عِبَادَتِهِۦ وَيَسْتَكْبِرْ فَسَيَحْشُرُهُمْ إِلَيْهِ جَمِيعًا ﴿١٧٢﴾ فَأَمَّا ٱلَّذِينَ ءَامَنُوا۟ وَعَمِلُوا۟ ٱلصَّٰلِحَٰتِ فَيُوَفِّيهِمْ أُجُورَهُمْ وَيَزِيدُهُم مِّن فَضْلِهِۦ ۖ وَأَمَّا ٱلَّذِينَ ٱسْتَنكَفُوا۟ وَٱسْتَكْبَرُوا۟ فَيُعَذِّبُهُمْ عَذَابًا أَلِيمًا وَلَا يَجِدُونَ لَهُم مِّن دُونِ ٱللَّهِ وَلِيًّا وَلَا نَصِيرًا ﴿١٧٣﴾﴾ [النساء: ١٧٢-١٧٣]

Allah ﷻ says, too, regarding the Messiah عليه السلام: **{Never would the Messiah disdain to be a servant of Allah, nor would the angels near [to Him]. And whoever disdains His worship and is arrogant – He will gather them to Himself all together. And as for those who believed and did righteous deeds, He will give them in full their rewards and grant them extra from His bounty. But as for those who disdained and were arrogant, He will punish them with a painful punishment, and they will not find for themselves besides Allah any protector or helper.} [Qur'ān 4:172-173]**

فهذا بحث عظيم يجب معرفته، وبخاصة في أوقات الجهل والخرافة.

In short, this is a subject of great importance that should be understood, especially in an era of ignorance and false beliefs.

المتن

(٢٠٦) وَنُؤْمِنُ بِأَشْراطِ السّاعَةِ: مِنْ خُرُوجِ الدَّجّال.

(206) We believe in *ashrāṭ al-sā'ah* (the Signs of the Hour), such as the emergence of the Dajjāl.

الشرح

الأشراط: جمع شرط، وهو العلامة، ومنه سمي الشرطي: شرطيًا؛ لوجود العلامة عليه.

Ashrāṭ is the plural of *sharṭ,* which is a sign (*'alāmah),* and thus a *shurṭī* (policeman) is named as such, because of a mark or sign that he carries.

وأشراط الساعة: علاماتها الدالة على قرب وقوعها، قال سبحانة: ﴿فَهَلۡ يَنظُرُونَ إِلَّا ٱلسَّاعَةَ أَن تَأۡتِيَهُم بَغۡتَةٗۖ فَقَدۡ جَآءَ أَشۡرَاطُهَاۚ﴾ [محمد:١٨] فقوله: ﴿فَهَلۡ يَنظُرُونَ﴾ أي: ينتظرون، وقوله: ﴿بَغۡتَةٗۖ﴾ أي: لا يعلم وقتها إلا الله، قال سبحانه: ﴿ثَقُلَتۡ فِي ٱلسَّمَٰوَٰتِ وَٱلۡأَرۡضِۚ لَا تَأۡتِيكُمۡ إِلَّا بَغۡتَةٗۗ﴾ [الأعراف:١٨٧]

The Signs of the Hour are the signs that point to the nearness of the coming of the Hour. Allah ﷻ says: **{Then do they await except that the Hour should come upon them unexpectedly? But already there have come [some of] its indications.} [Qurʾān 47:18]** His saying, here, *fa hal yanẓurūn* (do they wait) means *yantiẓirūn* and His saying, *baghtah,* or *unexpectedly* means that no one knows when it will be besides Allah. Allah ﷻ says: **{It lays heavily upon the heavens and the earth. It will not come upon you except unexpectedly.} [Qurʾān 7:187]**

وقال جبريل للنبي صلى الله عليه وسلم: «أخبرني عن الساعة»، قال: «**ما المسؤول عنها بأعلم من السائل**؟» قال: «أخبرني عن أماراتها»، قال: «**إن تلد الأمة ربتها، وأن ترى الحفاة العراة رعاء الشاء يتطاولون في البنيان**».

Jibrīl once said to the Prophet ﷺ: "Tell me about the Hour." He replied: "The one who is asked about it knows no more than the one who is asking." He said: "Tell me about its signs." He said: "That a slave-girl gives birth to her mistress and that you see the barefoot and naked shepherds competing in raising tall buildings."[138]

وقد ذكر العلماء أن أشراط الساعة على ثلاثة أقسام:

The scholars of Islām have noted that there are three types of signs ahead of the Hour:

القسم الأول: العلامات الصغرى، وهذه حصلت وانقضت.

One. Minor signs which have already come and passed.

القسم الثاني: العلامات الوسطى، هذه ما تزال تحدث مثل ما حدث في زماننا من تقدم الصناعات والاتصالات، واستخراج الكنوز من الأرض، وتقارب البلدان،

138 Al-Bukhārī, no. 50; Muslim, no. 9-10.

حتىٰ كأن العالم قرية واحدة، واجتماع اليهود في فلسطين انتظاراً للدجال، وتوطئة للملاحم التي ستقوم هناك.

Two. Medial signs: These continue to occur, and among them are advancements in industry and communication that have taken place in our times as well as the extracting of treasures from the earth. They also include the convergence of lands to the extent that the world has seemingly become one town, the gathering of the Jews in Palestine in anticipation of the Dajjāl and the precursors of the large scale bloodshed that will occur there.

القسم الثالث: العلامات الكبرىٰ، من خروج الدجال، ونزول عيسىٰ عليه الصلاة والسلام، وخروج يأجوج ومأجوج، وخروج الدابة، ثم طلوع الشمس من مغربها، فهذه إذا حصل أحدها تتابعت البقية.

Three. Major signs, such as the emergence of the Dajjāl, the descent of ʿĪsā ﷷ, the emergence of Gog and Magog, the emergence of the Beast and then the rising of the sun from the west. When these events occur, the rest will follow in succession.

وقوله: **(من خروج الدجال)**: هو أول العلامات الكبرىٰ، وهو من اليهود، ويدّعي الربوبية، ومعه خوارق شيطانية، تفتن الناس، يأمر السماء فتمطر، ويأمر الأرض فتخرج ما فيها من الكنوز والنبات.

"The emergence of the Dajjāl": This is the first of the major signs. The Dajjāl is one of the Jews. He will claim divinity and satanic paranormal occurrences will take place at his hands. He will be a trial for mankind. He will give a command to the sky and it will rain and he will give a command to the earth and treasures and vegetation will come forth from it.

والدجّال هو أشد الفتن؛ لأن الذين يفتنون به كثير؛ لشدة ما معه من الفتن، ومعه جنة ونار، ويأتي علىٰ جميع الأرض إلا مكة والمدينة، وهذه الفتنة تميز المؤمن من الكافر، وسُمّي دجالاً من الدجل، وهو الكذب؛ لكثرة كذبه، وسمي المسيح؛ لأنه يسير في الأرض ويمسحها بسرعة؛ لما هيأ الله له من وسائل المواصلات السريعة، التي هي أسرع من الريح، وقيل: سمي بذلك لأن عينه

ممسوحة، فهو أعور، ويسمىٰ: مسيح الضلالة. فيخرج الدجال فيتبعه اليهود، فيقودهم، ويحصل بسببه علىٰ المسلمين فتنة عظيمة، وما من نبي إلا حذر أمته منه، وأشدهم تحذيراً منه نبينا صلىٰ الله عليه وسلم؛ لأنه آخر الأنبياء، وأمته آخر الأمم، وأقربها للدجال، وأمرنا النبي صلىٰ الله عليه وسلم بعد التشهد الأخير من الصلاة: «**أن نتعوذ بالله من أربع: من عذاب جهنم، ومن عذاب القبر، ومن فتنة المحيا والممات، ومن فتنة المسيح الدجال**» فهو فتنة عظيمة وشر كبير، فينزل عيسىٰ عليه الصلاة والسلام من السماء فيقتله بباب «لد» فيريح الله منه المسلمين، ثم يحكم عيسىٰ بحكم الإسلام، فهو تابع للنبي صلىٰ الله عليه وسلم؛ لأنه ليس بعد نبينا نبي، وليس بعد شريعة الإسلام شريعة.

The Dajjāl is the greatest trial of faith and many will be seduced by him because of the great trials that he has. He has a paradise and a hell and will go to all places on earth besides Makkah and Madīnah. These trials of faith distinguish the believers from the disbelievers. The Dajjāl gets his name from the root *d – j – l* which denotes *deception,* or *lies,* because of his frequent lying. And he is called the *masīḥ* because he travels and journeys (*yamsaḥu,* from *m – s – ḥ*) the earth quickly, as Allah ﷻ gives him speedy means of transportation that will be faster than wind. But it is alternatively said that he is named so because one of his eyes is smoothed out (*mamsūḥah,* from *m – s – ḥ*). He is one-eyed and is also called the '*masīḥ* of misguidance' (*masīḥ al-ḍalālah*). The Dajjāl will emerge and will be followed by the Jews. He will lead them and be a cause of the occurrence of great trials of faith for the Muslims. There was never a prophet who did not warn his people of him and our Prophet ﷺ was the most ardent in his warnings, as he was the final prophet, and his community of believers is the final community of believers and the nearest of them to the Dajjāl. The Prophet ﷺ commanded us to seek refuge in Allah from four things after we recite the last *tashahhud* of the prayer: To seek refuge from the punishment of the Fire, from the punishment of the grave, from the trials of life and death and from the trial of al-Masīḥ al-Dajjāl.[139] Thus, his coming is a great trial of faith and an immense evil. Then, 'Isā ﷺ will descend from the heavens and kill him at the gate of Ludd, and Allah ﷻ thereby relieves the Muslims of him. Then, 'Īsā will judge by the law of Islām and is thus a follower of the Prophet ﷺ, as

139 Al-Tirmidhī, no. 3613. Al-Tirmidhī said: This *ḥadīth* is *ḥasan ṣaḥīḥ*.

there is no prophet to come after our prophet and there is no law after the law of Islām.

ثم يخرج في وقته يأجوج ومأجوج، وهم أيضـًا فتنة عظيمة، قال تعالىٰ: ﴿حَتَّىٰٓ إِذَا فُتِحَتۡ يَأۡجُوجُ وَمَأۡجُوجُ وَهُم مِّن كُلِّ حَدَبٖ يَنسِلُونَ ﴿٩٦﴾﴾ [الأنبياء:٩٦]، وهم أمة من الأمم من بني آدم، كانوا في زمان الإسكندر ذي القرنين، وبنىٰ دونهم السد، قال الله تعالىٰ: ﴿فَمَا ٱسۡطَٰعُوٓاْ أَن يَظۡهَرُوهُ وَمَا ٱسۡتَطَٰعُواْ لَهُۥ نَقۡبٗا ﴿٩٧﴾﴾ [الكهف:٩٧]

Then, in his time, Gog and Magog will emerge and they will also be a great trial. Allah ﷻ says: **{Until when [the dam of] Gog and Magog has been opened and they, from every elevation, descend.} [Qur'ān 21:96]** They are a race of humans who lived in the time of al-Iskander, "*Dhu'l-Qarnayn*". He built a dam to blockade them. Allah ﷻ says: **{So Gog and Magog were unable to pass over it, nor were they able [to put] in it any penetration.} [Qur'ān 18:97]**

فلا يستطيعون الصعود فوق الحائط، ولا يستطيعون نقبة؛ لقوته؛ لأنه من الحديد والبأس الشديد، ولكن إذا جاء وعد الله جعله دكـًا، فيخرجون ويفتكون بالعالم، وليس لأحد طاقة في قتالهم، ثم يهلكهم الله في ساعة واحدة.

They are not able to climb over the wall nor penetrate a hole through it, because of its strength as it is made of iron and mighty strength. However, when Allah's ﷻ promised time has come, it will be made level, they will eradicate people throughout the world and no one will have the power to fight them. Then, Allah ﷻ will cause them to perish in one hour.

المتن

(٢٠٧) ونُزُولِ عِيسَىٰ ابنِ مَرْيَمَ عَلَيْهِ السَّلامُ مِنَ السَّماءِ.

(207) And the descent of 'Īsā (Jesus), the son of Mary, from the heavens.

الشرح

ويسمىٰ بالمسيح؛ لأنه كان يمسح علىٰ ذي العاهة فيشفيه الله، ويسمىٰ: مسيح الهداية، ونزوله من السماء إلىٰ الأرض في آخر الزمان متواتر، ومن أنكر ذلك فهو كافر، قال تعالىٰ: ﴿وَإِنَّهُۥ لَعِلْمٌ لِّلسَّاعَةِ﴾ [الزخرف:٦١] وفي قراءة: (وإنه لعلم للساعة) - بفتح العين واللام - أي: علامة علىٰ قرب الساعة، قال الله سبحانه: ﴿وَإِن مِّنْ أَهْلِ ٱلْكِتَـٰبِ إِلَّا لَيُؤْمِنَنَّ بِهِۦ قَبْلَ مَوْتِهِۦ﴾ [النساء:١٥٩] وهذا في آخر الزمان؛ لأنه حي في السماء ولا يموت إلا بعد إنهاء المهمة الموكلة إليه، فيموت فيدفن في الأرض بعد أن يقتل الدجال والخنزير ويضع الجزية ويحكم بالإسلام.

He is called the *masīḥ,* or Messiah, because he wipes over (*yamsaḥu*) those who have disabilities and Allah ﷻ heals them and is named the '*masīḥ* of guidance'. His descent from the heavens to the earth in the end of times is something that has been concurrently handed down to us in the traditions. Anyone who denies this is a disbeliever. Allah ﷻ says: **{And indeed, Jesus will be [a sign for] knowledge *('ilm)* of the Hour.} [Qur'ān 43:61]** In one variant reading of the Qur'ān: *he will be a sign* (*'alam) of the Hour,* that is, an *'alāmah,* or sign for the nearness of the Hour. Allah ﷻ says: **{And there is none from the People of the Scripture but that he will surely believe in Jesus before his death.} [Qur'ān 4:159]** This is in the end of times. He is living in the heavens and does not die until the task entrusted to him is concluded. He will die and be buried in the earth after slaying the Dajjāl and the swine, imposing the *jizyah* tribute and judging by the law of Islām.

المتن

(٢٠٨) وَنُؤْمِنُ بِطُلُوعِ الشَّمْسِ مِنْ مَغْرِبِهَا.

(208) We believe that the sun will rise from the west

الشرح

الشمس مسخرة تجري بأمر الله، فتخرج من المشرق، وتغرب من المغرب، ثم إذا كان آخر الزمان وحان قيام الساعة أمرها الله سبحانه بالطلوع من المغرب، فتكون علامة للقيامة، وإذا طلعت من مغربها فلا يقبل الله توبة التائب، قال سبحانه: ﴿هَلْ يَنظُرُونَ إِلَّآ أَن تَأْتِيَهُمُ ٱلْمَلَـٰٓئِكَةُ أَوْ يَأْتِيَ رَبُّكَ أَوْ يَأْتِيَ بَعْضُ ءَايَـٰتِ رَبِّكَ ۗ يَوْمَ يَأْتِي بَعْضُ ءَايَـٰتِ رَبِّكَ لَا يَنفَعُ نَفْسًا إِيمَـٰنُهَا لَمْ تَكُنْ ءَامَنَتْ مِن قَبْلُ أَوْ كَسَبَتْ فِىٓ إِيمَـٰنِهَا خَيْرًا ۗ قُلِ ٱنتَظِرُوٓا۟ إِنَّا مُنتَظِرُونَ ﴿١٥٨﴾﴾ [الأنعام:١٥٨] فالكافر يسلم، ولكن لا يقبل الله إسلامه، والعاصي يتوب، ولكن لا تقبل توبته.

The sun is compelled to move by the command of Allah ﷻ. It rises from the east and sets in the west. When the end of time comes and the coming of the Hour approaches, Allah ﷻ will command it to rise from the west, and this will be a sign of Judgment Day. When it rises from the west, Allah ﷻ will not accept anyone's repentance. Allah says: **{Do they [then] wait for anything except that the angels should come to them or your Lord should come or that there come some of the signs of your Lord? The Day that some of the signs of your Lord will come no soul will benefit from its faith as long as it had not believed before or had earned through its faith some good. Say, 'Wait. Indeed, we [also] are waiting.'} [Qur'ān 6:158]** Then, a disbeliever may submit to Allah ﷻ as a Muslim, but Allah ﷻ will not accept their submission (Islām). Likewise, a sinner may repent but Allah ﷻ will not accept their repentance.

❁❁❁

المتن

(٢٠٩) وَخُرُوجِ دابَّةِ الأَرْضِ مِنْ مَوْضِعِها.

(209) And that the Beast will emerge from its place in the earth.

الشرح

قال سبحانه: ﴿وَإِذَا وَقَعَ ٱلْقَوْلُ عَلَيْهِمْ أَخْرَجْنَا لَهُمْ دَآبَّةً مِّنَ ٱلْأَرْضِ تُكَلِّمُهُمْ أَنَّ ٱلنَّاسَ كَانُوا۟ بِـَٔايَـٰتِنَا لَا يُوقِنُونَ ﴿٨٢﴾﴾ [النمل:٨٢] تخرج هذه الدابة فتسم المؤمن والكافر، أي: تضع عليه علامة يتعارف الناس بها، فيتخاطبون، وهذا يقول: يا مسلم، وهذا يقول: يا كافر، ومعنىٰ قول الله: ﴿تكلمهم﴾ بكلام خارق للعادة. وليس عندنا خبر ثابت عن موضع خروجها، لكن نؤمن بخروجها من موضعها الذي يعلمه عالم الغيب والشهادة، قال سبحانه: ﴿أَخْرَجْنَا لَهُمْ دَآبَّةً مِّنَ ٱلْأَرْضِ تُكَلِّمُهُمْ﴾ [النمل:٨٢].

Allah ﷻ says: **{And when the word befalls them, We will bring forth for them a creature from the earth speaking to them, [saying] that the people were, of Our verses, not certain [in faith].} [Qur'ān 27:82]** This Beast will come forth and brand every believer and disbeliever. That is, it will place a mark upon each person whereby people will recognize and address each other. Some will say, 'O, Muslim!' and some will say, 'O, disbeliever!' In the verse, '*speaking to them*' means in a paranormal manner. There are no confirmed reports of the place from which it will emerge. Even so, we believe that it will come forth from a place known by the All-Knower of the unseen and the manifest. Allah ﷻ says: **{We will bring forth for them a creature from the earth speaking to them.} [Qur'ān 27:82]**

المتن

(٢١٠) وَلاَ نُصَدِّقُ كاهِناً وَلاَ عَرّافاً.

(210) We do not believe in diviners or fortune-tellers;

الشرح

سبق أن ذكر المؤلف الكرامات وضابطها، وأن الكرامات حق ثابت، ولا يجوز الاعتماد عليها، ولا يظن بأن للأولياء مرتبة يُدعون فيها مع الله عز وجل، كما يقوله القبوريون والخرافيون، فيتعلقون بالأولياء والصالحين من أهل هذه

الخوارق.

The author has already mentioned *karāmāt* (miracles) and the guiding principle regarding them. He also mentioned that *karāmāt* are an established truth, and that it is not permissible to rely on them. It is not to be believed that *awliyā'* have such a status as to be supplicated to besides Allah ﷻ, as grave-worshippers and some superstitious people believe. They attach themselves to the *awliyā'* and righteous people who are associated with these paranormal occurrences.

أما قوله رحمه الله: **(لا نصدق كاهنًا ولا عرافًا)** ففيه بيان الفرق بين الكرامة والكهانة والعرافة والسحر والشعوذة والتنجيم، فهذه - أي التي مع الكهان والعرافين - خوارق شيطانية وأعمال حذقوها وتعلموها بسبب تقربهم من الشياطين فيظن الناس والجهال أن هذه كرامات وأنها بسبب ولا يتهم لله، وهذا غلط، إنما هي من فعل الشياطين؛ لخضوعهم لهم وموافقتهم علىٰ الشرك، فالسحرة ما توصلوا إلىٰ السحر إلا لخضوعهم للشياطين، فالسحر من عمل الشيطان وهو كفر بالله، فلا يغتر بهم، فهم يقولون: هذه كرامة أو أعمال رياضية أو أعمال بهلوانية، ويحضرون في المحافل والنوادي، ويتركون يعملون السحر أمام الناس، ويقولون: هذه أمور رياضية، ليضلوا الناس وليأكلوا بسحرهم الأموال، فيجب التنبيه علىٰ هؤلاء وبغضهم وعداوتهم؛ لأنهم أعداء الله ولرسوله.

As for his ﷺ statement, **"we do not believe in diviners or fortune-tellers,"** it displays a distinction between *karāmāt* on the one hand, and fortune-telling, divination, sorcery, witchcraft, and astrology on the other. The latter (which fortune-tellers and diviners do) are satanic paranormal activities and practices that such people have mastered and learned in order to seek favour of the devils, and people (especially those who are ignorant) believe that they are miracles and that they happen because those people are *awliyā'* of Allah ﷻ. This is a mistake. They are nothing more than acts of the devils, as those people are subjected to them and go along with them in their polytheism. Thus, whatever sorcery the sorcerers have learned is because of their subordination to the devils. Sorcery (*siḥr*) is among the works of the devil and amounts to disbelief in Allah ﷻ, so one should not be deceived by it. They often say that these things are games or stunts. Magicians appear at assemblies and clubs and are left to perform magic in front of people, and say that they are entertainment and deceive people to take their money with their magic. It is necessary to warn of such people, to hate them and treat them as enemies, because they are the enemies of Allah ﷻ and the Messenger of Allah.

والسحر علىٰ قسمين:

There are two types of magic:

القسم الأول: سحر حقيقي: وهو ما يؤثر في بدن المسحور فيمرضه أو يؤثر علىٰ عقله أو يقتله، فهذا عمل شيطاني.

One. Real magic. This type has an effect on the body of the bewitched person, causing one to be sick, altering their mind or even killing them. This is a satanic act.

القسم الثاني: سحر تخييلي، قال الله تعالىٰ: ﴿يُخَيَّلُ إِلَيْهِ مِن سِحْرِهِمْ أَنَّهَا تَسْعَىٰ ﴿٦٦﴾﴾ [طه:٦٦] وهو ما يسمىٰ: القمرة، فيعملون شيئًا علىٰ أعين الناس، وهو ليس له حقيقة، فيظهر منه أن يضرب نفسه بالسيف، وأنه يأكل المسامير أو النار أو الزجاج، أو يدخل في النار، أو أن السيارة تمشي عليه، أو ينام علىٰ مسامير، أو يجر السيارة بشعره، أو يأتي بأوراق عادية، ويروج علىٰ الناس أنها نقود، وإذا ذهب سرحه عادت الأوراق إلىٰ أصلها، كما يحصل من النشالين. ومن أعمال السحرة أيضًا: أن يأتي أحدهم بجعلٍ، وهي الحشرة المعروفة، ويُظهر بسحره أمام الناس أنها خروف، وكذلك فهم يروجون علىٰ الناس أنهم يمشون علىٰ خيط دقيق، وهو ما يسمىٰ السرك، أو ما يسمىٰ بالبهلوان.

Two. Illusionary magic. Allah ﷻ says: **{And suddenly their ropes and staffs seemed to him from their magic that they were moving [like snakes].} [Qur'ān 20:66]** This is called *al-qumrah*. They do something to people's vision but it is not real. So it appears that the person is striking himself with a sword, or eating nails or fire or glass, or entering a fire, or that a car is running over him, or that they are sleeping on nails, or that he is dragging a car by his hair or that he is turning normal pieces of paper into money. When the illusion is finished, the paper turns back to normal as with pickpockets. Other magic acts include presenting a beetle, the known insect, and making it to appear to people as a lamb as well as trying to convince people that one is walking a tightrope. This is called circus acting or stunt artistry.

فهذا كله كذب وتدجيل علىٰ الناس، وسحر لأعين الناس، وهو سحر تخييلي، إذا ذهب هذا السحر عادت الأمور كما هي، فيجب علينا أن لا نغتر بهم ولا نصدقهم ولا نمكنهم من أولادنا ولا بلادنا من أجل ترويج سحرهم.

All of these things are lies and fraudulent and are also a form of magic to people's eyes. They are called illusionary magic, because when the magic disappears, everything returns back to normal. Therefore, we should not be deceived by such people, and we should neither believe them nor allow them to promote their magic to our children or in our lands.

وأما الكاهن: فهو الذي يدعي علم الغيب وقد أخبرنا النبي صلىٰ الله عليه وسلم أن الشياطين يسترقون السمع فيسرقون الكلمة، فيخبرون بها الكاهن فيكذب معها مائة كذبة فيصدقه الناس في كل ما قال بسبب تلك الكلمة، قال سبحانه: ﴿ هَلْ أُنَبِّئُكُمْ عَلَىٰ مَن تَنَزَّلُ ٱلشَّيَٰطِينُ ﴿٢٢١﴾ تَنَزَّلُ عَلَىٰ كُلِّ أَفَّاكٍ أَثِيمٍ ﴿٢٢٢﴾ يُلْقُونَ ٱلسَّمْعَ وَأَكْثَرُهُمْ كَٰذِبُونَ ﴿٢٢٣﴾﴾ [الشعراء:٢٢١-٢٢٣]

A diviner (*kāhin*), on the other hand, is someone who claims to have knowledge of the unseen (*al-ghayb*). The Prophet ﷺ told us that devils eavesdrop what they can of what is spoken in the heavens and tell the diviner. The diviner, though, tells a hundred lies along with that one word; and so people believe in everything that he says because of that one word. Allah says: **{Shall I inform you upon whom the devils descend? They descend upon every sinful liar. They pass on what is heard, and most of them are liars.} [Qur'ān 26:221-223]**

وكانت الكهانة في الجاهلية كثيرة، فكان في كل قبيلة كاهن يتحاكمون إليه ويسألونه عن الأمور الغائبة، ولما جاء الإسلام أبطل الكهانة ومنع النبي صلىٰ الله عليه وسلم من الذهاب إلىٰ الكهان، قال عليه الصلاة والسلام: «من أتىٰ

كاهناً لم يقبل منه صلاة أربعين يوماً» وهذا الحديث في صحيح مسلم.

There was much divination in the pre-Islamic period of *jāhiliyyah* (ignorance). Each tribe had a diviner (*kāhin*) that they referred to for judgment and asked about matters of the unseen. When Islām came, divination was put to an end and the Prophet ﷺ forbade going to diviners. The Prophet ﷺ said: "Whoever goes to a diviner, their prayer will not be accepted for forty days."[140] This report is in *Ṣaḥīḥ Muslim*.

وجاء في السنن **«من أتىٰ كاهناً أو عرافاً فصدّقه بما يقول فقد كفر بما أنزل علىٰ محمد»**، ولما سُئل عن الكهان قال: **«ليسوا بشيء»**، وقال النبي صلىٰ الله عليه وسلم: **«لا تأتوهم»**.

It has been presented in the *Sunan* literature that "whoever goes to a *kāhin* or an *ʿarrāf* and believes what he says has disbelieved in what was revealed to Muḥammad."[141] And when asked about diviners, he said: "They are nothing." And the Prophet ﷺ said: "Do not go to them."

فالكاهن: هو الذي يدّعي علم الغيب، بسبب تعامله مع الشيطان.

A *kāhin* is someone who claims to have knowledge of the unseen because of his dealings with the devil.

وأما العراف : فهو الذي يدّعي علم الغيب، لكن ليس بواسطة الشياطين، وإنما بالحدس والتخمين، فيقول: يمكن أن يقع كذا وكذا، بناء علىٰ تنبؤات كاذبة.

An *ʿarrāf*, on the other hand, is someone who claims to have knowledge of the unseen not through devils but rather through intuition and guesswork. He would say 'it's possible for such and such to happen' based on false predictions.

وقال بعض أهل العلم: إن العراف هو الكاهن، كل منهما يخبر عن الأمور الغائبة لكن باختلاف الوسيلة، فيجب علىٰ المسلم أن يكفر بالكهانة والعرافة،

---

140 Muslim, no. 2230.

141 Aḥmad, 2/429; al-Ḥākim, 1/8. Al-Ḥākim said: This is an authentic *ḥadīth* according to the criteria of al-Bukhārī and Muslim.

ولا يصدق أهلها، فهم ليسوا من أولياء الله، إنما هم من أولياء الشيطان، ومن أراد التوسع في هذا فليراجع كتاب «الفرقان» لشيخ الإسلام.

Some of the scholars said that an *ʿarrāf* is a *kāhin*. Each one of them tells of matters of the unseen but through different means. It is incumbent on all Muslims to disbelieve in all divination and fortune-telling and not to trust those who practice them. They are not among Allah's *awliyāʾ* but are rather allies of the Devil. If one would like to seek more extensive content on this matter, then the book *al-Furqān* by Shaykh al-Islām may be referred to.

وأما التنجيم فالمنجم: هو الذي يخبر عن الأمور المستقبلة بواسطة النظر في النجوم، إذا طلع النجم الفلاني يحصل كذا، وإذا غرب النجم الفلاني يحصل كذا، والبرج الفلاني فيه نحس أو فيه سعادة، وهكذا يستندون إلىٰ هذه الأعمال الكاذبة.

As for astrology (*tanjīm*), a *munajjim* (astrologer) is someone who predicts the future by looking at the stars. If a certain star rises, such and such will happen; and if a certain star sets, such and such will happen; or a certain constellation is a sign of misfortune or happiness. They use such fallacies as bases for their predictions.

فالتنجيم: (هو نسبة الحوادث الأرضية إلىٰ الأحوال الفلكية) كما عرفه شيخ الإسلام. والتنجيم من أمور الجاهلية، قال عليه الصلاة والسلام: «**أربع في أمتي من أمور الجاهلية لا يتركونهن: الطعن في الأنساب، والفخر بالأحساب، والنياحة علىٰ الميت، والاستسقاء بالنجوم**»، أي: طلب السقاية من النجوم.

Thus, *tanjīm* is the attribution of events on earth to astronomical events, as defined by Shaykh al-Islām. *Tanjīm* is something that was practiced in the pre-Islamic period of ignorance (*jāhiliyyah*). The Prophet ﷺ said: "There are four matters of *jāhiliyyah* that my *Ummah* will not leave: attacking [the reputations of] lineages, boasting of noble descent, wailing for the dead and asking the stars for water."[142]

قال سبحانه وتعالىٰ: ﴿فَلَآ أُقۡسِمُ بِمَوَٰقِعِ ٱلنُّجُومِ ۝٧٥ وَإِنَّهُۥ لَقَسَمٞ لَّوۡ تَعۡلَمُونَ

142 Muslim, no. 934.

عَظِيمٌ ﴿٧٦﴾ إِنَّهُۥ لَقُرْءَانٌ كَرِيمٌ ﴿٧٧﴾ فِي كِتَٰبٍ مَّكْنُونٍ ﴿٧٨﴾ لَّا يَمَسُّهُۥٓ إِلَّا ٱلْمُطَهَّرُونَ ﴿٧٩﴾ تَنزِيلٌ مِّن رَّبِّ ٱلْعَٰلَمِينَ ﴿٨٠﴾ أَفَبِهَٰذَا ٱلْحَدِيثِ أَنتُم مُّدْهِنُونَ ﴿٨١﴾ وَتَجْعَلُونَ رِزْقَكُمْ أَنَّكُمْ تُكَذِّبُونَ ﴿٨٢﴾﴾ [الواقعة:٧٥-٨٢]، أي: تنسبون ما يحصل لكم من الرزق للنجوم والحوادث الفلكية، فهذا من اعتقاد الجاهلية، فالنجوم إنما هي خلق من خلق الله مسخرة، وخلقها الله لثلاث حكم:

Allah ﷻ says: **{Then I swear by the setting of the stars, and indeed, it is an oath – if you could know – [most] great. Indeed, it is a noble Qur'ān in a Register well-protected; none touch it except the purified. [It is] a revelation from the Lord of the worlds. Then is it to this statement that you are indifferent and make [the thanks for] your provision that you deny [the Provider]?} [Qur'ān 56:75-82]** That is, you attribute the sustenance that you are given to the stars and astronomical events. This is among the beliefs of the pre-Islamic *jāhiliyyah*. The stars are among Allah's ﷻ creations and they are under Allah's subjection. Allah ﷻ created them for three reasons:

الأولى: أنها زينة للسماء الدنيا.

One. To be an adornment for the lowest heaven.

الثانية: أنها رجوم للشياطين.

Two. To stone the devils.

الثالثة: أنها علامات يهتدي بها في ظلمات البر والبحر.

Three. To be guiding signs in the darkness in the land and the sea.

فمن اعتقد أنها لغير ذلك فهو قد أضاع نصيبه.

If anyone believes that they are there for something else, then they have lost whatever good was given to them.

وإذا تدبرت القرآن وجدت أن الله ذكر للنجوم ثلاث فوائد، أما ما يحدث في الأرض من حوادث فليس للنجوم فيها تأثير، وإنما المنجمون يُدَلسون ويكذبون

علىٰ الناس، ويقولون: إن هذه الحوادث بسبب النجوم، قال سبحانه: ﴿وَٱلنُّجُومُ مُسَخَّرَٰتُۢ بِأَمۡرِهِۦٓۚ﴾ [النحل:١٢]، فهذه الأمور تخل بالعقيدة، ويبطل إيمانه إذا صدق أن النجوم هي التي فعلت هذا الشيء بالكون.

If you reflect upon the Qur'ān, you would find that Allah ﷻ has mentioned three benefits of the stars. However, whatever events happen on earth are not at all affected by the stars. Rather, astrologers falsify information and lie to people. They say that such events occur because of the stars. Allah ﷻ says: **{...and the stars are subjected by His command.} [Qur'ān 16:12]** These matters abdicate [Islamic] creed and render one's faith invalid if one believes that stars themselves are what cause things to happen in the universe.

❁❁❁

المتن

(٢١١) وَلاَ مَنْ يَدَّعِي شَيْئًا يُخالِفُ الكِتابَ والسُّنَّةَ وإجْماعَ الأُمَّةِ.

(211) Or anyone who claims anything contrary to the Qur'ān, Sunnah and the consensus of the Ummah.

الشرح

أي: لا نصدق أحداً يخالف الكتاب أو السنة أو الإجماع؛ لأنها الأدلة التي يعتمد عليها، فما خالفها فهو باطل، سواء من الأقوال أو الأعمال أو الاعتقادات.

That is, we do not attest truthful anyone if he says something contrary to the Qur'ān, Sunnah, or consensus (*ijmā'*), because evidence is based on these things, so anything that runs counter to them is false, be they statements, actions, or beliefs.

❁❁❁

المتن

(٢١٢) وَنَرَىٰ الجَماعَةَ حَقًّا وَصَوابـًا، والفُرْقَةَ زَيْغـًا وَعَذابـًا.

(212) We consider unity (*jamāʿah*) right and correct and we consider division deviation and punishment.

الشرح

نرىٰ - معشر أهل السنة والجماعة - أن الاجتماع حق والفرقة عذاب، فالاجتماع للأمة علىٰ الحق رحمة، والفرقة بينها عذاب، وهذا من صميم عقيدة أهل السنة والجماعة، فيجب الاجتماع ونبذ الفرقة، قال سبحانه وتعالىٰ: ﴿وَٱعْتَصِمُواْ بِحَبْلِ ٱللَّهِ جَمِيعًا وَلَا تَفَرَّقُواْ﴾ [آل عمران:١٠٣]، فحبل الله القرآن والإسلام، وقوله: (جميعاً) أي: اجتمعوا علىٰ القرآن والسنة، وقوله: (ولا تفرقوا) لما أمر الله بالاجتماع نهىٰ عن الفرقة، وأخبر أن الاجتماع يكون علىٰ حبل الله، وهو القرآن، ولا يجوز الاجتماع علىٰ غيره من المذاهب والحزبيات، فهذا يُسبب الفرقة.

We, Ahl al-Sunnah wa ʾl-Jamāʿah, hold that unity is truth and division is a punishment. The unity of the *Ummah* upon the truth is mercy, and their division is a punishment. This lies at the heart of the creed of Ahl al-Sunnah wa ʾl-Jamāʿah. It is incumbent to unite and to reject division. Allah ﷻ says: **{And hold firmly to the rope of Allah all together and do not become divided.} [Qurʾān 3:103]** The *rope of Allah* ﷻ is the Qurʾān and Islām. His words, *all together,* mean "be united upon the Qurʾān and Sunnah". ...*And do not become divided:* Having commanded unity, Allah ﷻ forbade division and He proclaims that unity is to be upon the *rope of Allah,* that is, *the Qurʾān,* and it is not permissible to unite for the sake of any other doctrines or groups. This causes division.

فالاجتماع لا يحصل إلا علىٰ كتاب الله، قال سبحانه: ﴿وَٱعْتَصِمُواْ بِحَبْلِ ٱللَّهِ جَمِيعًا وَلَا تَفَرَّقُواْ﴾ [آل عمران:١٠٣].

Thus, unity does not take place except upon the Book of Allah. Allah ﷻ says: **{And hold firmly to the rope of Allah all together and do not become divided.} [Qurʾān 3:103]**

فأمر الله سبحانه بالاجتماع ونبذ الفرقة في الآراء وفي القلوب، فالمسلمون مهما تفرقوا وبعدت أقطارهم فإنّهم مجتمعون علىٰ الحق، وقلوبهم مجتمعة،

ويحب بعضهم بعضاً، أما أهل الباطل وإن كانوا في مكان واحد، أحدهم إلىٰ جنب الآخر، فهم مجتمعة أبدانهم متفرقة قلوبهم، قال سبحانه: ﴿تَحْسَبُهُمْ جَمِيعًا وَقُلُوبُهُمْ شَتَّىٰ﴾ وقال تعالىٰ: ﴿وَلَا تَكُونُوا۟ كَٱلَّذِينَ تَفَرَّقُوا۟ وَٱخْتَلَفُوا۟ مِنۢ بَعْدِ مَا جَآءَهُمُ ٱلْبَيِّنَٰتُ ۚ وَأُو۟لَٰٓئِكَ لَهُمْ عَذَابٌ عَظِيمٌ ﴿١٠٥﴾﴾ [آل عمران:١٠٥]، وقال سبحانه: ﴿وَلَا تَكُونُوا۟ مِنَ ٱلْمُشْرِكِينَ ﴿٣١﴾ مِنَ ٱلَّذِينَ فَرَّقُوا۟ دِينَهُمْ وَكَانُوا۟ شِيَعًا ۖ كُلُّ حِزْبٍۭ بِمَا لَدَيْهِمْ فَرِحُونَ ﴿٣٢﴾﴾ [الروم:٣١-٣٢]، وقال سبحانه: ﴿أَنْ أَقِيمُوا۟ ٱلدِّينَ وَلَا تَتَفَرَّقُوا۟ فِيهِ﴾ [الشورىٰ:١٣].

Allah ﷻ commands us to unite and to reject the division of our views and hearts. However much the Muslims are split and however far their lands are from each other, they are still united upon the truth, their hearts are united and they love each other. The people of falsehood, on the other hand, regardless of whether they are in one place or one of them is right next to the other, their bodies are united but their hearts are divided. Allah ﷻ says: **{You think they are together, but their hearts are diverse.} [Qur'ān 59:14]** Allah ﷻ also says: **{And do not be like the ones who became divided and differed after the clear proofs had come to them. And those will have a great punishment.} [Qur'ān 3:105]** Allah ﷻ also says: **{And do not be of those who associate others with Allah, [or] of those who have divided their religion and become sects, every faction rejoicing in what it has.} [Qur'ān 30:31-32]** Allah ﷻ also says: **{...to establish the religion and not be divided therein.} [Qur'ān 42:13]**

فالواجب علىٰ المسلمين أن يكونوا أمة واحدة في عقيدتها وفي عبادتها وفي جماعتها وطاعتها لولي أمرها، فتكون يداً واحدة، وجسماً واحداً، وبنياناً واحداً، كما شبهها النبي عليه الصلاة والسلام، وهذا رحمة للمسلمين، تُحقن دماؤهم، وتتآلف قلوبهم، ويأمن مجتمعهم، فإذا حصل هذا درت عليهم الأرزاق. أما إذا تناحروا وتقاطعوا وتباغضوا تسلط عليهم الأعداء، وسفك بعضهم دماء بعض.

It is incumbent on the Muslims to be united in their creed, worship, community and obedience to their leader. And they should thus be one hand, one body and one structure, as the Prophet ﷺ likened them to. This is a mercy to the Muslims. Their blood would be spared, their hearts would be brought together and their societies would be safe. When this happens, they will receive abundant good. But if they rival each other, break relations and hate each other, the enemy will gain the upperhand over them, and they will shed each other's blood.

والاختلاف علىٰ قسمين:

There are two types of differing:

القسم الأول: اختلاف في العقيدة، وهذا لا يجوز أبداً؛ لأنه يوجب التناحر والعداوة والبغضاء ويفرق الكلمة، فيجب أن يكون المسلمون علىٰ عقيدة واحدة، وهي عقيدة لا إله إلا الله، واعتقاد ذلك قولاً وعملاً واعتقاداً، والعقيدة توقيفية ليست محلاً للاجتهاد، فإذا كانت كذلك فليس فيها مجال للتفرق، فالعقيدة مأخوذة من الكتاب والسنة، لا من الآراء والاجتهادات، فالفرقة في العقيدة تؤدّي إلىٰ التناحر والتباغض والتقاطع، كما حصل من الجهمية والمعتزلة والأشاعرة والفرق الضالة التي أخبر عنها النبي صلىٰ الله عليه وسلم بقوله: «**ستفترق هذه الأمة علىٰ ثلاث وسبعين فرقة، كلها في النار إلا واحدة**» قالوا: من هي يا رسول الله؟ قال: «**من كان علىٰ مثل ما أنا عليه وأصحابي**» فما يجمع الناس إلا ما كان مثل ما عليه النبي صلىٰ الله عليه وسلم وأصحابه.

The first type is differing in creed (*ʿaqīdah*). This is never permissible because it causes disputes, enmity, hate and disunion. So it is incumbent that the Muslims have one creed, namely, the creed of *lā ilāha illa ʾllāh* (there is no God but Allah) and to believe in that in word, in action and in the heart. Moreover, creed is something that has been prescribed and is not a matter of personal judgment and therefore, there is no possibility for division. Furthermore, creed is derived from the Qurʾān and Sunnah, and not from opinions and personal judgments of scholars. Division in creed results in bitter fighting, hate, and the breaking of relations, as occurred with the Jahmīs, the Muʿtazilites, the Ashʿarites and all other deviant sects that the Prophet ﷺ prophesied of in his statement, "This *Ummah* will divide into seventy-three sects. All of them are in the Fire except for one." It was said,

"Which one, O Messenger of Allah?" He said: "The one that is in conformity with what I and my companions are upon."[143] Thus, there is nothing that unites people except what is in conformity with what the Prophet ﷺ and his Companions followed.

القسم الثاني: اختلاف في الاجتهاد الفقهي، وهذا لا يوجب عداوة؛ لأن سببه هو النظر في الأدلة حسب مدارك الناس، والناس يختلفون في ذلك، وليسوا علىٰ حد سواء، فهم يختلفون في قوة الاستنباط وفي كثرة العلم وقلته.

The second type is differing in matters of discretionary judgment in jurisprudence (*fiqh*). This does not cause enmity because it amounts to the study of evidence according to the perceptions of people, and people differ in that respect. They are not all the same. They differ in their ability to draw inferences from the evidence and in the extent of their knowledge.

فهذا الخلاف إذا لم يصحبه تعصب للرأي فإنه لا يفضي إلىٰ العداوة، وكان الصحابة يختلفون في المسائل الفقهية، ولا يحدث بينهم عداوة، وهم إخوة، وكذلك السلف الصالح والأئمة الأربعة يختلفون، ولم يحصل بينهم عداوة، وهم إخوة، وكذلك أتباعهم، فإذا تعصب أحدهم للرأي فإن ذلك يوجب العداوة، ويجب علىٰ المسلم أن يأخذ الأقوال التي توافق الدليل من الكتاب أو السنة، قال سبحانه: ﴿فَإِن تَنَٰزَعۡتُمۡ فِي شَيۡءٖ فَرُدُّوهُ إِلَى ٱللَّهِ وَٱلرَّسُولِ إِن كُنتُمۡ تُؤۡمِنُونَ بِٱللَّهِ وَٱلۡيَوۡمِ ٱلۡأٓخِرِۚ﴾ [النساء:٥٩]، وقال سبحانه: ﴿وَمَا ٱخۡتَلَفۡتُمۡ فِيهِ مِن شَيۡءٖ فَحُكۡمُهُۥٓ إِلَى ٱللَّهِۚ﴾ [الشورىٰ:١٠] فيرجع في الخلاف إلىٰ الكتاب والسنة ويؤخذ ما ترجح بالدليل .

This kind of differing (as long as it does not reach the level of bigotry to a view) does not result in enmity. The Companions differed in matters of jurisprudence and no enmity occurred among them. They were brothers. Moreover, the righteous early Muslims and the Four Imāms differed, and no enmity occurred among them. They were brothers. This is also the case for their followers. If any of them were to have fanaticism for an opinion,

143 Abū Dāwūd, no. 4569; Ibn Mājah, no. 3991; Aḥmad, 2/332; al-Ḥākim, 1/128. Al-Ḥākim said that it is sound.

it would result in enmity. It is incumbent on every Muslim to adopt the opinions that are in agreement with the Qurʾān and Sunnah. Allah ﷻ says: **{O you who have believed, obey Allah and obey the Messenger and those in authority among you. And if you disagree over anything, refer it to Allah and the Messenger, if you should believe in Allah and the Last Day.} [Qurʾān 4:59]** Allah ﷻ also says: **{And in anything over which you disagree – its ruling is [to be referred] to Allah.} [Qurʾān 42:10]** So, differences of opinion are to be referred back to the Qurʾān and Sunnah, and that which has the weightiest evidence is to be adopted.

المتن

(٢١٣) وَدِينُ الله في الأرضِ والسَّماءِ واحِدٌ، وهُو دينُ الإسْلَامِ.

(213) Allah's religion is one in the heavens and on earth. It is the religion of Islām.

الشرح

والإسلام عبادة الله وحده لا شريك له، فهذا تدين به الملائكة في السماء والإنس والجن في الأرض، وهو دين الإسلام، ومعناه بمفهومه العام: هو الاستسلام لله بالتوحيد، والانقياد له بالطاعة، والخلوص من الشرك، كما عرفه شيخ الإسلام ونقله عنه الشيخ محمد بن عبد الوهاب في الثلاثة الأصول، فالإسلام دين جميع الأنبياء وأتباعهم، فكل نبي دعا قومه إلىٰ ذلك، وكل من اتبعه علىٰ ذلك فيعتبر مسلماً، سواء من أول الخلق أو آخرهم، فهو مستسلم لله بالتوحيد ومنقاد إلىٰ الله بالطاعة، فدين الأنبياء واحد، وشرائعهم شتىٰ ومختلفة بسبب حاجة البشر في كل زمان ومكان، ففي الحديث: «**الأنبياء إخوة لعلات، أمهاتهم شتىٰ، ودينهم واحد**» وقال تعالىٰ: ﴿لِكُلٍّ جَعَلْنَا مِنكُمْ شِرْعَةً وَمِنْهَاجًا﴾ [المائدة:٤٨].

Islām is to worship Allah, He who has no partners, alone. It is the religion of the angels in the heavens and of man and jinn on earth. It is the religion of

Islām. In its general sense, it means to submit to Allah ﷻ while singling Him out (*tawḥīd*), to yield to Him in obedience and to purify oneself of polytheism, as defined by Shaykh al-Islām, and as quoted by al-Shaykh Muḥammad b. ʿAbd al-Wahhāb in *al-Thalāthatu 'l-Uṣūl*. So, Islām is the religion of all of the Prophets as well as their followers. Each prophet preached it to his people. Anyone who follows this message is a Muslim [lit. one who submits or surrenders to Allah], be they from the earlier or the later people, as such a person submits to Allah ﷻ, serves Him as one God and yields to Him in obedience. The religion of the Prophets is one, but their laws vary and differ because of different human needs in each time and place. According to one *ḥadīth*, "Prophets are paternal brothers. Their mothers are different, but their religion is one."[144] Allah ﷻ also says: **{To each of you We prescribed a law and a method.} [Qur'ān 5:48]**

فالله يشرع لكل نبي ما يناسب قومه ويناسب مصالحهم، ثم ينسخ الله لأمة أخرىٰ بحسب مصالحها، فمن كان علىٰ دين نبي قبل أن ينسخ فهو مسلم، فعبادة الله بما شرعه لذلك النبي، ولكن بعد البعثة المحمدية صار الدين واحداً ونسخ الله ما قبله، وصار الدين المعتبر دينه عليه الصلاة والسلام، فلا يجوز لأحد أن يبقىٰ علىٰ دين من الأديان السابقة؛ لأن رسالته ودينه عليه الصلاة والسلام عام لكل الخلق، وشامل لكل زمان ولكل جيل.

Allah ﷻ prescribes a law to each prophet as is appropriate and best for his people. Then, Allah ﷻ abrogates the law for another people according to what is best for them. So whoever follows the religion of a prophet before it is abrogated, then they are a Muslim. Allah is to be served according to what He has prescribed for that prophet. But after sending Prophet Muḥammad ﷺ, Allah ﷻ abrogated all religions that preceded it, and there became only one religion that counts and that is of the Prophet Muḥammad ﷺ. So it is not permissible for anyone to continue following any of the preceding religions, because his message and religion are universal to humanity and encompassing of every time, [place] and generation.

---

144 Al-Bukhārī, no. 2365; Muslim, no. 3443.

المتن

(٢١٤) قال الله تعالىٰ ﴿إِنَّ الدِّينَ عِنْدَ اللهِ الْإِسْلامُ﴾ [آل عمران: ١٩]، وقال تعالىٰ ﴿وَرَضِيتُ لَكُمُ الْإِسْلامَ دِينًا﴾ [المائدة: ٣].

(214) Allah the Most High also says: *{Indeed, the religion in the sight of Allah is Islām.}* [Qurʾān 3:19] *{...And [I] have approved for you Islām as a religion.}* [Qurʾān 5:3]

الشرح

فهو الدين الذي رضيه لعباده من بعثة محمد صلىٰ الله عليه وسلم إلىٰ أن تقوم الساعة.

It is the religion that Allah is pleased with His servants to follow, from the time of the sending of Muḥammad ﷺ until the coming of the Hour.

المتن

(٢١٥) وَهُوَ بَيْنَ الْغُلُوِّ والتَّقْصِيرِ.

(215) It is a middle course between excess and negligence;

الشرح

فالإسلام وسط بين الغلو، وهو: الزيادة والتشديد، وبين التقصير، وهو: الجفاء، فدين الإسلام وسط لا تشديد فيه ولا تحلل منه، فكلا الطرفين مذموم، والوسط خير، ولهذا قال سبحانه: ﴿يَٰٓأَهۡلَ ٱلۡكِتَٰبِ لَا تَغۡلُواْ فِي دِينِكُمۡ غَيۡرَ ٱلۡحَقِّ﴾ [المائدة:٧٧]

Islām is a middle course between *excess* (*ghulūw*), i.e. additions and doing that which is beyond one's capacity and *negligence* (*taqṣīr*), i.e. to have an aversion (to something). The religion of Islām is a middle course and one should neither do what is beyond one's capacity nor slip away from it. Each of these is blameworthy. Steering a middle course is best. **{Say, 'O People of the Scripture, do not exceed limits in your religion beyond the truth.'} [Qur'ān 5:77]**

وقال عليه الصلاة والسلام: «**هلك المتنطعون**» قالها ثلاثـًا، والمتنطعون هم المتشددون في أمور الدين، ولما قال نفر علىٰ عهد النبي صلىٰ الله عليه وسلم... قال أحدهم: أنا أصوم ولا أفطر، وقال الآخر: أما أنا فأصلي ولا أنام، وقال الثالث: أما أنا فلا آكل اللحم، وقال الرابع: أما أنا فاعتزل النساء، فقال عليه الصلاة والسلام: «**أما إني أتقاكم لله وأخشاكم لله، وإني أصوم وأفطر، وأصلي وأنام، وأتزوج النساء، وآكل اللحم، فمن رغب عن سنتي فليس مني**»؛ لأن هذا تشديد ما أمر الله به، قال سبحانه: ﴿يَـٰٓأَيُّهَا ٱلَّذِينَ ءَامَنُواْ لَا تُحَرِّمُواْ طَيِّبَـٰتِ مَآ أَحَلَّ ٱللَّهُ لَكُمْ﴾ [المائدة:٨٧] يعني: من باب التدين، وقال سبحانه: ﴿وَلَا تَعْتَدُوٓاْ﴾ [المائدة:٨٧] فالآية شملت الطرفين، فالدين وسط.

The Prophet ﷺ said: "The *mutanaṭṭi'ūn* are doomed," three times[145]. The *mutanaṭṭi'ūn* are those who go to excess in matters of religion. During the Prophet's ﷺ time, a group of men said such things as, 'I will fast and never break my fast,' another said, 'I will engage in the prayer and not sleep,' a third said, 'I will not eat meat,' and a fourth said, 'I will live whilst abstaining from women.' The Prophet ﷺ said: "But I am the most pious and fearing of Allah, and I fast and break my fast, I pray and sleep, I marry women and I eat meat. Whoever forsakes my *sunnah* is not of me."[146] This is because this hardship is not commanded by Allah. Allah ﷻ says: **{O you who have believed, do not prohibit the good things which Allah has made lawful to you} [Qur'ān 5:87]** – that is, as a matter of one's practice of religion. Allah ﷻ says: **{...and do not transgress.} [Qur'ān 5:87]** Thus, the verse includes both groups, and the religion of Islām is a middle course.

145 Muslim, no. 2670.

146 Al-Bukhārī, no. 5063; Muslim, no. 1401.

المتن

(٢١٦) وَبَيْنَ التَّشْبِيهِ والتَّعْطِيلِ.

(216) Between *tashbīh* (likening Allah's attributes to the creation) and *taʿṭīl* (divesting Allah of His attributes);

الشرح

أي: في العقيدة، بين التعطيل والتشبيه، بين تعطيل أسماء الله وصفاته، وبين تشبيه المخلوق بالخالق، والعقيدة وسط، فالمعطلة غلوا في التنزيه، فنفوا الأسماء والصفات، والمشبهة غلوا في الإثبات حتىٰ شبهوا الله بخلقه، والعقيدة، وسط، قال سبحانه: ﴿لَيۡسَ كَمِثۡلِهِۦ شَيۡءٞۖ﴾ [الشورىٰ:١١] هذا رد علىٰ المشبهة، ﴿وَهُوَ ٱلسَّمِيعُ ٱلۡبَصِيرُ ١١﴾ [الشورىٰ:١١] هذا فيه رد علىٰ المعطلة، -ونحن معشر أهل السنة والجماعة - نثبت ما أثبته الله لنفسه، وما أثبته له رسوله، من الأسماء والصفات، ولا نعطلها ولا ننفيها، ولا نشبه الله بأحد من خلقه، بل: نقول أسماء الله وصفاته تليق به سبحانه وإن كانت هذه الأسماء والصفات موجودة في البشر، لكن الكيفية مختلفة، والصفة تابعة للموصوف.

That is, in terms of belief, it (the creed of Islām) lies between *taʿṭīl* (divesting Allah ﷻ of His attributes) and *tashbīh* (likening Allah's attributes to those of the creation or roughly: anthropomorphism). The correct creed is the middle course. The adherents of *taʿṭīl* are excessive in their affirmation of Allah's transcendence (*tanzīh*) and thus, deny all of Allah's ﷻ names and attributes. And the adherents of *tashbīh* are excessive in their affirmation (*ithbāt*) of the names and attributes and therefore, assimilate Allah ﷻ to created things. The right creed is the middle course. Allah ﷻ says: **{There is nothing like unto Him.} [Qurʾān 42:11]**This is a refutation of the proponents of *tashbīh*. **{And He is the Hearing, the Seeing.} [Qurʾān 42:11]** This is a refutation of the proponents of *taʿṭīl*. But we, Ahl al-Sunnah wa ʾl-Jamāʿah, affirm the names and attributes that Allah has affirmed and those that the Messenger of Allah ﷺ has affirmed. We do not deny them or divest Allah of them and we do not compare Allah to any of His creations. Rather, we say that the names and attributes of Allah ﷻ befit Him. Although those names and attributes exist in humans, the manner is different and an attribute is in accordance with that which it is attributed to.

المتن

(٢١٧) وَبَيْنَ الْجَبْرِ والْقَدَرِ.

(217) Between fatalism *(jabr)* and the denial of *qadar*.

الشرح

مذهب أهل السنة والجماعة وسط بين الجبرية والقدرية، فالجبرية يغلون في إثبات القدر حتىٰ يسلبوا العبد عن الاختيار، فيقولون: العبد ليس له اختيار، أفعاله كلها مجبور عليها، فهو آلة يحركه القدر، فصلاته وصيامه وأعماله ليس له فيها اختيار، فهو يحرك كما تحرك الآلة، وهذا مذهب باطل. والقدرية غلوا في إثبات اختيار العبد فنفوا القدر، حتىٰ جعلوا العبد يستقل بأفعاله ويخرجونها من إرادة الله ومشيئته، وأن العبد له إرادة مستقلة، فقالوا: هو الذي يخلق فعل نفسه، وليس لله فيها تصرف، وهذا مذهب المعتزلة.

The doctrine of Ahl al-Sunnah wa 'l-Jamāʿah is a middle course between the Jabriyyah sect and the Qadariyyah sect. The Jabriyyah sect are so excessive in their affirmation of predetermination that they deny the fact that people have any choice. They say that a person has no choice and that one is compelled to do all of one's actions. One is only an instrument that is moved by predetermination. Thus, one's prayers, fasting and other deeds are not by choice. One is moved in the same way that an instrument is moved. This is a false doctrine. The adherents of the Qadariyyah sect are excessive in their affirmation of choice, or free-will, of people and thus, negate *qadar* (predestination). In fact, they believe that people are independent in their actions, are beyond the will of Allah ﷻ and that a person has an independent free will. They say that individuals are the creators of their own actions and that their actions are not under Allah's ﷻ control. This is the doctrine of the

Muʿtazilites.

أما أهل السنة والجماعة فتوسطوا في هذه المسألة، وقالوا: إن العبد له اختيار ومشيئة، يفعل باختياره، ولكنه لا يخرج عن قضاء الله وقدره، فأفعاله خلق الله، وهي فعله وكسبه، فهو الذي يفعل المعاصي ويفعل الطاعات، ولكن الله هو المقدر، فلذلك يعاقب علىٰ جرائمه، ويثاب علىٰ طاعته، ولو كان يفعل هذا بغير اختياره ما حصل علىٰ الثواب ولا العقاب، فالمجنون والصغير لا يؤاخذان، وكذلك المكره الذي ليس له اختيار لا يؤاخذ.

Ahl al-Sunnah wa ʾl-Jamāʿah, on the other hand, follow a middle course when it comes to this issue. They say that a person has a choice and free will and that one acts by one's own choice, but he is not beyond the decree and predetermination of Allah ﷻ. One's actions are creations of Allah ﷻ, but they are one's own actions and work. It is the person who commits the sin or act of obedience, but Allah ﷻ is the one who predetermines it. And therefore, Allah punishes people for their offenses and rewards them for their obedience, and if one were to do so without choice, he would not receive any reward or punishment. Thus, an insane person and a minor are not accountable. Likewise, someone who does something under compulsion or duress is not accountable if they do not have a choice.

المتن

(٢١٨) وَبَيْنَ الْأَمْنِ والْيَأسِ.

(218) And between loss of fear [of Allah's punishment] and loss of hope [of Allah's mercy].

الشرح

كذلك، هذا من عقيدة أهل السنة والجماعة، وهو الوسط بين الأمن من مكر الله والإياس من رحمته، فهم يرجون رحمة الله، ولا يأمنون من مكر الله، ولا من

العذاب والفتنة، لكن لا يقنطون من رحمة الله، فيجمعون بين الخوف والرجاء، وهو ما كان عليه الأنبياء، قال سبحانه: ﴿إِنَّهُمْ كَانُوا۟ يُسَٰرِعُونَ فِى ٱلْخَيْرَٰتِ وَيَدْعُونَنَا رَغَبًا وَرَهَبًا ۖ وَكَانُوا۟ لَنَا خَٰشِعِينَ ﴿٩٠﴾﴾ [الأنبياء:٩٠]، فهؤلاء هم الأنبياء، فخوفهم من الله لم يحملهم على القنوط من رحمة الله، قال سبحانه: ﴿إِنَّهُۥ لَا يَا۟يْـَٔسُ مِن رَّوْحِ ٱللَّهِ إِلَّا ٱلْقَوْمُ ٱلْكَٰفِرُونَ ﴿٨٧﴾﴾ [يوسف:٨٧]، وقال سبحانه: ﴿وَمَن يَقْنَطُ مِن رَّحْمَةِ رَبِّهِۦٓ إِلَّا ٱلضَّآلُّونَ ﴿٥٦﴾﴾ [الحجر:٥٦]، وأيضًا: رجاؤهم من الله لم يحملهم على الأمن من مكر الله، قال سبحانه: ﴿أَفَأَمِنُوا۟ مَكْرَ ٱللَّهِ ۚ فَلَا يَأْمَنُ مَكْرَ ٱللَّهِ إِلَّا ٱلْقَوْمُ ٱلْخَٰسِرُونَ ﴿٩٩﴾﴾ [الأعراف:٩٩].

This is also a part of the creed of Ahl al-Sunnah wa 'l-Jamā'ah, namely, following a middle course between being fearless (*amn*) of Allah's ﷻ plan (*makr*) and despair (*iyās*) of Allah's ﷻ mercy. In their view, one is to have hope in Allah's mercy but not to be fearless of Allah's plan, or punishment or trials of faith (*fitnah*). Nonetheless, one should not despair of Allah's ﷻ mercy. Thus, one should combine both fear and hope. This is in conformity with the way of the Prophets. Allah ﷻ says: **{Indeed, they used to hasten to good deeds and supplicate to Us in hope and fear, and they were to Us humbly submissive.} [Qur'ān 21:90]** This refers to the Prophets. Their fear of Allah ﷻ did not lead them to despair of His mercy. Allah ﷻ says: **{Indeed, no one despairs of relief from Allah except the disbelieving people.} [Qur'ān 12:87]** Allah ﷻ also says: **{And who despairs of the mercy of his Lord except for those astray?} [Qur'ān 15:56]** Furthermore, their hope for Allah ﷻ to have mercy on them does not cause them to be fearless of Allah's plan (*makr*). Allah ﷻ says: **{Then did they feel secure from the plan of Allah? But no one feels secure from the plan of Allah except the losing people.} [Qur'ān 7:99]**

فإبراهيم أبو الأنبياء يقول: ﴿وَٱجْنُبْنِى وَبَنِىَّ أَن نَّعْبُدَ ٱلْأَصْنَامَ ﴿٣٥﴾﴾ [إبراهيم:٣٥] فإبراهيم ما أمن على نفسه، ولكنه خاف الفتنة؛ لأنه بشر.

Ibrāhīm, the father of the Prophets, said: **{'My Lord, make this city [Makkah] secure and keep me and my sons away from worshipping idols...'} [Qur'ān 14:35]** Thus, Ibrāhīm ﷺ was not fearless over what might happen to him. He feared that his faith would be tested because he was human.

فلا يأمن الإنسان علىٰ نفسه ويقول: أنا رجل صالح، بل يخاف علىٰ نفسه، مع عدم القنوط من رحمة الله، قال تعالىٰ: ﴿قُلْ يَٰعِبَادِىَ ٱلَّذِينَ أَسْرَفُوا۟ عَلَىٰٓ أَنفُسِهِمْ لَا تَقْنَطُوا۟ مِن رَّحْمَةِ ٱللَّهِ ۚ إِنَّ ٱللَّهَ يَغْفِرُ ٱلذُّنُوبَ جَمِيعًا ۚ إِنَّهُۥ هُوَ ٱلْغَفُورُ ٱلرَّحِيمُ ﴿٥٣﴾ وَأَنِيبُوٓا۟ إِلَىٰ رَبِّكُمْ وَأَسْلِمُوا۟ لَهُۥ﴾ [الزمر:٥٣-٥٤].

So one should not be fearless of being punished and say, 'I am a good person' but one should rather fear for oneself while not despairing of Allah's ﷻ mercy. Allah ﷻ says: **{Say, 'O My servants who have transgressed against themselves [by sinning], do not despair of the mercy of Allah. Indeed, Allah forgives all sins. Indeed, it is He who is the Forgiving, the Merciful.' And return [in repentance] to your Lord and submit to Him.} [Qur'ān 39:53-54]**

فالواجب علىٰ الإنسان: أن يفعل أسباب الرحمة، وهي التوبة وإسلام الوجه لله سبحانه، عند ذلك يحصل علىٰ رحمة الله، فرحمة الله قريب من المحسنين، والإحسان سبب الرحمة، هذا مذهب أهل السنة والجماعة، وهو بين مذهب المرجئة الذين يقولون: لا يضر مع الإيمان معصية، فإذا كان الإنسان مؤمناً بقلبه فلا تضره المعصية، فهؤلاء أمنوا مكر الله، ويقولون: الأعمال لا تدخل في حقيقة الإيمان، فيدخل الجنة وإن لم يعمل شيئاً عندهم، وهذا مذهب أفسد الدنيا، تحلل الناس من الدين بسببه، وقالوا: ما دام أننا ندخل الجنة، فلا حاجة إلىٰ الأعمال، فيفعلون ما يشاءون.

It is incumbent to do what is a cause of mercy, namely, repenting and submitting oneself to Allah ﷻ. It is then that mercy is attained. Allah's ﷻ mercy is near to those who are doers of good, and doing good is a cause of mercy. This is the doctrine of Ahl al-Sunnah wa 'l-Jamā'ah, and it is a middle course between that of the Murji'ites, who say that sin is not an inherent detriment of faith[, and between the *wa'īdīyah* Khārijites.] As per the Murji'ites, if someone believes in their heart, then sin is of no effect on them. Those people do not fear the plan of Allah ﷻ, and say that deeds are not an intrinsic part of the nature of faith. In their view, one enters Paradise even without doing anything. This belief has caused much corruption in the world and many have gradually slipped away from the religion because of it. They say, as long as we are to enter Paradise, there is no need to do good deeds, and so they do what they want.

وبين الوعيدية الخوارج الذين يُكفِّرون بالكبائر التي دون الشرك، ويرون إنفاذ الوعيد الذي ذكره الله على من عصاه، فإن الله توعد العصاة، لكن قال: ﴿إِنَّ ٱللَّهَ لَا يَغْفِرُ أَن يُشْرَكَ بِهِۦ وَيَغْفِرُ مَا دُونَ ذَٰلِكَ لِمَن يَشَآءُ﴾ [النساء:٤٨]. فهم تحت المشيئة، وهذا مذهب أهل السنة والجماعة، وهو الوسط.

The *wa'īdīyah* (those who are labelled as deviating in the matter of *wa'īd*, or threats) Khārijites, on the other hand, declare others to be disbelievers on account of major sins that are less serious than polytheism. They believe that the threats that Allah has mentioned will be enforced on those who disobey Him, as Allah has posed certain threats against those who disobey Him. However, He says: **{Indeed, Allah does not forgive association with Him, but He forgives what is less than that for whom He wills.} [Qur'ān 4:48]** So, people are under Allah's will. This is the doctrine of Ahl al-Sunnah wa 'l-Jamā'ah. It is a middle course.

والقول الحق مع أهل السنة والجماعة الذين توسطوا بين الأمن والرجاء، والخوف والقنوط، ولهذا يقولون: الخوف والرجاء بالنسبة للإنسان كجناحي الطائرة، ولابد من سلامة الجناحين، فكذلك الخوف والرجاء لو اختل أحدهما سقط، فلابد من التعادل كما يتعادل جناحا الطائر.

The right belief is that of Ahl al-Sunnah wa 'l-Jamā'ah who tread a middle course between fearlessness and hope on one hand, and fear and despair on the other. Hence, they say that fear and hope to a human are like the wings of a bird. The wings have to be flawless and sound. Similarly, if either of one's fear or hope is flawed it will fall, so there has to be balance as there is with the wings of a bird.

المتن

(٢١٩) فَهَذا دِينُنا واعْتِقادُنا ظاهِرًا وَباطِنًا، وَنَحْنُ بُرَآءُ إِلَىٰ اللهِ مِنْ كُلِّ مَنْ خالَفَ الَّذِي ذَكَرْناهُ وَبَيَّنّاهُ.

(219) This is our religion and belief, outwardly and inwardly. We dissociate ourselves from anyone who opposes what we have said and explained here.

الشرح

أي: ما ذكرناه في هذه العقيدة من أولـها إلىٰ آخرها، فهو ديننا معشر المسلمين، ونحن براء من كل من خالفه؛ لأنها عقيدة حق، وما خالفها فهو باطل.

That is, what we have said in this statement of creed, from beginning to end, it is our religion, the religion of the Muslims. We wash our hands of anyone who opposes it, because it is the right creed so whatever opposes it is false.

المتن

(٢٢٠) وَنَسْأَلُ اللهَ تَعالَىٰ أَنْ يُثَبِّتَنا عَلَىٰ الْإِيمانِ، وَيَخْتِمَ لَنا بِهِ.

(220) We ask Allah to make us steadfast upon the faith and to allow us to die upon it;

الشرح

هذا تأدب مع الله، لما بين عقيدة أهل السنة والجماعة، سأل الله أن يثبته عليها، فلا يكفي أن الإنسان يعرف العقيدة، فالعالم يَزِلُّ ويخطئ، فلا يغتر الإنسان بعلمه، ولا يأمن الفتن، فهل علمه يعادل علم إبراهيم عليه الصلاة والسلام؟ وقد دعاء الله فقال: ﴿وَٱجۡنُبۡنِي وَبَنِيَّ أَن نَّعۡبُدَ ٱلۡأَصۡنَامَ ٣٥ رَبِّ إِنَّهُنَّ أَضۡلَلۡنَ كَثِيرٗا مِّنَ ٱلنَّاسِۖ﴾ [إبراهيم:٣٥-٣٦].

This is the proper etiquette toward Allah ﷻ. After explaining the creed of Ahl al-Sunnah wa 'l-Jamā'ah, he (the author) asks Allah to make him steadfast upon the faith. It is not enough for someone to know the right creed. A knowledgeable person may fall into error or make mistakes, so one should not be deceived by one's knowledge and feel safe from trials of faith. Is one's knowledge equal to that of Ibrāhīm ﷺ? Who prayed to Allah, saying: **{My Lord, make this city [Makkah] secure and keep me and my sons away from worshipping idols. My Lord, indeed they have led astray many among the people.} [Qur'ān 14:35-36]**

فالإنسان يسأل الله السلامة والعافية، فكم من عالم زل وانحرف عن الدين، وكم وكم.. فالأعمال بالخواتيم.

So, one should ask Allah for salvation and well-being. How many knowledgeable people have deviated from the right faith? Indeed, deeds are judged by the last of them.

المتن

(٢٢١) وَيَعْصِمَنا مِنَ الْأَهْواءِ الْمُخْتَلِفَةِ، والْآراءِ الْمُتَفَرِّقَةِ.

(221) And to keep us from the many inclinations and diverse opinions;

الشرح

ما أضل الناس إلا الأهواء، قال تعالى: ﴿وَمَنْ أَضَلُّ مِمَّنِ ٱتَّبَعَ هَوَىٰهُ بِغَيْرِ هُدًى مِّنَ ٱللَّهِ﴾ [القصص:٥٠]، وقال سبحانه: ﴿أَفَرَءَيْتَ مَنِ ٱتَّخَذَ إِلَٰهَهُۥ هَوَىٰهُ وَأَضَلَّهُ ٱللَّهُ عَلَىٰ عِلْمٍ﴾ [الجاثية:٢٣] فالإنسان يسأل الله السلامة من الهوى، وأن يهديه الحق، وإن خالف هواه، وقال الله عز وجل في اليهود: ﴿أَفَكُلَّمَا جَآءَكُمْ رَسُولٌۢ بِمَا لَا تَهْوَىٰٓ أَنفُسُكُمُ ٱسْتَكْبَرْتُمْ فَفَرِيقًا كَذَّبْتُمْ وَفَرِيقًا تَقْتُلُونَ ﴿٨٧﴾﴾ [البقرة:٨٧]، فالهوى خطير جداً.

There is nothing that has caused people to stray from the path other than the inclinations of the soul (*ahwāʾ*). Allah ﷻ says: **{And who is more astray than one who follows his desire without guidance from Allah?} [Qurʾān 28:50]** Allah ﷻ also says: **{Have you seen he who has taken as his god his [own] desire.} [Qurʾān 45:23]** One should ask Allah ﷻ to be kept safe from one's own whims and desires and to be guided to the truth, even if it is contrary to one's inclinations. Allah ﷻ says in respect to the Jews: **{But is it [not] that every time a messenger came to you, [O Children of Israel], with what your souls did not desire, you were arrogant? And a party [of messengers] you denied and another party you killed.} [Qurʾān 2:87]** Therefore inclinations are very dangerous.

المتن

(٢٢٢) والْمَذاهِبِ الرَّدِيَّة.

(222) As well as the evil doctrines;

الشرح

وهي الفرق التي أخبر عنها عليه الصلاة والسلام بقوله: «**ستفترق هذه الأمة على ثلاث وسبعين فرقة، كلها في النار...**» الحديث؛ لأنها خارجه عن الحق، إلا من سار على مثل ما سار عليه رسول الله عليه الصلاة والسلام وأصحابه، فإنهم ناجون من النار، ولذلك سموا بالفرقة الناجية. والمذاهب بمعنى الآراء.

This is a reference to the sects that the Prophet ﷺ has told of when he said, "My *Ummah* will divide into seventy-three sects: all of them are in the Fire..."[147] - on account of them being apart from the truth, except for those who tread a path like that of the Messenger of Allah ﷺ and his Companions. They are saved from the Fire and are thus called *al-firqah al-nājiyah* (the saved sect). 'Doctrines' (*madhāhib*) here means views or opinions.

---

147 Abū Dāwūd, no. 4596; Ibn Mājah, no. 3991. Aḥmad, 2/332; al-Ḥākim, 1/128. Al-Ḥākim said that it is *ṣaḥīḥ*.

المتن

(٢٢٣) مِثْلَ الْمُشَبِّهَةِ.

(223) Such as those of the Mushabbihah;

الشرح

هم الذين شبهوا صفات الله بصفات المخلوقين.

They are those who liken Allah's attributes to those of created things.

المتن

(٢٢٤) والْمُعْتَزِلَةِ.

(224) The Mu'tazilah;

الشرح

هم الذين عطلوا صفات الله ونفوها، بحجة أنهم ينزهون الله، فغلوا في التنزيه، وهم أتباع واصل بن عطاء، وعمرو بن عبيد، وكانا من تلاميذ الحسن البصري، وكانوا يحضرون في حلقته، فسئل الحسن البصري عن صاحب الكبيرة، فأجاب بما يوافق الكتاب والسنة، وقال: هو تحت المشيئة، ولا يكفر بالكبيرة، وهو ناقص الإيمان، فعند ذلك أنكر عليه واصل وقال له: هو في منزلة بين المنزلتين، ليس بكافر ولا مسلم. فاخترع هذا المذهب الباطل، واعتزل مجلس الحسن، واجتمع حوله الناس الذين هم من جنسه، فكونوا جماعة سُمُّو بالمعتزلة.

They are those who divest Allah of His attributes and deny them based on the argument that they affirm Allah's transcendence. They are the followers of Wāṣil ibn 'Aṭā' and 'Amr ibn 'Ubayd. These two individuals were students of al-Ḥasan al-Baṣrī and were attendees of his [teaching] circle. Al-Ḥasan al-Baṣrī was asked about those who commit major sins, and he answered according to the Qur'ān and Sunnah, saying that those people are under Allah's will, and that they are not disbelievers on account of their major sin but are lacking in faith. At that point, Wāṣil criticized him and said that such people have an intermediate state of salvation (*manzilah bayn al-manzilatayn*) and that they are neither disbelievers nor Muslims. And so he invented this false doctrine and retreated from the circles of al-Ḥasan. Those who were like him gathered around him, and they became a group known as the *muʿtazilah* (those who retreat).

المتن

(٢٢٥) والْجَهْمِيَّةِ والْجَبْرِيَّةِ.

(225) The Jahmiyyah, the Jabariyyah;

الشرح

وهم أتباع الجهم بن صفوان الترمذي، تبنّىٰ مذهب شيخه الجعد بن درهم، وهذا أخذه عن طالوت اليهودي، الذي أخذه عن لبيد بن الأعصم الذي سحر النبي صلىٰ الله عليه وسلم، وهذا المذهب هو القول بخلق القرآن، ومن أقوالهم: الجبر؛ أن الإنسان مجبور علىٰ أعماله وغيرها، ولذلك نُسبوا إلىٰ الجهم، وسموا بالجهمية، فالجهم أخذه من الجعد الذي كان في أواخر دولة بني أمية، وقتله خالد بن عبد الله القسري، كان خالد يخطب في عيد الأضحىٰ، فقال: ضحوا أيها الناس، تقبل الله ضحاياكم، فإني مُضحٍّ بالجعد بن درهم، فإنّه يزعم أن الله لم يكلم موسىٰ تكليماً، ولم يتخذ إبراهيم خليلاً.

They are followers of Jahm ibn Ṣafwān[148] al-Tirmidhī, who adopted the

148 Abū Maḥraz al-Rāsibī, one of the founders of misguidance and a leader of the Jahmīs, was a man of intelligence and dialectic. He denied the attributes of Allah ﷻ on account of (as he purported) his affirmation of Allah's ﷻ transcendence. He said

doctrine of his *shaykh,* al-Ja'd ibn Dirham[149], who in turn learned it from Ṭālūt, the Jew, who learned it from Labīd ibn al-Aʿṣam, who had placed a magic spell on the Prophet ﷺ. This is the doctrine that views the Qur'ān as being created. Also among their views is the doctrine of *jabr* (fatalism), that people are compelled (*majbūr*) in respect to actions and other things. This is why they are associated with al-Jahm and are called al-Jahmīyah. Al-Jahm learned it from al-Ja'd, who lived to see the end of the Umayyad dynasty. He was slain by Khālid ibn ʿAbdullāh al-Qasri. Khālid was giving the sermon on *Eid-ul-Adha* (Feast of Sacrifice) and said: "Sacrifice your animals, O people. May Allah accept your offerings. I am to sacrifice Ja'd ibn Dirham, for he claims that Allah has not spoken to Mūsā and that Ibrāhīm is not the friend of Allah."

فنزل من على المنبر فذبحه؛ لأنه زنديق، فقتله واجب، وشكر ذلك أهل السنة والجماعة، ولذلك قال ابن القيم في النونية:

He came down from the pulpit and slaughtered him for being a heretic, so executing him was an obligation. Ahl al-Sunnah wa 'l-Jamāʿah have shown appreciation for this. Ibn al-Qayyim said in his *Nūnīyah:*

ولأجل ذا ضحىٰ بجعدٍ خالدُ الـ　　قسري يوم ذبائح القربان

لقد شكر الضحية كل صاحب سنة　　لله درك من أخي قربان

On account of that, Khālid al-Qasri sacrificed Ja'd on the day of the sacrificial offerings.

Every adherent of Sunnah gives thanks for that sacrifice, your goodness be attributed to Allah, my brother and associate.

فخلفه الجهم، فنُسب المذهب إليه؛ لأنه هو الذي أظهره، فجمع بين الجبر

that the Qur'ān was created and that Allah ﷻ is in all places. He also said that faith is the belief of the heart, even in cases of disbelief. See *Siyar aʿlām al-nubalā',* 6/26-27.

149 He is Mu'addib Marwān, the donkey. He was the first to introduce the heresy that Allah ﷻ did not take Ibrāhīm ﷺ as a friend and did not speak to Mūsā ﷺ. Al-Madā'inī said: "He was a heretic". Ibn Wahb said to him, 'I believe that you are one of those who are doomed. Were it not for the fact that Allah told us that He has a hand and an eye, we would not have said so.' Not long after, he was crucified. See *Siyar aʿlām al-nubalā',* 5/433.

والتجهم.

Jahm was his successor and the doctrine is attributed to him as it became manifest by his doings. He combined the doctrine of fatalism with his own doctrines.

ولهذا يقول الشاعر:

Hence, the words of the poet,

عجبت لشيطان دعا الناس جهرة   إلىٰ النار واشتق اسمه من جهنم

I am astonished at a devil who openly called people to the Fire, and has a name derived from jahannam (Hell).

المتن

(٢٢٦) والْقَدَرِيَّةِ.

(226) The Qadariyyah;

الشرح

مثل نفاه القدر، وهم المعتزلة، يقولون: أفعالُ العباد خلقهم، وليست داخلةً في خلق الله ولا إرادته، ولذلك سُمُّوا بمجوس هذه الأمة؛ لأن المجوس أثبتوا خالقين: خالق للخير، وخالق للشر، أما القدرية فأثبتوا خالقين متعددين مع الله.

Such as those who deny *qadar*, namely, the Muʿtazilites. They say that the actions of people are their own creations and are not within the realm of Allah's creation or will. This is why they are called the Zoroastrians (*majūs*) of this *Ummah*, because the *majūs* believe in two creators: a creator of good and a creator of evil. The Qadarīyyah, on the other hand, believe in multiple creators alongside Allah.

المتن

(٢٢٧) وَغَيْرِهِمْ، مِنَ الَّذِينَ خالَفُوا السُّنَّةَ والْجَماعَةَ، وَحالَفُوا الضَّلالَةَ.

(227) And others who have gone against the Sunnah and the *Jamāʿah* (united community), and aligned themselves with error.

الشرح

من الذين خالفوا الكتاب والسنة من سائر الفرق الضالة.

Referring to those who belong to any other misguided group that opposes the Qurʾān and Sunnah.

المتن

(٢٢٨) وَنَحْنُ مِنْهُمْ بَرَآءٌ، وَهُمْ عِنْدَنا ضُلّالٌ وَأَرْدِياءُ وَبِاللهِ الْعِصْمَةُ والتَّوْفِيقُ.

(228) We dissociate ourselves from them, and to us, they are astray and evil. And Allah ﷻ is our saviour and helper.

الشرح

فنحن نبرأ منهم، ونعاديهم في الله، ونبغضهم؛ لأنهم أهل ضلال وباطل، فالواجب هجرهم وبغضهم، والرد عليهم وعلىٰ باطلهم.

We dissociate ourselves from them and treat them as enemies and hate them for Allah's ﷻ sake, because they are people of misguidance and falsehood. It is obligatory to desert them and detest them, and to refute them and their falsehood.

فنحن نتبرأ ممن يقول: إن كل الفرق تحت اسم الإسلام، ويجب أن نتغاضىٰ عن هذه الأمور، أخذاً بحرية الكلمة وحرية الرأي، فالفرق كلها تدخل تحت الإسلام. وهذا مذهب باطل وخطير علىٰ الأمة، وحرية الكلمة والرأي مقيدة

بالكتاب والسنة وما عليه سلف الأمة. والفرق المخالفة كلها في النار إلا الفرقة التي علىٰ ما كان عليه الرسول صلىٰ الله عليه وسلم وأصحابه.

We also dissociate ourselves from those who say that all of the sects fall under the name of Islām and that these matters should be overlooked in the name of freedom of speech and freedom of opinion, and so all of the sects fall under Islām. This is a false belief and it is dangerous to the *Ummah.* Freedom of speech and opinion are restricted by the Qurʾān, the Sunnah and the way of the predecessors of the *Ummah.* All of the sects that oppose this are in the Fire, except for one sect, and that is the one conforming with what the Messenger of Allah ﷺ and his Companions followed.

والإنسان عُرضة للخطأ، العصمة والتوفيق والحول والقوة بيد الله، فالإنسان لا يضمن لنفسه النجاة، إنما يرجو الله ويخافه.

People are prone to error. Being unerring, and having success, power and strength are in the hands of Allah ﷻ. A person should not feel assured of one's salvation but should rather have hope and fear in Allah ﷻ.

وبهذا انتهت هذه النبذة المباركة، المشتملة علىٰ جُمَل عظيمة من اعتقاد أهل السنة والجماعة، فنسأل الله أن ينفعنا بها، وأن يجزل لمؤلفها جزيل الثواب علىٰ ما بيّن، وعلىٰ ما وضح وعلىٰ ما كتب، وعلىٰ ما نصح للأمة، فجزاه الله خيراً وسائر أئمة المسلمين.

Now ends this blessed concise work (on creed) which contains a great part of the creed of Ahl al-Sunnah wa ʾl-Jamāʿah. We ask Allah ﷻ to make it of advantage to us and to reward the author greatly for what he has explained, clarified and written, and for his counsel to the Muslims. May Allah reward him abundantly as well as all of the *imām*s of the Muslims.

والله أعلم، وصلىٰ الله وسلم وبارك علىٰ نبيّنا محمد وآله وصحبه أجمعين.

Allah ﷻ knows best, and may Allah confer His blessings on, and grant peace to, our Prophet Muḥammad and his Family and Companions.

We would like to thank Aaron Josiah Hernandez for translating this work, Khadija Nasseredin for revising it, and Nagwan Noaman and Khadija Nasseredin for proofreading it. We would also like to thank Shaykh Shadi al-Nu'man for his invaluable input throughout the project.

Ilm Islamic Translation Services